A HISTORY OF SCOTLAND

A History of
SCOTLAND

Rosalind Mitchison

ILLUSTRATED BY GEORGE MACKIE

METHUEN & CO LTD
11 NEW FETTER LANE LONDON EC4

First published 1970 by Methuen & Co Ltd,
11 New Fetter Lane, London EC4
© 1970 by Rosalind Mitchison
Printed by Richard Clay (The Chaucer Press) Ltd
Bungay, Suffolk

SBN 416 14450 0 (HB)
SBN 416 27940 6 (UP)

Distributed in the U.S.A.
by Barnes & Noble Inc.

To Murdoch, who saw this coming before I did.

Contents

'Vie in this cingdum ar will ffull, proud, and nesiesitus eivin to begarie.'
Lord Rothes, Chancellor of Scotland

'Any shuckle can write a book: it takes a Man to herd the Merrick.'
Anon.

Author's Note

THIS BOOK HAS BEEN written with a mind to the problems of students of Scottish history at the moment of writing. It has therefore been over-weighted in the space and emphasis it gives to the key period for the understanding of modern Scotland, the seventeenth century. It has been finished at a time of considerable debate on the future government of the country. Within a few years the epilogue may be in need of revision. I ask the reader to bear in mind that in its own way this is a historical document, to be viewed in the light of changing events.

I have endeavoured in this book to make full use of the conclusions of modern research and to relate Scottish history to the current interests of students of history. In the present dearth of modern outlines of Scottish history it has seemed to me best that it should be written as independently as possible. Perhaps it is typical of a small country that there should be a wide gulf between the opinions of the current generation of working scholars and the popularly held truisms about its history. The version of Scottish history generally accepted, for instance in Scottish schools, has received little major change since Scott enshrined it in his *Tales of a Grandfather*, except that it has been extended to include some nineteenth-century events. Yet work has been done in this century that has undermined this received opinion, and the enthusiasm for new work to be seen in the biennial Scottish History Conference shows that many people are dissatisfied with the popular myths. There cannot be many historians working on a country of a little over five million inhabitants, and historians dislike disagreeing with the public except in the narrow field of their own specialisms. As a result the changes in opinion have not often been stated clearly at a popular level. When these have been stated, historians have tended to use a traditional phraseology and a similar tone of voice. In an attempt to offer an independent opinion, structure, emphasis, and style, this book has been worked at in isolation and kept away from authoritative criticism. As a result there are sure to be inaccuracies and mistakes in it. I shall be glad to be informed of these by readers.

In the matter of personal names I have tended to adopt the spellings of the *Complete Peerage* and the *Dictionary of National Biography*. An effort has been made to assist clarity in financial matters by reserving the sign £ for sterling money. The word Scotch has been used in the period when it was the adjective Scots applied to themselves. The notes at the end of chapters are to help the reader to distinguish individuals from one another, and are not intended as miniature biographies. The notes at the end of the book are there to help a reader find his way about the chapters and main events.

History is a co-operative and kindly profession. This book owes a great deal to other practitioners of it. In particular it owes more than I can easily express, and for more than I can ever repay, to a lifelong friend, Sir Llewellyn Woodward, whose advice and counselling have been generously given at all stages. Though he has no responsibility for my opinions and my errors, he has given me detailed advice on the general problems of writing outline history. I have received a great deal of the stimulus to my historical thinking from conversations with Dr T. C. Smout, and could not imagine what this book would be without his contribution. There are also many others from whom I have gathered ideas, criticism, or information. Among these are Mrs Jennifer M. Brown, the Reverend Dr James P. B. Bulloch, Professor Gordon Donaldson, Professor A. A. M. Duncan, Dr Bruce Webster, Dr Ranald Nicholson, Dr W. F. H. Nicolaisen, Dr Gweneth Whitteridge, Dr I. B. Cowan, Eric Linklater, the Reverend Campbell Maclean, Dr Atholl Murray, Dr N. Phillipson, Mrs A. L. F. Smith, and Father Anthony Ross. Futhermore I am intellectually in the debt of all those with whom I have associated in teaching over the last few years, both pupils and colleagues, as well as to members of my own family for stimulus, tolerance, and help.

One element of help is impersonal and cannot be thanked. It is the living record of the past in the features and lie of the land. The opportunity of thinking of history in tranquillity in the environment that helped to shape it has come to me mainly on the hills of Scotland.

Chapter 1

Before 1100

GO AND STAND ON the castle rock of Stirling and look about you. That is the quickest way to comprehend the basic features that have dictated Scottish history. You will see the Highland line, one of the great geological faults to which Scotland owes its shape, a wall of hills rising sharply from the plain a few miles to the north. It runs as an irregular diagonal across the country. To the north-east lies its screen of outliers, the Ochils. Above the main ridge individual mountains, those of three thousand feet, Ben Ledi, Ben Vorlich, Ben Lomond, overlook their fellows. To the north-west runs the flat and now fertile carse with the great golden corn stacks and haystacks in ranks perpendicular to the road. But, for our ancestors, before the improvers of the eighteenth century drained it, this carse land was a bog covered with peat, across which the little sluggish streams took themselves to supply the still tidal Forth. The river Forth comes through Stirling in a series of big loops, and, four miles to the east as a hypothetical crow might fly, but many more as a boat's crew would row, it widens into the arm of the sea, its firth. South of Stirling the wall of the Highlands is reflected by the lesser ridge of the Campsies. To pass in reasonable safety and comfort from southern to northern Scotland a man must cross the Forth within a mile or two of Stirling.

Stirling is the brooch that holds together the two parts of the country. It is right that the most decisive battle in Scottish history should have been planned and agreed to for the ownership of Stirling castle on its rock above the vital bridge. Scotland as we know it began when the various peoples that made up the medieval population linked together with the aid of this brooch. The division to be overcome was not the modern cultural and economic one between Highland and Lowland but the older one between north and south of the Forth.

At Stirling the sharpness of the Highland line reveals the Highlands as a region of low fertility. It has old hills with deep valleys that stand in sharp contrast to the rounded hills of the Lowlands. The fault that makes the main block of Lowland hills, the southern uplands, runs along the edge of the Lammermuirs and Moorfoots south of Edinburgh and builds a structure which reaches the top of its dome with Broad Law in Ettrick. This structure, though it can go up to two and a half thousand feet, has hills not mountains, and many of the hills have been an aid rather than a hindrance to communication. The treeline in Scotland is low, and you walk a lot drier at two thousand feet than at one thousand. Old tracks for man and cattle run along the ridges and over the cols; by them the farms and townships in the valleys can communicate with other centres. But in the scooped-out valleys of the Highlands communities are much more cut off, and the hill land is of negligible fertility; there the lines of contact often lie by water rather than by land. The geography of the Highlands makes the small chieftainship over a population held together by kin a natural political unit, in the same way that the little mountain-ringed plains of Sicily and Greece lead naturally to the city state. The creation of larger political units would be easier in the Lowlands. The diagonal of the Highland line leaves areas geographically low-land in the North of Scotland. These include the broad, fertile valleys of Strathearn and Strathmore, the coastal strip round the Mounth (the old name for the central block of the Grampians), the low, rolling country of Aberdeenshire, and the warm and sheltered plain of Moray.

In historic times we know of five peoples to whom we can give names who occupied the territory now called Scotland. School text-books still remind children that in 843, or thereabouts, two of these peoples, the Picts and the Scots, were united by Kenneth MacAlpin, a king of the Scots. But in the ninth century there were also British or Welsh tribes in the south of Scotland, still holding a line of principalities from the outskirts of modern Edinburgh to Carlisle. In the thirteenth century the descendants of these were to give Scotland one of her greatest heroes, William Wallace, whose name means 'the Welshman' and who came from Clydesdale. In Lothian, Berwickshire, and Roxburghshire there were Anglo-Saxons, probably mixed with the British. The Norsemen from Norway were colonizing the islands and estuaries of the north and west, and threatening the political survival of the other peoples. Beneath all these Celtic or Germanic populations the river names of Scotland carried, and still carry, the reminder that other people had been there earlier. Even if, by the ninth century, these people had lost their political identity, and perhaps their language, they still contributed to the future: perhaps in local cults and superstitions, perhaps in the extraordinary words on Pictish monuments, by cairns and barrows and the crumbling walls of early shelters.

Of the five historic peoples the one that was doing worst in the ninth century was the British. The Kingdom of Strathclyde, with its fortress at Dumbarton, straddled Clydesdale and the northern English counties on the west, and elsewhere there were lesser princes ruling smaller areas. We know something of these Britons from Welsh literature. The Welsh epic, the Gododdin, written down in its final form in the twelfth century but carrying stanzas three centuries older, is about the great tribe of the Votadini, who at one time had a town on Traprain Law. This poem and other Welsh poems do not tell us of an organized kingdom but of princes who fought with one another and held court, who hunted and banqueted, listened to their bards, and counted wealth in flocks, jewellery, and splendid weapons. Just as Celtic art in its greatest phase was non-representational, so these poems shirk telling us clearly what has happened, and pass on instead to give us the lyric intensity of instants of feeling. For those lacking ancient Welsh and unsympathetic to the grouse-moor image of this way of life it is depressing: here we have the broken picture of a people who failed to organize themselves as a political force and who, in spite of occasional revivals, were to be defeated because of this. They failed to develop economically and have left us little in material relics, but we can hear of the sixth-century battle for a lark's nest (Caerlaverock perhaps) or of the desolation of Powys under Anglo-Saxon attack. Little survives of the days when the Votadini held their own with the other big political units. The importance of these British tribes to Scotland lay in the fact that they were the source of Scottish Christianity. The religion came through St Patrick to Ireland, and via Irish saints innumerable to Argyll, and through the Columban church there to Pictland and Northumbria.

Pictland was the country north of the Forth and, by the seventh century, east of the long mountain range that makes the 'spine' of Scotland. Mystery hangs about the Picts for two reasons. On the one hand we have a people who were defeated and whose language was obliterated. In this case there was no refuge for it in Wales. Pictish ceased to be spoken, and because it was not spoken the records (whatever they were, annals, histories, laws, genealogies) failed to be copied in later centuries and were lost totally. This alone would not make the mystery. That comes from the coupling of this silence with the most coherent, precise, and detailed artistic symbolism of the Dark Ages. The Picts have left their animals, real and imaginary, and their symbol stones all across north-eastern Scotland, as evidence of some articulate mythology, belief, or scale of values that was neither dependent on Christianity nor hostile to it. They have shown that from this they could develop a school of sculpture, simple and vivid. Hard facts about the Picts are confined to their royal inheritance, which came through the female line as it seems to have done in the Germany of Tacitus's day, to special places and areas, and to a language surviving in place names that belong to the P-Celtic division, as does British.[1] We know that they had sacred hills, Ben Ledi and Schiehallion for instance; and that special districts were important to their kingship – the Tay valley, Fife, Morayshire. We can trace them in 'Duns' or forts, Dunnottar, Dunkeld, Dunnichen. Perhaps they lived or kept their cattle in souterrains. Scone, 'Scone of the high shields' as the Irish annals call it, was in some ways a special centre, and it was here that Kenneth MacAlpin, King of the Scots, is

1. The great body of Celtic speaking peoples had split many centuries before into two sections, P-Celtic and Q-Celtic. Of present or recent languages, Welsh, Breton, and Cornish belong to the former, Irish, Manx, and Gaelic (the language spoken by the Scots) to the latter.

said to have slaughtered many of the Picts, luring them to a feast 'by their excessive potation and gluttony' says Giraldus Cambrensis, so that they could be killed by the 'innate treachery' of the Scots, 'in which they excel the other nations'.[1]

Like all the other peoples of ninth-century Scotland the Picts were at least partly pastoral. The late ninth-century Scottish King Constantine II is called 'the cowherd of the byre of the cows of the Picts' in one of those bogus Irish prophesies which were written after the events they foretold. This is a reminder of what was wealth to all these people. Minor details of evidence suggest that the Picts were not very thick on the ground, and were not a unitary kingdom but a federation or collaboration. We hear of kings of North Picts and of South Picts in Bede; we see the later separatism of Morayshire; Fife has always been remembered as a kingdom; the Caledonii had their Dun at Dunkeld. Part of this federation may have been dominated either by a people who still used a non-Aryan language and inscribed it on their great stones, or who had it surviving in personal names, or who collected impossible collections of consonants out of the initials of significant texts or sayings. We shall not know which of these explanations is the right one until we can interpret things like 'ettocuhetts ahehhttannn hocvvevv nehhtons'. Federations, even apparently strong ones, crumble more easily than unitary states under outside pressure. Another source of Pictish weakness may have been their old-fashioned matrilineal inheritance, through the sisters of kings, especially as some at least of these royal heiresses married foreign princes. Perhaps they all did. Certainly there were Pictish kings with English, British, or Scottish princely fathers, as there were Scottish kings with Pictish names. For a generation in the seventh century the kings of Northumbria were overlords of the southern Picts, until they were defeated in the great battle at Nechtansmere[2] in 685. In 741 the Pictish King Oengus had some sort of overlordship over the Scots. We have no record of this dominance ceasing until a great battle in 839 saw the slaughter of kings of both Picts and Scots by Norsemen. Before this date a Pictish King Constantine had put his

1. Giraldus, a Welshman at the court of Henry II of England and Anjou, could hardly resist a jab at other nationalities, and is not always reliable as evidence of national characteristics.
2. Probably near Dunnichen in Angus.

son upon the throne of the Scots, and among his successors it appears that a father was succeeded by his three sons, marking the end of the Pictish rule of succession. But these were among the last of Pictish kings, so shadowy that they are no more than names, and names that appear in only one Irish list. Almost immediately afterwards we find a Scot, Kenneth MacAlpin, ruling the Picts, and various stories of the Pictish overthrow, of the slaughter at the banquet, showing that this was not simply a Scot inheriting the kingdom through a Pictish mother: the Scots had won. They proceeded to turn what might have been merely a temporary overlordship into a general take-over.

The Scots historically are intruders – they came from Ireland and built the Kingdom of Dalriada on land which had once been Pictish, in the west of Scotland, in Argyll and the Isles. By the mid-sixth century they held a sizeable kingdom lying north of the Britons of Strathclyde and stretching up beyond the Great Glen, and they named it after the district in Ulster from which they took their royal house. The spine of Scotland (as Adomnan calls it in his life of St Columba, the *Druim Alban*), the big hills of the west, effectively cut their grazing grounds and small patches of arable off from the Picts. This country includes some fertile islands, notably Bute, Islay, and the traditional fair-weather corn-growing Tiree; the good land at the south end of Kintyre and the straths of Knapdale; but if a people there were to increase and turn steadily more and more to corn-growing they would need to look eastward in their imperialism to drier country. East lie the belts of the old red sandstone which still to this day give the best farmland of Scotland, from the red earth of the East Lothian plain to the flat-bedded fields of Caithness. The drop in annual rainfall as you go east in Scotland is more than an inch a mile, and to primitive farmers this is very important. As a people become more agricultural, expansion becomes more a matter of conquest than of infiltration or of gradual pressure. Pastoral peoples can be shifted slowly and more easily than a community of farmers. We know no facts about the demography of this period, but our suppositions and estimates of climatic history offer us a vision of a warmer and more even climate in north Europe than that of today. In the ninth century Norse voyagers laid courses farther north than we can do today without risk of ice. So of the two semi-independent variables that dominate the history of numbers, disease and climate, we can allow that if disease did not prevent it, the Scots in Dalriada could have been a fast-growing population. They gave the names of individual princes to areas of occupation, for instance, Comgal to Cowall. They had their strategic fortified centres: Dunadd, commanding movement down the sound of Jura; Dunolly, controlling the western approaches of the Great Glen. In the mid-sixth century they added to their territorial imperialism the great saint of the day, Columba.

Columba had come to Scotland in his forties, already a notable man, a member of a royal house, a scholar and ascetic in a country where these qualities were prized, and had persuaded the Pictish king to give him Iona for the founding of his monastery. We do not know if he came because he had made Ireland too hot to hold him: the wish to live a monastic life may have been the only reason. Yet his coming was bound to be a political event. Iona became the centre of the Columban church, creating and dominating other monasteries in Dalriada and Pictland. This church was run by monasteries under their abbots, and these abbots had even greater authority when they were princes. Bishops might be attached to monasteries to provide for ordination, but the rule of bishops and the delimitation of dioceses was unknown. The Celtic church kept its admiration for hermits and monks. Saints, however genuinely they may have abjured the world, provided outlets for the competitive emotions of their admirers. This is clearly shown in the Irish annals. The austerities of the saint, his learning, his monastic skills, were all points in a championship or competition, and his miracles not only showed his prestige but were the means by which he looked after his people. The stories of Columba show what the Scots valued in a saint; second sight for instance, and calligraphy. We see the monks of a century later rowing over the sea in coracles to Iona, towing behind them the timber for his church, and grumbling to the saint because he had not arranged better weather to let them get home in time for his feast day. The prestige and influence of the great saint was part of Scottish imperialism. Because of this, the authentic missionary activity of other saints, St Maluag of Lismore for instance, or of any or all of the saints of Pictland, have been swamped by the cult of Columba. It was in Iona that the Scottish kings were buried in the hope of picking up benefits hereafter from the proximity of the great saint.

By the ninth century the Columban church was no longer a separate unit. Conformity with the practices of Rome – the Roman calculation of Easter and the other movable feasts, the Roman shape of the tonsure – had been accepted by the Pictish King Nechton, says Bede, and even in Iona. But it took longer to get the Roman form of church government systematically established, and the wars of the ninth and tenth centuries did not provide a good setting for reorganization. The Church in Scotland, as in England and Wales, saw a decay of real monasticism and learning, and a continuation of proprietary habits – hereditary abbotships in princely families for instance – until cleaned up at the end of the eleventh century.

The Scottish kings continued to be buried in Iona after 843, but otherwise they turned their backs on the west. Scone and the area round it became their base: they were enthroned on the sacred stone there. Gaelic speech and culture, remarkably intrusive at this time, spread with Scottish power across Scotland almost to Edinburgh. This was a drastic change, even though for the most part it replaced another Celtic language. The gap between P- and Q-Celtic was already deep. Columba had needed an interpreter when speaking to the Pictish king, which implies that Pictish and Gaelic were then farther apart than, say, Italian and Castilian are today. Gradually the name Scotia divorced from its old meaning of Ireland and came to mean all Scotland north of the Forth, which had hitherto been called Alba. This area was now predominantly occupied by people speaking Gaelic and owning a Scottish king, though they might differ as to who he ought to be.

To the south of Scotia lay the Anglian kingdom of Northumbria, populated by Angles from across the North Sea, but with a fair-sized British element too. These 'English' were probably already more geared to agriculture than their northern neighbours. Perhaps as a result of this their society was less exclusively masculine. Women figure in their stories not merely in the form of Celtic goddesses reincarnated as Celtic saints, but as princesses and rulers, abbesses of large monasteries, and missionaries in the great Anglo-Saxon mission field in Germany. The northern part of Northumbria, Bernicia, had its Dun at Bamburgh, its great missionary monastery on Lindisfarne, but it extended well beyond the Tweed. St Cuthbert, its special native saint, came from near Coldingham, and the St Abb whose headland still carries her name was an English-princess Ebba. Neither the Tweed nor the Tyne provides the sort of natural frontier of the Forth. Invasion into or from Bernicia was relatively easy, and for a time the Bernician Empire had dominated as far as the Tay. What destroyed this Anglian kingdom and its civilization was the force that shaped Scotland in the ninth and tenth centuries, the invading Norsemen. In 793 they sacked Lindisfarne. The 'black gentiles', as the Irish called them, sailed down the west coast of Scotland too and in 794 Skye and Iona and all the islands were pillaged by 'this valiant, wrathful and purely pagan people'.

Men had been sailing, visiting, exploring, colonizing, and occasionally trading up and down the western screen of Scottish islands for generations. The old routes ran across to Ireland, and thence to Cornwall, Brittany, and Spain. Mediterranean pottery has been found at Dunadd. But the Norsemen at sea were a different matter from Irish saints or Irish warriors in coracles. The viking long-boat, seventy feet long, strongly built and beautifully curved along its gunwale, carried thirty oars and could row the North Sea. It could and did fight naval battles. Not for nothing was his boat in some special way of religious significance to a viking ruler, so that he would be buried in it with his broken gear around him. On land the Norsemen added a touch of ruthlessness to the already bloody battles of primitive peoples. At first they came as pagan looters and destroyers of other civilizations: a generation later the emphasis was on conquest and settlement. By the late ninth century all those who found the growth of a powerful monarchy under Harald Fairhair of Norway an intolerable restriction on their enterprise looked for a better field abroad. Ketil Flatnose, for instance, went to Scotland: 'wide lands were known to him there, because he had plundered there widely'; he stopped paying tax to his king, conquered the Hebrides, and lorded it over them. It was these settling 'Norsemen' from Norway, bringing their families with them, and their laws, looking for good trading bases and building up private empires, who destroyed the central and northern English kingdoms. They also occupied all the islands of Scotland and much of the coast of Britain and Ireland, and founded earldoms in Caithness and Sutherland. It was their pressure on the Scots and Picts that produced the smashing military defeat of these two together in 839, a defeat which seems to have led to the Scottish take-over. In the wake of the Norsemen came other pirates, in particular the *gall ghaidhil* or foreign Gaels, perhaps a mixture of Scots and Norse, who were raiding and settling the coast of what was to take its name from them and be called Galloway.

The Norsemen created the literary form of the saga, the realist prose narrative, strong on character and biting conversation. Though the sagas which were eventually written down, and so have come to us, date from a good deal later than the ninth century, and have often improved on history, they carry the real flavour of a people. By the thirteenth century, and probably well before, these people combined a taste for narrative founded in character with an appreciation of the effects and limitations of violence. It is not that the sagas have weak or unmilitary values but, unlike the Celtic stories that survive, they realize that there is more to life than war and saintliness. In them we can see the whole of a way of life and the characters that made it. We have Turf Einar, who conquered Orkney and discovered the use of peat as fuel; 'ugly, one-eyed and sharp sighted'. We have Aud the deep-minded, the daughter of Ketil, coping as the rich ruler of a big household with political troubles after the death of her son; building a ship secretly in the woods that were then Caithness (but would probably be part of Sutherland now) and sailing away with her family, thralls and treasure to Iceland; distributing her granddaughters in marriage on the way; visiting her brother, even though she disagreed with him on religion, and finally settling the Dale lands of Breida-fiordr. There is Arneid, the daughter of an Earl of the Hebrides, and later a bondswoman, whom Ketil Thrymr married because she worked hard and had fair hair. Under cover of an expedition to gather nuts she showed him where there was a treasure of silver hid, because he treated her decently. It is one of the great misfortunes of Scottish history that its traditional emphasis ignores the Norse element because in the end the Norse in Scotland were conquered and absorbed into a kingdom based on a culture of mixed Gaelic and English influences. The kings were Gaels, and in the twelfth century and later the English part of the kingdom provided the means by which English and European influences entered it. So Gaelic and English ways of life are considered as mattering. But about the former we have little information. The Scots and other Irish used history as a record of war and genealogy, with an occasional miracle thrown in to show the saintliness of someone. This type of history is 'vexing and wearying', as Catherine Morland complained, 'the men all so good for nothing and hardly any women at all'. The Norse material has to be left on one side for the shadowy tale of political history, which is only a shadow of reality at best.

In the tenth century the Norsemen picked up Christianity, taking to it gradually in a businesslike way, often with a sharp eye to material advantage. This and intermarriage, both at the princely or noble level and with bondswomen, did much to assimilate their communities with the others already in Scotland. In material matters, climate and geography imposed similarities. Scotland, lying far into northern latitudes, with little warmth even in the long days of summer, has a climate that encourages pastoralism. The treeline is kept low by the strong winds and the rapid drop in temperature that comes with height in moist and northern lands, so that the tops of the plateaux are more like the arctic than like other European mountains. 'Forest', loose mixed woodland, probably covered much of the low-lying land of Scotland, except for the islands and Caithness, but it would leave a lot of the hills available for grazing: the temperature rarely falls low enough to kill grass in the winter. As the valleys were gradually cleared of trees by axe or by grazing on the young shoots, corn-growing spread, but until the discovery of techniques of draining much of the valley land was wet. The spring sowing was late, in May or even June, and the harvest consequently late and liable to frost damage. Corn will support a denser population than cattle, but in Scotland it has always supported it precariously. Fortunately few parts of Scotland are far from water, and northern waters abound in fish. Until the late sixteenth century it is unlikely that the peasantry were reduced to an almost exclusively cereal diet. The crops that will grow well in Scotland are the spring corns, oats, and barley. Wheat will grow in the Lothians, as the proud badge of these counties shows, but spring corn is a safer crop. Flax is also possible, but men in early Scotland probably dressed in wool all the year round, as many Scots still do.

The coming of the Norsemen marked the last of the great mass movements of peoples that seems to have gone on from the third to the ninth centuries. In the tenth century things began to stabilize. The English kingdom of Wessex extended itself and gradually reclaimed from the Norse the north and midlands of England. About 930 it destroyed the old British kingdom of Strathclyde, weakened by attacks from all sides, and in 937 the English king Athelstan defeated a combination of Scots, British, and Norse at 'Brunanburh', which may have been near the Solway. The destruction of Northumbria had given the Scots their chance to expand and control Alba, and though the English king claimed some sort of overlordship for the whole island, his rule was slight. There is the famous scene in 973 of Edgar of England being rowed on the Dee by eight under-kings, among whom were Kenneth, King of the Scots, and Malcolm, his nephew, King of 'Cumbria', the southern part of Strathclyde. This shows what had happened to Cumbria. In 945 the English king had accepted Scottish rule in a dependency which was far from the Wessex base, in return for the sort of overlordship which might be pictorially conspicuous on special occasions, as in this bit of oarsmanship, but which was unlikely to lead to real restriction of liberty of action. Only occasionally, when a king of England came north, would a Scottish king or sub-king have to decide between battle or subservience.

If it was the ninth-century Norse invasions that created the pressures and opportunities to bind Scotia together, it was the renewal of these attacks in the late tenth and eleventh centuries, not as mass invasions of England but as incidents in Danish power politics, that enabled Scotia to extend its power southwards. The overlordship of Cumbria was one part of this process, though it did not prevent invasions of the north of England. In the 970s, says an English source, the English king 'gave' Lothian to the Scottish king, so that the latter would be his helper. But we do not know what the bounds of this Lothian were, whether it was the area between the Forth and the southern uplands, or extended as far south as the Tweed. South of Lothian there was an English earldom of Northumbria, and when the Scottish king Malcolm II tried to get this too in 1006 he was defeated by the earl and lost Lothian. The Danish attacks on England went on to culminate in 1016 with Cnut seizing the crown of England. In the struggle that lay behind this *coup*, in which an earl of Northumbria had opposed Cnut, Malcolm seems to have regained Lothian from the earl, and again tried to extend it. He won a victory at Carham, just south of the Tweed, probably in 1018, but Cnut was not the sort of man to take liberties with, and a few years later Malcolm appears to have been holding Cumbria and the country north of the Tweed only by some nominal subservience to England. The Danish attacks had expanded Scotland to include lands south of the natural frontier of Forth and Clyde, and the line of the Tweed was to remain the division; but another century of pressure and bargaining was to go on before the Scottish kings' claim to 'Cumbria' was to mean only that part of it north of the Solway.

One of the reasons why the Scots failed to gain more was that they were having problems in their own kingship. Scotland was not a single unit: the old pieces that made up Pictland still had a life of their own, Atholl and Gowrie, Fife and Fortriu (or Fothrif, which may have been Kinrosshire), Angus and Mearns, Mar and Buchan, and most distinctive of all, Moray and Ross. These pairs of districts were ruled by 'mormaers', or stewards of the sea, perhaps offices somewhere between an Anglo-Saxon earldom and a sub-kingship. Mormaers were great men, and some at least were kin to the royal house. The office was not strictly hereditary, yet descent was an important element in it. The Scottish kingship lay in the near descendants of earlier kings. Any adult great-grandson of a monarch was near enough to succeed. In normal practice the kingship moved from one line of descent to another of near cousins, or 'tanists'. Thus Kenneth II was succeeded not by his son Malcolm but by Constantine III, the son of his first cousin; Constantine was killed by Kenneth III, nephew to the earlier Kenneth, and Kenneth III by Malcolm II. 'Tanistry', or succession by cousinage, meant that there was always an adult king on the throne, and no problem of royal minorities. It also brought into the succession men whose power and lands lay in different regions, and helped to hold the country together. But it meant too that there was always an adult rival for the throne who was unlikely to wait for the succession until his kinsman of a similar age died naturally. The result was frequent war and murder; a high wastage rate of the royal kin.

With Malcolm II the Scottish kingship begins to emerge from the mists of historic darkness, to be almost at once covered by the fog of literary invention. We can see that Malcolm was a powerful king by the length of his reign (1005–34), the number of his tanists that he killed, and his determination, leaving no son, to keep the throne in his line in the person of his grandson Duncan. So Duncan was put in to the exclusion of the surviving kinsmen, Macbeth and his wife Gruoch, who were both of the royal kin and who represented also the mormaers of Moray. Malcolm II and Duncan based their power on the Tay valley and Fife. Duncan was a young man (not the old king of Shakespeare's *Macbeth*) and Macbeth was not, and not prepared to wait. The result was a feud. In 1040 Macbeth killed Duncan and exiled his sons, Malcolm and Donald Ban. Seventeen years later he was himself killed by Malcolm. Malcolm went on to kill Lulach, Gruoch's son by her earlier marriage to a Moray mormaer, and make himself king. All these slaughters took place in the north, and this suggests that the wars were not only dynastic but also represented Moray separatism. Unfortunately they were written up by Hector Boece in the early sixteenth century. He combined a romantic and nationalist enthusiasm for early history of the Scottish monarchy, a belief that if history was not known literary standards demanded that it be invented, and an ignorance of the facts of the early Scottish method of succession. Perhaps this is not simply unfortunate, since it has led to Shakespeare's great study of what the act of murder does to the murderer, but it means that the first Scottish king of whom we know more fact than fiction is Macbeth's slayer. This was Malcolm III, nicknamed Canmore, the 'big-headed', who seized the throne in 1058 and was determined to continue his great-grandfather's work and keep it in a single male line.

The historian setting out to write the history of Scotland has to start by postulating anachronisms: that the later national state of Scotland is the natural end of the evolution of its peoples in the Dark Ages, and that when these people join together they create something that we can recognize as a state. The unit of government in early times was not the state but the monarchy, the person of the king. It was this that held together diverse peoples. Monarchies might in theory be independent or subordinate, but the facts of geography meant that any single power was in practice limited. Lesser units existed which should not be thought of as simply 'under' the monarchy. If the right political and personal conditions obtained these might grow to statehood. One such was the earldom of Northumbria, others were the Norse earldoms which occupied large parts of what is now Scotland; for instance the earldom of Orkney. There was also a Norse principality of the western islands, the 'Sudreys', sometimes regarded as a kingdom, with its royal base in Man. The royal families of England and Scotland were of greater prestige than these, because they commanded richer lands and more men, and because they had more distinguished royal genealogies, but they were not yet different in kind, nor were there any nationalist reasons why the kings of these units should not try to bring one or more of the semi-independent earldoms under real control. To do so would be a mixed process, calling for military power, personality, and some rights by inheritance. William Duke of Normandy reversed this process in 1066 by adding a kingdom to a semi-independent duchy by a process that was weak on the inheritance side but strong on the others. If the Scandinavian kings could produce a successor to Harald Hardrada of similar quality they might change the course of empire back: at any rate they would probably have a shot at regaining Northumbria, which had been ruled by a half Danish earl, Tostig Godwineson, until the Northumbrians threw him out. Before that Northumbria, under the rule of Earl Siward, uncle to Malcolm, had been the place of refuge of Malcolm from Macbeth. Of all parts of England Northumbria was the most difficult to dominate: William of Normandy tried hard to conciliate feeling there, and then decided on coercion and slaughter with the terrible 'harrying of the north' in 1070. Finally he executed the native earl Waltheof, son of Siward, in 1076.

In this setting Malcolm had several cards he could play over Northumbria, but he played them crudely and badly. He failed to increase his hereditary claim by marriage. Instead he married Ingibiorg, widow of Thorfinn. Thorfinn had been a Norse fighter who had conquered a large part of Orkney and Caithness and who had left two sons, later earls of Orkney. Ingibiorg gave Malcolm at least one son, Duncan. In 1070, or thereabouts, Malcolm married again, Margaret, sister of Edgar Atheling, of the house of Wessex. It seems to have been a love-match of people of widely different cultures. Margaret had been partly brought up in Hungary, and had come to England with her brother when it seemed likely the crown there might go to him. She was deeply pious; like many of the Anglo-Saxon aristocracy, but unlike Malcolm, she was educated and literate.

Hungary was a country recently converted to Christianity, and it had shown her what monarchy could do in religious matters and what community in the Catholic Church could and should mean. The marriage cannot have been well received by the Norman King of England. The Scottish court was already a centre for English refugees. Tostig had come there in 1065, and Cospatrick, who had claims to the earldoms of Cumbria and Northumbria, in 1069; but Malcolm failed to meet and use English feeling in his attempts to gain Northumbria. He invaded five times, starting in 1061: in 1072 his invasion, coupled with his marriage, brought William on a land and sea campaign to Scotland. The two kings met at Abernethy, in the heart of Pictish Scotia, right up by the Earn, a fact which suggests that William's force had been irresistible. There Malcolm 'became William's man', accepted some sort of overlordship, and gave his son Duncan as a hostage. An English chronicler's comment on Malcolm's invasion is biting: that it was done 'not to help him at all toward the kingdom but because it would annoy William'. His homage of 1072 did not stop him invading again; 1079, 1091, 1093. These attacks by ill-disciplined and looting followers effectively destroyed the value of any claim he might have had to the support of the Northumbrians against the Normans, and did much to fix the frontier at the Tweed. In his last English attack Malcolm and Edward, his eldest son by Margaret, were killed near Alnwick. Imperialism had not paid. William I had shown he meant to hold Northumbria by a policy of castle building, and in 1092 his son William II had taken Cumberland from the son of Malcolm's protégé, Cospatrick, and fortified Carlisle against the Scots.

What Malcolm's reign and second marriage had done though was to turn the interest of the monarchy of Scotland away from her Norse associates to England. This became marked when, on Malcolm's death, his inheritance was disputed. There seems to have been some reason why Margaret's sons regarded Duncan as illegitimate: Malcolm and Ingibiorg were probably related, and if so a closer knowledge of canon law might have brought their marriage under the blight of uncertainty which the chaotic church law on marriage laid over the medieval world. Malcolm's brother Donald Ban claimed the throne as tanist, and indeed held it for two brief periods in an atmosphere of reaction towards things Celtic. William of England put in the anglicized Duncan, who had grown up at the English court, as vassal. He was killed by Donald Ban, whom William replaced with Margaret's eldest surviving son, Edgar (1097). After Edgar came his brother Alexander (1107), who also held the kingship as vassal of England, married the illegitimate daughter of the English King Henry, and gave him back his own sister in marriage. An era of Scottish–English marriages kept up close relations between the countries, but the question of vassalage was to depend on the persons and powers of the kings concerned in the next hundred years.

NOTES

The children of Malcolm III (Canmore):
 by Ingibiorg, Duncan II (reigned 1094)
 by Margaret, six sons and two daughters:
  one daughter married Henry I of England
  of the sons, three succeeded to the throne:
  Edgar (reigned 1097–1107)
  Alexander I (1107–24)
  David I (1124–53).

Chapter 2

1100–1286

Inchcolm: building the monastery

TO SAY THAT SCOTLAND was a monarchy in the eleventh century is to stress the personal element that held together its varied cultures. Kingship was a fact: to call yourself a king you had to be of the royal house, accepted, enthroned, and ruling. That as king you might, or might not, acknowledge a superior, was not particularly important. If there had been no English overlordship of Scotland there might well have been a Norse one, for Norse power was reviving. Magnus Bareleg, King of Norway, had conquered and reclaimed the Norse earldoms. By agreement in 1098 his part of Scotland included all the islands and Kintyre, which is almost an island. The Scottish kings had lost their ancient burial site of Iona, but the kings of Margaret and Malcolm's line, turning their backs on the Celtic past, were buried in their new Benedictine abbey in Dunfermline. Kingship gave wide scope for personal influence, and where, as in their case, this was linked with Margaret's reputation not just for piety but for saintliness, the sphere of the monarchy could expand. She and her youngest son, David, eventually David I, were able to lead the country in secular and religious changes. Most of the kings could not hope for such special influence, but they would have particular support from some particular region in the kingdom while claiming to be king of the whole. Their material support came in dues of grain and cattle and hospitality, so that to receive these the king had to move, or send men, about. He had rights of 'cain' and 'conveth', cain being a due in grain, conveth in hospitality. There was a general obligation of military service, 'Scottish' service as it was later called. The king did not make law, for law was regarded as already existing, but in practice he declared it. We hear of David I sitting in justice 'at the entrance of the royal hall'. These rights and powers were only enlargements of those that other men exercised under him: the mormaers, or earls as they became, were almost sub-kings, and there were men called 'britten' or judge, who also gave out law. If the king was not there in person someone else would have to collect his grain dues.

Under the king, life was held together by concepts and facts of kin and chieftainship. There were 'thanes' who may have been the men in charge of the king's own lands. In the north a chief or 'toisech' existed, perhaps as a leader of the army. National and royal duties would not be separated in men's minds. Within the larger relationship of kin were special ties produced by the old Celtic custom of fosterage – as the life of St Catroe states, a foster father 'provides aid thenceforward in everything'. But otherwise this was a society lacking in formal institutions and clear obligations. Dealings between men were settled by personality, power, and kinship.

In the same way the Church lacked organization. There were bishops in Scotland but not with fixed areas of action. Hermits could be found, and semi-monastic groups, the Celidé or Culdees, but not a settled monastic way of life with a written rule. Religious functions, except near to one of these groups, must have been only occasionally discharged by a visiting priest or wandering holy man.

For most people the bounds of experience and life were narrow, even though the habit of moving stock to upland pastures each summer took families away from a single base. The land was not closely settled: perhaps between a quarter and a third of a million people lived in old Scotland. Material possessions were few. Iron was a precious commodity, used to tip tools otherwise made of wood. Houses were huts of stone and turf, probably shared on equal terms with the cows. They would be filled with smoke since nothing as elaborate as a flue could yet be built. Cleanliness, the first luxury of primitive peoples, was difficult to attain. That important artefact, soap, is not mentioned as an object of commerce in Scotland before the seventeenth century, but it is known to have existed as a domestic manufacture in most of Europe since the ninth century. It is also relatively easy to make a lye with wood-ash which will help in washing. But the primitive hearths and houses of early Scotland must have meant that all except the greatest were used to a lot of soot and mud around them. Cleanliness was stressed as part of knightly courtesy in the upper-class literature of the thirteenth century, but, like much else of the knightly code, was probably a rarity in practice. We hear that Queen Margaret enormously impressed her contemporaries by introducing them to material luxuries. Under her guidance both nobles and king dined off gilded vessels; the Scots were 'compelled to buy clothes of different colours . . . with various ornaments', and the palace was hung with silken cloths.

A society such as this could move closer to the rest of Christendom, or it could stay where it was for several centuries. Sooner or later political or economic pressures would force it into the European community. It was because of the decision of the sons of Margaret, particularly of David I, that this change was to take place in the twelfth century and not be postponed, as it was in Muscovy, until the coercion of Peter the Great at the end of the seventeenth century, or as in Ireland, till the actions of the conquering English. In the unsettled period after Malcolm's death some of his sons had grown up at the English court, in the full flush of Normanization. The Normans were the men of business of all Europe at this time, providing the tools of government, a literature, and a common standard of values from Sicily northward. They understood things in terms of a mixture of military force, law, and organization. It was the Normans who

believed in counting and measuring, in defining rights and obligations. Particularly they knew how to use the specialized soldier, the
mounted mailed man, the 'tank' of primitive battle. Norman society
was not confined to those with a family base in the Duchy of Normandy, for the Normans as imperialists were not nationalists. They
assimilated those who would share their speech and way of life,
providing a common upper crust across Europe, so that an enterprising man might find land and a career a thousand miles from his place
of upbringing, or a girl in England might speak casually of cousins in
Sicily. There was a sense of the kinship of Normans all the world
over, which, if in many cases meant a real cousinship also meant
a cultural affinity, with the use of northern French speech. By the
conquest of England the Normans added their system of feudal law,
landholding, and military service to a country which had already gone
a long way farther in the creation of formal governing institutions
than had Scotland. It was from this new amalgam that Alexander I
(1107–24) and his brother David I (1124–53) brought the elements
that reorganized Scotland.

A society in which the means of production are almost exclusively
confined to the land, one where wealth is in crops and stock and where
international trade barely exists, must tie the provision of the functions of government to land or disintegrate. Pre-Norman Scotland
had no coinage of its own, a fact which gives the measure of its
commercial life. Feudalism is a way of organizing and delegating
government through the land: its basic concept the conditional
holding of land in return for service of a specialized kind. Feudal law
creates the unit of the fief, the estate held hereditarily and inalienably
by the vassal in return for the performance of precise services to his
lord. Landholding is a contract: loyalty and service, whether at war
or in court, are owed by the man, and protection by the lord. Land-
lordism is the same as overlordship, the rights of both relate to a
particular estate. Service includes service at court, the duty of advice
or of receiving justice, as well as military duty or castle guard.

The two most important functions of government, justice and
defence, thus get tied up with landholding, and so strong was the
prevailing structure of feudal law that this system of delegated power,
and the supporting system of two or more men having inalienable
rights in a piece of land, continued long after the economic need for

this form of social structure. Theoretically the form of military service is an accident of the current techniques of war in a feudal society. The specialized warrior might be the two-sworded samurai fighting on foot, as in Japan, or the mailed knight and the defender of castles, as in feudal Europe and Palestine. In practice the form of the specialization did something to dictate the size of feudal units. Mail was expensive, so was a horse capable of carrying a man and his armour. Both of these got dearer still when mail gave way to plate armour in the late fourteenth century. So the basic knight's fief had to be a sizeable estate – a group of townships or a village. Till the fifteenth century the art of fortification remained well ahead of the techniques of siege, so the great lord in his castle, with his knights and men of arms under him, remained relatively immune to unrest from those below him, or to royal discipline. The early twelfth-century castle might be only 'motte and bailey', an artificial or natural mound with a wooden or stone tower ringed by a palisade and ditch, but more formidable buildings came in by 1200 and in the thirteenth century there developed the elaborate and carefully angled keeps, gatehouses, and curtain walls that show that warfare had its own science. The powerful castles of the later Middle Ages, for instance Tantallon, Dunnottar, Dunstaffnage even, combining strong fortifications with natural features, would be a tough proposition for military force, and were practically impregnable to local peasantry. Yet in the mountainous parts of Scotland the peasantry continued to have a military function. Scottish service under the earl was still of military importance on terrain unsuited to cavalry.

In the feudal state all land eventually is owned by the king, since he personifies civil authority, but his real authority may be limited or shadowy, as was for instance that of the King of France over his vassal the Duke of Normandy. Even more vague was that of the English king over his 'man', Malcolm Canmore, or Alexander I. Meanwhile it suited the sons of Margaret and Malcolm to preserve the relationship: it kept out rival claimants, the line of Ingibiorg or the mormaers of Moray, and gave the kings a chance to establish claims on Cumbria or Northumbria. Since the frontier of Tweed and Solway was not, at least in the east, a real natural break, nor on either side a cultural one, it was entirely reasonable to hope to expand. When Alexander I inherited from his brother Edgar, Strathclyde and southern Lothian were bequeathed to his younger brother David, who became earl of southern Scotland. David married an heiress with claims to the old Northumbrian earldom, and the right to an earldom in southern England, in Huntingdonshire and Northamptonshire. This southern earldom was clearly David's, and he and his successors did homage for it to the King of England. Scottish historians have sometimes complained that this territorial possession led the Scottish king into an undefined subordinate position to England, but the hope of reuniting and dominating the old kingdoms of Northumbria and Strathclyde made it worth while, and for a century and a half the Scottish monarchy allowed itself to be woven closer and closer into the English by intermarriage. More immediately Earl David found advantages in the Normans who were his vassals in his English earldom, and transferred some of them to holdings in his Scottish earldom. David had an intelligent and receptive mind. He was in England when the new monastic orders were being taken up with enthusiasm; he had worked as a judge in Henry I's court there. He was technically trained in feudal war and understood the value of castles. Even more than his mother he had a taste for foreign goods, which would have to be bought. When therefore he became king he brought in the institutions he had met abroad. He transferred his friends and followers; some to smallish holdings as individual knights, some to bigger tracts of land such as the lordship of Annandale, given to the de Brus family. He built castles; examples of these are Roxburgh and Berwick. He borrowed the idea of officers of state from England, of Constable, Marischal, and Steward. The 'sheriff' was a useful servant though his function in Scotland was not as an administrator of a shire court, for these courts did not exist, but as a royal servant who looked after the king's rents and held a royal castle,[1] and who may have been an adaptation of the old thane. The English writ came to Scotland as the 'breve' but its function, as a brief and businesslike administrative order, was unchanged. In David's lifetime, feudalism and the presence of Normans stopped at the Forth, but the creation of a central machinery using Norman techniques

1. The word sheriff covers three very different institutions today, all of which carry some of the old Anglo-Saxon features of the office – in the United States he is a policeman, in Scotland a judge, and in England the formal representative of the local gentry.

B

meant that eventually they would spread into Scotia, so that even the earldoms, those outposts of Celtic life, would be feudalized. Great feudal landowners brought up their own Normanized followers from the south; an example of this was the grant of Romanno by Robert de Quinchy (whose family came from Flanders) to a follower of his called Hugh. De Quinchy and others retained land in both England and Scotland. A few of the great names, and more of the lesser, had lands in both kingdoms, which might create problems of personal allegiance, but not yet of national loyalty since this was not at issue. Under David's grandson, William the Lion (1165–1214), feudalism entered Scotia proper and knights were planted in Angus, Gowrie, and Mearns. Probably in this reign the family of Comyn came into Badenoch and built up a powerful network of holdings based on the earldom of Buchan, acquired by marriage. Feudalism's conveniences were not ignored by the older nobility. Duncan, Earl of Fife under William, held his earldom by knight service, and the earls of Strathearn and Angus had knights under them. But there were still areas with very little in the way of feudal tenures, notably the far north, and Galloway which still sat loose to the monarchy under its own earls and laws. The king's own knights, so useful in an army even when they only numbered a score or so, were not obtained by mass demands on great lords for thirty or so, but by individual grants of land, and this meant that the Scottish tenant-in-chief or 'baron' was often the owner of a small estate – the Dolfin of Dolphinton or the Simon of Symington in Clydesdale for instance.

The late tenth century had seen a monastic reform in Burgundy and Lorraine which had spread over the continent and reached England. The eleventh had seen a drastic reform of the secular Church. Neither of these movements had had a direct effect on Scotland until Alexander and David remodelled the Church there. But the personal holiness of Margaret and her attempt to remove particular anomalies – irregularities over the timing of Lent, peculiar features in the Mass, and an obligation to marry a stepmother or sister-in-law are examples – had started the tradition that the Church should be a special area of concern for the royal house. Margaret's introduction of Benedictines to the new abbey at Dunfermline had turned the monastic emphasis of Scotland away from the more disorganized Celtic tradition. All medieval kings tried to exercise control in the Church, to have as bishops the men they wanted, understandably since a bishopric was a great unit of landholding and local power. Almost all held a special devotion for some saint or other, and all expected, and knew they needed, a spiritual return from benefits to monasteries, ease of their souls after death. But the early twelfth century was a period of specialization: kings were feudal soldiers. As such it was not their business to understand fine points of doctrine, nor in the early part of the century to read Latin.[1] Whereas Henry I of England would give ecclesiastical and lay office to a priest who pleased him by getting through mass in record time, his brother-in-law David held a different set of values in church matters. It was under him that the secular Church was given coherent organization. The territorial diocese with its bishop, its episcopal centre, and under this the beginnings of a parish structure, date from his reign. This gave Scotland a church structure similar to that of the rest of Europe, except that her nine bishoprics did not include an archbishop, and were, in some inadequately defined way, until 1192 under the see of York. After that date the Scottish Church was a special daughter of the see of Rome. Her bishops were men of international calibre who knew what the reforming papacy was about, and were prepared to try and do something about the standard British system of married and hereditary clergy. The kings, particularly David, brought in the new monastic orders with a care and deliberate selection that shows they understood the different facets of religious life the orders represented – Cistercians from Rievaulx with their stress on labour and plainness at Melrose; Cluniacs with their elaborate services in the Isle of May; Tironensians at Kelso; Premonstratensians at that loveliest of sites, Dryburgh, where the pinkish grey stones now lie in ruins under big trees beside the Tweed; Austin canons at Holyrood, Jedburgh, and Cambuskenneth. This was not just an enthusiasm for fashionable developments in monasticism. The monastic life has to be lived as a challenge if at all, and it was in the new orders that this approach would most readily be found. Royal pressure gradually transformed the last vestiges of the old Celtic Church, the communities of Culdees, into Austin canons – at St Andrew's and Monymusk and perhaps at

1. This had changed by 1200. There is for instance the well-known scene of the English Richard I (not a bookish type) showing up his archbishop's bad latinity to a court which could appreciate the joke.

Scone. The Scottish Church became, not just in theory but fully in practice, a branch of the Catholic Church organized like the other branches.[1]

In another important feature of civilization the Scotland of David came into Europe. This was the creation of formal town life, in the burghs. In one sense nothing seems more organic than the growth of towns: communities of merchants and craftsmen at key communication centres, providing a market for local food surpluses and importing or making the specialist products needed even by a primitive economy. But in fact burghs have to be created, given a special corporate existence, a special law, and put into special relationship (financial and judicial) with the central government. Though no burgh charters survive from David's reign it seems that this was when they started. Dunfermline, Berwick, Roxburgh, Edinburgh, Perth, Stirling, and Aberdeen at least appear to date from then. The next big batch dates from David's grandson William, and includes Dumfries, Ayr and Dundee. In many of these cases the burgh was created at a place with some life of its own already; perhaps trade moved there already because of a vital river crossing or harbour. Creation of a burgh means confirmation and definition of rights of trading, and strengthening them by monopoly, by the exclusion of others from trade in a defined area. A rampart or a wall is set up as protection for the privileged traders. Sometimes there may be a royal castle too. The burgh and its men, the burgesses, are organized at least partly to govern themselves: this is necessary because they will have to use special law and speedy procedure, and will have special needs.[2] In return for these advantages the burghs are expected to pay money, customs duties on important exports, and a rent or 'ferme'.

Towns were being founded all over twelfth-century Europe. Sometimes the aim was political. In the German conquests over Slav lands towns were founded as nuclei of German power. In France the king,

1. In an effort to reduce the total period of control by the papacy some Presbyterian church historians have often unduly extended the life of the Columban Church and behaved as if the differences between Scotland and the rest of Christendom in the tenth and eleventh centuries were not simply irregularities but a sign of incipient protestantism.

2. The law of the burghs came to be what was known as 'the Laws and Customs of the Four Burghs' (Edinburgh, Roxburgh, Berwick, and Stirling), and this was based on the late twelfth-century customs of Newcastle-on-Tyne.

who after all stood in theory for law and order, gained enormously politically by encouraging the creation of towns, for instance the *villes neuves* of Louis VII. The Scottish kings probably had similar motives. In 1174, according to William of Newburgh, the most accurate of English chroniclers, the towns of Scotland were 'known to be inhabited by the English'. Town life was part of David's cosmopolitanizing policy. In the same way that Scottish monasticism, almost exclusively of royal foundation, gave its own prestige to a monarchy still insecure enough to appreciate it, so did the burghs. They were either from early days the king's own burghs, founded by him and holding of him, or gradually became regarded as in some way 'royal'. They contributed to royal funds. Any effective privilege or the right of self-government needed an explicit royal grant. Besides prestige they gave another needful thing to the Crown, money. The kings of Scotland were adjusting their habits to those of the general upper crust of Europe and this meant needs that could not be met at home – good armour and weapons, expensive fabrics, books such as the gold-lettered gospels that St Margaret used to read, spices for their food, wine. Money already moved about slowly in Scotland, but not till David did any king coin his own. The new pennies that David's urban policy produced were crude coins of sterling silver[1] (Scottish coins do not merit any aesthetic appreciation until the reign of David II). Whereas the king's lands paid their dues in kind and his followers theirs in service, the towns gave hard cash, and this opened up the economic life of king and nation. By the late thirteenth century the burghs provided an eighth part of the king's revenue. Each burgh lay enshrined in its own little area of privilege. 'I firmly forbid any foreign merchant within the sheriffdom of Aberdeen from buying or selling anything except in my burgh of Aberdeen,' runs William the Lion's charter. At first the burghs were full of foreigners speaking outlandish tongues from England or Flanders. In practice they could not remain so cut off. For one thing most of these burghs were tiny; they had little mercantile activity and got a good deal of their bare living from the land. Burgesses had to grow at least a part of their own food and until the eighteenth century the burgh's lands and grazings were important. In 1174 the Scots and Galwegians in the army of

1. It was probably not so much in imitation of England that sterling was used but because this degree of alloy provides a good working material. Pure silver is too soft.

William the Lion had felt sufficiently hostile to these strangers, the townsmen, to fall upon them and slaughter them after his defeat at Alnwick. A hundred years later the townsmen were not strangers. They shared the local speech in south-east Scotland because their own English had been adopted there. They also recruited part of their populations from the countryside: all towns had to do this at least until the later eighteenth century to survive, since towns were killers. Even the minute burghs of Scotland would form dangerous concentrations of disease in an age totally unsanitary.

The Crown and aristocracy needed merchants, whether strangers or no, for the things they brought in. As military techniques developed, so did the specialization necessary to serve them. The wealth of the great Italian cities in the thirteenth century set a new level of luxury for the upper classes elsewhere to copy, which could not be provided by rural craftsmen. Neither standards of living nor techniques could be fossilized, and so enonomic development was eventually to break up the feudal society the burghs were designed to serve. But at first the burghs were a necessary anomaly.

The new institutions did not come painlessly into Scotland. The entry of a foreign aristocracy, gradual though it was, meant adjustment. Scots lost lands or positions to the newcomers. The discomforts of this could soon be eased by intermarriage, yet there were feelings of hostility. A distaste for the newfangled feudalism was shown in 1160 when the young King Malcolm IV came back with his brother from an expedition to Toulouse in the army of Henry II of England, on which he had been knighted by Henry, and found six Scottish earls in arms against him. Support for the old Celtic method of tanist succession continued, and sometimes allied itself with regional separatism. Moray, the strongest separatist element, kept a line of earls and mormaers from Lulach until 1134, when David I annexed this earldom to the Crown. Either he or his successors fastened a particularly detailed administrative structure on it, planting castles and burghs, for instance Elgin and Forres. In Argyll there reigned Somerled, almost independent, a semi-king. He had driven out the Scandinavians and controlled Kintyre and some of the islands. Only in 1164 was he defeated and killed by Malcolm IV. Galloway was fiercely separate under its own law, and wearing its own clothing: the Galwegians fought in battle 'half naked'. The reason why local independence was dangerous to the monarchy was that at best David I and his grandsons had a claim to the throne that needed some explaining. Duncan II had left a son, William, from whom came a line of 'MacWilliams', and this form of nomenclature indicates that their base was in Gaelic Scotland. Donald MacWilliam, grandson of Duncan II, made a revolt in the north in 1181 which was not suppressed till he was killed in 1187. As late as 1239 the slaughter of an infant of this line by methods a good deal cruder than those used by John of England against his rebel nephew Arthur shows us that the monarchy was aware of weakness in its title. Politically as serious was the threat by another claim, that of Malcolm Macheth in 1130. Malcolm may have been an illegitimate son of Alexander I. This may not seem much of a claim but it was made dangerous by an alliance with the Earl of Moray, and this was the background to, and explanation of, the royal annexation of the earldom. A few years later David I had to meet another rebellion by a Moray pretender, Wimund, Bishop of Sodor and Man (a twelfth-century bishop was often of necessity a man of war and politics).

So the monarchy needed all the prestige its new institutions could give, particularly as the kings were not particularly successful militarily. The crisis that showed they were winning came on the death of David's son, Earl Henry. David's own succession had been obvious, for it fulfilled both the Celtic system, as his brother's heir, and the feudal one of primogeniture. To prevent a reversion to one of the rival lines he had associated Henry with himself in the kingship, a practice common among the other feudal monarchies: 'deo propitio heres et rex designatus' Henry was called. But Henry died ten months before his father. David then bent all his great personal influence to securing the succession of his grandson Malcolm, a child of twelve. The boy was sent through Scotia in the company of the Earl of Fife and a large army, and proclaimed heir. The king's influence prevailed and Malcolm inherited, but the survival of the MacWilliam claim meant that control over the Highlands, both by himself and by his brother and successor William, was slight.

The eyes of the twelfth-century kings were anyway not on the Highlands but on southern expansion. When the civil war in England broke out between Stephen and Matilda, the Scottish King David, as a vassal of the old King Henry I, had sworn allegiance to Matilda.

She was David's niece, but another niece was the wife of Stephen. David stayed neutral until called in by Matilda, and then charged in unsuccessfully in the hope of grabbing Northumberland. He tried again in 1138 but was defeated at the famous Battle of the Standard after a campaign that led to a flood of atrocity stories in the English chronicles (it was the Galwegians particularly who annoyed the English). In spite of defeat, the uncertain position of Stephen enabled David to get hold of Carlisle and the earldom of Northumberland. But the year of the Standard marks a watershed in frontier history: the old community of northern Anglo-Saxon Britain was broken. In Yorkshire the Scots appeared as foreigners. A national breach between England and Scotland was bound to become defined in the twelfth century at some point. If it had not come from the slaughters of the Standard campaign it would have been created by the formal body of law and institutions which later kings of both countries, particularly Henry II of England and William the Lion of Scotland, built up. The breach was not yet recognized by the kings, who went on playing a game of beggar-my-neighbour with each other, each taking advantage of any weakness in the other's position. As David had snatched the northern earldom in civil war, Henry II took it back during Malcolm's minority, in breach of treaty, and William the Lion entered into the struggle between Henry II and his son, the young Henry, in 1173 on a promise of it from the young Henry. Another attempt led to William's capture at Alnwick in 1174, which coincided with a rising in Galloway. The Scots king could not afford to quibble over terms with the English, made at Falaise, but in the end these were generous. William had to accept English overlordship, swear fealty, and do homage, liege homage, and his barons with him, and hand over his main southern castles. But these were interpreted leniently, understandably when you look at the English king's position. He had just had the most serious rising of his reign, which had split the loyalty of the English kingdom deeply. Explicit overlordship of Scotland might be useful if it led to real friendship and peace. Territory, to a king who owned a third of Europe yet could not control it, was less important than good relations. So the Galloway rising was not exploited, only three castles were occupied, and William's brother David was granted the earldom of Huntingdon. In 1189, when Henry's successor Richard wanted money for crusading, the whole treaty was surrendered by the quitclaim of Canterbury for 10,000 merks.[1]

But the Scottish king still wanted that English northern earldom. Both kings continued to chip in on any troubles that might afflict their neighbours. So in 1209 William nearly got an invasion from John, and compromised instead on a complicated financial and matrimonial bargain. In 1237 Alexander II, by appearing to join in Henry III of England's Welsh and baronial troubles, secured the Treaty of York, abandoning Scottish claims to the northern counties for an estate in the north as Henry's vassal. Other families in Scotland held lands in England, and one such, the de Brus, later called 'Bruce', is said to have fought on both sides at the Standard. Correspondingly the great church of Durham had been given lands in Lothian by kings and nobles who did not feel that devotion to St Cuthbert stopped at a frontier. In the thirteenth century, with peace between the countries and the habit of accepting payments instead of military service, these mixed possessions caused no more difficulties than are created today by an international portfolio of stocks and shares. And the century was one of peace. Henry III did not leave Scotland alone but his interventions were more those of a father to the young Queen of Alexander III than of someone with pretensions to suzerainty. Overlordship might be talked about occasionally, but did not go beyond talk.

David I is the last king for nearly two centuries of whom we have a clear impression of personality, and that comes more from the total sense of vision in his work than from personal accounts, though we are left with a convincing picture of his affectionate relationship with his son Earl Henry. Scottish records, confiscated and lost on two later occasions by English invaders, and probably sparser than in England even before these occasions, are now traditionally regarded by the public as non-existent. This is not true, but official documents before the mid-fifteenth century are to be counted only in hundreds where the corresponding English material numbers tens of thousands. The surviving 'Acta' of Malcolm IV comprise a hundred and sixty-one documents, and are mainly gathered from private cartularies. What is more, the main chronicle sources for the twelfth and thirteenth centuries are English rather than Scottish, and their

1. A merk is two-thirds of a pound.

picture of Scottish rulers and affairs lacks the vigour and pungency, as well sometimes as the systematic bias, found in their accounts of English affairs. Perhaps the Scottish kings after David I were men without the daemonic qualities of the Angevins. Alexander II (1214–49) and III (1249–80) were adequate for their function. If they did not play as big a part in reshaping the country's institutions as their predecessors of the twelfth century, this was because that work had now been done. With peace on their southern frontier they could work at incorporating more fully the two areas of separatist traditions, the north and Galloway. William the Lion had intervened in the 1170s in a dispute between the sons of Fergus, Lord of Galloway, and had eventually secured the division of the lands, so that Galloway proper went to one claimant, and southern Ayrshire became the lordship of Carrick, later an earldom. Rivalry between the two lines and districts was reawakened at the end of the thirteenth century when by marriages these came to represent two separate claims to the throne, those of the houses of Bruce and Balliol. Galloway was still so separate that it had to have its own Justiciar, to rank with the other Justiciars for Scotia and Lothian. For a time in the 1230s it looked as if separatism there might link up with Norse power in the islands, but this was prevented by a mixture of force and luck.

The north was a longer issue because it was a bigger area and beyond lay the foreign power of the Norse-held islands. There were also the rival claimants to the throne, the MacWilliams. Gradually these were exterminated. The crucial area of the central Highlands with the bleak but essential Drumochter pass, connecting north and west with the south, was made into the lordship of Badenoch and given to the Comyn family to hold by castles and discipline. This settled, Alexander II was able to assert overlordship over Argyll and plan the conquest of the western isles.[1] He went westwards with an army and fleet in 1249 to take advantage of the death of an earl of the Hebrides, but died suddenly in Kerrera, a small grassy island lying in the mouth of the bay of Oban. Settlement with the Norse had to wait till the maturity of his son Alexander III.

1. The Isles could be regarded as *Scótia Irredenta*, but since they had been held by Scottish kings their own civilization, the nature of kingship, and even the meaning of the word 'Scotia' had drastically changed.

Alexander III tried to buy the Norwegians out in the Isles. On their refusal he provoked a vast invasion plan from Norway in 1263. The old King Haakon IV (whose name still survives in Kyle Akin) sailed out from Bergen in his dragon-headed ship 'to avenge the warfare that the Scots had made in his dominions', took a levy from the inhabitants of Caithness, plundered Kintyre, and, taking boats across the narrow isthmus at Arrochar, looted the Lennox. For all that the islands belonged to him, they gave him little help, and that grudgingly. The Scottish king had an army but lacked the mobility of Haakon's fleet. Things swung in his favour with damage by an October storm to the Norse fleet riding at open anchorage in the Cumbraes, and a disorganized fight on land near Largs. The Norwegians abandoned the initiative and retreated to Orkney where the old king died. His saga gives us a picture of his last days, the king being read to, first in Latin, and then, as he weakened, in Norse, first the stories of saints and, at the end, of his great ancestors, the conquering kings of Norway. His successor decided to let go the distant islands, perhaps because they were uncooperative. He made the Treaty of Perth in 1266, giving Man and the western islands to the Scots for a lump sum and an annual rent. The Scots seem to have been backward in their payments, but the treaty was effective because it marked, not so much a Scottish victory, as the admission by Norway that the viking age was over, the tide of conquest had passed.[1]

So in Alexander III's reign the area known as Scotland became much as it is today, with the striking exception that the northern isles still belonged to Norway. Caithness had become securely held by the Scots earlier in the century. With the king building fortresses along the west coast and the islands it looked as if a new era for the Scottish state was opening. Later events were to gild this reign with the

1. Man did not stay long in Scottish hands. It was taken by the English in 1290 on a claim of misgovernment by the Scots (probably justified): regained for a while in the fourteenth century and then held under English suzerainty for several centuries as an almost independent principality, by the Stanleys. In the eighteenth century it passed to the dukes of Atholl, and later sovereignty was bought back by the British Parliament. Eventually it settled down under a form of Home Rule. The separateness of Man has enabled it to provide useful economic services at various times: a refuge for debtors and a smuggling base in the eighteenth century, an outlet for gambling or motor-cycle racing in the twentieth.

reputation of a golden age, a time 'Of wine and wax, of gamyn and glee'. Lacking documentation we have only scraps of information to use as confirmation or denial. There had been political disturbance from 1253–7, a mixture, it seems, of factions among the aristocracy and intervention by Henry III of England, and these produced the first example of the Scottish habit of kidnapping the king. But it looks as if these divisions had healed and certainly the English king had afterwards been so deeply involved in troubles of his own that he had no time to spare for Scotland. We know that agriculture was increasing in the thirteenth century. In 1214 it was ordered that any peasant rich enough to have four cows should get land from his lord to plough and sow: but this reminds us also that much of Scotland's wealth was in stock and game – cattle, salmon fishings, deer. A turn to agriculture is evidence of growing population. Scotland's peasantry, particularly the large class of unfree, owed their lords heavy rents in kind, and also occasional special labour services. They do not seem to have been regularly bound to work on his demesne. They were 'bound' to the soil unless they could get to a town and live and work there for a while, but they do not seem to have had the security of tenure of a manorial villein in England. Since their value was as rent payers and since it would be a long time before Scotland was fully occupied and farmed, their lords usually wished to retain them. A network of duties and obligations held them to him: they had to use his mill, fetch his needs, cut his turf, pay him conveth. In the south the land was farmed in small townships, with the arable in strips; in the north in homestead units or 'davochs'. Between townships, at least in the valleys, there was still a lot of open woodland, the most famous of these areas of forest being that of Selkirk which stretched across the Borders and parts of Lothian, and provided the king with his hunting. In the Borders, sheep farming, associated especially with monasteries such as Melrose, was already important, and there and elsewhere rapidly denuded the country of trees. Wool was also already a major product in Strathmore. The rivers of Scotland held salmon, which could be pickled for winter, and the large bays of the sea were visited by herring.

The natural features of Scotland's geography gave her her primitive trading goods, wool, skins, and fish. The eventual problem of an economy of this type is that it has definite limits of expansion. As the

population grows, and of necessity turns more to agriculture, both
pasture and areas for game become restricted. The peasantry eat
worse, if more regularly. By the time we can get details of their food,
in the eighteenth century, it is definitely a diet deficient in protein,
even though saved from utter inadequacy by the fact that the Scottish staple, oats, has the highest protein content of all the grains. At
the same time wool and hides cannot be produced on the old scale
with the land needed for corn. At what point the failure to expand
becomes serious is not known, since we do not know the size of Scotland's population before the mid-eighteenth century. In 1258 the
country was sufficiently dependent on grain to suffer the same
dearth from a bad harvest as did England: we hear of another dearth
in 1200. There is no notable evidence of shortage of farmable land
before the sixteenth century. The general signs are that Scotland
enjoyed the 'boom' found all over Europe in the thirteenth century,
and her setback came from the later wars rather than from the weakness of over-population which was affecting much of Europe in the
early fourteenth century.

   This boom saw a period of increasing population, the expansion of
the area under plough, the growth of towns, increasing technological
skill, and more trade. The thirteenth century is the period when city
life flowered in Italy and the Netherlands, when the fulling-mill
transformed industry in England, and when all Europe learnt of
better techniques of ship-building and rig. Most materially it has left
across Europe the ruins of elaborate castles and town walls, complicated structures of dressed stone. Scotland's share of all this was real
but probably small. We hear of her wool in the European markets,
coarse stuff, classed below the English, but of value; of coal working
in the Lothians, probably only of outcrops; of salt-pans on the coast,
even in the mid-twelfth century. From the twelfth century the towns
of Scotland were making cloth. Berwick was the burgh that specialized in the export of wool and hides, and in 1286 Alexander III
was able to use its customs as surety for a loan of over £2,000 (this
does not mean that they were worth that sum, but only its annual
interest at some extortionate medieval rate: interest rates were always
high for kings). The duty must already have been very valuable.
Berwick by then had the full paraphernalia of town government, by
a mayor and four 'praepositi' (grieves) and twenty-four burgesses

elected by the community, with a gild merchant to exercise her privileges and regulate the sales and industry of the town. Whenever there was peace a large proportion of Scotland's trade went to England. Perhaps the expansion of trade and the growth in scale and activity of burghs is the explanation of the most mysterious feature of Scottish history in the Middle Ages, that Gaelic speech, having spread across almost the whole country by the end of the eleventh century, should by the late thirteenth have been supplanted by English in much of the south and east.

RULERS OF ENGLAND, SCOTLAND, AND NORWAY

England	*Scotland*	*Norway*
Edward the Confessor 1042–66	Malcolm III (Canmore) 1058–93	Harald Hardrada 1047–66
Harold 1066	Donald Ban 1093–4 1094–7	Magnus II 1066–9
William I (of Normandy) 1066–87	Duncan II 1094	Olaf III 1069–93
William (Rufus) II 1087–1100	Edgar 1097–1107	Magnus III (Bareleg) 1093–1103
Henry I 1100–35	Alexander I 1107–24	Olaf IV 1103–16
Stephen (Civil War) 1135–54	David I 1124–53	Eystein I 1103–22
Henry II (of Anjou) 1154–89	Malcolm IV 1153–65	Sigurd I 1103–30
Richard I 1189–99	William the Lion 1165–1214	[Civil Wars 1130–1240]

John	Alexander II	Haakon IV
1199–1216	1214–49	1217–63
Henry III	Alexander III	Magnus VI
1216–72	1249–86	1263–80
		Eric II
		1280–99

Chapter 3

The War of Independence

ON 18 MARCH 1286 Alexander III, riding home from Queensferry late on a dark night to his new young wife at Kinghorn, lost his way, fell from his horse in the dark, and broke his neck. The fact that all his children had already died transformed a tragic accident into a political crisis. At first the great men of the country carried it. They met at Scone six weeks later and acknowledged Margaret, Alexander's three-year-old Norwegian granddaughter and only direct descendant, as inheritor of the kingdom, unless the king's widow should bear a child. They also appointed a Committee of Guardians composed of six, two earls, two bishops and two barons, to govern until a ruler should be enthroned. That an earl and a baron were both of the same great family of Comyn is interesting; part of the family's importance at this time lay in the fact that it was not one really close to the throne. The two leading claimants to the kingship after Margaret, Robert Bruce of Annandale and John Balliol of Galloway, brother-in-law of the Comyn baron, could not, obviously, be Guardians. One of them, Bruce, immediately showed that he was not going to co-operate in keeping the peace, by seizing some castles, two of them royal and one a Balliol one, and making a local band or alliance at his own castle of Turnberry. The band announced loyalty to the line of Alexander but showed that Bruce would have an independent view of what loyalty meant.

Most medieval kingdoms could keep their administration going for a year or two after a king died, but sooner or later the Guardians would need more direct royal authority. By 1289 two Guardians were dead, one naturally and one by murder: if peace was to be kept the heiress must come, and she would need strong support from some-where. The obvious helper was Edward I of England, who had a considerable European reputation, was already closely related to the Scottish monarchy, and had a son and heir of almost Margaret's age. A treaty was made at Birgham near Berwick in March 1290 in which the remaining Guardians and a large body of clergy and nobility agreed that Margaret was to come to Scotland, that she should marry the young Edward of England, and together they would rule the two separate and independent kingdoms. Two centuries of royal intermarriage were to culminate in bringing the two countries together, but Margaret was not yet formally betrothed. She was Edward's great-niece, and it was in his interest as well as hers that she should find a peaceful kingdom. Edward's own children had had a high mortality, and it was conceivable that she would inherit England as well as Scotland. The 'Maid of Norway' set out in the late summer, but died in Orkney on her way, in the arms of the Bishop of Bergen. In recognizing that her death precipitated a national and international crisis, we should also spare some pity for the royal children of ages past, dedicated to politics from birth and forced for the sake of peace into strange homes, arduous journeys, and sometimes lonely deaths.

Even before the news of Margaret's death was certain the two chief claimants started asserting themselves, and one of the Guardians wrote to Edward urging him to intervene. Edward had till now been busy in Gascony, but had given a little attention to the Scottish issue as a good neighbour and near relative. However, he had an aim of his own, the reassertion and acknowledgement of his overlordship. Feudal overlordship had indubitably existed a hundred years before: it had twice been claimed by his father and once by himself, in 1278, when Alexander III came to Edward's Parliament to do homage for his English lands. We have two different accounts of this scene, one from the English Close Roll and one from the cartulary of Dunfermline. In the English account there was some ambiguity in the definition of the homage done, and the right of homage expressly for the kingdom of Scotland was reserved for later discussion: in the Scottish account this right was expressly denied by Alexander in ringing phrases. Neither document is undeniable proof of what happened, but the English is the better evidence by historical standards. The Scottish version, though it appears to have had echoes circulating in 1299, was not written down in the form we have it till after 1320, and it is hard to place much credence on spirited back-chat recorded nearly two generations later. Both accounts agree that the English claim to suzerainty was made, and neither show it as accepted.

With a disputed succession, something could now be done to clarify things in the English interest. Edward could play the game Scottish and English kings had played all through the twelfth century, that of taking advantage of each other's weaknesses. The royal house of Scotland had not been prolific since the days of Malcolm Canmore, and the claims all went back to the children of Earl Henry, or even farther. Earl Henry's youngest son David, the younger brother of Malcolm IV and William, had left three daughters, and from these came the lines of disputing successors. There was also the Count of Holland, descended from Earl Henry's sister. Fourteen competitors put in claims, but of these only two were really important, John Balliol's, as grandson of Earl David's eldest daughter, and Robert Bruce's, as son of the second daughter. Though by the modern rules of primogeniture, already at that date widely accepted in feudal Europe, Balliol's claim was the better, the Bruce claim of nearness of generation embodied the ancient Celtic method that the house of Canmore had systematically repudiated, and was not negligible. There was another issue. Was Scotland to be treated as a Kingdom, which must stay as a unit, or as an earldom or some lesser estate which would be divided among heiresses? The Scots were turned to a decision by Edward's legal machinery as the alternative to civil war. The leaders, the 'high men', met him at Norham on the Tweed in May 1291, and there he demanded that they recognize his overlordship. The Scots, after chewing it over for three weeks, made a famous and fairly diplomatic reply. 'They know full well you would not make so great a demand if you did not believe you had good right to it, yet of any such right they know nothing.'

The first part of this statement is true. Edward's respect for the letter of the law meant that he would not have claimed such a right unfounded. The second half was simply dishonest: whatever version of the meeting of 1278 was then current in Scotland it must have involved the story of the English claim. Some of the individual 'high men', Bruce for instance, had been present then. The English claim had indeed some grounds (the important issue was not whether it existed but how good it was), and to acknowledge it now would not be to regain, for instance, the relationship of William of Normandy and Malcolm Canmore. Edward was the master of the most over-governed kingdom in western Europe, and at the period of the height of its creative changes, the law-making era. He had recently shown how he could transform a claim of feudal overlordship into direct control by the conquest, or what he then thought of as the conquest, of Wales, just as his rival Philip the Fair was trying to do in English-held Gascony. The struggle between the two great kingdoms of England and France was further to centralize both monarchies. Not all of this can have been clear to the 'high men' when they framed their disingenuous answer. The only person who could properly answer the king, they said, would be the King of Scots. But Edward had them caught. No more than a modern historian could the leaders of Scotland then prove that his claim was false: if they did not accept it the country would disintegrate in civil war. Edward changed his demand, and turned from the 'high men' to the competitors. Most of these were not Scots, and they acknowledged his overlordship. Fealty by Guardians and magnates was sworn on the grass by the Tweed, and Edward as overlord put into action an enormous court with eighty Scots representing the two leading claims of Bruce and Balliol, and twenty-four Englishmen of his council. After patiently investigating some very bogus side-lines, the court decided for Balliol as king. At least half the Scottish magnates and prelates were already on his side, and Balliol was enthroned in November 1292. The interregnum had apparently ended with general assent, and the country had carried itself through the crisis.

Having got rather more than he could have anticipated, Edward then overplayed his hand. He had asserted that his court was open to Scottish pleas, and a few cases dribbled up to it, not enough to show that the Scots appreciated the developed state of English law, but enough to embarrass and annoy both the Scottish king and the kingdom. (Edward had cases regularly going from his courts in Gascony to the court of the King of France, so he had good reason to regard this as normal.) Then the shadow of the cumulative crisis of Edward's reign loomed: the French attack on Gascony early in 1294, the Welsh rising of 1294–5 that toppled the great castles of the king, the enormous military and financial effort needed for a war on two fronts, and from all this the constitutional crisis of 1297. Edward was over-driving his own realm, sending it nearly to rebellion. It is not surprising that in the process he found the Scots in arms against his overlordship. The most visible relic of this crisis today is the ring of Edwardian castles in Wales. The great walls of Conway, Beaumaris looking across the straits: these show what Edward had to do to reconquer Wales. Their appalling cost is both the explanation of the Scottish reaction and the reason why, in the long run, he could not hold Scotland too. But that is the long story: the short one is of Scottish failure. Edward demanded military service in Gascony (not a direct Scottish interest) from king and magnates in 1294. The Scots, humiliated, and perhaps thinking that the events of the interregnum had shown that Scotland was a country that could manage her own affairs, put pressure on Balliol to refuse. They went on to ally with the French in 1295: the alliance was to be held together by royal marriages, and there was to be no unilateral peace-making. But the Scots were not united. Not surprisingly, the Bruce family and some of its supporters behaved as loyal subjects of the English king, which indeed they were for they had lands in England, and refused the summons to the Scottish host. Scottish kings had not shown themselves skilled or inventive fighters for two centuries: Balliol was no exception. Edward, on the other hand, who had out-manoeuvred and defeated the de Montforts at Evesham when he was twenty-six, had been on a crusade, and campaigned in Wales, knew his business well and now in 1296 approached war with a combination of efficient organization and inventive flair. He took Berwick easily, slaughtered the townsmen, defeated the feudal army of Scotland in a pitched battle outside Dunbar, and then, riding this way and that for several months across lowland Scotland, showed that he was master.

Edward treated Scotland as a conquered country. He deposed the king with all possible humiliations. Prisoners were taken and sent south as hostages, and every man of note was called on to swear fealty in person. The English bureaucracy provided men for the king to use in Scottish positions. The Scottish records and regalia, and most important of all, the Stone of Destiny, on which Scottish kings were enthroned, went south as symbols of conquest. The result of this was, of course, another revolt. Not under a king this time, for there was none, and with little leadership from the magnates, many of whom were being held as hostages, but from a lower stratum. It was William Wallace, a young man and younger son of a knightly family in Clydesdale, who sparked it off by killing an English sheriff of Lanark. The revolt was general. It has all the appearance of a movement national in inspiration, caused by resentment of foreign domination and national humiliation. It ranks with other surprisingly nationalist movements of this period, the Sicilian Vespers of 1284 and the Matins of Bruges of 1302. But both Sicily and Flanders were parts of Europe with sophisticated cultures and a relatively advanced economy. Scotland was not. In fact one of its features that aided the rebellion was the great tract of forest over southern Scotland into which Wallace and his men could disappear and hide. The general support for the revolt meant that from the first it was conceived in terms of restoring Scotland's independent government. Wallace fought in the name of King John (Balliol), put into office Scots as officials, and raised his men by the old summons. But he also fought a different war from that at which the feudal host had recently failed so conspicuously. In 1297 he caught the English army at Stirling Bridge, and massacred it, infantry defeating mounted knights. On the grave of the foreign administration the Scots recreated their Guardians: Wallace at first alone on behalf of Balliol, and then later a system of joint Guardians. The French alliance was reaffirmed and the Scots started invading northern England. But they could not cope with a renewed attack by Edward. In 1298 at Falkirk, Edward showed that English knights and Welsh archers, properly deployed, could defeat and slaughter the half-trained peasants fighting with spears in their great but unmanoeuvrable unit, the schiltrom or spear ring.

Wallace was undeniably the stuff of which heroes are made. He was unselfish and unyielding. But he had not the royal authority of kingship. Nor had later Guardians. Efforts were made to get an effective committee of Guardians, but the men did not work well together. The difficulty seems to have been to combine harmoniously the great houses of Comyn and Bruce (the latter now represented by the old competitor's grandson, Robert Bruce, Earl of Carrick). The nominal king was in refuge in France and had declared he would never come back. It was impossible for the magnates of Scotland not to wonder about the future of the Crown, nor for them to forget that some of them were English barons. A lot of modern national opinion has commented on this lack of patriotism without recognizing that the concept of patriotism was created by the war. National feeling already existed, but when men thought in terms of obligation they thought in feudal terms of fealty, and most of the landowners of Scotland (though not Wallace) had sworn fealty to Edward. It was difficult to replace this with loyalty to an abdicated and inactive king. Only by doing things in the old way, by using Balliol's name and reasserting the French alliance, could the government of the rebel country hold insecurely together. For no period of history does the anachronistic modern concept of the all-embracing national state more corrupt our judgement. We should no more expect nineteenth- or twentieth-century standards of patriotism from our ancestors than we should expect a European patriotism from ourselves – yet already there exists a sense of European community, and an attack from outside might crystallize this incipient supra-nationalism into a real loyalty. In the same way only sustained and brutal pressure would make a Galwegian think of himself first as a Scot. The grimness of the years of war after Falkirk provided this.

The years of war showed that the English could capture and hold the southern castles, but less easily move north. This meant that much greater pressure was put on the resolution of men in the south of Scotland than on those in the north, and particularly on those in the south-west. For Edward found this a useful route into Scotland, along which he could use supplies from Ireland. The war was concentrated on the great castles of the south-west, notably Caerlaverock and Bothwell, and went by sieges and executions. This is not enough in itself to explain the fact that one of the first great men to defect from the national cause was young Robert Bruce of Carrick. Bruce had been made a Guardian, first with John Comyn of Badenoch, head of the Red Comyns, then with Comyn and the bishop of St Andrews. There is a scene recorded of the first joint Guardianship, in a Council at Peebles, with the rivalries of their followers leading to blows between Comyn and Bruce. Probably both were difficult men to work with unless they were allowed to dominate. The war was also fought diplomatically, especially in the court of the great imperialist Pope, Boniface VIII, who used the Scots as a lever in his handling of the dispute between the two powers he feared, France and England. Boniface's neutrality was French-biased, for the French had bullied him more effectively than the English in the great quarrel over taxing the clergy in 1296. In 1300 it began to look as if papal pressure would get Balliol returned: not surprisingly Bruce gave up the difficult job of the shared Guardianship and early in 1302 he made peace. There was no obvious reason why he should fight for another to hold an inheritance he thought should at least partly belong to his own family.

But the plan that France and the Pope should put back Balliol was broken by another national resistance, the Flemish rebellion and the battle of Courtrai in July 1302. Like Edward, Philip of France was overstretched in imperialistic wars, and now met defeat. 'Trust not for freedom to the Franks.' The French and English patched up a peace, and the Scots had to carry on alone. By the end of the next year Edward had campaigned through Strathmore and taken Stirling. In 1304 the Scots submitted. Edward reimposed his administration in a carefully thought out 'Ordinance'. He had seen that he must use Scots in it, so they were coupled with English on the Council and as justices. Some were used as sheriffs, and it was a Scot who held the crucial castle of Stirling. Some at least of the Scottish magnates who held lands in England were readmitted to them, but Wallace was hunted down and captured, taken to London, tried for treason, and executed by hanging, drawing, and quartering, the new and beastly technique for traitors.

Edward was now in his late sixties, and Bruce was a young man of twenty-eight, inheritor of great estates and two earldoms, and with large views of his rights. Perhaps it was unwise of the old king to trust in his submission. There appear to have been meetings between Bruce and two of the leading patriotic bishops, Glasgow and St Andrews. Then in February 1306 Bruce met the Red Comyn in the Greyfriars church at Dumfries: we do knot know what plan or proposal was put by Bruce to Comyn, but only that two men, who had been at blows before, fell out, and Bruce stabbed Comyn with a dagger in front of the high altar. In the confusion and fighting among their supporters Bruce seized the castle of Dumfries.[1] His crime had

1. The story that Comyn was finished off in another attack by a companion of Bruce's 'to mak siccar' is unfounded. There is no reason to believe that Bruce and

been appalling, the murder of the chief obstacle to his personal ambition in a consecrated place, but he was supported by a surge of national feeling, and enabled by it to snatch the main castles of the firth of Clyde. He rode to Scone and was enthroned and crowned as king with as much of the ancient ceremony as could be carried out with several of the Scottish magnates and the Stone of Destiny missing.

His rule collapsed almost at once. Edward sent Aylmer of Valence to fight him with no holds barred. The Scots had only begun to learn the military lesson of the War of Independence, to avoid pitched battles, to destroy the castles and rely on the forest, on mobility and difficult terrain, and on scorched earth. Bruce was caught out and defeated at Methven and ran for the Highlands. Many of his followers, including his wife and daughter, were caught, but he got out and away from the country. He came back again in the winter and started a campaign from the hills of the south-west, his own land of Carrick. Edward came north for the last time, in 1307, to deal once and for all with the rebellion, and died by the Solway.

Bruce had been made king, a fact of enormous importance; there was a functioning administration for him to capture, and he had the support of many of the bishops and of some of the great laymen. Three areas particularly stood out against him, not necessarily from lack of patriotism but from allegiance to Balliol: Galloway, Balliol's own earldom; Buchan, which was Comyn country; and Argyll, under the Macdougalls of Lorne. These took the brunt of his attack, at first with the odds on the defenders, as in Buchan. Here after an unexpected victory Bruce systematically devastated the earldom; the 'herschip' or harrying of Buchan that, says Barbour in his great poem, men lamented for fifty years. Even if the direct slaughter of people was less than that of livestock, for a countryside with limited resources devastation and plunder in the depth of winter are equivalent to murder. The effect was such that the Gaelic speech of Buchan gave way to Scots as newcomers recolonized the land later. In the next year, 1308, Bruce outwitted an ambush in the vital cleft to the west, the pass of Brander, and defeated the Macdougalls; his surviving

his immediate followers spoke English: Anglo-Norman or Gaelic or both are all more likely. Scottish history is full of biting phrases such as this which have no contemporary authority.

brother Edward Bruce (the rest had been executed by Edward I) went down into Galloway to teach the lord and peasants there to foget their Balliol allegiance, and gradually over the years to retake the castles.

From having nothing, not even a base, in a few incredible years Bruce had become king. By 1313 he was acknowledged throughout northern Scotland and the south-west; he had held Parliaments, issued charters, got bishops appointed, and opened diplomatic relations abroad. Even if he had not gained this position by gentleness, the support for him was real. The English had not been loved, and Edward I's brutal punishments on all he could capture in 1306–7 had forced any who at first had offered half-hearted assent to Bruce as king to realize that only by ardent support of him could they hope to survive. Bruce himself, in Buchan and later in Ireland, was capable of ruthlessness, but even in the conviction of the rightness of his claim he did not make the mistake of over-indulging in punishment. Edward's son and successor, Edward II, had not inherited his father's locked-on purpose, and had given up the campaign of 1307 as soon as he had become king. Most of his reign was taken up with disputes at home, some caused by the political and financial difficulties created by his father's imperialism, others by his own deplorable tastes and affections. The expeditions he had made against the Scots had not been taken seriously, even by himself. One by one Bruce's attacks captured the great castles of the south-east. Many of these were then systematically destroyed. It would take an English re-occupation a good three or four years to rebuild them. In the capture of Perth Bruce himself had waded the moat neck deep and climbed the ladders. His supporters raided the northern English counties, forcing them to purchase truces expensively, and were threatening Man.

Among the castles still held by the English, Stirling was outstanding. In 1313 Edward Bruce, unsuccessfully besieging it, agreed with its commander, Sir Philip Moubray, that unless an English relieving force arrived within three leagues of the castle by midsummer 1314 it would surrender. In spite of Bruce's decision to avoid pitched battles, this thoroughly medieval bargain set the stage for the greatest battle of Scottish history.

Both kings had unwillingly to take up the challenge. Characteristically, Edward II was almost late – it was Sunday 23 June when an enormous English army, some fifteen or twenty thousand men, came up the Roman road from Falkirk, and Moubray admitted that they had fulfilled the bargain. The Scots lay mustered in the Torwood ahead of them. Moubray advised Edward to postpone battle; but Edward had cavalry, lots of it, and cavalry meant noblemen anxious for a display of their technique and skills, noblemen who were only partially under the control of a king, for whom they had very little respect. These pushed on and started fighting that evening, and brought the English army into a restricted position between branches of the Bannock burn, so that next day they had to fight hemmed in by boggy alluvial ground.[1] The tremendous Scottish victory was partly the result of this physical restriction to the only dry areas of ground available, areas big enough to be used effectively by the Scottish schiltroms but not big enough for the proper deployment of the English cavalry, who got in the way of their own archers. The other element seems to have been practice and discipline. The Scottish soldiers had fought hard and often in the last six years (those raids into England produced a double dividend) whereas the English, though led by a king and aristocracy trained for war, had not in practice been at it on this scale. It was hard fighting on both sides, but utterly decisive, and ended with Stirling surrendering and the English king in flight through the Lothians to Dunbar where his ships lay. Bruce's associate Sir James Douglas rode after him:

> He leit thame nocht haf sic laseir
> As anys wattir for to ma

says Barbour, a commanding description of the discomforts of hard riding in hot weather and full armour.

Bannockburn ought to have been, but was not, the death knell of the mounted knight as an instrument of war, though those intelligent enough realized that the future lay with properly used archers and spearmen. It also ought to have marked the end of the war, but did not. Edward II had not the character to make a decision so damaging to his prestige, nor was he king enough to care for the harm that the Scots proceeded to inflict on his northern counties. The Scots forced these counties to buy them off. In 1315 Edward Bruce got the O'Neills to put him up as 'King of Ireland' and crossed over for a destructive

1. Improving landlords of the eighteenth century have made it impossible for us o appreciate how boggy this ground was.

campaign there, in which for a time the Scottish king joined. In the end Edward Bruce was cut off from Scottish supplies and killed, so that the attempt to tie up the two kingdoms in a revived Celtic confederacy did not come off, but it stopped the English using Ireland as a base for further attacks. Edward of England managed to make a few raids into Scotland but he could not protect his north country. The crisis of his reign and his deposition disrupted defence, and it was his fifteen-year-old son and successor who made the Treaty of Northampton in 1328 with Bruce.

By this time Bruce was in his last illness, and his only son David was a boy of four. Bruce's own authority in Scotland had been so strong that immediately after Bannockburn he had declared the disinheritance of all those who did not admit it unconditionally. The treaty accepted this situation, and Scotland's independence, but there was to be compensation of £20,000 to the English for the surrender of their claims. David was to marry the child sister of the English king, and did so at once. The terms of the treaty were obvious and overdue: the surprising thing is that they were so rapidly undermined and repudiated.

Yet is it so surprising? A few years later there was a child on the Scottish throne, a young and active king on the English one, anxious to regain prestige, a large body of disinherited and a claimant, Edward Balliol, son of John, with the will to enforce what was basically a good claim. Clearly a good many in Scotland were uneasy about the crowning of the two Bruces. In 1320 in an attempt to dissuade the Pope (John XXII, a long-lived and often mistaken, old man) from denouncing Robert Bruce, the clergy of Scotland had produced, and the nobility had assented to, the splendid Latin prose of the Declaration of Arbroath, an announcement of independence and allegiance to Bruce 'as being the person who hath restored the people's safety in defence of their liberties'. Its basic statement was that 'For so long as there shall but one hundred of us remain alive, we will never consent to subject ourselves to the dominion of the English'. But now, when there was a genuine issue about the right to the kingship, combined with a large group of disinherited and an English king ashamed of the treaty, the whole question was re-opened.

In August 1332 Edward Balliol landed a tiny army, mainly English,

at Kinghorn, and by skill and determination defeated a big army
under the Earl of Mar, Guardian of Scotland for the child king, at
Dupplin Moor. The victory was so devastating that it could be taken
as evidence of divine approval of the Balliol cause. It raised again the
issue of Scotland's survival. The Scots had reverted to the unsuccessful tactics of pitched battles by armoured knights on bad
ground. Edward III had pretended neutrality, but after the battle he
received from Balliol acknowledgement of suzerainty over Scotland,
and a general promise of a great piece of southern Scotland in return
for military help. His army regained Berwick for England by a battle
at Halidon Hill soon after. The war then dragged on, breeding the
forces that kept it alive. Edward III could not, even at first when he
had no other military entanglements, fortify and hold more than the
southern part of Scotland against the resistance of many of the
inhabitants and the organization that the new Scottish leader, Sir
Andrew Moray of Bothwell, built up. A big castle might cost eight,
nine, or ten thousand pounds to build, and involve the importation of
several hundred workmen; a cost which meant a large part of the
skilled labour force and perhaps a tenth of the King's normal revenue.
It would then have to be occupied by expensive soldiers. Edward III
spent about ten thousand a year on garrisons. He could only extract
about two thousand from southern Scotland. The crucial fact, in
the words of a modern historian, was 'the relationship between the
income of a king and the pay of a soldier'.[1] He could conduct short
expensive campaigns, or he could let his men sit tight in castles, but
he could not sustain activity. Meanwhile the diplomatic activity of
the Scots widened the war by turning one of the frequent troubles
between French and English in Gascony into a major war, the Hundred Years' War.

The continuing war clarified the issue of nationality versus personal loyalty. The Balliol cause in Scotland found itself unable to
retain the support even of the disinherited. For others, it was for
Scotland rather than for a particular king that they fought: 'they held
of the Lyon', the heraldic emblem of the Scottish crown, was the
phrase used by patriots. This distinction had been foreshadowed in
the Declaration of Arbroath. Eventually in 1355 Edward III took

1. J. Campbell, 'England, Scotland and the Hundred Years' War in the Fourteenth
century', in J. R. Hale (ed.), *Europe in the late Middle Ages*, p. 186.

over Balliol's claims on his own behalf, and the war became openly what it had long been in fact, one between two states, not two claimants.

Almost immediately after this things ran into a stalemate. The widening of the war to include France had not at first helped Scotland much, except that for seven years France provided a safe refuge in Normandy for the royal children. Later, as the Scots abstained from pitched battles, the English hold on southern Scotland slackened and the castles fell to the Scots until by 1342 only two main ones, Berwick and Lochmaben and their hinterlands, were held by the English. David II was brought back from France in 1341: his exile had, however, meant that he was out of touch with the realities of Scottish politics and government and in touch instead with fourteenth-century ideas of chivalry. Rather than trying to work the primitive machinery of government effectively, he looked to military excitement. In 1346 he took a large army into England and was defeated, wounded, and captured at Neville's Cross, near Durham.

The king's eleven-year captivity brought out the problem which fourteenth-century warfare was creating all over western Europe, the great magnates, the over-mighty subjects. Scotland had long had the great earldoms of Scotia, the big territorial units that spanned the two cultures of Celtic and Anglo-Saxon speech lying in only partially feudalized relationship to the Crown. War had also given influence, lands, and eventually status and power to the close companions of Bruce, particularly to the house of the Black Douglas, the descendants of Sir James Douglas, who were building up a landed power in the Border, and to the Stewarts. Walter, High Steward of Scotland, had been left in charge of the kingdom when Bruce made his attack on Ireland, and he had married Bruce's only daughter Marjorie well before David II's birth gave Bruce a male heir. His son Robert 'the Stewart' was David's nephew, though older than the king, and his heir presumptive. Political favour at first, the dynastic connection in the case of the Stewart, the great Marcher lordship that the Douglases built up, made these two houses the particular examples in Scotland of baronial power. A Marcher lordship was one geared to war. Its wealth lay in arms and men rather than in rents and produce. Loot and ransoms, the former of which could be got from both sides in the disorganized and half-civil warfare of the period, kept it going and provided its aim. By the end of the century the great lords on either side of the frontier conducted war and foreign policy on their own, and the nominal relations between the two kingdoms were more an issue of Douglas–Percy dealings on the Border than of the two kings. The interests of kings and kingdoms lay in ending the war, but far more effective in practice were the immediate interests of those who often profited by it, and even when they did not, held their lands and position by virtue of being leaders in this war-based society. The Marcher lordships were extreme examples of the character of chivalry, that system of aristocratic values and training which blended together snobbery of birth, athleticism, honour, military skill and sheer greed, and in which kings and nobles alike were educated. David II had wanted to invade England because warfare was expected of this society. His captivity left his nephew, the Stewart, who had run away at Neville's Cross, in the predominant position in Scotland. David had no children, and though he was still young his captivity reduced the chances of a direct heir, even though towards the end his wife (by then over thirty, which was late for the commencement of child-bearing) joined him. When at last the renewed attacks by the English forced the Scots to negotiate his ransom he found a kingdom led sleepily by the heir presumptive into a general rundown. Effectively there had been no personal government for nearly a quarter of a century. Scotland's primitive machinery of government depended on the person of the king.

As far as we can see, after 1357 David worked hard at the job of ruling, and discharging the backlog of business. The enormous ransom he had to pay, nominally £160,000, made parliaments and special taxations necessary, and gradually over half of it was paid. The king also had to meet, and did meet with considerable effect, rebellions from his own bumptious subjects, in which both Douglas and Stewart joined. David learnt rather late to balance the pressures upon him, to negotiate with friendliness and skill with the English king, to hold the great nobles in check, and to reduce the payment on the instalments on his ransom even though the country could afford to pay. In 1363 he attempted to solve the problems of the future by an agreement with the English that the two kingdoms should be joined in a personal union under Edward III or his heir, after David's death, with safeguards to the separate continuance of the kingdoms.

The scheme was much like that worked out for the marriage of the Maid of Norway: it might have worked, and at least it would have spared Scotland the first two Stewart kings. We do not know if David really wanted it, but in any case the Scottish Parliament, unwilling to see the rights of existing heirs overruled, repudiated it. Probably David had got out of it what he really wanted, the realization by the Stewart that he had better behave if he was to hope to inherit. The rest of the reign passed much more peacefully, both at home and abroad. By David's death in 1371 the question of the relationship between Scotland and England had entered into a stage of recurrent mutual animosity with no real expectation of conquest. Fighting and badly kept truces alternated for another century. The militarization of society gave the king and court ideas much like those dominant in other courts, and this tended to sever the court from the Celtic part of its inheritance, which more vigorous monarchs, Alexander III and Robert Bruce, had been able to hold. War also always hurt Scotland more than England. You have only to cross the Border at Carter Bar to have a vivid impression of how much more, absolutely as well as proportionately, of Scotland's wealth was at the mercy of England than English wealth open to Scotland. The French alliance, the 'Auld Alliance' as it became called, which had been of real value in the 1330s and 1340s, developed less attractive aspects in later years, and it became a habit of the French to drag the Scots into the bigger Anglo-French dispute when they might well have stayed out. The effects of the war were thus long-term. But as a war of independence the issue was settled in David II's reign.

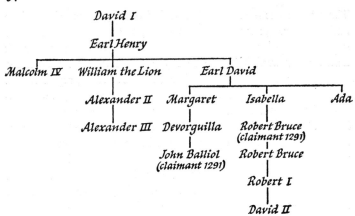

Chapter 4

Robert II to James I

Seafight: capture of James

THE FOURTEENTH CENTURY IS most generally remembered as a century of pestilence and disaster. From 1348–50 the Black Death, the start of three and a half centuries of a pandemic of plague, swept across the totally unimmunized population of Europe, to return at least every generation. The disaster was not just a private one for the families of those who died. Almost everyone was deeply involved, since the initial mortality, of which estimates vary upwards from 20 per cent, meant that no one escaped the shock. The population was brought down sharply and kept down for much of the century. As a result the whole economic life of Europe was affected by it, in dislocation and in the drop in demand, and took a long time to

C

adjust. The century is often labelled as a period of 'depression', and to this decline in economic activity was added the closing of the eastern trade routes by the Mongols and a great deal of warfare. Those indices we have all show production failing to regain its late thirteenth-century level. This depression hit the upper classes, but meant that the peasantry, once the plague was in abeyance, had a better economic position, more chance of enough to eat, more land, more opportunities. Even before the Black Death there had been famines and epidemics which suggest that Europe's population was getting beyond its food supply. Things would now be easier. Population may have begun to rise again before the end of the century. Technical change went on, particularly in mining and metal work, as well as improvements in navigation. New areas of prosperity developed while old ones declined, altering the main trade routes of Europe. Depression was not the whole picture for the fourteenth century.

Scotland received the plague late, in the winter of 1349–50. It was politically embarrassing because her propaganda had attributed the outbreak of it in England to moral shortcomings of the English. That it came in winter makes it probable that it came in the pneumonic form, spreading by droplet infection. People do not recover from pneumonic plague. On the other hand the impact may have been reduced by Scotland's sparse population and bad communications: districts might well not receive the infection at all. Plague returned again for 1361–2, and again apparently in pneumonic form. Together these two outbreaks made a traumatic experience. But after they had scythed through the population it looks as if Scotland did not again suffer many losses from plague. Future attacks were bubonic in form, carried by rat fleas, which like a temperature in the seventies (Fahrenheit) for breeding, and this is a rarity in Scotland. Burgh records frequently refer to alarm over plague, which broke out every few years, but it was an urban affair only. Fleas could easily be exchanged in the filthy, stinking small towns of the day, but not so easily over the country as a whole. It became usual for those who could afford it, to run away, remove to the country, when plague showed up in a town. The burghs of Scotland had never included much of her population. They now became more unhealthy than ever, but the change was not so great as to dislocate a still primitive economy. More serious was the impact of plague on the great cities of Europe, and on the outside demand for Scotland's crude products. The long-term effects of the plague in Scotland were probably not demographic.

Scotland's exports were the product of her pastoralism – wool and skins and, later, salt fish. Eventually the growth of population would reduce the land available for pasture, but we do not know when this happened. Great inroads were made into her woodlands in the fourteenth and early fifteenth centuries, but these were more probably the result of unrestricted grazing than of clearing for the plough. It looks as if in the fourteenth century the country still had commodities to send overseas if people would pay for them. But it had been the burghs in the south-east that carried the bulk of her trade, and these took the brunt of the war. War damaged the country directly, and indirectly by the lawlessness it encouraged. At the same time it entrenched in position a nobility who easily learnt high standards of expenditure from abroad. Standards of armour and castle-building in the late fourteenth century were expensive. Doune and Tantallon, which both date from then, cost a lot to build, and were built to be occupied by mercenaries, who were expensive too. Great men tended to have many followers and hangers-on, even if they did not formally hire them. Splendid fabrics were available for the nobility, at a price. A knight would need three or four destriers, big, well-trained horses capable of carrying a lot of weight, and costing about a hundred pounds apiece. The upper classes wanted money, but that fact is not necessarily a sign of economic decline.

Scotland was probably less severely hit by the economic troubles of the fourteenth century than other countries. But she was already poor, and the upper classes found it hard to raise the funds for the style of life they thought should be theirs. The Crown, too, was hard up, and responded by depreciating the currency. David II increased the number of pennies coined from a pound of silver from 252 to 352, and the Stewarts followed on, till by the late fifteenth century the pound of silver made 1,680 pence. Depreciation should not be regarded as always unfortunate. At times it may have encouraged exports. The cheaper penny would enable money transactions to take place among people with little to sell. But it was a way of raising money from the commercial classes which was unsettling, and it was bad for prestige to have the Scottish pound drop to about a quarter of the pound sterling (for depreciation hit the English less than other European coinages).

A more realistic sign of Scottish poverty was the development of the habit of Scots serving abroad in other people's armies. Impecunious and ambitious members of the nobility had often done this before, and it had been made easy by the conquest of much of Europe by the Normans, with their strong sense of family ties. A knight would go abroad to fight and hope to take or be given land. In the more commercial atmosphere of the fifteenth century we find a lot of Scots fighting abroad for pay. In 1418 Albany, regent of Scotland, sent an army to France under one of his sons, and in 1424 the fourth Earl of Douglas had a large army in the French service, perhaps 7,000 Scots, and got a French dukedom for it.[1] They and he were slaughtered by the English at Verneuil in that year. Later the Scots formed the personal bodyguard of the French kings. Early in the sixteenth century Scots fought for the Danes, and for a time for the Swedes as well in their wars with the Danes, and in the seventeenth century they served in large numbers in Sweden, Poland, Germany, Russia, and the Netherlands. All this was for pay. The only difference between the Scottish mercenary of the late Middle Ages and the English soldier was that the former got his cash from the King of France, the latter from his own king. The difference lay not in the cash nexus but in who paid it: the Scottish king could not afford the scale, ranging from 2d. a day for a common soldier up to 13s. 4d. for a duke (or even 20s. for the Prince of Wales), so someone else had to pay for the fighters that Scotland produced. War was a matter of careers and business. Booty and wages kept men in it as a profitable occupation, and the occasional ransom provided the jackpot. Elaborate rules and organization were created to settle and administer claims to ransoms.

Not all the urge to fight could be used up in war in France or on the Border. There were two notable engagements in the Scotland of the early Stewarts caused by an excessive desire to indulge in military activity. The first was the almost legendary battle on the Inch at Perth in 1396 between two Highland clans which cannot today be

1. The French were appalled at the amount the Scots ate: international cooperation often produces this reaction.

identified for certain.[1] Thirty a side they fought, in a specially prepared enclosure, and however hard it is to believe that such formal set-tos occurred outside fiction, the Exchequer Roll provides us with the note of 'xiiii li. iis. xid' for the enclosure for 'sexaginta personarum pugnancium in Insula de Perth'. In 1411 a complicated inheritance dispute between the Lord of the Isles and the Earl of Mar over the earldom of Ross led to a major battle at Harlaw where the Lord of the Isles was defeated. But these two battles both occurred in a period when the monarchy was in eclipse. No king who had any real respect for his kingship would have tolerated the latter one for it involved estates and men closely related to the Crown.

The monarchy was in eclipse for personal reasons. Robert II inherited from his uncle David II at the age of 54. Though he had been anticipating this for several years his expectations had not prevented him from entangling his descendants in a typically medieval uncertainty about their legitimacy. His eldest son had been born ten years before Robert had obtained the dispensation for his marriage within the prohibited degrees. Could subsequent legitimization overcome this? The king had later married again. Both marriages had been prolific and the children of them were marrying into all the leading houses. A parliament settled the succession by the seniority of age of the king's sons, but this naturally did not satisfy the sons of the indubitably legal second marriage, the Earl of Strathearn and the Earl of Atholl. Fifty-four was old by medieval standards, and medieval government needed a king who could get on a horse and ride off for a campaign against trouble-makers. It is difficult for a man who has spent a long life as a leading trouble-maker to appreciate the point of view of the other side. Whether out of sheer senility, bodily weakness, or mental habit, Robert II failed to provide the drive the government needed to make it work. In 1384 his eldest son, the Earl of Carrick, later Robert III, was commissioned by the King's Council to execute the law for him. In 1388 the commission was taken from the earl because of his infirmity (he too could no longer ride) and passed to a younger brother, the Earl of Fife. The prospect was not good when Robert III, also in his fifties, succeeded in 1390. For a time the Earl of Fife's commission was continued. Robert III, whose only recorded remark was to describe himself as 'the worst of

1. Clan Chaltan was probably one: Clan Cameron may have been the other.

Kings and the most miserable of men', would even leave the drafting of diplomatic correspondence to his wife. By the early years of the fifteenth century the situation was out of hand. The king's elder son, the Duke of Rothesay, had been made Lieutenant for his father and was running wild. The king's youngest brother, Alexander, had earned the title of the 'Wolf of Badenoch' in a part of the world where people were used to savage behaviour. The Earl of Fife, now promoted Duke of Albany, had a grudge against the throne, and a series of parliaments were demanding better government and regular parliaments, so that the king's 'subjectis be servit of the law'. By the end of 1406 Rothesay was dead in mysterious circumstances and the Duke of Albany had again been made Lieutenant. The old king had tried to ship his surviving son, James, to safety in France and the boy had been kidnapped on the way by the English, probably in breach of truce (neither side kept a high level of truce observance). Robert III had died on hearing of this, so the twelve-year-old captive was nominally king. The English showed no signs of letting him go and Albany was ruling a kingdom he could well feel would soon be his in title as well as in something near to fact.

With James I's succession began the string of Scottish minorities. For over two hundred years no monarch was to succeed as an adult: the first four Jameses were to die violent deaths while still young men. This meant long minorities, but often ones in which there was no obvious alternative if the young king's life should fail, and as the disputed marriage of Robert II grew further away, unruly nobles were less and less willing to reopen the whole difficult succession issue. The monarchy paid in reduced efficiency for its long stretches of infancy, but it gained in one aspect, that the kings were brought up in the knowledge of their kingship. Never again would the throne be occupied by someone like the first two Stewarts, each regarding himself as an earl who had come up in the world. The first four Jameses might fail as kings, but at least it was a royal policy they pursued, not a private one. They had active and forceful foreign policies, and as part of these they looked to foreign dynasties for their wives; they tackled, sometimes too abruptly, the problems of the country.

All this lay ahead. Meanwhile the kingdom moved into the twilight rule of Albany. The surrender of the Roberts from government had been personal: under Albany it became institutionalized. Government was deliberately by-passed. The Regent and the great feudatories made agreements as to how the peace was to be kept which removed large areas of function from the Crown. These agreements were a development of the kind that had been made in England during the civil war between Stephen and Matilda. We have surviving an indenture made in 1409 between Albany and the fourth Earl of Douglas in which they agree to settle between themselves by arbitrators any disputes that may arise between themselves and their followers, and which leaves no place for royal justice. The lands of Douglas and Albany and their followers comprised a good deal of Scotland, and there were other such bargains. Some of these deals are explained by the lack of a parliament. Albany, as governor for an absent king, could not call a parliament, since it was peculiarly the king's court, yet there were disputes that needed some authoritative settlement. But Albany also allowed the run-down of government funds. It is in this period that we find noblemen both refusing to pay customs on their own goods, and looting the customs of the money paid by others. In 1413 the Earl of Douglas refused to pay seventy pounds levied on him as customs, and took a further six hundred and thirty pounds out of the customs too. In 1420 he took the whole net receipts of the customs of Edinburgh. It is clear that Albany, who made no attempt to have the king ransomed, hoped to get the crown one day, but his policy would have ensured that it meant very little when he did.

James's imprisonment came to an end more through English events than because of Scottish demands. He had grown up in England, an intelligent boy interested in English methods of government, while the two countries wrangled over the rights and wrongs of his capture. In 1409 Albany's son Murdoch was captured too, but Albany negotiated a ransom for him in 1415. This made it clear to the young James where the loyalty of the house of Albany lay. In 1420 Murdoch succeeded his father in the regency. James had been taken to France by Henry V of England in the renewed attempts of the English to conquer France, and Henry used him as an excuse for hanging Scottish mercenaries who fought for the French king and had the bad luck to be captured. They were in arms against their king. (By the common standards of chivalry no such excuse was really necessary for inhumanity to the lower orders of society.) On Henry's early death the regency government of England was prepared to negotiate more seriously on the Scots king's ransom: weaker than a king it could see advantages in diplomacy. James could be used to detach the Scots from France. So in 1424 James bought his way home. He agreed that no more Scots should go to France to fight for the French king, promised to pay 50,000 merks as expenses for his keep, and to take a Lancastrian lady as queen, Joan of Beaufort. If we believe his poetry he was in love with her anyway, and he seems, understandably, to have had little intention of paying off the ransom, so it was not a tough bargain in the end. In return for his freedom he had to give hostages, and in this way he got out of the kingdom a lot of the more troublesome nobles, including two with an interest in the throne through the other line, Malise of Strathearn and a member of the house of Atholl.

James came back to Scotland with a clear idea of what he intended to do; perhaps too clear an idea. The traditional remark attributed to him, that if God would grant him life he would see 'that the key keep the castle and the bracken bush the kye',[1] shows his aim. Government was to be restored, made effective. This involved cleaning up the royal finances, establishing courts and judges, and insisting on his authority being obeyed. It also involved drastic action against the house of Albany. In 1425 James wiped out the line by judicial execution, and he also secured the death of the Earl of Lennox, Murdoch's father-in-law. If we admit that Murdoch was aiming at the throne we must accept that at least one of these deaths was probably pure self-defence, but the batch process brought the claims of the other line nearer, and was not only ruthless but unwise. The widespread linkages of the royal house meant that nearly half the nobility were Stewarts and tangled in the succession. Who could tell where the king would stop?

James's main weapon in his renewal of government was Parliament. He had seen the uses of the English Parliament to the Lancastrian kings, and was prepared to copy. Parliament had existed in Scotland since the late thirteenth century. It was in some special way the king's chief court, a reinforced form of his Council which met at regular, or at least foreseeable intervals, so that pleas and lawsuits could be

1. The remark may be genuine: by this date Scottish kings spoke English, not Gaelic.

referred to it. To this special court, where the king was sure to be, political as well as judicial business was bound to come, and so it would be in a parliament that the king would take the opinion of his leading men. So Parliament became the instrument for two important aspects of government that could not be done without some measure of consent; changes in the law, and special payments of money to the king. Since money was more easily extracted from the burghs than from any other part of the kingdom, it became normal to demand that they send representatives to any Parliament that had to consider taxation. By the fourteenth century burgh representatives were usual at a parliament even if money was not involved, but with David II's ransom taxation had often to be raised. To Parliament, along with the prelates and noblemen, came 'freeholders', who were probably individual gentry of standing. Individuals could give their own opinion, and burgh representatives, if taxation were pending, would be asked to come with full powers. Parliament would show the king at his most kingly. There would be feasting, and clearly there was no need to keep humble people expensively at court for this. So before the end of David II's reign it became normal to give the burgesses leave to go home early, leaving a small nucleus to function as a parliament in commission. By James's reign Parliament was the usual place for discussion of matters of importance, but it was still more closely associated in men's minds with justice, the 'serving of the law'. Lawsuits cannot be settled without due warning, so there developed the forty days' notice necessary for the calling of a parliament. Much business that would be carried through in a parliament, if there was one at the right time, would be done in the king's Great Council if there was not, and this Council could be enlarged to make it more representative and meet at less than forty days' notice. So the Great Council in the fifteenth century developed into a body parallel in many of its activities to Parliament, almost as powerful and more flexible, known as the Convention of Estates. It was in Parliament that complaints were made of misgovernment under the Roberts; 'it is deliveryt that the mysgovernance of the reaulme and the default of the kepying of the common law sulde be imput to the Kyng and his officeris'; and it was in Parliament that their lieutenants had been appointed. Albany had not been king enough to hold a parliament, and now with the start of the active reign of James Parliament emerged as legislator. Through it the king got statutes insisting that his officials be competent and serve him, or be replaced; 'that ferme and sikkir pece be kepit', that men should not ride abroad with vast and unpaid followings (but should leave them at home); that the customs and rents of the burghs be paid to the king and not to anyone else; that the law be the same for everyone in the realm; even that football be totally forbidden so that men should spend their spare time in practising archery. (James's son was also to forbid golf in an equally vain attempt to boost the quality of Scottish military archery.) This programme of good government was to be repeated in the Parliaments of later fifteenth-century monarchs, and carried out with vigour in their brief periods of adult reign.

In 1426 and 1428 James's desire to copy England showed in his attempt to widen the structure of Parliament by calling up the small barons, or minor gentry; first of all by calling them all to Parliament, later by asking for representatives. He was too hasty. A lot would have to be done in security and economic prosperity for this class before it would be independent enough to be worth consulting, or rich enough to come. But the Acts show that James's ambition was to be a king in Parliament for all his people. Whether or not we should think of the Lancastrian period in England as one in which there was a 'parliamentary experiment', we must allow that it was from his enforced stay there that James had gathered an idea of the advantages of sharing responsibility and spreading support by the use of Parliament.

Passing statutes was not enough. Late medieval Parliaments in both England and Scotland provide a mass of exhortation and prohibition, most of it of no more effect than their prohibition of golf. Enforcement was the crux, and for this money was needed. The ransom provided the Crown with an excuse for taxation, and it was little more than an excuse, for most of the money so raised did not go to England. James showed the country the advantages of a king prepared to move around. When in 1429 a mixed set of Highland clans raided and burnt Inverness they found a king who, for all that he was short and very fat, was prepared to follow them across the Great Glen and defeat them by a mixture of fraud and force. The great Lord of the Isles found himself in ward in Tantallon, after a dramatic scene in which the Queen begged for his life. Less dramatically he was let out again soon after and used as the king's lieutenant in the west. James was enough of a realist to know that a major show-down with the Highlands would have to wait.

Law needs its courts, and James created a new court. The Chancellor and certain 'discreet' men from Parliament were to meet three times a year and settle disputes. This is the origin of the Session, which in the next two reigns was to be tidied up and eventually, under James IV, to be turned into a regular court of law held by members of the king's Council sitting in Edinburgh. It was a court with limited function. Only in some areas and over some people had it jurisdiction. The justice it gave was limited in quantity and by the amateurish nature of those who at first administered it. These limitations are reflected in the quality of Scots law at this time. In the twelfth and thirteenth century the law had followed a course similar in development to English. The creation of original writs in England was reflected in Scotland, though with significant differences in wording that indicate the cruder quality of the administrative and judicial machinery, but there had been nothing in Scotland like the great thirteenth-century proliferation of these writs in England. In both countries the Common Law was growing out of administrative needs and processes. The kings had to keep order and in doing so created procedures and remedies, and thus created law. But the Scottish kings' lesser authority, the fact that their servants were not simply their own, left their law weaker and their procedures fewer. Their courts were less useful and less used. Even this new central court could not eradicate habits that had grown up, jurisdictions that had become established, the relics of two generations of spineless government. Scottish Common Law became concentrated on one main process, the writ of right, it covered only part of the country and some aspects of life, and so succumbed in the sixteenth century to the renewed enthusiasm for Roman Law. So Scotland had a 'reception' where English Common Law was strong enough to muddle through.

James's emphasis on Parliament, his new use of it – he was the first to 'prorogue' a Parliament – and particularly his heavy taxation, brought forward the burghs in the life of the country. Townsmen were still few, and still formed an enclave. The merchant burgesses, the urban upper-class, were few, engaging in a hereditary profession, protected by privilege and set in a privileged society. It did not occur to men that there was anything odd in this: civil rights were largely a matter of special liberties and privileges. It was normal that trade should be controlled and restricted, confined to the burgesses and exercised in fixed ways. The burghs were experimenting with the idea of a staple, a named port in the Netherlands that should receive all the main exports of Scotland to that region and which would grant special rights to the Scots, such as lower duties or wharf fees. Many countries had their pirates, and in chronic warfare it is difficult to distinguish between piracy and legitimate self-defence. There was anyway no distinction between navy and merchant marine in the type or main use of ships. So a fixed trade outlet would make things safer for all. The system of control and privilege made it easier for the king to collect customs, so it had royal encouragement. The Scots bargained around in the Netherlands in the fourteenth century for the best staple port. They tried Middleburg first. In 1407 they transferred to Bruges with a treaty that promised them privileges as great as those already exercised by Germans. Bruges was the greatest town of the north and the dukes of Burgundy understood the importance of trade to their dominions and were fostering it. But perhaps Bruges was too great a centre for the Scots to be of value. Better a port which would give more to get the Scottish trade, yet would be big enough to absorb all Scottish produce at good prices. The Scots negotiated with Holland, went back to Middleburg in Zeeland, and then tried Bruges again in 1427. They settled finally on Campvere[1] in the early sixteenth century. Here they could have a good harbour, a sympathetic government (the Emperor Maximilian), their own wharf, a governor, special houses, and, effectively, a completely Scottish community. Probably the choice was wrong. By then the Scottish trader needed fiercer competition, more will to experiment.

All this bargaining and manoeuvring held the community of burghs together. Their representatives to Parliament would meet also elsewhere to do their joint business. Parliamentary legislation affected them closely. There were the consistent efforts of fifteenth-century kings to deal with bullion shortage by statute, either forbidding money being taken out of the realm, or insisting on it being brought in, fine declarations of wishful thinking which paid little attention to costs. To make a trading venture which carried goods only one way

1. Campvere, sometimes spelt Campveer or Campveere, is today usually called Veere.

and money the other sent up the freight costs of the goods, so that no merchant would do it unless the market forced him to. But if the market made it necessary, he would do it or lose his occupation. So James I's attempts, for instance, to see that barrelled salmon only went out of the realm if forty pence of money came in, or James II's similar attempts to burden the cattle trade to England, were probably ineffectual. Fifteenth-century governments were suspicious of traders who took food out of the realm for gain: their primitive economic thought prevented them seeing anything but the fact that a food shortage might make itself felt. With interference of this sort going on in Parliament the burghs had to be attentive to their joint interests. Gradually the non-parliamentary meetings of the burghs crystallized till in 1552 we find the full-fledged Convention of Royal Burghs, a semi-legislative body. It would make joint regulations for the burghs, allot their shares of taxation and manage the Scottish staple. This lay a long way ahead, but the events of the early fifteenth century helped to shape it.

For all this, trade cannot have been very lively because standards of expenditure were low and money was still not much used. The vast amount of regular payments in Scotland, rents and dues, went on in kind. A great magnate such as Huntly in the early seventeenth century was still getting much of his rent in this form, in grain, cattle, lambs, poultry, eggs, and dairy produce, and usually getting it irregularly. The result was that even when it was not necessary the produce would be eaten by his vast household and military following rather than traded – what else can you do with over 5,000 eggs arriving at uneven intervals through the year? Payment in kind was the symptom of an undeveloped economy: it was also an encourager of backwardness and of the social structure that tolerated it. Rents in kind made it normal for the nobility to have large followings and to keep open house for them and live on a grand scale. Below the nobility, standards of life were tough. Fifteenth-century kings moved around from one palace to another, or stayed in the bigger monasteries, not only because they had no fixed capital but because they had to move on when the privies became intolerable. They would carry vast amounts of ordinary equipment with them in carts because only a few people had even the simplest luxuries of life, and therefore these could not be bought at short notice. The glass in the royal palaces, even under James IV, arrived there only when he did: at other times the palaces would be almost as bleak and empty as they are today, and certainly as damp. No wonder his wife's clothes and equipment occupied thirty-five carts when on the road. We can trace James I's trip to Coldingham to discuss his ransom with his uncle-in-law, Cardinal Beaufort (James was not going to pay), by the entry of nineteen shillings in the Exchequer Rolls for moving the king's feather bed from Haddington to Dunbar. James and his queen deliberately encouraged fine living among the nobility. This was not softness learnt in England but a recognition that it encouraged the merchant element in the country, the craftsmen and the traders; and these were the people who valued the Crown's peace.

Probably most of the country appreciated firm government, even though many of James's statutes were hopeful rather than effective. But there was a nucleus of hostility. James's savage blows at the houses of Albany and Lennox had frightened many and left the house of Atholl near the throne. The other rival line from Robert II was represented by Malise Graham who was a hostage in England and had been forced to exchange his earldom of Strathearn for a lesser one, so that James could pacify the house of Atholl with Strathearn. But Atholl was not pacified, and there were resentful Grahams too. A conspiracy developed between the Atholl Stewarts and Malise's uncle, Sir Robert Graham. We have a detailed account of the last terrifying scene in James's life in the Blackfriars house at Perth in 1437; the king and queen play chess and read romances with their companions until it is time to go to bed; then the curtain is drawn and the king stands on a sheet to undress, putting on his nightgown and furred slippers while the conspirators put planks across the ditches and quietly approach the undefended house. Then the attack, the noise, the weapons, a door that will not bolt. The king seizes the tongs as a weapon and jumps down to hide in the privy outlet. There he waits in the intolerable smell while the murderers push the terrified women aside and search for him. Finally there is the desperate fight in the filth between the two men, James and Graham, one of them unarmed, with the inevitable result. But the infant prince was not there, and the country did not rise to put the line of Atholl on the throne. All it came to was a lot of brutal executions and another royal minority.

often have looked at Scottish history with eyes accustomed to English, and searched for parallels between the primitive administration of Scotland and the most advanced bureacracy of the day, ignoring the rest of Europe. Till the seventeenth century the Scottish exchequer still ran on a system of accounting similar to that of England in the early twelfth century, a few weeks in the year in which the King's servants made their statements of charge and discharge. The contrast between this and the elaborate structure of English government finance was not evidence of Scotland's backwardness, so much as of England's abnormal forwardness. The Scottish kings faced problems familiar to the kings of France, rather than to the kings of England. The great noblemen, in both countries, looted the customs and other royal revenues, and probably did it better in France in that there was more to loot. At any rate this feature was not caused by the special poverty of Scotland and her king. The Duke of Brittany could declare for neutrality in the Hundred Years' War and the Duke of Burgundy take up a position that was not even neutral, in a way which is very similar to the actions taken together by the great Border lords, Douglas and Percy, when their respective governments threatened to disturb the *status quo* on the Border. The Duke of Brittany, who claimed to rule *Dei gratia*, had an inaugural ceremony for his reign in Rennes Cathedral which was almost a coronation. The Lord of the Isles, the great Macdonald ruler of the Western Highlands, was installed in a ceremony that imitated the ancient installation of the kings of Dalriada. The new Lord, clad in white, put his foot in the hollowed footstep in the special square stone, and received a white rod and a sword to symbolize power and protection. At least one bishop, and if possible two bishops and seven priests, attended, as well as all the leading chieftains under him. Mass was said, the new ruler was blessed, gifts were given to monks and bards, and everyone feasted for a week. The ruler had his own council, meeting at a special stone table, his own records, and even his own weights and measures. The difference in the two lordships, Highland and Breton, was that a prince in France had under him a functioning bureaucracy, whereas in Scotland he had his kin, the men who bore his surname, or the dependent surnames, and perhaps those nearby lords of lesser status who found it best to stand in with him. In so far as he had officials they were hereditary, and this shows the different emphasis of the civilization. They were bards and genealogists. The actual governing machinery of his principality depended on personal influence and force.

James's reign mirrors successively the different types of 'baronial problem'. First he was beset by the Livingstones, a small house that had risen rapidly by collecting Crown offices. There is no real parallel for this in France because the greater elaboration of land-holding and the bonds of society prevented the rise of such fly-by-nights. We know from a hostage price-list of 1424 how the Living-stones rated before their sudden rise; they were well down the list, fourteen great lords being priced above them. Yet by 1449 they had the offices of justiciar, chamberlain, comptroller (the chief financial position), and master of the mint, and held four royal castles. This was too much: James, eighteen and just married, suddenly turned the lot out, executing two of them. This palace revolution may have been instigated by his new queen, Mary of Gueldres, a niece of the Duke of Burgundy, who had been granted the customs of Linlithgow as part of her dower, and found them held by Livingstones. But at no crisis of the reign could the Crown win unless some at least of the great powers among the nobility were on its side. The greatest of them all at this date, the Black Douglas, seems to have backed the king. It was this house which provided a melodramatic crisis of its own a few years later.

In 1440 the Livingstones, while still dominant, had organized the murder of the teenage sixth Earl of Douglas and his brother at dinner with the child king. The Douglas sister, heiress for the Galloway part of their estates, had married her cousin the eighth earl. The Douglases, who had already joined together the great Galloway power that the Scottish kings had broken in the thirteenth century, now added to this a wedge of land across the Border, Ettrick, and the wardenships of West and Middle Marches. Two other Douglas brothers had earldoms on their own, and though a fifteenth-century earldom was no longer the great semi-separate governmental unit it had been in the twelfth and thirteenth centuries, it was a mark of wealth and power. The Douglases were descended from both of Robert II's marriages: if they had tried for the Crown they would have been a real menace. Instead they aimed alternately at general political domination, for which they would ally with other houses, or at effective separation. In 1451 a 'band' or agreement between Earl William Douglas, Crawford, and the Lord of the Isles precipitated a crisis. The king had Douglas to supper in Stirling under safe conduct, and when Douglas refused his urging to drop the band, stabbed him to death in anger. (Riotous and violent behaviour was not confined to the barons.) The breach was now open. The new earl, brother of the murdered man, held his estates together by marrying the widowed heiress of Galloway. He began to build up an alliance with the rising Yorkist party in England, and secured the release from England of Malise Graham. It looked dangerous for the Crown. But the Yorkist bid for power in England was only successful for a while, and James was either very clever or very lucky. He won parliamentary exoneration for the murder, which indicates that many men were uneasy at Douglas power and appreciated the need for an effective monarchy. But it also implied that his actions needed justifying. King and Parliament would back each other up because they were necessary to each other in the government of the realm. The king could use Parliament, as James II did, in a body of legislation aimed, like his father's, at good government. James went on with a policy, which he shared with many successful monarchs in Scotland, of building up a new nobility among the houses favourable to royal power. He had already built up the Gordons and now he favoured some that felt Douglas oppression, the lesser Galloway family of Kennedy and the rival, illegitimate Douglas Earls of Angus, the 'Red' Douglases. He persuaded the Gordons to oppose Crawford and won over the Hamiltons by frightening them. In 1455 it came to fighting and two of the Douglas brothers were killed. James captured their castles of Abercorn and Threave, and the Earl of Douglas took refuge in England.

The capture of Threave was significant. James was an enthusiast for the new military arm of artillery. There had been guns before his reign. The first Scottish mention was in 1384: 'pro uno instrumento dicto gun' says the Exchequer Roll, billing it at four pounds (it must have been a small one). In the last year of his reign James I had spent £590 on workmen constructing 'bombards'. These early guns were crude things. It was long before a barrel could be cast in one, so they were made of bars of wrought iron bound together with iron hoops which were tightened with wedges. Since the range was short and accuracy poor,[1] early development concentrated on the mass of shot. The great fifteenth-century survival, Mons Meg, still on Edinburgh castle, weighed six and a half tons, had a twenty-inch bore, and used a hundred and five pounds of powder. The shot would travel nearly two miles and was either 1,125 pounds of iron or 549 pounds of stone. Stone was cheaper but apt to blow to bits and endanger the gun crew more than the enemy. Guns were a tremendous prestige point, both national and royal. Minstrels accompanied Mons Meg down the castle hill in 1497 at the cost of thirteen shillings. Artillery was an exorbitant expense. First of all it had to be bought abroad, then skilled foreign gunners and smiths had to be hired to use and maintain it, and foreign powder bought. A host of unskilled workmen with mattocks, spades, horses, and tows were needed to move it about. The royal artillery in the tragic raid of 1513 took fourteen days to cover forty-eight miles. In 1497, for the raid on Norham, the use of artillery meant the hire of two hundred and twenty-one men and ninety-three cart-horses, at seven shillings a week each. This was only just within the realm of the financially possible for the king, and quite outside it for the magnates. It meant that if the King really decided to he could take any baronial castle he wanted. For the king to assert himself in this way in the Lothians would give useful practice to his gunners. Farther afield, and travelling at three-and-a-half miles a day, he would only take action if he must. Threave, Caerlaverock, Dunnottar, the more distant great castles, would continue to be safe to their owners in minor disputes, but not in major ones. The function of these great fortresses had changed, but not been destroyed. They were still of enormous value in the forays and slaughters of great men against each other and humbler folk; of definite but limited use in teasing the king.

The Douglas crisis led to a major piece of legislation in 1455, the Act of Annexation, which declared various sources of money and points of power inalienable from the Crown. The Crown must be secured in the whole customs as they stood at James I's death, in many of the now forfeit Douglas lands, in the key castles of Edinburgh, Stirling, and Dumbarton and in various lordships. Heritable offices were revoked. Merely putting this statement into a statute did not

1. James II had a Frenchman whose gunnery did not err by more than a fathom, and this was a matter of wonder.

make it effective, yet it was more than a mere declaration. It put on record the view of Parliament and king that there was an irreducible minimum that the king must have. Meanwhile it helped to pay for James's expensive toys and a foreign policy that took advantage of civil war in England.

It was not simply an accident, but an expectable outcome of his enthusiasm for the new techniques and an assertive foreign policy, that marks James II's death in 1460 when besieging Roxburgh, after a brief but vigorous attempt to give his country sound legislation and firm government. One of his cannon exploded and a flying wedge killed the king, who was standing too near for safety. James had already similarly lost one of his valuable French gunners. The war went on. The Lancastrians let the Scots have Berwick back for a generation while the Yorkists made an agreement with the great magnates, the Lord of the Isles and the exiled Douglas. This 'treaty' of 1462, sometimes called the treaty of Ardtornish after the Macdonald base, is a clear indication of what the magnates thought feasible and desired. With English help, the kingdom of Scotland was to be destroyed. In its place the Douglas, the Lord of the Isles, and a kinsman of his would divide the country north of the Forth, and in the south the Douglas was to get back his estates. All were to hold of Edward IV. That nothing came of this could be forecast from the fact that the lion's share went to Douglas, who would of necessity contribute least in forces. In any case Edward IV was not secure enough in England to do much, and the Lord of the Isles, John, the fourth Lord, was not the man to drive anything through consistently, even against a king who was a minor. In 1474, when the Crown learnt of the treaty, James III was old enough to show his opinion, and it was some time before the Lord of the Isles could regain a degree of royal tolerance, and that only by surrendering Kintyre and the earldom of Ross and agreeing to hold his lordship feudally. The king now knew that here lay the greatest threat to the kingdom and kept an eye on the Macdonalds. He also prevented a second Douglas power building up in the Border. The Earls of Angus, the rising house of the Red Douglas, were forced to exchange their southern lands for territory in the north.

James III was not a fool. His long introspective face was, if anything, over-intelligent. He had already dealt with a baronial take-over bid by the Boyd family. This set of upstarts had kidnapped him in his minority and held him for two years while they dug into the royal revenues. James got free only during the negotiations for his marriage, in 1468.

The marriage was a far-sighted one, to Margaret, daughter of the King of Denmark and Norway. She brought the Danish king's lands and rights in Orkney and Shetland as successive pledges for her dowry, and when the Danish king failed to find the cash the Scottish Crown foreclosed. Repeated later attempts to unmortgage the islands were repulsed. It was a successful piece of sharp practice. Sympathy goes to the islanders, starting three centuries of Scottish oppression.

James III followed on the policy of building up a new nobility. Conspicuously among the early Stewarts, he believed in making his mark on foreign affairs. His reign bears the stamp of activity and assertion. This makes it difficult to understand why the reign should have ended in failure. Failure it indubitably was, because he could not govern his great men with any sense of security to himself, or with approval from them. The difficulty of understanding is not lessened by the detailed and spirited historical narratives which survive, and which were written nearly a hundred years later. From these we hear of James's low-class favourites who pandered to his unmilitary tastes. While James's brothers, the Earl of Mar and the Duke of Albany, were good, chivalrous characters who liked fighting and jousting, James was avaricious and spent his time with musicians, architects and tailors. The king quarrelled with his brothers and imprisoned them, which led to Albany's gallant and romantic escape from Edinburgh castle and his alliance with the English king as a pretender to the throne. The nobles made a demonstration against James and hanged his upstarts over Lauder bridge in 1481 or 1482. A renewed crisis, mixed with civil war and foreign threats, led to a band of nobles getting hold of James's eldest son and meeting James in battle at Sauchieburn, near Stirling, in 1488. The king lost the fight, and we are given a detailed and totally unsubstantiated account of his murder after it. It all makes an excellent moral tale, stressing the need for a good, martial, and impecunious spirit in a king. Unfortunately there is little particular reason to believe much of it. Some parts of the tale we know to be untrue. This is, after all, a period for which the official records give a good amount of detail. All the spirited back-chat has to be discarded as unauthenticated, including the long discussion among the nobles as to who was to take on the king before Lauder bridge, to 'Bell the Cat'. James's close associates were not all upstarts, even allowing for the fact that some of them so named never existed at all. But there was certainly a quarrel with Albany, which brought in the English and led to the final loss of Berwick in 1482. The English occupied Edinburgh and James held out in the castle. James managed this crisis successfully, mixing force, negotiation, and appeals to the country for support, and had the sense afterwards to try and treat Albany leniently. Only after a second invasion was the duke forfeited. Something drastic certainly did happen at Lauder bridge at some time or other. The place passed into the folk memory of the upper classes as the scene of a brutal humiliation of the king. And in the 1480s we can see signs of suspicion and hostility between the king and his nobles. The king has a royal guard. He quarrels with influential families, the Homes for instance, and even with the Earl of Argyll, whose house normally backed the Crown. There was a bargain earlier in 1488 between the king and his opposition in which peace and friendliness were promised. Then the king is seen looking for allies, and the final breakdown, battle and death occur.

A king had failed to get on with his nobles. Probably the failure had been more from personality than policy. A lot of the nobility had remained neutral in the crisis. James may have annoyed the others by a touch of paranoia. What is unusual in the dealings between Crown and baronage in Scotland is that they should have led to the killing of the king. Scottish politics were not usually that dangerous for the monarch: on the whole Crown and nobility worked together.

The implications of the received story of James III are also interesting. They show the popular or literary hold of the chivalric myth, that the life of the king and aristocracy was expected to be one of jousting and ceremony, all good, clean, upper-class fun, with no attempt to discipline the magnates. A king could be disapproved of for avarice and for patronage of the arts. It is as if today public opinion demanded of a head of state philistinism and a high performance at water-skiing. True, horsemanship had some relevance to the business of government: a man too infirm to ride at all could not rule. But it is worth remembering that the kingdom eventually received real government from a king who was a notoriously incompetent horseman, for ever falling off. Out of simple envy nobles resented a king who managed to collect money, and it is the nobles' point of view that the historians of the sixteenth century accepted. In so far as James appreciated beauty in word or stone, or in the metal of his delightful coins, he was a lot more in tune with the spirit of the day than were his joust-loving opponents. If this meant expense, perhaps the country could sustain it.

Evidence of more movement in the economy, more wealth in the country, is not clear, but this is a time when burghs were proliferating. These were the lesser burghs, not the old core, which now come to be called royal burghs, and to which additions were still being made, but the burghs of barony and regality. A royal burgh had privileges which included the right to trade abroad. The lesser burghs were for the home market only. Fifty-one of these were founded between 1450 and 1516. Each of these had its own area of privilege, in which it monopolized buying and selling, and craft work such as the finishing of cloth. A new burgh cut down the area of privilege of existing burghs, and so was not welcome to established interests. Inside both kinds of burghs a long contest for control of the town's affairs went on between craftsmen and merchants, in which the craftsmen were always being beaten. Merchants, especially foreign merchants, were more important and necessary than craftsmen. This suggests that trade was of increasing importance in the life of the nation. Scotland's exports now included the products of her fisheries in the form of barrels of salted herring and salmon, as well as wool and skins. That money was moving about more is shown by the growth of feu-ferm in the later fifteenth century. Lands were being assigned in feu-ferm, that is, granted by their overlord permanently to a tenant in return for a cash rent and a few clearly defined services. Selling feus was a way of raising money quickly, but it also involved more regular use of cash in the rent. The Crown had been feuing land occasionally since the thirteenth century, and in the late fifteenth century the practice became frequent. The tenants got security and the king got cash from it. The nobility and the Church later followed the Crown in taking to the practice. All sorts of 'middling' rank people got land in this way in the fifteenth century. Feus ranged in size from a single farm to the whole barony of Strathearn.

Feus were sought after, and even fought over. Sometimes they gave security to the man who already occupied the land, sometimes to an intruder. In any case the tenant had now to find cash for the rent, and therefore took care to get it out of those below him. But as the depreciation of the fifteenth and sixteenth centuries ran the coinage down, the burden of rent on the tenant decreased. The laird, as the tenant would be called, became financially stronger. The class of lairds gradually became of political importance. But feuing was often at the expense of existing small tenants, the 'kindly' tenants, who seem to have held by a tenure which was not precise and often had an element of kinship in fact or theory. Kindly tenants were a varied class: in some parts of the country their tenure was treated as permanent. But where this was not the case, feuing either meant that a laird was brought in over the heads of the kindly tenants, who had now to pay an increased rent, or in some cases that these tenants were able to scrape up the rent themselves and hold their own feus. These became the 'bonnet lairds', the small landowners who farmed their own land. In both cases landholding became more fixed, the relationships involved more certain and more financial. Below the feuar the small tenantry had no advantages from the system. Their rents went up but their insecurity remained, so much so that Major, describing Scotland in 1521, thought that the absence of leases for more than four or five years was the reason for the failure of the Scottish peasantry to build any but small mean houses, to plant trees or develop their land. But at the upper end the units, even the great aristocratic ones, were becoming more stable.

Scotland in the fifteenth century had other European concepts besides that of chivalry. There had been the great conciliar movement in the first half of the century, when the lay powers had worked together and put forward a programme of church decentralization and reform. The schism within the papacy had been deeply disturbing to all Christendom. It had been particularly exasperating to Scotland, for the country had been unable to send her scholars to English universities, because England backed another pope. This was one of the reasons for the creation of St Andrew's University, nominally in 1412 (but universities do not get to work in a single year). Active work to mend the breach in the Church brought the separate national Churches more under the leadership and control of their own kings, and these kings did not regard themselves as mere stand-ins for the papacy. Though the Scottish Crown did not cut the Scottish Church off from the papal appointments system, as did the English, it tried under James I to prevent both money and clergy going abroad. James III passed Acts in Parliament designed to prevent the Pope overriding the royal patronage and in favour of 'free' elections. The schism had already enhanced the nationalism that largely created it. At one heady but insecure moment the Scots had had a pope to themselves. Some of the great Councils had been organized under the system of 'nations'. Nationalism, as distinct from patriotism, was an emotion of the time, and the Scots shared it. They reverenced their own native saints, and at the end of the century under Hector Boece, an able Latinist and an unscrupulous historian, started inventing their own history. Nationalism, too, was responsible for the over-provision of universities. Two more, Glasgow and Aberdeen, were founded in the fifteenth century. It also was probably the power which gave Scotland her own metropolitan: the archbishopric of St Andrew's dates from 1472. The national spirit was reinforced by a real native culture, the blossoming of Scottish literature. The late fifteenth-century poets, and there were a lot of them, found that Scots gave them a rich vocabulary and an exciting diction to work with. They had a professional pride in their technique. We may be charmed by the freshness of the poetry, but the men who wrote:

Quhen Tayis bank was blumit bricht

or:

Empryce of pryss, imperatrice
Bricht polist preciouss stane

were not simple singers but skilled craftsmen balancing rhyme, rhythm, and alliteration. Dunbar, in his famous *Lament for the Makars*, lists over twenty poets gone before. If some of these men took James III's mind from horse-mania, we can sympathize with the king.

The Church's trouble encouraged not only nationalism, but anti-clericalism. It was with the help of laymen that she had refounded herself. Anti-clericalism is to be expected in a society where the clergy are numerous, the Church rich, and its wealth often misapplied. In the fifteenth century the clergy not only included those who had the cure of souls, but numerous men following professional careers of no special religious significance. It included clerks and administrators of all kinds, academics, and the court poets. Many of these did not lead lives that were particularly edifying or justified clerical status. There were literate and educated men outside the clergy, for instance among the kings of France and Scotland and the Italian princes. There was no reason why reverence should be assigned to some of the specialized careers still monopolized by the clergy in an age when a king of France could write serious sermons. Meanwhile it was easy to talk about abuse. The superstructure of the Church, the monasteries, cathedral chapters, and universities had all been created by filching revenue from the parishes. The parish clergy had been left too poor to do their work properly. It was time for the Church to redefine the function of the clergy in a more cultivated, richer, and better educated world. Instead, in the fifteenth century, the papacy was involved in reasserting itself against kings and General Council and trying to create a political system in Italy that would enable it to feel secure. In these circumstances the Church got its priorities wrong, and the parishes and the faithful were neglected.

The country was slowly growing the minimal instruments of government, and in the process Edinburgh was becoming the capital. Since 1466 Parliament had had its own records, separate from those of Council. Since James I's time its effective work had been done by the committee, the Lords of the Articles, which kept its discussions practical and short. The Session, the chief court, was becoming more professional in membership and widening its scope. The judges were members of the King's Council and sat in it when the Council was doing judicial work. The Session was not divorced from the king. He would sit in justice himself in Council and hear cases. James III had tried to tidy up his income, and organize its receipt better. It was still conspicuously too small for the things a king would want to do, even in peacetime, and as a result there was no regular system of salaries for his officials and judges. But even when the king could raise the money he did not aim at a salaried service. The concept is too modern. Instead he used men who owned land, or got his servants beneficed by the Church. Their service was to the monarch in person, rather than to the Crown as an institution.

The complexities of the fifteenth century made requirements of monarchy that were not yet depersonalized. To some degree the next

King of Scotland met these: at least he satisfied the wishes of his kingdom, and so held it with him in his aims. This is not to say that the aims themselves were wise. James IV, nearly of age at the time of his father's murder, was fully part of the community of European princes. Behind him lay a series of international marriages which tied Scotland into Europe. He combined the interests of the day with great enthusiasm, though with limited intelligence, and was popular for both reasons. His pop-eyed, eager face, his willingness to try anything, his restless delight in fast travel, were all sympathetic characteristics. Aeneas Sylvius, later Pope Pius II, had visited Scotland in his youth in James I's reign: in the famous pictures in Siena of his triumphant progress to the papal see (the local boy had made good) we can see that to a Sienese of the mid-fifteenth century Scotland was entirely a land of myth – the most mythical thing being the old white-bearded king.[1] By contrast, James IV's reign gives us the practical account of the diplomat Ayala, sent in 1498 by the Catholic kings of Spain to vet a possible candidate for the hand of their daughter. They wanted, and got, a practical account of both king and country. Ayala analyses James's abilities and character, the royal revenues, and the economic strength of the country in a way that shows it was no longer a land of mystery and excruciating hardship to the rest of Europe, but a province of European civilization.

James's enthusiasms extended to languages. He had more than a smattering of several, and even learnt a little Gaelic. For the first time for over a century it looked as if a monarch was going to bridge the growing gulf between the two civilizations of the country. He made frequent expeditions to the Highlands. Trouble between the Lord of the Isles and the Mackenzies had blown up. Perhaps it was an attempt of the Lord of the Isles to regain the earldom of Ross. James turned against him, and in 1493 forfeited the Lordship and broke up his confederacy in a series of short campaigns. The forfeited Lord was old and lacked decision. James was young and active.

1. Aeneas Sylvius, who writes of a miraculous tree in Orkney which had fruit that turned into birds, belongs to an old tradition of telling tall stories about Scotland. This dates back to Procopius, to whom Scotland was a land where the air was so poisonous that no human being or creature other than serpents could survive there more than half an hour.

Still it is surprising he got away with it. The king could destroy the lordship but he could not quiet the west. In the vacuum of power the lesser units developed more independence. This is the time when the clan chiefs begin to come forward and act as nearly independent rulers, and the 'clan system' is fastened on the Highlands. James could not sustain the task of keeping law and order there. The moment he left, disorder broke out again. In 1494 as soon as James's ships set out from Dunaverty he saw the captain he had installed there being hanged by the Macdonalds of Islay. To sustain his efforts for order he had to fall back on two growing and important kinships, the Campbells and the Gordons. In 1509 he made Huntly and Argyll heritable sheriffs, dividing the west between them. But these leaders were unlikely to act as disinterested servants of the Crown. Perhaps, to use James I's phrase, if God had but granted time, things would have been better; but God was not in the habit of granting time to the Stewarts. The appalling record of clan warfare in the sixteenth century seems to have been at least partly caused by the destruction of the dominant political unit of the Highlands. James IV's efforts to replace it with feudal lordship exercised by the heads of imperialist clans were not acceptable to those outside their kinships.

James's Highland expeditions were expensive, yet the country which had complained of his father's avariciousness supported them. It also allowed an enormous programme of palace building – the main relics of this are Falkland and Linlithgow. Like his grandfather, James was an enthusiast for guns, and this now meant naval guns as well as land ones.[1] James put a lot into his navy, the great achievement of which was the *Great Michael*, launched in 1511 from special quays constructed at Newhaven. She was said to have consumed all the wood in Fife except for that for the king's hunting at Falkland, and then to have needed timber from Norway: this probably means that there was already little in the way of full-grown woods in Fife. The monster was 240 feet long, with walls 10 feet thick, carried over twenty guns, 300 sailors, 120 gunners, and 1,000 fighting men. It was a shocking example of megalomania, of an undeveloped country indulging in the latest thing in expensive armaments without the skill to use it properly. The king's enthusiasm could not enable Scotland

1. Other European monarchs shared this enthusiasm, notably John II of Portugal; who also realized that gunpowder did not need a vast ship.

to equip this ship. The master gunners had to be got from abroad, and so did other special features: the iron came from Spain, the compass from Middlesborough. Gunpowder was not a native product yet, at least not in the quantities used by these big guns. Secondary armament stuck out like pins in a pincushion. True, she was the latest thing in naval design, with her gunports built into her sides to get the weight of the guns low, and with elaborate precautions to stop them setting her on fire. But she would soon be obsolete. She was too heavy to handle easily, and being unrelated in scale to other ships she could not draw on a body of skilled men. Her vast manpower would make her a focus of infection within a few weeks of going to sea. When the armed strength of the country was mustered the king had not enough skilled gunners for both land and sea, and in 1513 he put them in the wrong place, at sea.

The crisis and war of 1513 was the result of James's character, his mixture of quickness, enthusiasm, and lack of deep thought. He had married an English princess in 1503 after a good deal of deliberation. She was Margaret Tudor, the elder daughter of Henry VII, not as lovely as the younger sister but with a better claim to the throne. The marriage was the result of improving relations with England. Seven years before, James had been supporting the claims of the pretender Perkin Warbeck against Henry. It was in this cause that minstrels had accompanied Mons Meg down from the castle in 1497 to start the lamentable campaign against Norham which had been hurriedly dropped when the English Earl of Surrey brought an army north. That some deep political interests were determined that James should marry Margaret is suggested by the sudden death of his most influential light-of-love, Margaret Drummond, and her sisters. The marriage meant a treaty promising real peace. It was a comprehensive agreement arranging for the peaceful settlement of every sort of dispute, and invoking papal censure and excommunication on whoever broke it.

But James still had obligations of a vague kind towards France. In spite of requests by Henry he had not expressly cancelled the Auld Alliance. This was not of importance while Henry VII, who wanted peace, lived, but in 1509 he was succeeded by Henry VIII, young, belligerent, and ready to spend lavishly in self-assertion. Within a couple of years there was friction between the brothers-in-law over naval actions by the English against Scottish ships which the English claimed were pirates. Both sides constantly indulged in piracy in the narrow seas, and where piracy stopped and self-defence began was a fine point. It was the sort of situation that would be peacefully handled only with goodwill. Goodwill was markedly not one of Henry's characteristics, and soon James, too, was spoiling for a fight. Events in Italy drove matters to a breach. In 1511 there began to form the political alliance misleadingly called the Holy League, a band between the papacy, Spain, and Venice against France and French power in Italy. The League was enlarged in 1512 to include England. Both England and France demanded James's support, particularly the loan of the *Great Michael*. The Empire joined the League, and French pressure on James to help France in her encirclement mounted.

So matters moved to a totally unnecessary war. Neither James nor Henry cared deeply about the French position in Italy. But the two kings were already rivals, and even though Henry modified his remarks about piracy, peace could not hold. Henry invaded France, and James prepared himself for excommunication over his broken treaty. The Scottish fleet was promised to the French, who made little use of it and allowed the *Great Michael* to run aground. The best gunners went with her. It was the men of lesser skill who were in charge when James's seventeen great guns, pulled by 400 oxen, took the road to Coldstream at a snail's pace in July 1513. James's ability to carry his country with him, even the Highlanders, was shown in the vast host that answered the summons to Ellem in Berwickshire, and on into England.

For all that James boasted that he would be in York by Michaelmas, this could only be a border raid to distract the English. Indeed it did this, for it brought some troops back from France, a hard core of trained men. The Border castles held the Scots up for several days. Catherine, the English queen, sent Surrey north to raise troops. Surrey had already roused James's envy as a soldier, but he was also an organizer and had created an efficient machinery for mustering the north. The English gathered at Newcastle and slogged north; and in a wet and windy September, by skilful manoeuvring and hard marching, they got between the Scots, encamped on Flodden Hill, and the Tweed. The threat of being cut off from Scotland brought the Scots down to fight on foot on Branxton Hill, and there the two met. It is difficult to accept the vast numbers offered us by contemporaries for the battle of Flodden. There does not seem room for more than about fifteen thousand a side on the hill, perhaps a bit more for the Scots and fewer for the English. It was English bill against Scottish spear; guns brought to bear against guns firing in the air; more seriously it was Surrey's determined strategy and professional approach against James's enthusiastic desire to get to grips. Had not Ayala fifteen years before said of James 'he is not a good captain, because he begins to fight before he has given his orders'?

Flodden marks the point of no return in the struggle between the two countries. With every nerve taut to deploy men and guns, an able Scottish king was defeated, his army wiped out, his own life expended, in a struggle with the second string of the English. And because James had had unprecedented support, the slaughter struck home at every farm and household throughout lowland Scotland.

> Unto the deth gois all estaitis
> Princis, prelatis and Potestaitis
> Bayth riche and pure of al degre;
> Timor Mortis conturbat me.

NOTES ON DRAMATIS PERSONAE

The Earls of Douglas:

Archibald, fourth Earl (first Duke of Touraine), killed at Verneuil 1424: grandson of Robert I's companion, Sir James Douglas. Married to a daughter of Robert III.

His son, Archibald, fifth Earl, was one of the regents in 1437, married Euphemia Graham, descendant of the Stewart Earls of Strathearn. He died 1439.

William, sixth Earl, son of the fifth Earl, murdered with his younger brother 1440. His sister Margaret, 'the fair maid of Galloway', inherited Galloway.

The line then reverted to the younger brother of the fourth Earl, James, seventh Earl, famous for his fatness. His sons were:

William, eighth Earl, murdered 1452, and

James, ninth Earl, forfeited 1455, who made the treaty of Ardtornish, and died 1491. Both these married Margaret of Galloway.

After them the earldom became extinct.

The Lords of the Isles:

Donald (1387–1423). The battle of Harlaw was his attempt to claim the earldom of Ross as his wife's inheritance.

Alexander, his son (1423–49). He was granted the earldom of Ross.

John, his son (1449–93). He made the treaty of Ardtornish, 1462, which led to his temporary forfeiture, 1476. Died, after permanent forfeiture, 1498.

Argyll. Colin Campbell, created first Earl, 1457, Chancellor 1483–7, died 1493. Except for the period 1487–8 he pursued his house's policy of supporting the Crown.

Huntley. George Seton, later Lord Gordon, second Earl of Huntley, Lieutenant North of the Esk 1491, Chancellor 1498, died 1501. His house grew in power under him by his policy of supporting the Crown, and by his frequent marriages and divorces.

Surrey. Thomas Howard, Earl of Surrey, 1443–1524, created second Duke of Norfolk 1514, Earl Marshal of England.

D

Chapter 6

James V

A prudent ruler will prefer a bad name for parsimony without hatred
to a reputation for liberality which leads to extortion.

MACCHIAVELLI, The Prince

FOR HALF OF THE sixteenth century Scotland had a monarch under
age and was ruled in his or her name by whoever could retain the
regency for a few years. So at a time when many European countries
saw the emergence of strong monarchies, that of Scotland stood out
as condemned to weakness. Yet one of the most valuable possessions
of the Crown in these long minorities was the fact that the royal
child's life was the only safeguard against a complicated inheritance
dispute. However much baronial gangster forces might wish to coerce
and use the king, they could not afford to endanger his life. This
personal indispensability is one of the reasons why the country
achieved an adult status in government and politics by the end of the
century.

At first it did not look as if this sort of progress could happen. The
great historian Maitland has commented gloomily: 'In that mournful
procession of the five Jameses there is no break. The last of them is
engaged in the old task, and failing as his forbears failed.' It is an
occupational weakness of historians to prefer sharply marked out
issues (Protestantism versus Catholicism, England versus France) to
the disorderly struggles of great families. Just because of this there
has been a tendency to try to align political strife with issues which
may not yet have emerged. But the dominant character of James V's
reign cannot be found in the religious struggle of the Reformation,
nor even in foreign alignments, but in a new attempt of the Crown
to assert itself among its nobility. Maitland is right in saying that
James belongs with his forbears, but he also belongs to the new

despotism of the early sixteenth century, a period when foreign policy was conducted in dynastic terms and worked out by dynastic marriages. The great achievements of the Habsburgs in this idiom set the European stage and provided the main European alliances.

The baby who inherited after Flodden was himself the product of dynastic marriage, though of a union that had conspicuously failed to hold together the interests of the families concerned. In the disorder after the battle Henry VIII might have expected to exercise control over Scottish affairs with the help of his sister Margaret. In the event, Henry proved too impatient and Margaret too unstable for this. Like her brother, Margaret had a troubled matrimonial history; unlike him she did not use her passions in the service of her political aims.

The immediate problems in 1513 were defence, and some sort of government. Edinburgh's response to the emergency was to order the women to the churches to pray, the men to arms; but the English had their eyes on France and did not want to be distracted by an invasion of Scotland. England and France were soon negotiating a peace, and in the respite the Scots got their infant crowned and began to build the famous 'Flodden wall' round the capital. The Queen Mother was accepted as Regent and guardian, but she promptly threw herself in marriage at the Earl of Angus, Archibald Douglas. This marriage was ostentatiously on the rocks in a remarkably short time, even by Tudor standards, but it led the opponents of the Douglases to look elsewhere for the regency. The obvious choice was the first cousin of James IV, John, Duke of Albany: his limitations were that he spoke only French and was completely under the control of the King of France. So long as the feeling of the country was against England these were not insurmountable handicaps. Albany came, was accepted as Regent for a while, and during that while held the country together.

Albany naturally renewed the Auld Alliance in the Treaty of Rouen, which promised the infant king a French princess as bride. He also made a series of truces with England which would hold so long as France and England remained at peace. As an instrument of French policy this was expected of him, but Albany went on to give the Scotch nobility a taste of discipline. The Earl of Home and his brother were executed for treason, probably justifiably, but with the result that the Warden of the Marches, whom Albany put in in their place, was murdered by the Homes. Albany, and later James, had to learn the hard way that a Scottish king could only afford to discipline his Border barons when he had a sure peace with England.

English pressure and Albany's own French interests prevented his staying on. He left Scotland in 1517 and returned only in 1521 when war between England and France was imminent, to bring the Scots into it. But the Scots had learned something from Flodden: they would not invade their neighbour again. The French alliance was useful as a protection against dominance by England, but they had no mind again to risk lives in purely French interests. It was to take another forty years before the French Crown realized that Scotland had no wish to escape English power at the cost of French domination.

Albany finally returned to France, and his regency lapsed in 1524. This led to a struggle between the nobles for power, complicated by the uncertain alliances made by Margaret, and simplified by the enormous advantages that accrued to whoever actually had hold of the person of the king. In 1526 the Douglas faction, breaking agreements, got control of James, declared him old enough to govern personally, and kept him for two years. This was the period when, says the historian Lindesay of Pitscottie, 'Nane durst stryve with ane Douglas nor zeit ane Douglas man.' The Douglases and their allies filled all the valuable posts and supplied the vacant bishoprics (including the appointment of a bishop of Argyll who had to be dispensed for homicide). They were so outrageous in their nest-feathering that the rest of the nobility was almost welded into a united opposition. James was in his late teens, ready to assert himself and passionately resentful of tutelage. When, in 1528, he finally escaped, the attack on the whole Douglas connection was vindictive.[1] Douglases were outlawed, their castles taken, their allies destroyed, and even minor adherents executed on trumped-up charges. These actions ended the great days of the house, but they did not lead the rest of the baronage to trust the Crown.

The normal aims of the baronage had been well shown by the way the Douglases had been behaving: personal advantage, soft jobs in the Church for younger sons, geographical advantage, territorial power

1. There is in this a similarity to the resentment of Richard II of England to the Appellants.

over their neighbours. The minority had seen important manifestations of this, such as the awarding of Commissions of Lieutenancy to nobles to act for the Crown. As a result the Earl of Argyll, one of the more reliable and consistent of the nobility, was controlling the western sea-board far beyond his own lands, raising crown rents and holding on to them for himself. The Earl of Huntly was doing the same farther north. Elsewhere, even without commissions, control was in baronial hands. The Homes and Douglases held the south-east, almost the most unruly area of all, and both had been negotiating for greater strength, the Homes by parleys with the English, the Douglases by confiscating the king. Other families would treat with the English to do down their neighbours: it was always uncertain whom a Border laird would be most ready to attack, English or Scot. There is no need to condemn them for failure to abide by the modern concept of a national state and the loyalty we expect to it. Their first loyalty was to their own family or surname; if this was to be widened to a territorial idea, this would still be only the local one. James V also thought largely in dynastic and family terms; for the Stewarts, and against the Douglases. His ideas acquired a national tinge only because the nation was his patrimony. Margaret his mother thought even more simply in personal terms, and continued for many years to disturb politics by her efforts at getting her marriage to Angus annulled (Angus was young, so there was no reason to expect a convenient widowhood) so that she could marry her new choice, Henry Stewart, later Lord Methven.

With this intense localism active it may seem surprising that even the minimum aspects of government survived the long minority. But in fact government did more than survive, it grew. The developments that were to mean so much by the end of the century can be traced to this period and no earlier – the slow rise of new men and new families in crown service, useful servants with no great house behind them, and the increasing professional nature of the Court of Session. In 1528 the membership of the court ceased to be open to the Council in general: the judges were still mainly ecclesiastics, but they were professionals. James kept up this professional spirit in his service when he started to rule personally, perhaps because he saw its long-term possibilities, perhaps because he did not get on with his baronage.

The king took over his own government with a vigour and a personal direction which shows instantly in his correspondence. He had had a rough training in baronialism and baronial wars. There had been the fight in Edinburgh between Douglas and Hamilton in 1520 to which the Scots later gave the nickname of 'Cleanse the Causeway', and the much more bitter affair at Linlithgow in 1528 where the young Earl of Lennox had been killed in an attempt to rescue the king, and James had had a Douglas hand on his bridle. Now he would rule by himself, and he could hardly escape noticing that kingship could mean much more than it had done in the past. There were the new despots, Henry VIII and Francis I, to model himself on; the new, splendid, and very expensive courts of the Renaissance princes in Italy. It did not need the rough treatment of his minority to make this a more attractive image than the Scottish kingship of the past. James set out to rule and live as a Renaissance prince.

James was a shrewd man, active and self-assertive. He wanted to govern his realm in a more real sense than his forbears. He went some way towards this, making spectacular inroads into the two areas of least government. A long-planned circumnavigation through Orkney took him into the Highlands and Islands in 1540, the culmination of several visits, and gave him the chance to make a serious attempt to put his own officials into power instead of relying on one or another local faction. In 1530 he went down on the Border and hanged Johnnie Armstrong of Liddesdale and various other Armstrongs. Liddesdale was always the most difficult part of the Border to control, and a succession of Scottish monarchs, rightly or wrongly, came down on the Armstrongs as particularly reprehensible sources of trouble. Monarchs who 'raided' the Border were expected to do a certain amount of hanging of local thieves, *pour encourager les autres*. To make sure that no demoralizing acquittals took place they usually brought to trial only those whose guilt was pretty certain, and they brought their own juries with them for extra certainty. When Mary, Queen of Scots, had an attack of leniency in the Border it made trouble for her lieutenant Moray, who was not inclined that way at all. There is no evidence that James's hangings were more numerous than was usual when government was determined to keep order and have its authority respected.

James went on to increase and make more direct his hold on the Border. The offices of Warden of the Marches were taken away from the powerful families that had been holding them and given to lesser men, who relied for authority not on their own private influence but on their royal commission. Surprisingly, this worked for a time. But it added to the discontent of the nobles in general and made the loyalty of the great Border houses more uncertain even than usual. Discipline in the Border would be a sound policy only if the king could maintain such a peace with England that he would not have to call upon the Border lairds to fight for him. A dispassionate enthusiasm for law and order, which James may well have felt, must be a peace-time luxury.

In other ways James asserted the nature of his government. In 1532 he 'founded' the College of Justice. This meant securing the agreement of the Church to a personal tax of 10,000 pounds Scots on the bishops, to support a court for civil and ecclesiastical causes. The court was the old Court of Session unchanged, and the main issue was the bargaining with the bishops as to how much they would actually pay. The final compromise was 72,000 pounds, spread over four years, some of which got past James and was actually received by the judges. But the court was developing, even without James's attention, and a few years later the keeping of separate registers shows that it had finally cut adrift from the Privy Council. In the 1550s the creation of the 'inner' and 'outer' house equipped it to act both as a court of first instance and as a court of appeal. All that James's elaborate 'foundation' of the College had done towards this natural development was to endow the court with an income and use the structure to get money out of the Church. It is more part of the history of taxation than of his abstract interest in effective government.

It is James's constant drive for more money which more than anything else gives continuity and policy to his reign. Foreign policy, church policy, home affairs, all tie up with the search for extra funds, and this is so persistent and successful that it is impossible not to put money as his first objective. Some historians have attempted to account for this in terms of the well-known sixteenth-century price rise, which forced monarchs to find new financial resources. That prices all over Europe rose in the sixteenth century is undeniable, but they did not rise all the time, and in most parts of Europe they did not rise very far in the first forty years of the century. In any case there is no consistent evidence for any rise at all in Scotland between 1520 and 1540. James was raising enormous sums in taxation, especially from the Church, and even his 'ordinary' revenue by the end of his reign was more than three times what it had been under the Douglases, or as a fairer basis for normality, 50 per cent higher than his father's in 1507. James behaved about money as a dipsomaniac behaves with alcohol, tucking it away in all sorts of secret places. There were the king's mysterious boxes, full of gold and valuables, which enabled him to live in style on his visit to France, much to the surprise of his companions, and which also sustained the early days of his daughter's minority.

Of course a Renaissance prince had material needs. His court would be expected to show a certain sumptuousness; James was building great palaces. His authority ought to have military force behind it, and weapons were expensive. James's instructions to Albany over the negotiations for a French marriage show an appreciation of Scotland's lack in both these respects. If a dowry is mentioned, Albany is to press for 'a generous supply of royal furnishings, embroideries, tapestries, vessels of gold and silver, cloth of gold, silver and silk and so forth, also warlike munitions of divers kinds including gunpowder'. Repeated attempts by James to get ordnance abroad, gunpowder from France, metal from Denmark (particularly an urgent appeal to both countries for gunpowder in 1531 so that he could equip an expedition against the chiefs in the Islands), show that Scotland was not producing munitions. More important than weapons was money as the sinew of power. The king obtained an Act of Parliament allowing him to feu out the Crown lands for a greater return. The expedition to the Isles meant that at last they gave a revenue to the Crown. The forfeitures that were imposed by the king increased the Crown's wealth – not always justifiably, to judge from the rapid reversal of some of these immediately after his death. We hear that James's pacification of the Border enabled him to keep 10,000 sheep in Ettrick as safely as if they had been in Fife (it is a Fife man speaking) which suggests that the deforestation of Ettrick, if not already far advanced, soon would be. Henry VIII protested to James that this sort of direct farming was beneath his royal dignity, which obliged James to deny that he was doing anything of the sort. Henry felt that James should get his money by the more gentlemanly way of robbing the Church, and back him up in his own breach with Rome. James preferred to use the Church as a form of out-relief for his bastards, and found the split between Henry and Rome a useful means of putting pressure on the Pope: he could always remind the Pope, and frequently did, that without royal prevention heresy might seep into Scotland from her neighbour. The use of an acquiescent Church to James is shown in his most scandalous begging letter to the Pope:

> As I have three illegitimate sons . . . I am obliged to confess to your Holiness that the fault is my own (although it might indeed easily be attributed to youth[1]), and I acknowledge the error of human weakness. Yet that natural fatherly affection, common to all creatures, which nature prompts, urges every man to have regard for the welfare of his offspring as of himself; . . . We therefore beg your Holiness, of your clemency and courtesy . . . to dispense with these our sons, by the grace of your apostolic authority, that, notwithstanding their defect of birth, they may, when their age allows, be duly promoted . . . to all holy orders, even that of priesthood, and that at present, notwithstanding their minority as well as their defect of birth, they may . . . hold any church dignities whatsoever, . . . even two, three, four or more incompatible benefices. . . .

James had at least nine illegitimate children to look after, and did his best for them. The effect of this on the Church can be imagined from his remarks to the Pope when he tried to get a six-year-old bastard given the priory of St Andrews: 'the royal dignity of the boy will put a restraint upon the impious. . . .' The nobility moved in on the same racket, and on their behalf the king demanded bishoprics and abbeys for young men of the right families. Though it might have been difficult to expect *parvenus* to exercise authority in lawless

1. As James was barely twenty-one at this time, indeed it might be, though it is doubtful if youth is an adequate apology for a string of bastards by different women. That such lapses did not detract from the popularity of a monarch in the Middle Ages is shown by the nickname of 'the Good' given to Philip of Burgundy who owned the record number of twenty-six historically traced illegitimate children.

districts unless they had support from the great houses, the total absence of religious considerations in the letters of recommendation that James sent to the Pope for bishoprics is a significant warning of the Reformation. In 1535 Paul III allowed the king the right to nominate his bishops – another benefit from exploitation of the English situation. While sapping the Church from inside James gave his patronage to the pungent anti-clerical criticism of the *Satyre of the three Estates* by David Lindsay, with its crude sarcasm about the Church. This play offers, in theme, only the standard anti-clericalism that is to be found in both England and Scotland in the fifteenth and sixteenth centuries, but gives it life and character. The courtiers, all of them tied to relatives who held or aspired to church office, could and did laugh at the writing on the wall.

James's church appointments were not necessarily any worse than those of the regencies of his minority, but between them the two sets almost completely stuffed the Church with men whose main interests and activities were secular. Half the bishops had illegitimate children, and indeed Cardinal Beaton had almost as many as James.[1] Bishoprics and abbeys were handed over to laymen and children *in commendam*. Already the parish clergy had been deprived of most of the teinds: 85 per cent of parish churches were appropriated, which meant that the vicars in them had very little allowed to live on, the bulk of the income going to some institution. Now at the upper end of the Church the baronial and royal nominees were gaining the benefits of this shift in church income. Scotland had developed an episcopate which was baronial in its concerns – its members came from the great families and thought and lived for the interests of these. This is a peculiarly Scottish feature. Elsewhere we find great prince-bishoprics, but these carried their own territorial interest, even though they might be persistently held by the members of one family. It could even be argued that the papacy had become little more than a great prince-bishopric, too. The specially Scottish system was one where the bishops thought as members of their surname. So we have the dynasty of Chisholms in Dunblane, the three illegitimate Hamiltons (who included an archbishop), the Hepburns, the Gordons, and the Stewarts. This was not a new feature – immediately after Flodden one of the two candidates for the archbishopric of St Andrew's had been

1. Eight can be traced for the bishop.

besieging the other in purely baronial fashion – but it was enhanced now. It became natural to regard the Church as an organization about as much separated from ordinary lay life as the members of a particular golf club are from society at large today, an institution which gains its homogeneity from a narrow class background and particular common interests only. This being so, it was understandable for James to encroach on the funds that supported the club. The total revenue of the Church was some 300,000 pounds Scots a year; the 'ordinary' revenue of the state was under 50,000 even at the end of the reign. Not all the Church's wealth could be made to yield a share of taxation, but James worked at getting what he could. By 1535 the clergy were paying four separate taxes to him, and one of these, the 'Great Tax' for the College of Justice, was so heavy that the bishops had to ask permission to feu their lands to raise the money. Feuing meant a permanent alienation of the land in return for a small rent and a large sum at once: it was a way of mortgaging the future, more permanent than the usual rent and entry-fine method. It was also a way of entrenching the lay landowning classes in the Church's property, and increased the baronial tie-up with the Church. Between them, the king, the Pope, and the bishops were selling the Church to the nobility.

Feuing also altered the power structure of landholding, giving strength to classes below the nobility. Those who obtained feus profited by them in the sixteenth-century price rise. They became the emerging gentry, and showed their increasing economic and political importance for the first time in the crisis of the Reformation. In this aspect as well as in doctrinal and disciplinary matters the Church policy of the Crown produced its logical results.

That James should have followed Henry of England's lead and break with the Pope was never likely. For one thing James never questioned Catholic orthodoxy or papal authority: he was an automatic Catholic. The quality of his church appointments suggests that he was little more than an automatic one. In any case James could get money out of the Church without schism. Because Henry had been unreasonably thwarted in his matrimonial needs for political reasons, James found the papacy unusually conciliatory. On the rare occasions when it was not, James could use the threat of friendship with Henry as a means of putting the screw on for money or other advantages. In return he would repay favours by burning a few heretics. In 1534 some Lutherans faced martyrdom so that James could persuade the Pope to grant dispensations to his sons, and to give way over the royal right of nomination. In 1541 he snubbed Henry by agreeing to meet him at York and then failing to turn up. The Pope, gratified, allowed another tax on the Church. In the event James paid higher for the tax than he intended.

For by 1541 the foreign relationships of Scotland had gone back to those of 1513. James was bound to France by marriage. He had thought hard about a suitable match. The Emperor Charles V had offered him the hand of their cousin the Princess Mary of England, but James had declined her, pointing out that she was hardly Charles's to give away. He had considered a couple of French ladies, and even thought of marrying his current Scotch mistress, as well as making a half-hearted move for a Danish princess. What James wanted most was a marriage with a good dowry attached within the terms of the dominant French–English issue. In 1536 he went off to France where he put through two profitable pieces of business, the usual act of revocation of grants which Scottish monarchs who had been minors made in their twenty-fifth year and a well-dowered marriage. He persuaded Francis I to fulfil the Treaty of Rouen by giving him his daughter Madelaine. Francis had been stalling on this for many years, claiming reasonably enough the princess's youth or ill-health. James brought the poor child to Scotland without provoking a renewal of the English war, and in a few weeks she was dead. In her place the French court allowed James to marry Mary of Guise a year later.

Mary was a lucky choice, not merely for her dowry. She was an older woman, already widowed and with a child, a sister to the Cardinal of Guise and the Duke of Lorraine. The Guise family was an important branch of the Valois house, not yet a separate interest in the French state, and not yet the flag-bearers of Catholicism, but a great house, still under the sway of the French king's policy. Mary had lived in its warm and secure atmosphere both as a child and as a widow – they were a large and affectionate family of handsome and intelligent people. Yet she survived the move to the loneliness and discomfort of Scotland and the occasional attentions of her husband. James by now had aged a lot: his coins show a long thin face and pointed beard with haggard eyes. Mary's face is self-contained and tight lipped. She needed her self control. Her two sons, born in 1540 and 1541, both died suddenly in the spring of the latter year. She was pregnant again within a year.

The royal marriages meant that Scotland was again at the mercy of the French–English relationship. A lesser prize and smaller dowry, a princess from Scandinavia, for instance, would have been far safer, but James had never broken away from the issues of the French and English feud. Henry regarded a French–Scottish alliance as a likely base for a religious war against him, and though this did not happen, and France had other worries because of her quarrel with the Habsburg power, in 1542 relations with England were sliding into war. So the promised meeting of Henry and James at York was an important move for peace. But when Henry had moved his vast bulk north James did not come. Henry was not a man who could be snubbed with impunity. By the late summer of 1542 the two counties were as much at war as James could manage (this was not much in practice because his lords refused to fight). They staged a retreat when mustered on the east at Fala: in November James got them to Lochmaben on the west for an attack across the Solway but it was a fiasco. The Scots were led in a muddled way and ran away or surrendered on very little provocation. Solway Moss, as the battle came to be called, was not a credit to king or men. James's chosen leader, Oliver Sinclair, is cattily described by Knox in his *History* as 'fleeing full manfully'.

The reign was running down. James retreated from the Border, found time to stay with both his wife and his latest mistress, but collapsed and died within three weeks of the battle of Solway Moss. News that his wife had given birth to a daughter was brought to him, and his answer showed how little he had grown out of the family concentration shared by his great nobles. 'It cam wi' a lass and it'll pass wi' a lass,' he said. All the Crown meant to him at this juncture was its union with the house of Stewart.

We really do not know enough to analyse the reasons for James's failure. They may have been personal: a king had, in some way, to get on with his nobles, and James's handling of them shows he mistrusted them. Trust and mistrust are mutual things. The nobles could see what had happened to the Douglases and might happen to others.

Perhaps too many of them had been disciplined in one way or another. Since Flodden, the Scots would not be dragged into attacks on England. James seems to have wanted to go too fast, to take too high-handed a line, to try and turn the country too quickly into a state where the king's orders were obeyed and his law ran, without the long personal bargaining and balancing which was the way his grandson learnt to govern Scotland by the pen. However much the chroniclers, who were not nobles, admired James and said so, the policy had gone farther than was safe. James had been taking too much into his own hands, too much power and too much money. Here again the chroniclers supported him. 'He by his heich pollicye mervellouslie riched his realme and his selfe, both with gold and silver, all kinde of riche substance quhairof he left greyt stoir and quantyte.' Indeed he did. But some of the elements of that wealth must have led to discontent. The Exchequer's 'property roll' which was used to record forfeitures and escheats had to be supplemented with a second one for the last two years of the reign, so great was the business of this type. The aristocracy might just bear ruthless extortion if they got a say in policy, or institutional changes, as a *quid pro quo* – in this way Edward I of England just managed to ride out the storms he raised. Otherwise a reign in which the king enormously increases his revenue at the expense of his nobility is likely to be followed, as was that of the English King Henry I, by a sharp reaction. James had not the trained ability, his own or someone else's, to couple his financial extortion with reform. Maitland has over-simplified the position: James was engaged in a more ambitious task than that of his forbears. He was building up the money resources of the Crown. But he failed, just as the earlier Jameses had failed.

NOTES ON DRAMATIS PERSONAE

Albany. John Stewart (*c*. 1484–1536), fourth Duke, son of Alexander Stewart, second son to James II.

Angus. Archibald Douglas (*c*. 1490–1557), sixth Earl. His second wife was Margaret, the Queen Mother, who rapidly tired of him.

Argyll. Colin Campbell (died 1529), third Earl.

Beaton. David Beaton (1594–1646), Cardinal Archbishop of St Andrews. A smooth-faced politician in his portrait, a sincere but not austere churchman.

Chapter 7

Reformation

Dumbarton: the Queen embarks for France

1542 WAS NOT SIMPLY a reproduction of 1513. Some of the same elements were there – war with England in French interests, the prospect of a long minority, military defeat, a foreign queen-mother, baronial disagreements. But in important ways the setting had changed. For one thing the life of the baby queen, Mary, was vital to internal tranquillity. The alternative was a disputed succession issue between the houses of Lennox and Hamilton, arising from an uncertain divorce, a typically medieval problem, which gave the Hamilton line, in the person of the Regent, Arran, doubtful legitimacy. The Earl of Lennox had been captured at Solway Moss and was being softened up, by words and cash, by the English; he came back with other nobles whom the English called 'assured', coerced, or bought over to an alliance with England. Others came back from abroad – the Douglases returned to a reduced state, but by their very numbers and alliances were soon to be reckoned with. There were others who would dispute the Regent's control; Cardinal Beaton the primate, and the dowager Mary of Guise, a much more politic and consistent character than Margaret Tudor had been. Mary's main concern was her daughter's future. For a time she was prepared to think that this might lie in an English marriage, which would indeed be a valuable dynastic *coup*. The balance of power shifted uneasily from one Scotch group to another while Henry pressed his wishes.

Henry needed to break the Scottish–French alliance, but he wanted more than just that. If he could hold a strong party in Scotland he could look for an ally in his religious isolation. Scotland, he hoped, would break with Rome, and led on by England, instructed by a careful infiltration of the right English books, would avoid both the 'fancies and dreams of inferior persons' such as the Lutherans, and the 'corruption of hypocrisy and superstition' of the papacy. There was an unsatisfied demand in Scotland for vernacular Bibles and psalters: 'if a cartlode sent thither they wolde be bought, every one' reported his envoy. The existence of an infant queen, when he himself had an infant prince a few years older, was an obvious invitation to an arranged marriage which would unite the island.

It looked as if Henry had got most of what he wanted in the Treaties of Greenwich, a peace treaty and a marriage agreement. The young Mary was to leave for England at the age of ten already married to his son Edward by proxy, though the union of the kingdoms was to be a personal one, not an incorporation. But these treaties were the result of oscillations in the balance of power in Scotland which soon swung back. Arran needed church support to maintain his claims to legitimacy and hence the succession, and church support meant the Cardinal and hostility to Henry's religious position. In any case diplomacy with Arran was of doubtful profit because, as Mary of Guise said of him, he was 'a simple and inconstant man who changed purpose every day', a remark which might be applied to any of the leading Hamiltons for the next two centuries, and explains their relative lack of political success. Immediately after making the treaties Arran succumbed to the personal domination of the Cardinal, and within a few months Beaton was Chancellor of Scotland, ruling with the support of both the dowager and Arran. Henry had in any case wanted more than the treaties gave him, an immediate breach with France and the custody of the young queen, so he failed to ratify them and was then surprised to find the Scots reverting to their French alliance, and the Scotch Parliament passing an Act against heretics. Uncertainties between the Scotch leaders and Henry's haste had combined to prevent union between the countries, but Henry still had important forces working on his side: money, the real unwillingness of the Scots to attack their greater neighbour, and a growing common religious interest which was not at all what he had been aiming at.

You cannot treat religious ideas and information like bath water, to be turned on and off as desired. Books and ideas had been coming into Scotland, not only from England, and there may have been an organized body of heretics already in the country. Recent work in England has shown the inadequacy of our past appreciation of the survival of Lollardy and disproved the theory that there was a gap between the followers of Wycliff and the arrival of Lutheran ideas. We now know that active groups of Lollards continued to meet and recruit followers in many parts of England in the later fifteenth century, even though the sixteenth century's reissue of Lollard literature suggests a lack of strength and creativity in these groups. The episcopal records which might reveal a similar story in Scotland have been lost, and there are only a few signs of survival there; the trial of thirty Ayrshire Lollards in 1494, the existence in manuscript of a Scots translation of Wycliff's New Testament made about 1528 and significantly given a Lutheran preface. These are not enough to maintain the idea of a similar story for Scotland, but they show that there were individuals about who held Lollard opinions.[1]

1. One of the most quoted indications of Lollardy, the phrases 'Lamp of Lollardism' and 'Lollard Laureate' used by the poet Kennedy in *The Flyting of Dunbar and Kennedy* in the reign of James IV is really a counter-indication; in the same way a modern term of abuse is a pointer to the fact that we are not seriously perturbed today about the Bogomile heresy.

In any case Scots trading with the continent had been bringing in Lutheran books for some time. James V had admitted to Pope Paul III in 1537 that 'foul teaching' often came in with other merchandise in cargoes. There was a strong demand for religious literature in the vernacular, which at this date, before the Council of Trent decided against allowing unlimited access by the laity to the text of the Bible, was not necessarily connected with heresy, though it gave it a good opportunity. Patrick Hamilton had been martyred in 1528 for what looks like straightforward Lutheranism. Thereafter the elements of what the Catholic Church called heresy are more confused, and were welded on to a long-standing anti-clericalism, and this gained strength from the wretched situation produced by the war. Those, and they were many, who would prefer an English to a French alliance, if only Henry would behave reasonably, turned against Beaton both as principal agent of the Catholic Church in Scotland as well as head of state. They were reinforced by English bribes and by the very real fears of English attack held by those with lands in the south.

The *Gude and Godlie Ballads*, hymns and paraphrases of uncertain date, show something of the popular Protestantism of the 1540s. They are predominantly Lutheran: justification is by a faith which means more than intellectual assent, a total trust in salvation by Christ. There is an emphasis on the New Testament which is suggestive of Luther, but already there is a sign of the tendency to worship the literal text of the Bible which has been one of the weaknesses of Scottish Protestantism,[1] coupled with attacks on the ideas of intercession by saints, of purgatory, and very crudely of transubstantiation. The Calvinist doctrine of assurance and emphasis on the whole of the Bible are not yet there.

Henry was not used to failing in an object that seemed as easy as the dominance of Scotland: the lion knew his strength and was ready to use it. 'Put all to fyre and sword' ran Henry's orders to the Earl of Hertford, 'burne Edinborough town', and with special malice that showed he recognized the heart of the opposition, 'spoyle and turne upset downe the Cardinalle's town of St Andrews, as thupper stone

[1] For instance: My New Testament, plaine and gude
for quhilk I sched my precious blude
Zour onlie hope and Saulis fude. . . .

may be the nether, and not one stick stande by an other, sparing no creature alyve within the same'. In fact Hertford's invasion did not get to St Andrews, but he devastated the towns along the Forth. (Even this much was as expensive for the English as for the Scots, and caused a new devaluation of the English pound.) This was the 'rough wooing' of 1544–5, of which the scars can still be seen in the ruins of the Border abbeys. It marks the nadir of Anglo-Scottish relations. It did not push Scotland completely into the hands of France, but it gave Mary of Guise a stronger position on the Scottish Council and led to a good deal of support for a plan to marry the young queen to Arran's heir. French troops were sent over, and, more important, French money, to outbid even the bribes of Henry. Henry's only retort was to plan the assassination of Beaton.

The plots against Beaton were mainly the work of a group of Fife Protestants who opposed the Cardinal on three grounds – his pro-French foreign policy, his Catholicism, and local issues about land-ownership. The leader was William Kirkcaldy of Grange, one of the more straightforward of the Protestant landowners of the Reformation period: Henri II of France called him valiant, which indeed he was, and he was not much more bloodthirsty than many of his contemporaries of less evident sincerity and much less dash. At the English end of the plot there appears a Scot called Wishart: as it was with the name of George Wishart, the preacher of Protestantism, that the assassins finally struck down Beaton, it is natural to think that the agent in the plot and the preacher were the same man, but the identification cannot be proved and has therefore become a subject for dogmatic rather than historical speculation.[1]

Wishart had died in the flames at Edinburgh less than three months before, on 1 May 1546, for his opinions and still more for his success-ful preaching and organizing. Two years before he had brought back from abroad the ideas of the Swiss as well as of the German reformers, and had preached vigorously in Dundee and Perth and worked in Dundee through the plague. It is a striking thing that both Wishart and Beaton, knowing that there were men determined to kill them,

1. Wishart is neither rare nor common as a Scotch name: there are less than a column of Wisharts in both the Edinburgh and Glasgow telephone directories. Neither side in the religious disputes of the sixteenth century abhorred this sort of action.

continued in their work. Wishart had been the accepted spiritual leader of the Protestants, and at his arrest his companion, John Knox, felt that his mantle had passed to him.

Beaton's death took place at St Andrews. A group of sixteen conspirators broke into the castle, cleared out Beaton's servants, murdered the Cardinal, and when they found there was a lack of general support for this, garrisoned the castle with their friends and followers and held it through a long, incompetently organized siege all winter and much of the next summer, that of 1547. Until the murder the politics of the queen's minority had been conducted in unusually unbloodthirsty terms, and when the castle finally surrendered to French ships the treatment of its defenders was relatively humane. They went to the French galleys, from which several escaped, or were imprisoned in France. But they had held out long enough to publicize their aim, an English alliance, and to advertise the weakness of the Scottish government. Arran had come back to the Regency, but he also had a western rising on his hands, organized by the Earl of Lennox who had been in English pay since Solway Moss. Arran was unsure of both his position and his policy, whereas the calm and smooth-faced Beaton had known clearly where he stood. But the English failed to take advantage of his indecision. Henry VIII was sinking in January 1547 and at his death there was a period of adjustment within the Council of the child king, Edward VI. By the time Hertford had become Regent as the Duke of Somerset and attacked Scotland again, the alliance with France had been refurbished. Somerset pushed up towards Edinburgh with sixteen thousand men on the well-trodden eastern route of invasion within the line of coastal castles, and met a fully representative Scottish army at Pinkie. Arran may have been a bit put off by discovering in the castle of St Andrews a book with the names of two hundred Scottish noblemen and gentry in the pay of England, but when it came to the point anger held the country together against the English. Though the Scots were anxious to come to grips, perhaps because they were over-anxious and miscalculated, Somerset was able to win a crushing victory.

Pinkie is an example of a rare type of battle, militarily decisive and politically pointless. The English simply could not afford to continue the conquest at the price it was coming to in men and money, nor could they take the risk of whole-hearted commitment in the north without better relations with the mainland powers of Europe. So long as there was an English army devastating the Borders and the east coast, the very real element of opinion that the future of Scotland must lie in an English alliance was silenced. Men would buy safety for their lands by acknowledging English lordship with no intention of remaining 'assured' longer than was necessary. The independent Scots sent the five-year-old queen to Inchmahome Priory on the Lake of Menteith and by next year Mary of Guise had made plans for her future. She was shipped off from Dumbarton and round Ireland to France, to live with the royal family of Henri II and marry his eldest son. The French had beaten Henry to control of the queen, and with much less effort. Mary's childhood, unlike that of the other royal minors of this century, was passed in a family setting, material comfort, and physical safety. No modern child guidance clinic would recommend the background given to the young James V or to his grandson. Yet of the three rulers Mary was to be the one least ready for the life of loneliness and independence of a reigning monarch.

French money, and the French marriage now decided on, brought Mary of Guise the Scottish regency. In 1550 she followed her daughter to France, taking with her several leading nobles for softening up, and when she came back her way to power was easy. This in itself was no disadvantage for the country, for though she was more cautious than Arran she was more resolute too. (Arran had been bought off with a French duchy, and now called himself the Duc de Chatellerault.) Mary's weakness was that she had become the weapon of an excessively pro-French foreign policy, and to carry this through she had to make concessions in other matters. In particular she had to accept and work with a growing Protestant party among the nobles. It was to humour them that she revoked the forfeitures on those captured in the siege of St Andrews. Scottish Protestantism, with the accession in 1553 of Mary Tudor to the throne of England, did not necessarily go with a demand for an English alliance, but it did link up with extremist elements in English thought. Knox, for instance, when he returned from his stretch in the French galleys, became a Protestant preacher at Berwick and later in London. On Mary's accession he was among those who wisely left for Geneva,[1] but he was

1. His retreat would have been entirely respectable if he had not later on accused Queen Elizabeth of cowardice for keeping her head down and conforming in

back again in Scotland for a short time in 1555–6 when he organized the Protestants into a coherent political and religious group with a definite policy.

Reformation and Catholicism were not the only counters on the political board, and neither the kings of France, who had been ready to use Lutheranism and even Mahommedanism against Habsburg power, nor the house of Guise, had adopted the position of Catholic champions. In any case it was not yet clear that 'reformation', even in the Protestant sense of the word, must necessarily take place outside the Catholic Church.

The appropriation of this word 'reformation' subsequently by Protestantism alone, makes it easy to forget the ambiguities and scope of the whole question of reform at this time. No serious sixteenth-century ecclesiastic could deny that there were weaknesses in the organization of the Church and failures in its leadership. The papacy had been playing politics in Italy as if it were no more than a city state with spiritual as well as military weapons. The episcopate had for long been chosen for the type of compromise reasons that did its religious character little credit. Appointments had balanced the influence of one great baronial family against another, and recently in Scotland became a source of supply for the Crown and its dependents. The parish clergy too often had neither the funds nor the training to carry out their functions adequately. The movements for monastic reform of the twelfth century had been succeeded by the great new idea of the ministry of the friars in the thirteenth: in the fourteenth and early fifteenth centuries there had been serious attempts to improve the organization of the whole Church: but since then little positive leadership or new inspiration had been offered inside the Church, and one has the impression that this great institution had been living on its spiritual capital for over a century. The system had been running down because no attempt had been made to interpret its message in terms acceptable to a changing political and social world. Protestant and Catholic writers have spent a lot of ink on the issue of the exact condition and quality of sixteenth-century churchmen. We have a variegated picture which, by its very variety, seems

---

Mary's reign. No one can impugn Knox's genuine courage: his charity is another matter.

likely to be true. There were clergy who performed their duties sincerely and honestly: there were bishops who, even if not appointed for the best religious reasons, and even if not able in most cases to live chastely, administered their dioceses conscientiously and efficiently: there were monasteries where, at least in times of peace, the Hours were said and the Rule and its accretions observed. By masses and prayer, by bell and saint's day, the Church organized and carried through the daily life of the people. It was not enough.

Even without the express theological challenge of Protestant opinion it looks as if the Church could not have held and channelled the devotions of mankind. In providing means of mitigating the problem of sin, it had developed an armoury of tools and panaceas that could in practice stand between a man and his knowledge of God – this was the essence of the Lutheran attacks on Indulgences. Too much of the daily work of the Church was offered to the dead and dying in the arithmetical process of heaping up masses, and much too little to the task of explaining the meaning of Incarnation and Resurrection, or even of the sacraments, to the living. The starving of the parish clergy in favour of the monasteries and the cathedral clergy was only one aspect of this. The laity of the sixteenth century were in many cases richer and better educated than their ancestors of four centuries before. They were ready to study religion, to read for themselves, without taking monastic vows. Monasticism and withdrawal from the world were less easy to expect when the world itself was a more comfortable and learned place. These facts were realities to which the Church had not adapted. At the same time, in Scotland, the Crown and baronage had taken over the profitable side of the Church, her positions and lands, so that these were no longer her own. The failure of the clergy to achieve celibacy meant that they were not marked off from their flocks in their way of life.[1] In these circumstances drastic readjustment and internal reform were difficult aims – and aims that it was unrealistic even to hope would be consistently held to by the Church's own leaders.

1. How long-standing this failure had been is not known: what is known is that by the sixteenth century two-fifths of the legitimations of bastards were for the children of clergy. This is not proof that two-fifths of those born out of wedlock were priests' children: the clergy had more interest in legitimating their children than laymen had.

Lutheranism had torn Germany in two politically as well as religiously, and by the 1540s it was clear that the Church as then organized could not stand up to its competition. The answer to this situation was the great Council of Trent which opened in 1546. On the one hand the Council was to redefine the doctrines questioned by Lutherans: on the other to enable the Church to put itself on a fighting basis. It was not easy for Scotland to contribute to the Council. As Beaton complained, the English blocked all the obvious ways to Italy. The only Scot at Trent was Robert Wauchope, bishop of Armagh, a close ally of the papacy in its attempt at reform. Typically enough it was Scottish baronial resistance that had prevented him being given a see in Scotland, overriding him in favour of Arran's half brother, John Hamilton. But the Church in Scotland got regular reports of the decisions of the Council and held its own meetings to put forward plans of reform.

It was this John Hamilton, promoted from Dunkeld to St Andrews on Beaton's murder, who led the Church's attempt at reform. The instrument was a series of councils, in 1549, 1552, and 1559: the most serious product the catechism of 1552. This catechism was to meet the criticism that the Church did not attend enough to teaching. The ordinary parish clergy, whose main work was the administration of the sacraments, could not be expected instantaneously to turn themselves to the difficult task of preaching, but this exposition of what the Church held to be necessary belief would help them to instruct the laity. It was to be read 'clearly, articulately, and with attention to the stops' on Sundays and holy days, an instruction that reminds us how limited was the talent for expression of the ordinary run of parish priests. It is a good document, avoiding denunciation of the reformers, concentrating instead on the core of general belief. If it adopted a position on the central question of justification not far from that of Luther, and paid little attention to the papacy, these are reminders of what was acceptable as Catholic doctrine before the Council of Trent had finished its work of definition.

The legislation of these Scottish councils, generally well-meaning and conscientious, also shows the drastic limitations of the movement for Catholic reform at this time. The catechism was no more than a tool: it needed to be put to use. Yet the councils shrank from enforcing a better standard of performance. There was no attempt to improve the quality of candidates for the priesthood, and barely a mention of the need for systematic and frequent episcopal visitation. Yet these two matters were fundamental to any policy of reform. There are other serious matters in which the response of the councils was half-hearted. They made the usual condemnation of clerical immorality, but they accepted that the clergy, and particularly the bishops, could not be expected to live up to their profession, by formulating detailed regulations to prevent them from dowering their children with church property, leasing church lands to their mistresses, treating church offices as hereditary and maintaining their children in their households. The core of the attack on the established Church, that the clergy did not preach the Word of God, was poorly answered. If preaching could not be expected from the rank and file, who had not been trained to it, it could and should have been expected from the *élite*, from special lecturers and above all from the bishops, yet in 1549 all that a Scottish council could lay down for the bishops was that they must in person preach four times a year, and even that was not enforced. Ten years later, spurred on by a demand from some of the nobility for regular preaching, the council said that bishops must preach as often as they could and that parish priests must explain the meaning and inner significance of the sacraments to their flocks. This was a more realistic appreciation of the need of the day. But it came in 1559, and no more time was to be given to the Catholic Church in Scotland to decide its priorities, and to demand that its leaders be prepared to make life less comfortable for themselves.

That this demand was not made, or not answered, wrecked the reform movement. The Scottish episcopate was not prepared to upset the comfortable tenor of its way. Reform, in so far as it meant exhortation and agreement on general principles, was easy. Regulations flowed out, improving the working of church courts, setting up lecturers in cathedrals, limiting unpopular mortuary fees; but when it came to hard work and austerity of life, the bishops remembered that this had not been expected of them when they took up office, and only grudgingly changed their ways. The result of generations during which religious vocation had been the least of reasons for making a man a bishop were now made clear. Church offices and lands were often in the hands of laymen, since the baronage had followed the king in treating the Church as a form of out-relief for younger sons, legitimate or illegitimate, and the clergy did not shed their habits of baronial thinking when they took orders. Catholic historians have tended to blame Mary of Guise for the quality of her appointments, but she did no worse, perhaps a little better, than had been done in the forty years before she gained control. It is true that because of her preoccupations with the French alliance she did not try to suppress the Protestant movement politically till it was too late. But that the Protestants were strong enough to challenge royal authority at all is a comment on the failure of the church hierarchy to respond to the religious needs of the day. The Church was entangled in the outlook of Crown and nobility and could not think clearly in other terms. No institution that regularly appoints its officials for other reasons than their real fitness for the job can do anything but decline.

The challenge to the Church changed in the 1550s: it was now from Switzerland, not Germany, that ideas were coming, and what Knox brought back from Geneva in 1555 seems to have included a great deal of pure Calvinism – and Calvinism was a fighting faith with no trace of quietism. Like Lutheranism it satisfied the sense of infinity. Luther showed the infinite nature of man's corruption and Calvin the infinite gulf between man and God. Man's function was to know and glorify God across this gulf; and in the light of this vast difference between them, the aids and achievements that the Church had to offer paled into insignificance. In any case these aids had in practice and emphasis been taking too big a part of church life. There had been too many masses, too many indulgences, too many pilgrimages, for the content of real repentance. Routine performances were excluding the faith. Both Lutheranism and Calvinism expressed various arguments for the discarding of the features that most easily became mechanical, for their disbelief in the invocation of saints, the treasury of merits, the efficacy of good works, and even of the renewal of sacrifice in the mass, but it is perhaps more comprehensible if these dogmas are remembered as discarded in the single illuminating concept of the total corruption of mankind and the infinite power and goodness of God. (Later the discarded dogmas became negative shibboleths which could also stand in the way of true religious apprehension.) The tremendous contrast between God and man produces Luther's answer to the problem of redemption: the acceptance or justification by faith alone, that only a total surrender of the whole person in the face of the reality of the living God could bring man and God together. Calvin added to this an emphasis on the total powerlessness of Man and a doctrinaire concept of what omnipotence in God must mean in practice. These ideas, to a mind steeped in the determinist phraseology of the Old Testament, produced predestination, the doctrine that some are foreordained to union with God and others to eternal separation and reprobation. Predestination can only be lived with as doctrine if it is coupled with the notion that one oneself belongs to the unreprobate. This idea is formulated in the doctrine of assurance, that those who are saved have the certainty of it in their faith, that they know, however weakly at times, that they are of God's elect. The Church is the 'company and multitude of men chosen of God', and for the elect, as Lord Melbourne said of the Garter, there is no damn nonsense about merit in it, since human merit does not weigh in this scale.

Predestination and assurance become therefore the key doctrines of Calvinism, and in Scottish history the latter doctrine holds a much stronger position than it does in Calvin's own writings. Calvin laid even greater stress than did Luther on the Bible. Both reformers held the inconsistent position of refusing to acknowledge the early Councils of the Church as of authority while accepting the form of trinitarian belief hammered out in them. The Bible was to them the sole authority of the Church, but while Luther stressed the New Testament, and even used that selectively,[1] Calvin insisted that the evidence of God's nature had to be found in the whole of Scripture. In practice this led in Scotland to the exaltation of the Old Testament: there is so much more of it than of the New, and its language is so much more militant. Belief in predestination tended to lower the importance of sacraments in the Church. Baptism was not an absolute prerequisite of salvation, and the eucharist, though it was more than merely commemorative to a Calvinist, implying a spiritual union with Christ, was not an essential part of church life, since the gifts of Christ through the eucharist may also be given at other times. But Knox stressed the eucharist more than did Calvin, as the seal of the Church as a visible body under the headship of Christ, and it was his view that prevailed in Scotland.

1. The epistle of St James was to him, not surprisingly, 'an Epistle of straw'.

Calvinism was a fighting faith. It had its negative emphasis, the things it wished done away with, as convenient slogans and labels, but its strength came from the superb basic inconsistency of determinism. As with Marxism, men would act freely and strongly in its cause because they felt that it was inevitable that they should. Its weaknesses as a religion were not immediately apparent, except for its abandonment of the most primary tenet of Christianity, that Christ died for all men. It has not proved an easy faith for pastoral work because the Calvinist has little helpful to offer those who doubt their own or their dear ones' salvation except to say that such doubts deny the possibility of assurance. For those minds unable to grasp the infinity of God, Calvinism has a lack of the minor objects on which to fix devotion, a reason perhaps for the tendency to exalt the actual text of the Bible into the position the Koran occupies in Moslem thought, that of the direct and divinely inspired word of God. Calvin held that the Bible could not err, but he and the early Scottish reformers accepted that finding the full truth in it might not be easy. When they spoke of 'the Word of God' they meant not the text of Scripture but the total message of Christ. There is a long process of intellectual deterioration: first, from this position to that of the seventeenth century when Scripture had become a divine bran-tub or lottery, when the devout would make use of this store of divine wisdom by acting on the inspiration of any text that might be turned up on opening the book, or float into the mind. Later there was a further deterioration from this to the formal belief of many in the nineteenth century in the literal truth of every word in the Bible and its direct authorship by God. In the absence of critical historical and linguistic study this process, if not inherent in Calvinism, came easily to it. Calvinism in Scotland developed also a characteristic moral weakness. There is nothing in the doctrine in Calvin himself that is an invitation to spiritual pride, and his sense of the immensity of the gulf between man and God runs entirely counter to such a habit of thought, yet the doctrine of assurance and the very real belief of the early reformers in the constant intervention of divine providence in man's daily affairs could easily lead to a theory that God would support his own in worldly matters, or to a satisfied acceptance of being of the elect.[1] Scottish Calvinists

1. James Nimmo, customs official, faced with an unexpected inspection, illustrates this well: 'The uprightness of the upright shall deliver them ... I remem-

soon usurped God's own function and claimed to know his mind and his intent, as if the assurance of their own acceptability gave them an insight into that of others. They became people it was not possible to argue with, absolutely certain of God's intent and of their own place in it, and prepared to accept that their place in society was part of this too. Periods of vivid Calvinism in the Scottish church have not been periods of active social reform.

Calvinism, and organized Calvinist churches, spread with astonishing rapidity in both Scotland and France in the 1550s and took both governments by surprise. The Scottish council of 1552 was able to announce cheerfully that 'many frightful heresies . . . have now at last been checked and seem almost extinguished', and so they may have been for 1552. But three years later Knox was organizing a Calvinist group among the Scottish nobility, which included the Earl of Argyll and the eldest and most able of James V's bastard sons, Lord James Stewart, nominally prior of St Andrews. These men made the usual 'band' or semi-legal baronial pressure group, which later became known as the 'Lords of the Congregation'. Mary of Guise did not try to suppress it: her French policy was leading to unrest: there were too many Frenchmen in Scotland, too often in office, and she had to humour those she could until the marriage of the young queen was carried through. The Protestants were the more ready to be humoured by her in that they could hope for little help from the obvious source of opposition to France, England, so long as this was under the reign of the ardently Catholic Mary Tudor. In the spring of 1558 the marriage contract was signed in France, and among the representatives sent out from Scotland for this event were leaders of the Protestants. The contract stated that the marriage was to be merely a personal union of the crowns, even though the Dauphin was to be styled King of Scotland; the two countries were to remain separate and independent. But already in secret the young queen had signed away her kingdom to the French, promising them the Scottish succession in the house of Valois, and that nothing she would sign subsequently to the contrary would be valid. In this bargain the Guise family over-reached itself. There was nothing in the story of Scotland

bered there was a back door to the chamber . . . and there undiscerned gott in and filled up the bookes . . . I must say the Lord so marcifully did guid me in all this. . . .'

to suggest that such terms could be successfully enforced, even if the accidents of dynastic history were to leave the French in a position to try to enforce them.

In a series of rapid events the leaders of Europe were reminded that of the three basic elements in dynastic politics, births, deaths, and marriages, human beings can only control the last. In November 1558 Mary of Guise completed her policy by persuading the Parliament to grant the 'Crown matrimonial', equality of status with the Queen and the right to inherit, to the Dauphin: in the same month Mary of England died, to be succeeded by Elizabeth. In Catholic eyes, and even to many Protestants, Elizabeth was illegitimate, and though pressure by Philip of Spain prevented the Pope announcing this, it became open to Mary of Scotland to claim the inheritance of England through her grandmother Margaret Tudor, and entirely open for her to quarter the English arms. It looked as if the Guises were to own a network of inheritance across Europe second only to that of the Habsburgs, and one in which Mary would be the main strand. Elizabeth had become the hope of English Protestantism. Whatever her real religious opinions may have been, the accusation of illegitimacy forced her to take the Protestant side. At last the conjunction in Scotland between Protestantism and an English alliance, pending for the last thirty years, was achieved, and Scottish and English affairs were to be tied up for the future by the inheritance question. Calvinism was on the offensive now, both in Scotland and France. In June 1559 Henri II of France issued the Edict of Écouen, a signal for a full attack on it. Already in May when Mary of Guise attempted to suppress some extremist preachers she found herself faced by a Protestant mob in Perth, backed by the Congregation, ready to fight. The active Reformation in Scotland began with the destruction of the charterhouse and friaries of Perth, but its significance lay in the union of mob, nobility, and John Knox.

The nobility had their own particular reasons for joining in. Many were already of Protestant sympathy. For those that were not upholders of Protestant dogma the last belated attempts at reform by church councils inside Scotland provided a motive. The council of 1559 made what might have developed into a real attempt to regain for the Church control of her lands and teinds:[1] these were not to be

1. Teinds – the Scottish equivalent of the English 'tithes'.

feud or leased to any except to the tenants of the Church. The looting of church revenue by nobles had gone on for the last generation, and therefore cannot be regarded in itself as a cause for taking up Protestant opinion. But an attempt to put the clock back might well increase the acquiescence in the upper classes of leadership by Protestants.

John Knox is a figure whose importance to the Protestant movement is difficult to estimate because it has lost nothing in his own telling of the story. He was a man of immense determination and courage. If he is often to be found in strategic retreat, this is more a pointer to his frank appreciation of his own value to the Protestant movement than to any failure of nerve. It was not his intellect that gave him influence, but his force of character – indeed his strident anti-feminism proclaims him a second-rate intellect. He was a natural orator, and a man to whom, in speech and writing, words were living things. The Calvinism he brought from Geneva had features of his own, the most important historically being a total lack of deference to social or royal position. As Morton was to say at his funeral, he was one 'who neither feared nor flattered any flesh'. Calvin's church was prepared to accept the existing civil authority and co-operate with it, but the Calvinists of Britain, finding Catholic queens in both kingdoms, were less amenable. Knox in his tract *The First Blast of the Trumpet against the Monstrous Regiment of Women* rejected the idea of their having legitimate authority, and later was to claim the right for the leaders of the Church, himself in particular, to dictate to the monarch. It was to be all-important for the next century that the Scottish reformers first became articulate in political opposition.

The leading noble of Scotland, Lord James Stewart, was, as Cecil reported to Elizabeth, in appearance and intelligence fit to be a king. If this is a fair judgement, it needs to be borne in mind that it required more than ordinary royal qualities to make a success of sixteenth-century Scotland. Lord James had a skill in making friends, he was competent and reliable, and could keep his personal ambitions within the bounds of possibility. His long, bony, rectangular, and cautious face, with an intelligent and watchful glance, gives a clue to his limitations. He was physically brave, but he disliked committing himself politically: through all the crises of the next ten years he showed a talent for discreet absence. He 'looked through his fingers' said Maitland of Lethington of him, waiting off stage to see what would happen, and then joining in. Even now he was not with the Protestants until attempts to make a peaceful settlement had failed.

The reformers were acting within a well-marked Scottish pattern, armed resistance to the Crown while not denying its authority. At first their demands were only religious, the spread of Protestantism and the suppression of 'the mass' as idolatrous. (Protestantism opposed the mass as belittling the sacrifice of Christ and as attempting to propitiate a God already satisfied.) But the rebellion could not stay clear of politics. The Congregation was in secret communication with England, and was soon joined by Lord James. It moved against the French alliance. England, nominally at peace with France, could not afford to be open, but so long as Mary and Francis claimed the English throne, Elizabeth could not neglect the Scottish rebels. Then in July the political scene was altered by the tournament accident that killed Henri II of France. Mary and her teenage husband Francis were now ruling monarchs of France as well as of Scotland. Henri had been able to keep the Guises in their place while using them. His death pushed them into a party position in France.

When it came to fighting, the Scottish reformers had neither the men nor the military skill to beat the Regent and her French troops, even though joined in the autumn by Maitland of Lethington, Mary's Secretary of State. They were also strengthened by the escape of the young Earl of Arran from France, a cloak and dagger episode which allowed his father Chatellerault to come over openly. As he had a residual claim to the throne, he became nominal leader, and a plan was formed to offer young Arran as a husband to Elizabeth. The marriage never came off, which was just as well since Arran's mental instability would have made it as disastrous as most of the dynastic unions of the century. Chatellerault's adherence also allowed the reformers to declare Mary of Guise deposed as Regent. But neither side wanted to do any hard fighting, and both were as interested in propaganda as in fortresses. For a time the Protestant lords chased the Regent out of Edinburgh and held the south-east coast. But English money, even when it got through, was not enough, and by January 1560 the Congregation was in retreat. At last, after agonizing indecisions, Elizabeth and her minister Cecil saw that they could not afford to let it lose, and an English fleet arrived in the Forth, cutting

E

off further French help. The Congregation and the English made the Treaty of Berwick against France and the French troops, a treaty which would break the dynastic strand encircling England. It was a political treaty only, but since it acknowledged the Congregation as in power it meant that things would go the Protestant way. It took some time to reduce the French garrison in Leith, but peace came in the summer with the death of Mary of Guise. As the chill of death came on her she asked for Lord James and Chatellerault to stay with her till the end, and they saw the short summer night out with her. The formal peace was made in the Treaty, or Treaties rather, of Edinburgh, and Elizabeth, by keeping her sights low and having some tact, had done what her father had failed to do.

This marked the joint defeat of France and Catholicism, the apparent end of the Guise network. The French were excluded from Scottish offices, their troops were to go home. Francis and Mary were to cease displaying the arms of England, and to govern Scotland through a Council of which they would appoint only a minority. In practice the Congregation was in power, with English support. Already the reformers had offered to this Council two major statements on which to build a Protestant Church, the *Confession of Faith* and the *First Book of Discipline*. Protestantism had won, though how this was to be adjusted to royal authority and what was to support the ministry of the new Church had not been settled. A final event confirmed this victory, the death of Francis in December from a septic ear, and the consequent separation of the Crowns of France and Scotland.

All through the events of these two years the striking thing about the Scottish reformers had been their weakness, and consequently their hesitancy. This gives a particular point to the problem of the fall of Catholicism in Scotland. It fell in most of northern Europe, but nowhere else except in Iceland did it go down so easily to so weak an alternative. To find an explanation it is not enough to look at what Protestantism had to offer that was lacking in the religion of the day. We need a specifically Scottish answer, and it is to be found in the French alliance. In the long run the French showed time and time again that they had nothing to offer to Scotland. The English at times might offer doubtful wares. It was impossible to accept the relationship as Henry VIII wanted it, or Protector Somerset, and even the most anglophile Scots, such as Maitland, found difficulty in making Elizabeth's policy acceptable, but at least Elizabeth offered some real advantages; peace, safety from overseas invasion, a community of language which would lead to a community of thought (as it tends to today between Britain and America), and a literature. Catholicism lost in Germany because it was linked too closely to the Habsburg power: it lost in Scotland because it meant France, and a France which had other things than Scotland to attend to.

NOTES ON DRAMATIS PERSONAE

Arran. James Hamilton, second Earl (died 1575), son to the first Earl by a second marriage after a divorce of doubtful validity, Regent of Scotland. Created Duc de Chatellerault (often spelt Chatelherault) in 1549, after which date the title Arran was borne by his son James, third Earl (*c*. 1537–1609). The third Earl was an unsuccessful suitor to Elizabeth of England and in 1562 became permanently insane.

Beaton. As in Chapter 6, David Beaton, Cardinal Archbishop of St Andrews, murdered 1546.

Hertford. Edward Seymour (*c*. 1500–52), uncle to Edward VI of England, made Earl of Hertford by Henry VIII, Lord Protector under Edward VI and Duke of Somerset, executed 1552.

Lord James. Lord James Stewart (1531–70), first Earl of Moray, Regent of Scotland, 1567–70, James V's eldest and most competent bastard.

Knox. John Knox (1505–72), reformer, preacher, historian, and polemicist. In 1549 he was minister of Berwick on Tweed, 1551 Newcastle, 1559 St Giles, Edinburgh. One of the main shapers of the new Protestant Church in Scotland.

Lennox. Matthew Stewart, fourth Earl (1516–71), forfeited for treason 1545–65. He married Margaret Douglas, daughter of Margaret Tudor and the Earl of Angus. 'Lusty, beardless and lady-faced', he lived much of his life in England. He was the father of Mary Stewart's husband Darnley, and was killed in the war between the supporters of Mary and James VI.

Mary of Guise (1515–60), sometimes styled Mary of Loraine. Eldest child of Claude, Duke of Guise, married first to Louis, Duke of Longueville

(1534), and in 1538 to James V. Mother of Mary, Queen of Scots, who inherited her great height but not her interest in government. 1554–60 Regent of Scotland.

Wishart. George Wishart (*c.* 1513–46), leading reforming preacher in Scotland from 1544 till his execution for heresy in 1546.

Chapter 8

Mary, Queen of Scots, and the Regencies

Queen Mary's ride to Dunbar

THE POLITICAL VICTORY OF 1560 decided that Scotland was to be Protestant. Because it had been won by the nobles, and by a narrow margin, it made imperative personal and institutional moderation. The nobles did not want to tear up the existing fabric of the Church – far too many of their dependents were supported by it for this to be tolerable – but they wished to see Protestantism preached and practised. Even before the fighting finished, a committee of the clergy was drawing up the blueprint of the new Church. In a remarkably short time it produced the *Book of Discipline*. When Parliament met in August 1560 with a dominant Protestant membership which included for once a sizeable group of lesser landowners, it accepted a Protestant Confession of Faith, Calvinist in doctrine and English in language, and forbade the mass and all papal authority. But the *Book of Discipline* was another matter, too drastic for the nobility to accept.

The objection was not to the Book's approach to the structure of the new Church. Here was proposed a Church organized on parish lines under superintendents, who in their ecclesiastical authority resembled bishops.[1] Calvin had taken it for granted that there was no separation of episcopal and priestly orders in the early Church, but this did not mean that there was no place in a Protestant Church for difference in function. The minister of the parish was to be aided by laymen, annually elected as elders, the group together making the parish kirk sessions, and the superintendent, also elected, was to be aided or controlled by a provincial council of the ministers and elders. The whole Church was to be bound together by inspection and report, as well as by some vaguely adumbrated great council. Its religious life was to take place in a year with four communion services. There was to be a Bible in every church for the parish to use, and the minister was to read through it systematically in service time. The master of every household, in patriarchal fashion, was to see that his family and servants knew enough about their religion to answer an annual examination by the kirk session. Above it all should reign the Christian Magistrate, or king, controlling and purifying the Church. And because no one could hope to provide ministers for all the parishes at first, emphasis was laid on education. Each parish should have a school and schoolmaster, each town a college, and the universities were to be enlarged to train the children of the rich, and also, at the Church's expense, those of the poor. The courses there would be geared to an education which would culminate in Divinity and provide learned ministers for the infant Kirk. It was a fine scheme, even if it had no likelihood of coming off.

For this structure the Book claimed the whole of the old church revenue – and this was where the nobility struck. By the end of the year the great council of the Church, which we can now call the

1. A great deal of later Presbyterian effort has been put into disguising this fact, in spite of the clear language of the Book. Knox, who refers to Christ as the 'greit Bischope of our saullis', did not have the dislike of episcopacy of the later Kirk.

General Assembly, was reduced to advising the Protestant clergy to live on alms. Compromise on money by both nobility and General Assembly was necessary if the new Church was to survive. It was achieved under the pressure of political uncertainty.

Within a few days of the death of Francis, Elizabeth had turned down the suggestion of marriage to the Earl of Arran by which the Protestants hoped to unite the two countries. She was not prepared to sacrifice her private life to the cause of Scottish Protestantism. Mary, her international value sharply depreciated, was likely to present that Protestantism with the problem of a resident Catholic monarch. And Mary still had not accepted the treaty.

The Church and the nobility reached a surprisingly sensible bargain in 1561. One-third of most of the revenues of the old Church were to be handed to the Crown: the Crown would take a share and distribute the rest to the young Church. Maitland of Lethington said scornfully that all the queen would get at the year's end would be enough 'to buy her a pair of shoes', and so it would have been if the comfortable salaries proposed by the Book had been offered, and if there had been Protestant ministers available for all the parishes. But only about a sixth could be filled, and for the next four years the Crown and Kirk shared their revenue amicably. It was a bargain which would hold for a while, but would need revision.

The completion of the reformation was thus made in money, not as elsewhere in blood. It is probably going too far to claim, as is often done, that no Catholic priests lost their lives in the changeover. Mobs had been called up and would be again, and they are unlikely to have handled their opponents gently. But there was a resolute avoidance of creating, or dwelling on, martyrdoms. The blood that was shed in the Scottish Reformation was for political ends, and even here it was more by battle and assassination than by execution. To take the group of political leaders of this period and see how many died in their beds is an interesting revelation, but until the monstrous theory of witchcraft was allowed to dominate men's minds, after 1590, there was little in the way of edifying burnings. Knox knew that a minority Church, for such it still was, could not afford it, and Mary disliked bloodshed.

In August 1561, in a typical Edinburgh *haar*, the nineteen-year-old queen landed at Leith. She had already entered a diplomatic duel with Elizabeth of England over permission to enter Scotland through England, in which she had put Elizabeth neatly in the wrong, and for the next few years she was to make rings round her cousin-queen diplomatically. Mary liked active diplomacy, the bold stroke that would transform a political scene without much thought for the long-term results. Elizabeth liked waiting and compromising. Her intellectual preference for compromise merged with an inhibition about decisive action. But it was a pity that the whole of their long relationship should take the form of a chess tournament. The two countries and the two queens were bound together by complicated involvements, and scoring each other off failed to settle common problems. In particular the main diplomatic issue of the next few years, the ratification or amendment of the Treaty of Edinburgh, might have been settled if they had known and understood each other better.

Mary, her French position weakened, rightly regarded her claim to the English throne as her most valuable possession on the international market. Her right to quarter the English arms was a piece of property the Treaty would deprive her of. If she was to surrender this she would require compensation; she suggested acknowledgement by Elizabeth as her heir. But here she came up against a deep bar in Elizabeth's mind: the English queen had been her sister's heir and seen what this had meant in her sister's last days. There was to be no rising sun in England until she was dead. This was the sort of obstacle that Mary might have understood if the two had met. Meanwhile Mary saw no point in giving way. She was prepared to make considerable sacrifices for Elizabeth's goodwill, which also entailed the goodwill of the large pro-English party in Scotland. She would even agree not to marry a foreigner without English approval. It was suggested she might marry an Englishman, but the only nobleman Elizabeth could offer her was her own love, Robert Dudley, the upstart Earl of Leicester. The Dudleys were a family with the worst of political and social pasts, yet Mary would have had him if she had been promised the succession. Here again Elizabeth's block could not be overcome. An English and Protestant match would ease Mary's situation in Scotland: a foreign and Catholic one would be an international counter of importance. The difficulty was the shortage of good candidates.

Mary had grown up at the French court and learnt a taste there for the sort of politics the Valois and Catharine de Medici played. Unlike her mother she was never really interested in government. She had dazzled personally at court, and this was not merely because of the poor quality of the tail end of the Valois. The healthy baby that Mary of Guise had stripped to show to the English ambassador had become a woman of splendid physique, high spirit, and lively intelligence. She was undersexed,[1] athletic, something of a tomboy, and of absolute physical courage. She did not shirk battle, actual or diplomatic, but she had a distaste for ruthlessness. She was no judge of men, of whom to trust and whom to use, but for the first few years of her reign she played a brilliant political game, either on her own, or with the advice and help of Maitland of Lethington and her half-brother Lord James.

Mary adjusted to the change of climate from France – material, religious, political, and geographical – remarkably well, though she never came to like Edinburgh. She set herself to work the settlement of 1560 within her kingdom, and there are no grounds for believing she did not mean this sincerely. She took to the more moderate leaders in the Protestant party: her half-brother Lord James was given the earldom of Moray. This involved a breach with the house of Huntly, who had claims to some of its lands. Unwisely the Gordons put up a show of resistance and Mary went jaunting out with her soldiery to subdue them: it was her only regret, she told the English ambassador, 'that she was not a man to know what like it was to lie all night in the fields, or to walk upon the causeway with a jack and knapschall, a Glasgow buckler and a broadsword'. The ambassador called it 'a terrible journey for horse and man', but shamefacedly felt he must accompany her. Lord James won a small battle, the Marquis of Huntly dropped dead, and Mary reluctantly executed a Gordon. She had both asserted her authority and held her Protestants. Another moderate Protestant, William Maitland of Lethington, had become her secretary. Maitland, son to one of James V's new men, was of a family that was to remain for several generations conspicuous both for its close service to the Crown and for its learning. Though he

1. It has been pointed out that any woman with a normal enjoyment of sex can keep a marriage going for six months: yet both of Mary's adult marriages were visibly on the rocks well within that time.

was a Protestant, his policy came from his political conviction that the future of Scotland lay in junction with England (a dynastic probability since Elizabeth at twenty-eight was already an old maid by sixteenth-century standards), and that the wisest immediate policy was close alliance between the two. Maitland wished to combine service to the queen with the English alliance, and held to Mary longest of all her courtiers. Whereas Moray was pro-English because he was Protestant, Maitland held Protestantism as a common bond, but not as the basic reason for the alliance.

So, in spite of her Guise connections it is a mistake to see Mary at this stage of her career as a protagonist for Catholicism. Like her cousin Elizabeth she wanted to preserve the peace of her realm for both Catholic and Protestant. 'It is a sore thing to restrain the conscience,' she said to Knox, and insisted on the right to hear mass for herself. Her brother James held the door of her chapel against the mob on her first Sunday in Scotland. She did not attempt to change the law forbidding the mass to others, and she would consider a Protestant marriage. She ignored papal suggestions that life would be easier after the execution of a few of the leading Protestant nobles. The outbreak of religious war in France in 1562 showed her that she could not expect the help that her mother had had from France; personal Catholicism in a country officially Protestant was as far as she could safely go, and it was a feasible solution. Elizabeth in England was pursuing a not very different line. It won Mary a good deal of moderate support; nothing would win the approval of extremists such as Knox, but Knox was not the whole of Scotland. While Mary thus built up for herself a strong position she posed problems to the Kirk. Where was the Christian, and by assumption, Calvinist, magistrate who should be purifying and controlling it? The best prospect was to hope for a Protestant marriage and a Protestant prince. Of the personal conversion of Mary, Knox held no expectation: he was always prepared to know a lot more about God's plans than Calvinism prescribed, an attitude which was to be prevalent in Scottish Protestantism for a long time. But Knox was not as dominating a figure in the Reformation period as his history implies.[1] Until he had an undisputed heir, Protestants and Catholics alike had to

1. Buchanan's history of Scotland barely mentions Knox. This may be partly the result of rivalry, but it is significant that the story could be told without him.

accept Mary and her compromise: the alternative was civil and foreign war.

For personal, religious, and diplomatic reasons the question of Mary's future marriage thus came to occupy as big a part of politics as it had in the 1540s. Early in 1565 Elizabeth allowed Henry Darnley, son of the Earl of Lennox who had been forfeited for treasonable dealing with the English in the 1540s, to go to Scotland. As the heir to English lands and born in England, Darnley was Elizabeth's subject: as a grandson to Margaret Tudor by her unsuccessful marriage with the Earl of Angus he was also her cousin and a claimant to the succession. Like many of the nobility of both Scotland and England he was not firmly attached to either Catholicism or Protestantism. A match with him would score off Elizabeth splendidly by uniting the two claims to the throne and appealing to English unrest. But Darnley was of a type in which Elizabeth's court seemed to specialize, an arrogant young playboy with physical charm, athletic prowess, and a total lack of manners, sense, or principle.[1] It is a comment on Mary's political judgement that she paid more attention to his looks and charm than to his character. Darnley came to court, she allowed herself to be attracted, fell in love with him, and married him at the end of July without waiting for the papal dispensation their cousinship made necessary.

Because Darnley had already made many enemies in Scotland, and because the marriage was unacceptable to Elizabeth, the Protestant lords rose in ineffective revolt. Maitland stayed with the queen, though he and his policies were pushed on one side, though Moray was in arms against her. But there was little general support for this rebellion and Knox contented himself with an offensive sermon on the rule of countries by women and boys (Darnley was only nineteen). There followed a few months of the futile military adventures called the Chaseabout raid, the sort of thing Mary loved. At the end of it Moray with his companions took refuge in England, where he received a public lecture by Elizabeth on the wickedness of insubordination to legitimate rulers, and probably a private telling off for inefficiency too, and an enormous bill for troops was placed against t he thirds.

1. The Earl of Oxford was another of this type, and Essex had many of the same characteristics.

Mary and her second husband were already visibly at odds. Nominally the quarrel between Mary and Darnley was over the question of the 'Crown matrimonial': was Darnley to be king only in title, or was he to have as much real authority as Francis had been intended to have? Mary had insisted on his receiving the title but she kept the authority, and before the end of the year was exercising it again in her own name alone. Probably she saw with dismay what Darnley with power would be like. But having once fallen in love, she had now a taste for emotional support. She could not get it from Moray, for she would never forgive him his opposition. She turned for advice and company to a young adventurer who had come into her service from that of the Savoy ambassador, David Riccio. Darnley was out of power, and out of her confidence: as much as she could manage it, he was out of her company too. In revenge the young fool began to intrigue with his late enemies. Both he and the lords of the recent rebellion objected to the confidence Riccio enjoyed. A plot was soon on the way, with the full knowledge and connivance of Elizabeth.

It all hinged on the technicalities of Scottish procedure for treason. The rebellious lords could only be proceeded against and forfeited in Parliament, and Parliament needed forty days of summons. Mary had called it for 13 March 1566; she spent the 9th arranging the most favourable structure possible for its business committee, the Lords of the Articles. That evening Darnley and others of the conspirators broke in on her and Riccio at supper in Holyrood, and dragged him out screaming, to murder him on the stairs. Moray and the exiled lords were already riding in from the Border in arms. The next day Mary was locked in her bedroom while Darnley as king suspended the Parliament. As a *coup d'état* it was efficient, even if barbarous. Darnley and his allies had power, and legal action against them was impossible, at least for forty days. They would use Parliament, when it met, to confer on him the Crown matrimonial. No kindness had been meant to Mary herself. She was well on in pregnancy and even the limited obstetrical knowledge of the age included an appreciation of the risks of a dangerous miscarriage.

Mary did not miscarry. As always, her physical health supported her in an emergency. She regained control of her feelings, appeared agreeable to Moray, persuaded him to relax the guard over her, and then won Darnley away from his fellow conspirators by sheer force of personality. With him as ally she was able to escape and ride through the night to Dunbar, where they could appeal to those not in the Band, Huntly, Atholl, and the borderer Earl Bothwell. We have a picture of Mary frying eggs for breakfast for her following. It was as good as lying out all night in the field. A few days later she was back in her capital in power.

But compromise with the conspirators was necessary. They had sent Mary the bond they had made with Darnley, so that she would know how little she could trust him in future. A month later some sort of peace was made. The rebels came back to apparent favour, but affection for Moray was gone. However, it was to an apparently reunited kingdom that her son James was born in June. Scotland at last had an undeniable heir, and the future looked hopeful for Catholicism.

There remained the problem of Darnley, sulking in Stirling castle during his son's christening there, impugning his legitimacy, threatening to leave the country, intolerable company for everyone. At the end of November, Mary, staying in the relatively cosy Craigmillar castle outside Edinburgh, was discussing him with various of her courtiers, Maitland, Moray, and Bothwell. She insisted to Maitland that nothing must impugn the legitimacy of her child, or her own honour. Divorce was thus impossible. Maitland promised that the matter would be looked to and that she would see 'nothing but good and approved by Parliament'. Was it to be another 'great business' like that of Henry VIII or an old-fashioned Scottish murder? A bond, as usual, was being drawn up by the magnates. Moray, said Maitland, would take care not to know what was going on, he would 'look through his fingers'. Mary, disliking bloodshed, had the feminine ability to instigate plots that would necessitate it at a distance. But in fact there is nothing surprising about the fact of Darnley's murder at Kirk o' Field house, on the outskirts of Edinburgh in February 1567. No one who had annoyed so many of the great lords in Scotland was likely to live long in the fifteenth or sixteenth centuries. What made it dramatic was the method, the blowing up of the house.[1] What made

---

1. In 1605 James's first reaction to the rumour of what is known as the Gunpowder plot was, 'I remember that my father died by gunpowder. . . . Search the basements.'

it disastrous was the fact that Mary afterwards behaved with wild indiscretion.

Mary almost certainly did not know of the actual plan of the murder. Probably nobody knew it all, for more than one plot seems to have been a-growing. Gunpowder is a clumsy weapon, pointless as a method of doing in just one person. Mary was due to sleep in the house herself the next night as part of an apparent reconciliation. From two separate diplomatic sources we know that Mary was well on in pregnancy in the summer of 1567; she may well have been already aware of her condition, and it would be common knowledge that the child could not be Darnley's without some show of reconciliation. For this reason she had every interest in keeping him alive for a few more days. Popular opinion laid the guilt on Bothwell, a strong arm man with a gang of Borderers to do his dirty work. By favouring him openly, by making his trial for the murder a farce, and then by acquiescing in kidnapping and marriage, Mary brought the reputation of guilt for the murder also upon herself.

The magnates had not put Darnley out of the way to have Bothwell in his place. They could get popular support from an upsurge of moral indignation. The banner they carried to war showed the infant James praying for revenge beside his father's corpse, a piece of outrageous double-faced propaganda. The extremist section of the clergy whipped up popular feeling against the queen. With an heir in existence, Mary was expendable. When Mary and Bothwell met the rebellious nobility in battle at Carberry Hill in June her soldiery and her husband melted away from her. She was back in the hands of the nobles, and this time they meant to keep her safe.

By now Mary's name was mud throughout Europe. No one except Elizabeth would intervene for her, and Elizabeth aimed only at preventing her murder. The plan of the nobility had been to coerce Mary and use her as a 'front', but it changed into dispensing with her altogether. She was bullied into abdicating in favour of James. Moray came back from a conveniently timed visit abroad and took over the Regency. Mary was closely confined among the Fifeshire fogs in the castle on Loch Leven. Compromise with Catholicism was over as a policy. The country and the young king were to be Protestant.

Moray had risen as far as was possible for one of illegitimate birth. But the very fact of his Regency broke the unity of the nobility. In particular Chatellerault and the whole Hamilton connection felt passed over and resentful. To the Hamiltons, James VI's reign meant a Lennox usurpation of a crown to which they had been the heirs. In 1568 Mary escaped and appealed to the Hamiltons to fight for her. When it came to the point they preferred to run away. There was no future for Mary in her kingdom and very little hope even of physical safety. After a long ride she was a refugee in England, without money or followers, and with only the short frock of a servant to cover her.

The situation posed a diplomatic problem for Elizabeth. Mary was a queen and a cousin, a rival and a claimant. She had made a mess of things, and the Bothwell marriage, to which she clung, was disastrous and made it impossible for her to be used as a counter on the matrimonial market at home or abroad. It was also clear that her opponents were all deeply involved in the murder of Darnley themselves, the ostensible ground of her deposition. Elizabeth had no desire to encourage rebellion against a legitimate ruler – her own monarchy as well as Scotland's had so little as practical weapons that it needed all the moral force available. But Moray had led the pro-English faction. Was James's infant life sufficient security for any régime?

In the end Elizabeth allowed an inquiry which was not a trial: ostensibly it was of Moray and others for rebellion, but really it was their chance to state the case against the queen. She closed it without a decision, saying that nothing had derogated from the honour of either. This was not enough to strengthen the Regent much, but it prevented an open breach. The English waited to see how well the Regency would do before giving it the help that might have established it. While Moray failed to consolidate his power – he could hold neither the conservative Huntly clan nor the Hamiltons who resented a Lennox on the throne – the only clarifying of the situation that happened was that Mary's return became a real possibility and Mary herself a real danger to Elizabeth. At last she disowned the Bothwell marriage. She was still in her twenties. There was a plan to marry her off to the Duke of Norfolk, and out of this came a plot of an English Catholic rising. Memory of the scandals of 1567 became fainter. Then in January 1570 Moray was assassinated – shot by a Hamilton from a staircase window as he rode with his men up the long street of Linlithgow. The cold-blooded ambush showed how little he had consolidated his position. It also embittered politics. A 'queen's party' began to form as attempts were made to find a Regency that was both strong at home and acceptable to England, and this party included Maitland and Kirkcaldy of Grange. Kirkcaldy executed Archbishop Hamilton for connivance in Moray's murder and Knox denounced Kirkcaldy. The Protestant party, divided into king's and queen's men, fought savagely among itself. The leading nobles mostly found their way to the queen's side, but the king's men got support from many of the clergy, gentry, and townspeople, who wanted a Protestant prince. For a long time Elizabeth dithered over which side to help. Names which in the past had stood for the English interest could be found on both. It was the massacre of St Bartholomew in France as much as the king's predominance in Scotland that overcame her indecision and brought English troops and artillery to help the Regency in the long tragedy of the siege of Maitland and Kirkcaldy in Edinburgh castle. Artillery was decisive. The fall of the castle in May 1573 ended the queen's party. Kirkcaldy was executed, largely because Knox had threatened him with a bloody end and Knox had to be right. Maitland died, depriving both countries of the man who saw most clearly that their future lay together. Morton rebuilt the castle in the form it has today with the great half-moon battery dominating the narrow crowded ridge-town. It was typical of him to see to it that during his Regency Edinburgh would be kept in order.

Morton, Regent for most of the years 1572–80, was competent and drastic when he thought it necessary. He was a fair, square man, curt and authoritative in speech with a massive stolidity. He had been a leader in the murder of Riccio, and certainly knew something about that of Darnley. Mid-sixteenth-century politics were not velvet glove affairs. His policy now was order, the English alliance, and a church settlement in agreement with these. He made a mess of things financially: no sixteenth-century ruler after James V had strength to do more than live from hand to mouth, and none of them had enough grasp of currency and elementary economics to do even this in an intelligent way. Morton endowed his own bastards in almost royal fashion, and allowed a good deal of money to slide into the hands of the nobility. Rather than face the unpopularity of taxation he depreciated the coinage. It is in this Regency that the general sixteenth-century price-rise can be found clearly in Scotland. In terms of silver the rise is not very much, but with the government tampering with the coin, first with one unit, and then with another, the pound Scots slipped from being worth a quarter of the pound sterling in 1560 to a twelfth in 1600 (James was unable to forgo using Morton's devices). This playing about with currency at a time when anyway money was difficult to come by lost Morton the support of townsmen and merchants and put additional difficulties in the way of the country's meagre trading activities.

Morton's greatest achievement was his insistence on law and order. In particular he used both firmness and conciliation in the Border. Combined with the English alliance this at last gave the area some stability. He also tried to suppress the feuds and brawls of the greater nobles. It is characteristic of their dislike of this restraint that immediately on his loss of power in 1578 brawling broke out again and cost the life of the Chancellor, Lord Glamis. Morton regained control of king and government a few months later, but failed to secure his position with the affection of the young king. James, highly intelligent and precocious, was awed and irritated by his Regent and ready to fall in love. If Morton's fall would please the king, nobody would care enough for him to prevent it, and nobody did.

All the same Morton had shown a real sense of the needs of the monarchy and of the kingdom. He refused to govern in the interests of a small clique. He was prepared to make a real effort to solve the problems of establishing the Protestant Kirk. Since the compromise settlement made under Mary, things had changed. The Kirk had had a try at collecting the thirds on its own, failed dismally, and realized it needed the co-operation of the state. It was now living under a Protestant and presumably 'godly' king: it could perhaps feel that it had less need of defensive institutions than under a Catholic. At the same time the Kirk now had more ministers, could take on more work, and needed a bigger share of the wealth of the old Church than a 'third' divided with the Crown. But the Crown and the nobles were still filling benefices, sometimes with men who wished to work in the new Kirk, and sometimes with men who regarded them as convenient pensions. In 1572, after a row over the failure to get the new Kirk's approval to the appointment of a successor to the archbishop, an agreement had been reached which bound the bishoprics into the new Kirk. The Crown was to nominate to them, the chapter of ministers to approve, and the superintendents, who were openly regarded as Protestant bishops, would consecrate. Either an Act of Parliament or death would get rid of the non-Protestant incumbents and Scotland would have an established Protestant Church on the English model, inheriting a good proportion of the wealth of the old Church as well as her dignitaries and structure. It was the Presbyterian take-over bid from Geneva that prevented this solution.

Calvin had been succeeded at Geneva by Theodore de Beza, and the new party line, in which disciples were being trained, was a condemnation of episcopacy. Scripture, it was said, showed no examples of a superiority or rule by one pastor over another, and so the scriptural Church must be one with parity between its ministers. The word pastor should apply only to those who had direct rule over a single flock. Bishops should be replaced by presbyteries, regular meetings of groups of ministers and elders, and these elders were to be an order in the ministry to which men were appointed for life. These 'ruling elders' were no longer to be thought of as laymen, for laymen should have no share in the government of the Church. The new doctrine stressed, in Augustinian terms, the distinction between the earthly kingdoms and the Kingdom of God, the Church. For this reason the miscellaneous General Assembly as it had grown up in Scotland, with barons and burghers sitting in it as a great ecclesiastical Parliament, was to be replaced by a purely ecclesiastical body of clergy and elders.

It is difficult to account for the influence of Beza. He was not a theologian to hold a candle to Calvin. His history is inaccurate and his reasoning has sizeable holes in it. Rule by one pastor over others may not be discernible in Scripture, but then neither are presbyteries, universities, academic teachers, and ruling elders. When Lord Glamis wrote to him in 1576 a long letter asking for advice on the changes that should be made to accommodate the Scottish Kirk to the new situation of a 'godly' prince, he got back a long formless essay answering none of his specific points. But Beza's influence did not depend on his voluminous correspondence. He sent Thomas Cartwright back to England and Andrew Melville to Scotland in the 1570s, indoctrinated followers of his, to bring their native Churches into line with the new Geneva. These young men were 'doctors', teachers, and scholars without pastoral experience. Cartwright was also a skilled writer and propagandist. Melville, who had taught for four years in Paris, and six in Geneva, was a fine academic linguistic scholar who had added Greek and Hebrew to the high level of latinity admired in Scotland at this time. It is understandable that the Presbyterian polity, as he outlined it, should have a place for 'doctors' in the councils of the Church but not for 'bishops' or superintendents. A university principal, such as Melville at Glasgow, was not a mere teacher. He was head of a college which was training the boys who would make the ministry of the future, and training them in opinion and life as well as in knowledge. It was a pastoral function.

The strength of the new structure put forward for the Church was considerable. Presbyteries could be conceived of as an organic growth from the voluntary 'exercises' of groups of ministers, practising self-criticism and discipline. There would be one of these functioning in each small town, covering the town and its 'landward' area. They would be more numerous and more immediate as a base for ecclesiastical order than the bishop of one of Scotland's great dioceses. Bishops were, in practice, expensive, and the Church needed all her revenues for enlarging her parish ministry. Presbyteries did not suffer from vacancies or deaths, or failure in authority from infirmity. They would not be easily influenced by the personal persuasions of a ruler – a point that Morton, and James after him, readily appreciated. With parity between ministers in all church assemblies, influence would, in practice, lie with the most articulate, the doctors. There were, and are, a lot of positive advantages in the new scheme of church organization. It is one of the unfortunate things in Scottish history that what has usually been said has been negative, an attack on episcopacy as 'papistical', corrupt, or unscriptural.

The new movement was expressed in both England and Scotland in the 1570s. It led to a struggle between the government and the 'new men' in each country, and in England the monarchy was stronger than in Scotland, and opposition to its policy had more limited political resources. As Morton's Regency drew to its end both governments were facing this new challenge, and in Scotland the church settlement as yet achieved was obviously temporary. A trial of strength was coming. Meanwhile James was growing fast and eager to try his hand at ruling his kingdom. Mary was still in 'temporary' confinement in England, scheming and planning, with her Scottish hopes growing dimmer but her English claims still important.

It would be tempting to see the victory of Protestantism, first over the old Church in 1560, and then over the monarchy itself in 1567, as a sign of the rising importance of the middle classes in Scotland. But things are not so clear cut as that. True, Protestantism seems to have spread in the towns first, as evangelism usually does in a country with poor communications. True, also, that Catholicism lingered most markedly in parts of the Highlands and in the great aristocratic linkages of the north-east. The rising class of lairds seems to have contained many Protestants in 1560, but so did the nobility. It is not at all clear how far the urban 'middle-class', the merchants and burgesses, can be thought of as 'rising'. Some merchants were making money well; trade was probably expanding, but slowly, perhaps faster after 1570. The Scandinavian markets were certainly developing. Scots went to Denmark or Sweden as mercenaries in their wars with each other and stayed on after the war; with kin in foreign ports a Scottish merchant was more ready to try a new branch of trade. The Swedish monarchy preferred to have trade in the hands of other than its own nationals. The Convention of Royal Burghs became formalized in the middle of the sixteenth century, but this, though it gave a regular mouthpiece to burghs, did not necessarily indicate economic progress. The function of the Convention was the allotting of taxation burdens among the burghs, and organizing and supporting the staple port in the Netherlands for the export of Scottish commodities. The existence of a staple port, now fixed at Campvere in Zeeland, where Scots could have privileges in customs duties and docking and pilotage, their own court and Kirk, is a sign that things had been made easy for the members of the trading community, but not one of either economic initiative or increased turnover. If trade was expanding, the lines that were to be important in the future lay outside the privileged world of merchant burgesses and staple privileges, in the coal mines along the Forth and the salt-works attached to them that Queen Mary had encouraged, and these were the property of landowners. The French connection had given the Scots trading advantages in France and peace with England always meant easier trade there. But as far as we can see expansion was still slight, money was tight, and conservatism strong. The merchant was more ready to change his faith than the destination of his goods and ships.

NOTES ON DRAMATIS PERSONAE

Arran. James Hamilton, third Earl, son of Chatellerault. Insane after 1562.

Moray. Lord James Stewart, illegitimate son to James V, (1531–70). Created Earl of Moray 1561. Regent of Scotland. Murdered 1570.

Maitland. William Maitland of Lethington (*c*. 1528–73), secretary to Mary, elder brother to the Maitland in Chapter 9. Died at the end of the siege of Edinburgh. A long-faced, long-headed man of great political ability.

Darnley. Henry Stewart, Lord Darnley (1545–67), son of Matthew Stewart, Earl of Lennox, and Lady Margaret Douglas, who was the daughter of the marriage of the Earl of Angus and the Queen Mother, Margaret Tudor. Murdered 1567.

Bothwell. James Hepburn, fourth Earl (*c*. 1535–78). Uncle to the Bothwell in Chapter 9. Died in prison in Denmark, held there by the kin of a past mistress of his.

Morton. James Douglas, fourth Earl (*c*. 1516–81), younger brother to the seventh Earl of Angus. Regent of Scotland. Executed.

Chapter 9

James VI in Scotland

Border Justice

JAMES VI, THE INFANT for whom Moray and Morton had ruled, grew up to be the most intelligent of the Stewarts, the last intellectual to grace the throne of Scotland, and, more important, the biggest success of them all. He was conscientiously educated to do credit to his royal position, and responded to the education. At eight he was translating freely from French to Latin; at sixteen writing tolerable verses and a sound analysis of the principles of poetry. Unfortunately, the education, and the aptitude it displayed, ignored the more creative aspects of the intellectual life of the day. In all that James regarded as a proper subject for learning he was a good practitioner; at the classics, theology, the ancient world, literature, but it was all a study of past achievements. He never had an inkling of economics or finance, he was an amateur at military science, and he learnt his politics by watching and listening. His regents and tutors had done well for him, but they had not done as well, for instance, as Charles IX of Sweden did for Gustavus Adolphus, with his training in modern languages, mathematics, war, and government. It was as if James had taken first-class honours at a modern university in all the older and non-expanding subjects.

It is customary to sneer at the king for his pedantry and his coward-ice. But James had as much scorn of the pedant as anyone. His love of learning was natural and went deep, his command over language vigorous and effective. What other king has written and published books? Could any other have put it on record that 'it becometh a king to purifie and make famous his owne language'? What other, in this island, since Alfred, has done so? Perhaps only Elizabeth of England. Elizabeth showed a sense of style in her speech, but she had not James's academic interest in it. As for cowardice, the historian living in an age provided with policemen at home and peace abroad cannot help being astonished at the splendid nerve displayed almost in-variably by the public figures of the sixteenth century, but this came from a value of public reputation as well as from mere courage. James, physically uncouth, friendly, and informal, had little basic dignity, and though he loved furious and dangerous riding, had a marked distaste for shows of violence and the weapons that accompanied them. He gave this away every time he dubbed for knighthood with his eyes turned away from his own naked sword-blade.[1] We have an account of his horror and fear at the first rumours of the gunpowder plot, but he had good reasons for his terror. James often let it be seen that he was frightened, but he never allowed himself to be deflected from his chosen policy by danger. A typical *coup d'état* by one of his nobles could be terrifying while it lasted. Sir James Melville describes an attempt by the Earl of Bothwell and his friends in which the royal

---

1. Sir Kenelm Digby describes an unnerving accolade, when he was nearly spiked: 'il faillit à me donner dans les yeux avec la pointe, n'eut esté que le duc de Bou-quinquan (qui sçavait bien a qu'il est arriveroit) la guida avec sa main . . .' But Sir Kenelm, who was capable of taking on Venetia, was not the man to be easily unnerved.

palace was full of 'reilling, robling with halbertis, the clakking of ther colveringis and pistolles, the duntling of melis and forehammers, and ther crying for justice', in which the attackers tried to burn out James's Chancellor from his refuge in a tower; but through the very real risk that these alarms carried James remained constant. Early in his teens the movements for and against Morton began a series of *coups* and counter *coups*. James resented, as his grandfather had done, being the subject of this sort of baronial treatment, but instead of merely resenting it, he studied how to deal with it. First he had to learn to keep his own counsel – to restrain the tears of rage or the shake in his voice. Soon after the Ruthven raid of 1582 the English ambassador complained that he could no longer get hold of the little key to the box of James's private papers. As James grew older he continued to keep his policy in his own hands, but he was open about its general drift. Because of this his reign has no single great minister with whom he worked, no Burleigh of England, no Oxenstierna of Sweden. And in the book of advice he wrote for his son, the *Basilikon Doron* of 1598, he offers us a key to his general ideas on the government of his realm.

This book is valued by many for James's vivid comments on the differing elements of sixteenth-century Scotland. 'No kingdom,' he says 'lackes her owne diseases.' The Scottish nobility have 'a feckless, arrogant conceit of their greatnesse and power': their aim is 'to thrall [by oppression] the meaner sort that dwelleth neare them to their service and following': their relaxation, feuding. 'They bang it out bravely, he and all his kin against him and all his.' The greatest hindrances to good government are their heritable sheriffdoms. James was not above complaining of evils he was too weak to tackle. The merchants suffer from a belief that the state exists to ensure them a profit: they achieve this by taking out of the kingdom basic necessities and returning with mere luxuries: they personate to James the acting out of the balance of payments and get his disapproval for being 'the special cause of the corruption of coinzie, transporting all our own and bringing in forrayne upon what price they please to set on it'. The craftsmen go in for low standards of work and have a liking for riot. 'If they in anie thing be controlled, up must the blue blanket goe.'[1] The mainland Highlanders were still semi-barbarous –

1. The blue blanket seems to have been the badge and banner of this class. It was

those in the islands 'Wolves and Wilde Boares': but the Borderers, though in private James would point out that these too were 'even from their cradells bredd and brought up in theft, spoyle and bloode', would cease to be a problem once the Scottish king inherited the English throne. The section of society that draws his strongest language is the clergy: 'never rose faction in the time of my minority, no trouble sen-syne, but they were upon the wrong end of it'. They lead the people by the nose, and the aim of the new Presbyterian movement is to establish an equalizing system in both Church and state.

But the real interest of the little book lies in its explanation of James's own standards as a king. The history of his reign and the story of his success and of his failures is written in these. 'Forefault none but for such odious crimes as may make them unworthie ever to be restored again,' says James piously, but the list of such crimes is not what we might expect. Witchcraft has pride of place, followed by wilful murder, incest and sodomy, poisoning, and false coin. Treason is not one of the unforgivable crimes: it depends on the man and the circumstances. Dishonouring parents is unpardonable, and James adds to this that it is those men or families that had served his mother best that he had found most loyal (this explains his casualness about the murder of the Earl of Moray). A king must protect his people, and go among them regularly. He should rule in person, not by a single great servant. But he should not go out of his way to endanger his own life. For servants he should stick to the families that had served the Crown well. The Church must be kept out of policy making, and its meetings be controlled by the king. These were the lines adopted by a king almost without resources beyond his own brains, faced with a baronage in the old Scottish way, and a Kirk asserting its right to control the state. They show how little accident there was in James's achievement.

Even in his teens James had stated his desire 'to draw his nobility to unity and concord'. It did not at first look very hopeful. Royal authority was more nominal than real and James was alone among his nobility in not being able to count on armed force to protect him, even in his own home. His personal security was no greater than that

---

also used as bedding, for ordinary and extraordinary purposes, as by the girl in 'the Keach in the Creel'.

of his poorer citizens. He could stumble out of his privy in the morning, half-dressed, to find that the Earl of Bothwell had gained control of the palace while he slept and was now gesticulating with a naked sword in James's own ante-room. The Grahams and the Sandilands could fight it out on the steep slope of the Edinburgh High Street outside the court where the king sat giving justice, while his Chancellor looked on unable to stop the brawl. To prove that violence was not the privilege of great lords or distant Highlanders, the Foresters of Garden defied the government in Stirlingshire for many years and feuded bloodily with the Bruces of Airth. Theoretically the nobles of Scotland respected the Crown as a necessity in government. They had none of the traditional attitude of the Aragonese to their king, expressed in the famous oath of allegiance which begins 'We, who are as good as you, swear to you, who are no better than we . . .' But in practice the Scotch nobility could often ignore the Crown inside their own territories, and in general politics they had the habit of using it as a weapon by the well-tried method of kidnapping the king.

James V had tried to enlarge the Crown's power by getting money. His acquisitiveness had not been matched in his descendants. Morton's rule had seen a steady increase of the royal deficit. He had been a Regent too weak to raise money by taxation. The reformation and the secularization of church property that accompanied it had brought some more money to the Crown – a share of the thirds for instance, but, with the inflation of the sixteenth century, this was soon outrun. James was permanently broke. When he tried to find a new source of wealth – the Act of Annexation of 1587, which took the ecclesiastical temporalities for the Crown – he was to decide later that it had not been worth while for the ill-will it had caused. Raised in an atmosphere of deficit and financial incompetence, he never developed any sense about money, or the willpower to refuse to make the gifts demanded by his courtiers. 'Helpe now or never,' wrote James to his Chancellor when desperately scrounging money for the baptism of his eldest son, but his friends had to help continuously, and, in return, helped themselves whenever they could. Not unnaturally, the likelihood of inheriting the English throne, where deficit finance was practised on a bigger and more glamorous scale, floated like a mirage to distract the king's foreign policy. Meanwhile, until he should step into the world of mirage, he followed Morton's policy of staving off emergencies by the worst possible method, depreciation of the currency.

This deplorable technique upset the trade of Scotland and ran down the small customs revenue. In the 1580s the customs were farmed at only about 30 per cent more than their level in the later fifteenth century, with the value of money a third of what it had been then. The practice also annoyed the merchants, and by upsetting the markets for craft work, caused unemployment. It has also disturbed the historian by giving a misplaced impression of the effects of the great price changes of the sixteenth century in Scotland. Between 1540 and 1600 the money price of food in Scotland went up by eight times: but most of this was the result of monkeying with the currency after 1570. There was still a real change in the price of corn measured against the price of silver. Between 1540 and 1580 this doubled. In the shifting world of unstable currency the losers in the end were the small number of people who worked entirely for wages as skilled or unskilled labourers – masons, carpenters, 'barrowmen', and all. These suffered a loss in real standards of living of between 20 and 30 per cent during the sixteenth century, the loss being higher for the skilled than for the unskilled. Fortunately most of the population had resources other than wages, but for those who had not it was difficult to attain to the standard of life of their fathers, let alone better themselves. This real, though not very great, inflation suggests that Scotland shared with many other parts of Europe a rising population in the middle decades of the century, a time when Scottish observers thought that numbers were going up, and were worried about unemployment. It also seems from the famine of 1595 and the relatively stable prices of the period after 1600 that she had her share in the general European disasters at the end of the century, and that by then her population growth had slowed down or ceased. Thus James's personal reign would seem to lie in a period after a generation of population growth, and at a time when it was particularly desirable to expand the economy to accommodate the increased population. There are small-scale signs of improving economic conditions: coal mining was developing, and as a corollary of this, salt boiling on the coasts. There were men from France teaching Scots (as they were teaching the English) to make glass; attempts at bringing in settlers from Holland with new techniques of weaving; the English were displaying better methods of metal working and tanning for the Scots to learn. Scottish traders were to be found abroad in numbers: the English had a misguided fear of them as undercutters, claiming that they had a low standard of living, that Scottish captains ran their ships on the cheap by not arming them properly, that every sailor, even to the ships' boys, went trading on their own account instead of being soberly organized and regulated in monopolistic trading companies. More real evidence of their ubiquity is the number of traders labelled 'Schotts' in the Baltic states: they are so many that some historians have seriously thought that small-scale pedlars were automatically called Scots – but even this implies that Scots predominated in the trade of this type. In many ways one gets the impression of an economic life hesitantly expanding: it was to do better in the second half of the reign when James had not only given his country a taste for the benefits of government, but also, by his succession to the English throne, had settled once and for all the main problem of policy. But even then it was only a slow expansion. A lot of attempts at new industries, at soap works and glass works, at gunpowder making, were only partially, if at all, successful. Rough textiles and crude exports such as coal were the basic achievements of this period, and all in all the growth probably did not keep pace with the increase in numbers. In the seventeenth century Scotland was ready and anxious to export people.

The come and go of merchants as well as of youths taking an education abroad, political and religious refugees, diplomatic missions, all helped to keep the country in touch with the ideas of Europe. The Scottish universities emphasized good latinity, though Scotland's prize classicist, George Buchanan, who impressed his latinity on the behind of the young king, had learnt his skill abroad. Later, under Melville, Hebrew and Syriac were taught. Even if James himself had no understanding of economics there were men at the mint who knew how the exchanges worked. These included Napier of Merchiston, who in the early seventeenth century was to discover natural logarithms, an essential tool in the modern higher mathematics created in that century, and also, when reorganized by an Englishman, Briggs, a few years later, a convenient aid in ordinary calculation. Napier had other designs in mind that took longer to materialize, the image of the tank and of the submarine. There were art forms in sixteenth-century

Scotland of permanent value. The silversmiths designed the exquisite mazers with a complete assurance that does not rely on ornament. Builders were beginning on the tower houses that combine foreign styles, a need for elegance in cramped quarters, and an eye for the practical issue of defence. But the promise of a wider intellectual and artistic life was frustrated in the seventeenth century. James turned the Scottish imagination to a morbid preoccupation with witchcraft and its beastlinesses, and the rising Presbyterian party subordinated theology to an attempt to gain political control of the country.

The form in which the political views of the Presbyterians forced themselves on the young king was such as to ensure that the movement never had his affection. In 1579 the king's first cousin once removed, his nearest relative on the Lennox side, Esmé Stewart, Seigneur d'Aubigny, came to Scotland from France, perhaps to get what he could from the recent disgrace of the Hamiltons, and James fell in love with him. This first love affair of the king gave him the opportunity of finding out what a king could and could not do. He could make d'Aubigny Duke of Lennox, endow him with church lands, and put him into the Privy Council. He could put up a follower of his, one James Stewart, to accuse Morton of complicity in Darnley's murder and so get rid of irksome control by the Regent. Stewart was given the earldom of the manic Earl of Arran and allowed to make a mess of controlling James's policy for a couple of years. The dominance of 'Arran' and Lennox coincided with an outbreak of international Catholic plotting, and Lennox also resisted the dominant pro-English group at court. It is likely that Lennox's Protestantism was only skin deep: he and James tried to quiet the growing discontent of both English and ultra-Protestant factions by putting out the *Negative Confession* of 1581, a document which damned Catholic beliefs and practices at considerable length in the hope that this was a way to create sincere Protestantism. This was not enough for those who objected to Lennox on religious grounds, and they added to their number those who were annoyed by 'Arran's' policy of loot, or who felt that there too many Stewarts were in favour and not enough of the other great families. The result was the 'Ruthven raid', a *coup d'état* in August 1582 in which James was carried off under the leadership of his treasurer, the Earl of Gowrie (James was never sure of the loyalty of even his own servants). The house of Gowrie stood for extreme

Protestantism and the English alliance. It took James nearly a year to escape and during this humiliating period of control, which he was old enough to resent, the General Assembly of the Church met with the Presbyterian faction dominant and approved the raid.

Lennox left Scotland for ever during James's captivity. James put 'Arran' back in power for a while, had Lord Gowrie executed, and showed the Church his disapproval by the 'Black Acts' of 1584. These denounced presbyteries and asserted the power of the king over everyone in the kingdom, and the authority of bishops in the Kirk. Elizabeth overplayed her hand by sending her Secretary of State, Francis Walsingham, to lecture James as if he were a schoolboy. There was not much difference in James's reaction to Walsingham's ticking off for daring to choose his own ministers and that to Andrew Melville later pulling the king's sleeve and reminding him that he was 'God's silly vassal'.[1] James remembered that he was a king, and swung the policy of Scotland against England. Melville and a handful of his followers were exiled. But this was a flash in the pan. James was not strong enough to assert himself finally against the Melvillites and another English *coup* organized against 'Arran' forced him to see that the first condition for security at home, as well as for the hope of the English succession, was the English alliance. There was a good deal of hard bargaining but finally in 1586 James and Elizabeth made an alliance of necessity: she to respect his rights without defining what these might be, he to receive a small subsidy. The money started at £4,000 a year, but Elizabeth shaved it down whenever she could find an excuse. James had not openly secured the succession but it would be difficult to see it going elsewhere.[2]

It was of enormous importance to the future of both countries that this alliance bound together two people with an intellectual and emotional distaste for war. The alliance became fundamental to the reign. Eventually it gave James a freer hand in deciding his policy. Because of it he refused to make more than a diplomatic show over

---

1. Silly in this context means weak.

2. James's succession hopes were not certain by English law: Henry VIII's will had preferred the descendants of his younger sister Mary, through whom came the Greys, to his elder sister, Margaret's, and the force of this will was a matter of great complexity, depending on sovereignty, law, and the authenticity of the signature.

the execution of his mother by the English in 1587 – it might be derogatory to his royal honour to have his mother executed for plotting, but though her life was not as dangerous to James as it was to Elizabeth, he had not a secure title while she was alive. He also showed political caution by not joining England's enemies in the Armada crisis of 1588. He then showed that he was still young by dashing off to marry Anne of Denmark in 1589, and passing the winter abroad, drinking on the Scandinavian scale. Though his choice of wife was largely made on the grounds of her dowry, the marriage created a series of financial alarms: how to find money for the journey; frantic attempts to furnish on tick a royal palace decently for the returning queen; and the problem of getting rid of her Danish escort before it ate the country bare. James was able to visit Tycho Brahé's observatory and to learn that in foreign courts it was not usual for the nobility to barge in and out of the king's bedroom as they felt inclined. Anne was considered good looking. She had the cheekbones of a horse, but her complexion was admired and she suffers in modern eyes mainly from preceding the era when Van Dyck was court painter. The marriage was as much a success as could be expected when we remember that James was not interested in women, intellectually or emotionally, had no first-hand knowledge of family life, that by custom the queen's children were taken away from her at birth, and that James had dowered her with property which his Chancellor, Maitland of Thirlestane, thought was his. Anne was young and healthy enough for her first three children to survive infancy: Henry, born in 1594, for whom nominally James wrote the *Basilikon Doron*; the exuberant Elizabeth, 'first dochter of Scotland' in 1596; and Charles in 1600. It was a long time since Scotland had had a real royal family.

By 1590 James had apparently had little success in securing his own safety or in controlling and pacifying his kingdom, yet by 1600 it was clear that, irrespective of his hopes of a royal union with England, he had transformed the monarchy in Scotland. The '90s are thus a watershed in Scottish history, but they began dismally enough. James was having trouble with his nobles. There was a large conservative-minded group, mostly holding lands north of the Tay, either open or concealed Catholics, and ready to intrigue abroad with Catholic powers, the earls of Atholl, Crawford, Erroll, and, as leader, Huntly. By the 1580s the revived Catholicism of the Counter-reformation was sending Jesuit priests into the country, and the tangle of marriage alliances between Catholic and Protestant houses meant that many had not come over to Protestantism irrevocably. The leading Protestant house of Gowrie had been reduced to representation by infants only, but there was the young and unstable Earl of Bothwell, owning great power in the Borders, and posing as an ardent Protestant. He was at odds too with the Chancellor Maitland over the church lands of Coldingham. The Kirk, by now the most effective single pressure group on James, was urging him to drastic action against Catholicism, and also demanding a better financial settlement than that of a share of the thirds. There was also the democratic, or Melvillian, party in it, demanding Presbyterian government.

James desired to live in friendship with his nobles, and to have peace among them – not for nothing had he made them walk hand-in-hand when he celebrated his coming of age. He did not want to provide another political martyr to Catholic assassination, nor did he wish to annoy any great Catholic power. Yet he had a real concept of monarchical government, incompatible with the irresponsible lawlessness of the earls and with the attempt of the presbyterian party to control him. One step in this direction was the building up of those landowning classes below the great nobility. With the Parliament of 1587 he brought the rising gentry, the 'barons of the shires', to representation in Parliament, a political confirmation of the increased economic importance of the class of lairds. The tenants-in-chief of the shires were to send one of themselves for each shire, at first perhaps only to provide information. Later in the reign James was to use the temporalities of the old Church to create a new nobility of lesser figures, either from families that had gained land and influence all through the sixteenth century, the houses of Buccleuch, Glenorchy, Ogilvy, and Tullibardine for instance, or, more important, from those that had served the monarchy in office.

In 1590 there blew up the North Berwick witchcraft scandal. Unlike most later witchcraft cases, it looks as if in these the accused may have actually been trying their hands at nasty kinds of magic. But behind them, as the trials progressed, came to stand the sinister figure of the Earl of Bothwell urging them to such practices against the king. James was terrified: believing sincerely in the power of such arts, as did most of his contemporaries, he felt himself, his wife, and his whole kingdom in appalling danger. From this moment dated his irreconcilable hostility to the earl and his fascination with the whole subject of witchcraft. It was to be eighty years before witch trials in Scotland abated from the zeal kindled by this fascination.[1] Bothwell did not make things easier for himself by referring to 'the lovable custom of our progenitors at Lauder' – the alleged murders of James III's companions. The king detested the earl, but he was the Protestant champion. Presbyterianism has had some strange allies in its search for political backing, and the General Assembly, forced to admit that the earl was a pretty unsavoury character, called him the king's 'sanctified scourge', and urged James to concentrate on bringing the Catholic northern earls to heel and leave Bothwell alone. Bothwell, combining a splendid nerve with support from within James's household, could not be kept in prison, and made several attempts to kidnap the king. Meanwhile James refused to discipline the northern earls. Huntly was married to a daughter of James's beloved Lennox, and so sure of favour. The earls pressed the king to get rid of his Chancellor, Maitland, for they disliked the royal reliance on a man of lesser family. In their eyes the king's natural advisers were his great nobles, despite their unwillingness to put in the work office required. They knew also that Maitland stood for conciliation of the Kirk. But in all this manoeuvring and pressure on the king there was very little of basic principle. In 1589 Huntly and Bothwell had allied to attempt a *coup*. A few months later Bothwell was befriending Maitland against Huntly's attempts to get him out of office. In 1592 occurred the scandalous murder of the Earl of Moray, the 'bonnie Earl', by Huntly at Donibristle, in which Moray won a literary immortality he did not personally merit. This was a peculiarly unpleasant event because Moray had come to Donisbristle, just across the Forth from Edinburgh, so that James could try to end the long-standing feud between the two houses, which took its rise in Mary's gift of the earldom of Moray to her half-brother. James had known that violence was likely and had not tried hard enough to prevent it. Moray was cousin to Bothwell, and Protestant feeling was indignant. James had his own inherited grudge against the house of Moray and

1. It was particularly unfortunate that Scotland should indulge in this morbid preoccupation at a time when the rest of Europe was beginning to outgrow it.

F

showed it by going hunting on the day of the funeral. When the Kirk demanded action against Huntly, he insisted that Bothwell must stand trial for witchcraft first. This position was difficult to maintain, and required important surrenders on other issues. He had to put up with the English subsidy being halved as an expression of Elizabeth's meanness and displeasure, and to dismiss Maitland from court. More important, he had to allow the Kirk its 'Golden Act', a formal acceptance of the legal authority of presbyteries.

In this way the Kirk became Presbyterian in administration. Things had already been tending this way, for James had used presbyteries, where they existed, to present to livings. But they did not yet exist in all areas, nor did kirk sessions or even Protestant ministers. As James had refused to make any significant change in the financial resources of the Kirk it was difficult for it to fulfil its obligations on a national scale. Bishops were still there, but enough attention was paid to Melvillian ideas to ensure that these also had parishes to care for. There is a shadowy resemblance between the bishops, thus shorn of diocesan authority, and their position in the old Celtic church, but only a proportion of ordinations were being carried out by them at this juncture. The General Assembly was still the amorphous but natural body envisaged in the *First Book of Discipline*, with barons and burgesses as well as clergy, and it met at the time and place appointed by the king. Melville had only won half of what he claimed.

For the next few years James supported the Protestant side of things, and used the Kirk's support to help to bring the northern earls to submit to his authority and that of the Kirk. The main point where he and the Kirk still disagreed was over Bothwell. There was another foreign intrigue discovered in 1592, the affair of the 'Spanish Blanks', blank papers signed by Huntly, Erroll, and Angus which implied treasonable goings-on, but these may have been already known to the king. James had to make his second military expedition against the north, but eventually forgave the earls in return for nominal conformity. He also persuaded Parliament to forfeit Bothwell. The earl struck back with the nocturnal capture of Holyrood. James, finding himself powerless, stood by the window half-dressed and controlled his fright enough to parley. It ended with Bothwell running things for a few months so disastrously that soon James had an alliance of the nobility strong enough to force him out and restore Maitland to court. James had by now learnt enough not to want any chief minister again. In spite of another raid by Bothwell, and another coalition that included him, the king was winning. The year 1594 saw another expedition against the north, 1595 the departure of Bothwell for the continent, and 1596 the submission of the northern earls. Maitland had died in 1595. James wrote a sonnet in his memory, 'How rare a man leaves here his earthly part', but was content to exchange his dominating presence for the men trained in efficient service by him. James hated being bossed, even by his favourites, and Maitland had not beauty enough to become one of these. Finally in 1596 the extremist party in the Kirk overstepped itself – there was an intemperate sermon preached which personally attacked Anne, the queen, and asserted the supremacy of ministers over kings. James's Council moved against the minister. Other attacks on the king and his servants followed, and Melville lectured the king on his subordination to the Church. When the Council forbade preachers to attack the king or the Council, the city of Edinburgh broke into riots. This gave James a weapon against both Presbyterians and city. He forced both to admit his authority. He was ready to learn how to control the Kirk. Here James's main tool was the uncertain but real control the king was acknowledged to have over the meetings of the General Assembly. By shifting its meetings in place and time he emphasized that it met when he chose.

One last threat of violence to the king's person occurred, which had a connection with the Presbyterian party, the mysterious Gowrie conspiracy of 1600. Most of what we know about this is James's own story, and not entirely consistent. But there genuinely was a plot, in which the young men of the Gowrie family were involved. James was lured into a remote part of their tower, and then with him out of sight, the Earl of Gowrie tried to get rid of the royal escort by telling it that the king had left. James had gained a steady nerve in dealing with troubles by now, and he won out by asserting his royal authority at a crucial moment. The result was the slaughter of the Gowrie brothers, the representatives of the nobility that stood nearest to the Presbyterian party. This is as much as we know for certain about the episode. Perhaps violence had not been intended, only restraint in the good old Scottish manner, but it was direct violence that the plotters

received. The Gowrie threat in politics and religion was removed and
James had an opportunity of arguing with his churchmen over the
form of the story to be published.

By then James's main battle was over. He had tamed the Church
and won the confidence of the nobility. The principles laid down in
the *Basilikon Doron* had worked, rather surprisingly. It now lay with
him to fix his personal victory in institutions. His nobles for a large
part of the time had become prepared to pay attention to the law:
that is to treat it, not as a substitute for force, but as a continuation of
private war by other means. Slowly James worked at reducing the
scale of violence, at enforcing smaller retinues so that the armed followers of the nobles should not be free to fight it out on a large scale
when their bosses visited town. The Privy Council might bind over
quarrelling nobility, at least those not of the first rank. There were
even executions for crime; for instance that of Lord Sanquhar for the
vindictive murder of a fencing teacher who had cost him an eye in an
accident. At the same time the fashionable introduction of the rapier
and the conventions of formal duelling did something to equalize
things between the gentry and the nobility. James did not dare
abolish the great feudal jurisdictions, though he pointed out that they
remained the most serious obstacle to good government in the
country, but he made a strenuous attempt to get the royal judges to
try criminal cases on circuits twice a year. The failure of this was
probably a reflection of James's main weakness, finance. There was
nothing to pay them with. He also borrowed the idea of the unpaid
Justice of the Peace from England, but here the relative failure seems
not to have been men or money but the elaborate existing network of
private and public courts which left them no place. All this attack on
courts and administration was only a beginning, but it explains why
in the seventeenth century that the modern framework of the Scottish counties crystallized out of the older districts.

In 1617 James's Chancellor, Lord Binning, in a eulogy, gave an
exaggerated but not basically untrue statement of the achievement of
the king:

> I schew that the blessingis of justice and peace, and fruittis
> arysing thairof, did so obleis euerie one of ws, as no thing in oure
> power could equall it; desyring that it might be remembered, that

whairas the Ilanders oppressed the Hielandmen, the Hielanders
tirannised ouer thair Lawland nighbours; the powerfull and violent
in the in-cuntrie domineered ouer the lyves and goodes of thair
weak nighbours; the Bordourars triumphed in the impunitie of
thair violences to the portes of Edinburgh; that treasons, mur-
thours, burningis, thiftis, reiffis, hearschippis, hoching of oxin,
breaking of milnes, destroying of growand cornis, and barbarities of
all sortes, wer exerced in all pairtes of the cuntrie, no place nor
person being exemed of inviolable, Edinburgh being the ordinarie
place of butcherlie reuenge, and daylie fightis; the paroche
churches and churche-yairds being more frequented upon the
Sounday for aduantages of nighbourlie malice and mischeif nor for
Godis seruice; nobilmen, barons, gentilmen, and people of all
sortes, being slaughtered, as it wer, in publict and vncontrollable
hostilities; merchandes robbed, and left for dead in daylight, going
to their mercats and faires of Montrois, Wigton and Berwick;
ministers being durked in Stirling, buried quick in Cliddisdaill,
and murthoured in Galloway; merchandis of Edinburgh being
waited in thair passage to Leith to be maid prisoners and ran-
soumed; and all vther abominations, which setled be inveterat
custume and impunitie, appeirid to be of desperat remeid, had
bene so repressed, puneissed, and aboleissed be your maiesties
wisdome, caire, power, and expensis, as no nation in earth could
now compaire with our prosperities. . . .

Even taking away three-quarters of this as dictated by the need for
flattery and a well-rounded sentence structure, it was an achievement.

It was not solely the work of the king. The reign carried on and
enhanced the nucleus of almost professional administrators first
found under James V. Maitland was particularly tied to these men,
and James kept on the Chancellor's principal aides. In 1596 there was
a desperate attempt to tidy up the Crown's finances, and eight men,
called the Octavians, were put in as a commission to prevent mis-
spending. In the event neither the king nor his court could take this
degree of control and the commission lasted less than a year, but the
men went on in the king's service. Church property had enabled
James to build up his new peerage, the 'lords of erection'. Some of
these new lords were already extensive landowners, but the interest

lies particularly in the professional part of the list, Lothian families like the Earls of Haddington, a line of small lairds who had served the Crown on the Court of Session, or the Maitlands who became Earls of Lauderdale under Charles I.

If Scotland was to achieve a government, she would also have to learn to pay for it. Taxation became more frequent, though not yet regular, and the size of taxes went up, even allowing for the depreciation of the currency. In 1588, 1594, and 1597 James raised over a hundred thousand pounds. The customs, farmed in 1583 for four thousand pounds and thirty tuns of wine, were bringing in over a hundred thousand pounds in the seventeenth century. Still there was not enough. The English pension, which at its best was £4,000, helped. But the failure was not just one of cash: it was also one of machinery. The Exchequer was still, as it had been in twelfth-century England, a short season of accounting once a year, six or seven weeks in the summer, for which a special house was hired and the local receivers of royal money were expected to turn up and explain what they had been up to, either to the king himself or his officials. People might fail to attend, and the accounting was still by the old-fashioned method of Charge and Discharge, which made it difficult or impossible for the real income to be discerned. In any case James's spending always ran ahead of revenue, and sudden personal demands, frequent for a compulsive spender and giver, would be entered on any fund that had some money in it, however inappropriate. So the accounts of the mint contain a bill of eighty pounds for furs: the special tax of 1597 to support foreign embassies was used to buy the queen a clock she wanted. Most of Scotland still lived by goods rather than by money: money was a gloss on the realities of life. So the king and the nobility could be traditionally out of pocket without it surprising anyone. There was no close connection in the Scottish Parliament between grants to the Crown and political concessions, so impecuniosity was not politically dangerous. Chronic bankrupts can be left to conduct small affairs without much in the way of a disaster. But trouble was bound to come when James was translated to the richer kingdom of England where money existed and had to be attended to on a greater scale, and where even the mean-fisted Elizabeth had not been able either to live within her means or to extend them.

In 1603 Elizabeth lay down to die, and at last admitted that James was her heir. The news of her death made James's recently published book, the *Basilikon Doron*, an international best-seller. Foreign statesmen who had hitherto ignored Scotland wanted to know the mind and quality of the inheritor of England. A great, perhaps a too great, court waited for its new master.

As James had long known, the area to be most affected by his transformation was the Border. Though there were parts of the Border where people attempted to live peaceably, for instance in the Merse, far too much of the picture of Border society in the sixteenth century is of clan feuds, cattle thieving, and bloodshed. Those who could lived in peel towers for safety. 'The Scots ride as far as Morpeth as quietly as in Tividale' went an English description. 'The Tividales will ride ten or twelve in a company from town to town and call men by their names and bid them rise quickly. . . . The simple man thinketh all true that he heareth: he riseth and giveth his hand . . . to be a true prisoner and enter when he is called for, or else to pay such a sum of money as they agree of. . . .' The same went for the English. Both sets of Borderers raided their neighbouring clans, on their own and the other side of the Border. The main season for theft was the autumn, after the assizes, but bloodshed took place at all times of year. Blackmail, which meant protection money, was the least intolerable part of the system; vengeful cold-blooded murder the worst. And each side of the Border received and tolerated political refugees from the other side, and not all refugees were purely political.

Things had got better after the suppression of the revolt of the English earls in 1569. From then on, fairly firm government existed on one side, and improving stability on the other. The great walls of Berwick still show that Elizabeth was taking no chances. But improvement did not mean quietude. Whenever the Scottish central government was secure and could choose the right clan-leaders as Wardens of the Marches, and back them up with 'raids', the scene was internationally secure. But feuds and thefts went on. Regular 'raids' were necessary. Levies from other parts of Scotland would be collected and taken down to the Border, either by the king or by his lieutenant: the favoured times were after harvest and when the moon was big. Landowners were made to take the General Band, that is to become surety for their dependants, or hostages were taken. A well-planned raid would bring in a group of troublemakers, and would assert crown authority by burning a few barns and hanging some thieves. It would all have to be done again in another section of the Border a few months later. It was not a gentle form of government, and the Borderers were not gentle. As late as 1593 one of James's Wardens was murdered in a clan feud. Bothwell had had to apologize for the roughness of his Border followers when he brought them to the Edinburgh of Queen Mary. James used on Borderers language almost as strong as that he used of the Highlanders. Even their amusements were apt to be violent. A feud started in 1583 between two Border nobles from a foul at a game of football.

The treaty with England was a point of departure for the Scottish administration of the Border. Now that there was no likelihood of war, the Wardens of the Marches could be expected to be more severe on their followers. In 1597 there was the international incident of Kinmont Willie. The English broke Border law by capturing him at a day of truce, and refused from personal animosity to the Scottish Warden Buccleuch to hand him back. Buccleuch then rescued him from Carlisle castle. The subsequent outbreak of diplomatic huffiness was resolved by a joint English and Scottish commission. This marked the decisive point from which it became clear that neither side wished to sacrifice amity for minor advantage. The old days were ending. Still, on James's accession there was a final fling. A mixed force of Grahams, Armstrongs, Elliotts, and others rode down on Carlisle on the pretext that until James had arrived in London there was no law in England, and enjoyed itself in what became known as 'the busy week'. Some of them paid for it afterwards. James picked on the English Grahams as the main offenders, in the same way that Scottish governments in the past had usually picked on the Armstrongs of Liddesdale. The Border was now to be known as 'the Middle Shires'. This did not immediately transform its ways. In 1605 a stronger commission was set up, which hanged over a hundred troublemakers, and another followed in 1618. As late as 1629 Charles I was issuing a pardon that rang with the old nicknames of broken men of the border; 'Edward Armstrong of the Ash ... Edward Armstrong alias Kinmond, Hector Armstrong alias Stubholme and John Armstrong otherwise called John-with-one-hand. . . .' Even after 1660 the Register of the Privy Council contains special commissions appointed for Border troubles. But as a major problem the Border was finished, so much so that now at last Protestantism had a chance to get in there.

A certain sadness hangs over this: men no longer rode on raids silently on unshod horses to leave the red cock crowing on others' houses. Soon the men would not be there. Pacification led to depopulation. Already the area was noted for the smallness of its holdings. Little grain could be grown in the hills. Sheep farming came in. Many years later Scott was to write of the disappearance of the minor gentry:

> Each of these persons maintained his little style – had a few cottages round his old tower whose inhabitants made a desperate effort to raise corn by scratching up the banks of the stream which winded through their glen. These are all gone and their followers have disappeared along with them. I suppose it became more and more difficult for them after the Union of the Crowns to keep the 'name and port of gentlemen'; they fell into distress, sold their lands, and the farmers who succeeded them and had rent to pay to those who bought the estates got rid of the superfluous cottagers with all despatch ... I could name many farms where the old people remember twenty smoking chimneys and where there are now not two.

It was a foretaste of the settlement of the remaining disordered area, the Highlands.

NOTES ON DRAMATIS PERSONAE

'Arran'. James Stewart of Bothwellmuir, son of Lord Ochiltree. He was the accuser of Morton and brought about his fall, probably at James's instigation. He was created Earl of Arran, 1581, during the insanity of the Hamilton Earl, attainted 1585 and murdered in 1595 by a nephew of Morton's.

Atholl. John Stewart, fifth Earl (1563–95), married to a daughter of the second Earl of Gowrie: a Bothwell supporter. He was the last Stewart Earl of Atholl and died broke. In 1628 the Murrays of Tullibardine received the re-created earldom.

Bothwell. Francis Stewart (*c.* 1563–*c.* 1612). Son of one of James V's bastards by a sister of the Bothwell in Chapter 8. Created Earl of Bothwell. Died in exile.

Crawford. David Lindsay, eleventh Earl (*c.* 1527–1607): 'ane princely man, a sad spendrift': involved in the brawl that killed the Chancellor, Lord Glamis, in 1578.

Erroll. Francis Hay, ninth Earl (died 1631). These two earls represent typical features of the northern nobility: impecuniosity, constant trouble over treason or Catholicism, a life in and out of forfeiture or prison.

Gowrie. William Ruthven, second Earl, one of the murderers of Riccio. Executed for treason 1584 after the 'Ruthven raid'.

John Ruthven, fourth Earl, son to the above, born 1577 and killed with his younger brother in the episode known as the 'Gowrie conspiracy', 1600: his limbs were distributed round the leading royal burghs for display and the surname and title were abolished.

Huntly. George Gordon, sixth Earl and first Marquess (*c.* 1563–1636). The Huntly of 'Woe be to you, Huntly' in the great ballad on his slaughter of the Earl of Moray. Father of the Huntly in Chapters 11, 12, and 13.

Maitland. John Maitland of Thirlestane (*c.* 1545–95), younger brother to the Maitland in Chapter 8, Lord Chancellor 1587, peer 1590. He survived the siege of Edinburgh castle in 1573 and came back to politics after Morton's death. More cautious and perhaps less able than his brother, he survived in a safer reign and founded the house of Lauderdale.

Moray. James Stewart (*c.* 1568–92), who obtained the earldom of Moray by marrying the elder daughter of Regent Moray. His slaughter at Donibristle in 1592 has earned him a poetic fame that even the good looks he was so proud of hardly merited.

Chapter 10

The Union of Crowns

Because I hope ye shall be King of moe countries then this; once in
the three yeares to visit all your kingdomes: not lipening to Vice-roies,
but hearing your selfe their complaintes.

Basilikon Doron, BOOK 2

JAMES HAD ALREADY PROVED himself as a statesman of skill when in
March 1603 the welcome news came through that Elizabeth was
dead and the throne of England waiting for him. It was a great
moment. The prospect of spendthrift living on what to Scotland was
an enormous scale was attractive: so was the fact that it was over a
century since an English monarch had been kidnapped or had
failed to die in his bed. More significant, if less personally so, was the
fact that England was an important unit in the European community of states, with influence on international affairs. These
attractions were more apparent than the problems of governing his
new realm. James may have known that English nobles were not as
turbulent as those of Scotland by about two generations of pacification. He was not aware of the rising temper of the English Commons
or the complexities and difficulties of the whole overstrained system
of government, though he had shrewdly written 'no Kingdome lackes
her owne diseases'. He hastily borrowed 10,000 merks from the city
of Edinburgh and set off to ride down through his new kingdom.
Outside Musselburgh he was held up by the funeral procession of his
mother's servant, Lord Seton. When this solemn reminder of an older
Scotland had passed, he mounted and rode on. It was long since a
Scottish king had ridden through the open gates of Berwick. His
family, indulging in a spree of new clothes buying on an unprecedented scale, were to follow later.

New clothes might be taken as symbolic of the forces that were to cut the monarch off from his ancient kingdom. James in the *Basilikon Doron* had urged on his heir not to stay away from Scotland: he himself promised to come back every three years. But the journey would be long and expensive, even though much of the cost could be cut by living parasitically on the country houses of England. More serious, James soon learnt to enjoy a level of comfort that he could not hope to maintain in Scotland, so that it was a point of real significance when the Venetian ambassador, beginning to pay attention to this new personality on the international stage, recorded in June that James had begun to live like an English monarch. No longer would he 'be waited on by rough servants, who did not even remove their hats'. Professor Lawrence Stone records that from 1608 to 1613 James's accounts show that he bought 'a new cloak every month, a new waistcoat every three weeks, a new suit every ten days, a new pair of stockings, boots and garters every four or five days, and a new pair of gloves every day'.[1] Against this picture has to be set that of James in his Scottish days borrowing a pair of stockings from the Earl of Mar so as to be able to receive the Spanish ambassador. James could not expect to live in Scotland in English style except on English funds. The Scottish nobility were beginning to indulge in conspicuous forms of sumptuousness in their country houses and castles. We have accounts of Sir Colin Campbell of Glenorchy spending 3,000 merks on hangings for his two houses in 1632, of the plaster work of the drawing room at Winton carrying Lord Winton's arms, of the great velvet chairs at Tyninghame. But none of this could compete with the sort of hospitality which James could extract from the English nobility, for instance the five days visit to Theobalds in 1606 which cost the Earl of Salisbury £1,180 sterling.

A visit of the king to his native country must therefore mean either a sharp drop in living standards or the transport of a great deal of English cash and goods. James came to like other things in the south besides luxury: he made friends there, and though at first he took with him a group of Scottish courtiers who annoyed the English by doing well out of the move, as well as by bringing their lice with them, he had in a few years dropped his Scottish favourite, Carr, for the Englishman, George Villiers. Villiers, ennobled as the Duke of Buckingham, moved in on the court and organized rackets and

1. *The Crisis of the Aristocracy*, p. 563.

extortions, sales of honours and economic privileges, on a scale that made all previous attempts at this mere pickings. Not many Scots could afford to keep up with the court on these terms, and those that did tended to slip out of touch with Scottish feeling and affairs. English politics were more clamant and time-consuming than Scottish, and the new country had dealings with foreign powers that had never meant much to Scotland. All in all it is not surprising that James only once managed to return to Scotland, in 1617, and that his son paid only a single visit before the crisis of his reign forced him to try to woo the Scots.

This change meant that the next king, Charles I, grew up in greater safety than he would have known in Scotland, but without getting to know his Scotch subjects, to speak their tongue, or share their pleasures. He could not follow his father in teasing them in colloquial Scots. He could not know the dominant features of their lives, the small amount of money moving round the country, the emphasis on kin as the basis of the groupings of men, as much the case in the Lowlands as in the Highlands, the smallness of the burghs, which struck English visitors as more like villages than towns, and the intense localization produced by geographic barriers and by poverty. Though the greater nobility would be familiar with his court, and even a few of the Highland chiefs (those with a relative lack of legal processes on foot against them) might get through to him, Charles did not go on the long summer hunting expeditions into the Highlands where political bonds and real friendships could be built up. We do not see him sitting in judgement in his court in Edinburgh, or marching into the brief annual session of the Exchequer to try and clean up his accounts, ticking his officials off for being unpunctual. Charles was never in a position to gauge the likely reactions of his Scottish nobility to plans he might make, nor was he able to spot and bring forward the administrators of the future.

The dynastic union of Scotland and England was the latest of the important junctions caused by the dynastic marriages of the sixteenth century. These unions mostly lasted a generation and a half before serious difficulties in government came to a head. Dynasties that joined together countries which, in their institutions, had not much in common, found themselves faced with a series of revolts. The best known of these is of course that of the Netherlands against

Spain, but there were also in 1640 the revolts of the Portuguese and Catalans, and earlier the rebellion of Sweden against her junction with Poland. There had also been the revolt of the *commuñeros* in Spain against Charles V's decision to leave the country and attend to his other territories. Absentee monarchy, in a period of bad and expensive transport, was apt to prove unsatisfactory to the smaller of the pairs of kingdoms joined together, and taxed to the full the primitive machinery of government.

England was still a foreign country to the Scots. In spite of similarities in doctrine, church organization, and language, not many Scots went to live there. There were more, of course, in England than admitted to it: In Elizabeth's reign officially only forty Scots were resident in London, the rest finding it convenient to claim origin in the north of England. As the peace between the two countries had stabilized, Scottish merchants and divines would move increasingly to England, but for education the Scottish upper class sent its youth to France. There, a Scot could move from one to another of the towns held by the Calvinists under the Edict of Nantes, and study a law which would be useful at home. We have a picture from the Erskine family leaving Bourges in 1617: 'If we had stayed still in Bourges we could not have lernit the Frence, in respek of the great number of Scotsmen that is there for the present, for we met efery day together at our exercise, so that it was impossible for us not to speak Scotis.' Since 1558 there had been no formal barrier of nationality between France and Scotland. Those of the nobility still positively adhering to Catholicism might send daughters to religious houses in northern France or Belgium (Protestantism provided no such convenient way of settling undowried daughters), or get Jesuit chaplains from abroad. Scotland's trade with the Netherlands was thought by many to be her most important economic outlet, and one that was growing while the French trade declined. This meant not only the presence of small groups of Scots at a lot of ports, but a big colony at the staple port of Campvere. Scots went to Europe to fight, and many more were to go when the Thirty Years War dominated European politics. In some ways England was a more unfamiliar foreign ground than other north European countries.

James had tried at once to unite his two realms. He started off by getting the customs between the two countries abated for a few years while he tried to put through a parliamentary union, a church union, and free trade. The grand scheme broke on the English fear of 'beggarly' Scots undercutting them, and in the end all that James salvaged was the legal decision that the *post-nati* (those in either kingdom born since the personal union) could not be treated as foreigners. In economic matters both countries reverted to their own customs system, but this was not yet a protective structure, and in any case since their economic resources were different, was not unreasonable. Scotland had not the export of fine woollen cloth, nor the growing number of small luxury manufactures of England, so there was no strong case for common economic policy. The king also tried to persuade his courtiers to bring the two countries closer together by marriages, but few would attempt this. The first example of it was not encouraging, the marriage of one of the Chandos heiresses to a Kennedy who turned out to be already married in Scotland, and a thorough-going bad hat into the bargain. The few other instances tended only to involve the younger sons of the English nobility, who were regarded as expendable.

So long as James personally controlled things the situation in Scotland was as tranquil as it had ever been. James had taught his nobles to consider the use of law as at least a parallel weapon with violence, a possible way of procedure in quarrels. It was not so much a substitute for force as a continuation of action by other means. He had also some success in subduing the other major unruly element in his kingdom, the Presbyterian wing of the Church, the weapons of which were words rather than swords. He learnt to manipulate the General Assembly. Without ever formally abrogating this body, for in fact he accepted it as the leading element in legislation for the Church, he established that it must meet where and when he chose. 'When' involved a tussle in 1605 because twenty-nine ministers defied James's proroguing of an Assembly in that year indefinitely. James imprisoned thirteen of these, and banished six of them later. He would probably have acted more drastically if the Privy Council had not dragged its foot over the prosecution. The numbers dealt with suggest a real hard core of determined opposition, but not a large one. James followed this up by imprisoning Andrew Melville, and later exiling him and some of his followers. None of this was particularly fierce as discipline: it did not silence or suppress the Presbyterian minority, but it made it clear that it was out of favour, and, since Melville's talent at speech was not matched in his writings, it deprived it of leadership. More effective was James's ability to keep troublesome ministers on short commons when sharing out the Kirk's revuenue.

The moving of the General Assembly from town to town was a more subtle means of control. Very few ministers would travel more than sixty miles to an Assembly, so James learnt to keep it from meeting in the two Presbyterian centres of Edinburgh and St Andrews. In 1610, for an Assembly at Glasgow, James made sure of adequate representation from the north by paying the expenses of those who came from a distance. This technique of control probably made the Assembly more, not less, representative of the full range of opinion within the Kirk. But, coupled with the exiling of the Melvillians, it showed that the king was going to have his authority obeyed. In the reaction after the Edinburgh riots of 1596 he had obtained a standing commission of the Assembly, nominally to advise the Crown, but in practice acting as a vehicle for James's influence on the kirk leaders. He went on to get the bishops, who had never been abolished in the Kirk though they had been by-passed, restored to use and control – as permanent 'moderators' or chairmen of synods, as members of the standing commission and as representatives of the Church in Parliament. By repealing the Act of Annexation he was able to provide them with more funds, though most of the old temporalities of the Church had to remain with the lords of erection, his new nobility. In 1609 the bishops got back jurisdiction over wills and marriages and in 1621 they were used to give the Crown complete control of the committee of the Articles, which conducted parliamentary business. This was now to be made up by the nobility choosing eight bishops and these bishops choosing eight nobles, and the two sets together choosing eight lairds and eight burgesses. Only if there were not eight noblemen of the king's persuasion would this committee oppose his policy, and as James had his allies in the new nobility this was unlikely. James even managed to emphasize the spiritual function of his bishops by obtaining consecration from the Church of England in 1610 (the apostolic succession in England being unbroken).[1] His initial motive in church matters had been a dislike

1. The Scottish church appears to have lost this succession, not of necessity but

of the Presbyterian principle of 'parity', 'the mother of confusion' he called it, as well as a danger to the state, 'by the example whereof ... they think (with time) to draw the political and civil government to the like'. If the monarchy had gone no further than this in the re-dressing of the Presbyterian swing of the late 1580s we would be congratulating the Kirk of Scotland on a successful combination of the strengths of both presbytery and episcopacy into a flexible organization.

Unfortunately James, perhaps because of years of keeping com-pany with the Anglican Church, went on to a liking for some of the forms of Anglican practice. He was not the only Scot to find these attractive, but the others were not in a position to encourage changes at home. In 1617, after his only return visit to Scotland, he put for-ward at a General Assembly at St Andrews (an unwise location) a set of five new regulations for observance in the Kirk, and when these were refused, pushed them through, partly by royal warrant and partly by much more careful management of the Assembly, at Perth, the next year. These re-established the main festivals of the Christian year, permitted baptism and communion in private, re-asserted the need for confirmation, and ordered kneeling for the reception of communion. These features did not bear directly on Protestant dogma, but they bore on shibboleths that had become as important as dogma to extremists. No one could find the Christian year laid down in the Bible, least of all in the Old Testament: private sacraments reduced the emphasis on the function of the whole com-munity, and also implied that the salvation of the individual was affected by such rites, and therefore not immutably decreed: con-firmation emphasized the function of bishops. The only one of these 'five articles of Perth' that had a real impact on the worship of the whole body of the laity, kneeling at the reception of the sacrament, was in fact doctrinally almost neutral,[1] but it enabled the more out-spoken of James's opponents to talk about bowing the knee to Baal. James got his articles, but at the cost of ill-will. He was determined

---

from indifference, in the 1570s when superintendents, some of whom became bishops, were 'consecrated' by presbyters.

1. The only argument that puritans could level against it was that Catholics knelt for a mass that Protestants considered idolatrous: therefore kneeling implied idolatry: it was a flawed syllogism.

to give them all the authority he could, so they were pushed through Parliament too, but in a way that showed he was putting a strain on the allegiance of his normal allies, the burghs and the lords of erection. Substantial opposition votes came from both these groups, a more menacing sign for the future than the fact that he had a group of ministers against him. The ministers could be disciplined, and James's severity was partly toned down by the Privy Council, but the lay opposition made it clear that he could not go on to provide a better liturgy for the Kirk. No General Assembly was to meet again till 1638. James had shown too openly how close a control he wished to exercise over the whole Church and in a matter that affected the entire body, clerical and lay.

In other spheres of life James's hold was less obvious, but it must have been clear by the end of his reign that the main outlets for expression were under royal control. Parliament was more a place where laws that the king required could be passed, than a body that made the law itself. The king had a second instrument for legislation and taxation, the Convention of Estates, which was an enlarged form of the Privy Council, and to which he had, by tradition, a fairly free hand in summoning whom he wished. But during this period, perhaps under English influence, the tradition was decaying, and the approved membership of the Convention of Estates approximated more and more to that of Parliament. In 1621 James failed to raise money through a Convention of noblemen only, a point which reduced the value of the institution to the Crown. But even in a parliament the Crown still had the initiative. By a careful choice of its functioning committee, the Lords of the Articles, the work of Parliament could be defined in advance. Laws as the king wished could easily be got: enforcement of them was another matter. Here James worked through his Privy Council. This body cannot be strictly paralleled with the modern Cabinet. It contained the leading nobles of the country, the king's officials, the judges, and a few bishops. In some ways it resembled the Swedish *Riksrad*: it was a means of getting the aristocracy to work for the state. But in this aspect James was far less successful than Gustavus Adolphus of Sweden, and so less successful in welding together the two main divisions of officials and aristocracy. The magnates, who objected to decisions being made without their involvement, also objected to being expected to turn up and carry on the routine and detailed work of the Council. The men who attended regularly and made the thing work were the office holders, the Chancellor, the Secretary, the Treasurer, and the judges, and this group comprised more than half the nominal members of the Council. Still, the Council provided an outlet for aristocratic opinion, and this, coupled with the personal trust and affection that James showed to all his great nobles except the Earl of Argyll, kept things tranquil. But this safety valve could easily be shut off by his successor.

James's government was at its least successful in the Highlands. There was a lack of sympathy here. James's view of the Highlanders as barbarous has been much criticized, but it was a natural reaction to the events of his day. The sixteenth and early seventeenth centuries are full of Highland bloodshed, and James was in no position to assess how much of this was the long term result of his great-grand-father's action in destroying the Lordship of the Isles and failing to fill the power vacuum it left. We hear of clan battles and affrays all through the century, of Macdonalds putting eighty Macleans to death at the rate of two a day, of people being burnt alive by the churchfull in Skye in 1520 or in Ross in 1603, of two hundred and eighty Macleans killed at Gruinard in 1598, or a hundred and forty Colquhouns at Glenfruin in 1603. Even if we drop off the last nought in most Highland accounts of inter-clan warfare, the fact remains that the slaughters were on a much larger scale than was now likely to occur in the Lowlands. Ever since the siege of Donibristle the Low-land nobility and gentry had confined their murders to two or three at a time, and though this relative level of civilization was new, it was important. Feuding, too, though it existed in the Lowlands, had ceased to be the full scale bloodfeud taken up by the whole kindred. This is shown by a famous dispute that lay across Aberdeenshire in the 1630s, the affair of the burning of the tower of Frendraught, part of the Crichton homestead which went up in flames one night in October 1630 with a son of Huntly and Gordon of Rothiemay, and their attendants, inside. It was never established that this was not merely a ghastly accident, but the Gordons were passionately resent-ful. Huntly took the quarrel to the Privy Council. The Council investigated repeatedly, tortured a servant or two for information, executed a hanger-on of no great social status, but failed to gain evidence against Crichton of Frendraught. Dissatisfied, Huntly let in broken men from the Highlands to ravage Crichton land, and for years the north-east was troubled by burnings, looting, and kidnapping. Though Huntly turned his back on his kinsman, the Earl of Sutherland, who refused to break with a nearer kin, Frendraught, and resisted the pressure of the Council for reconciliation, the matter never became a full-scale bloodfeud of the old type. Even so, it drained away the wealth and lands of the Crichtons in the next fifteen years. Still, the dispute shows that it was with the moral superiority of gamekeepers whose immediate ancestors had been poachers that James and his Lowland nobility looked down on Highland and Border feuding.

If there was contempt in the royal attitude to these areas, there was also wariness. The clan structure of Highland society, and the parallel surname system of the Border, produced a society unamenable to extending law. Bloodshed was a matter of concern for the kindred or the clan: it would either be taken up by the clan as a whole, or the killer disowned. The chief had to decide each case on its merits. If he decided too readily to abandon a follower to justice or revenge he might find his clan deposing him from the leadership, as happened to a Macdonald of Keppoch. James, like other Stewarts before him, stressed the tie of feudal lordship, under which it was easier to bring pressure to bear on overlords, and through them on the men. The monarchy attempted to enlarge its influence in the disorderly areas by giving grants of land or overlordship to certain favoured leaders, irrespective of whether these lands contained their clansmen or someone else's, and by formal commissions and lieutenancies to one or another great noble to subdue districts or clans. These policies produced insecurities over the ownership of land, and these insecurities, in an area over-populated for the available agricultural land, produced bitter disputes. It was the more fertile districts that suffered, especially Kintyre, the lower ground in Skye, Lewis, the straths of Kintail. The great lords, to whom commissions were usually given, Huntly and Argyll in particular, could not be expected to be mere instruments of the Crown: they looked to the political and territorial aggrandizement of their own houses at the expense of their neighbours. Attempts to insist on justice done by law courts rather than by violence led to further difficulties. Only those chiefs whose clans were not already in trouble with the Privy Council for feuding or cattle stealing, could safely answer a legal summons to Edinburgh. Small clans, pressed on by greater neighbours, might easily find the charters of lands they thought were theirs, or felt ought to be, in the hands of more favoured enemies. This meant that to survive they needed skill in diplomacy as well as in war, and absolute unity within the clan, to make bargaining effective. The Macdonalds, though still a great clan, failed to show these qualities and therefore declined. The Macgregors failed to temper their bloodthirstiness with policy, and under pressure from their neighbours, particularly the Campbells of Glenorchy, and also Murrays and Stewarts, broke into violence that could not be tolerated. Feudal superiority, given to other lords, meant an attempt by these to extract military service from hostile tenants, and failure to give this could lead to eviction: ineffective attempts to evict would start a clan war. Once up against the law in this way a clan would have to go from outrage to outrage, or cease to exist as a unit. This is the sort of story behind the Macgregor case. A series of disturbances began with the murder of a royal forester in 1589. This was not a casual homicide, but a deliberate slaughter by the clan, and of the servant of a king who held wilful murder to be an unpardonable crime. Things went on, with the breakdown of effective control by the chief, to culminate in the slaughter of the Colquhouns in an ambush at Glenfruin in 1603. No doubt the Colquhouns had asked for it, and perhaps the Earl of Argyll had encouraged the Macgregors in their outrages; but this was a direct challenge to the Crown, which had just given the Colquhouns a commission against the Macgregors. What is more, it took place in the Lennox on the edge of Highland and Lowland, where violence could not be ignored. The Privy Council decreed the destruction of the clan as a unit, the outlawry of those who had fought, the disarming of them all, the end of the name, and called on the neighbouring chiefs to make this effective. After ten years the survivors of the clan were disguised under the name and protection of other chiefs, and the house of Argyll had done well out of the event, as it usually did, being rewarded with the gift of Kintyre. By contrast the Camerons, also a bloodthirsty lot, but farther away from the centres of power, survived by acknowledging the superiority of Argyll and Huntly and leasing some lands to the Macintoshes. The vital element in their survival was the maintenance of a united headship by Lochiel, in spite of attempts by Huntly to divide them, and this was marked in 1616 by the execution of sixteen dissidents by Allan Cameron of Lochiel. A century and a half later the Camerons were still famous as a clan that had a short way of dealing with dissidents. It was this sort of bloodthirsty event which inspired the most notable attempts of James at 'pacification' of the Highlands.

One of these attempts was moderately successful. In 1608 Bishop Knox of the Isles was sent to tame his diocese, and got hold of many of the principal chiefs by inviting them on board ship to hear a sermon, and then imprisoning them. They secured release the following year by accepting the Band and Statutes of Icolmkill (Iona), an agreement to support the reformed Church, to pay its stipends and accept its discipline, to send their eldest sons to school in lowland Scotland, to disarm, to expel their bards, and to hand over offenders to the Law. The combined attack on disorder and on Gaelic culture worked for a time, calming things down. The other attempt was a failure; it was a scheme to settle lowlanders in the outer Isles. A family split in the Macleods of Lewis and an argument over title deeds between them and the Mackenzie's of Kintail enabled the king to declare Lewis forfeit: 'the maist fertile and commodious pairt of the haill realme . . . with an incredible fertilitie of cornes and plentie of fischeis', which 'would rander mainst inestemable commoditeis . . . gif the barbaritie of the wyld and savage inhabitantis thairof wald suffer . . . peceable trade' went the advertising-copy prose of one of James's proclamations. There was a plan for burghs to be founded in the Highlands, one in Lochaber, one in Kintyre, and one in Lewis. The island was to be granted for a rent to a band of Lowland colonists called the Fife Adventurers, headed nominally by the Duke of Lennox. The adventurers arrived, backed by soldiers, and built the town of Stornoway, but were prevented by the hostility of the Macleods from exploiting the 'inestemable commoditeis'. In the end the Mackenzies of Kintail bought up their rights, and James had merely exchanged one Highland clan for another in the Isles.

After 1603 James was forced on further by his English inheritance in attempts to pacify the Highlands. In the past, restless chiefs or groups of broken men had passed over to Ireland, sometimes with the goodwill of the Scottish Crown, to make trouble for the English government there. Obviously this could not go on. But there were close ties of language and culture between the Highlands and Ireland, and in many cases, of kin. The Macdonnells of Antrim were a branch of the Macdonalds of Dunnyveg, who had been in possession of Islay and Kintyre. The house of Dunnyveg was split by a bloodthirsty family quarrel, and the Crown exploited this in order to force from it the surrender of Kintyre. Kintyre went to the Earl of Argyll, and from him to his younger son. With royal approval, a burgh was founded in Kintyre, and marked the transfer of the peninsula with the name of Campbeltown. In 1614 Campbell of Calder managed to get the Macdonalds out of Islay too, by a mixture of diplomacy and force. The whole situation in the south-west Highlands was unstable because the Macdonalds had not acquiesced in these losses and the Campbells had their own family diversions. The seventh Earl of Argyll had married for a second time in 1610, turned Catholic, and gone abroad to fight for the King of Spain. He was declared traitor, but this did not mean that the Macdonalds got back Kintyre or Islay: most of the Argyll estates, which were in a bad way financially, were managed by Lord Lorne, his elder son, but till 1636 Kintyre was in the hands of the son of the second marriage. So long as the house of Argyll, which till this point had always worked in close alliance with the monarch, was officially in disgrace, there was still hope for the Macdonalds.

The reign of James VI did not bring stability or peace to the inner Highland areas – instead, by encouraging the expansion of MacKenzies and Campbells, it introduced new elements of uncertainty. James was never able to look on the Highlands as anything but a problem of law and order, as a society distorted by bloodshed and feud. This view seems to be shared by most historians of the Highlands. To read the chapter analyses of these is depressing: 'Dispute between the Earls of Sutherland and Caithness – Feud between Macdonald of Slate and Sir Roderick Macleod of Harris – Dreadful excesses in Skye and Uist – Defeat of the Macleans in Skye. . . .':[1] one would be justified in forgetting that there was such a thing as Highland civilization. An important element in that civilization was in government eyes closely connected with the feuding habits of the chiefs, the bards who sang the stories of the clan to the chiefs and people. For

1. James Browne, *A History of the Highlands and of the Highland Clans* (1849), analysis of Chapter XI.

those like James who were ignorant of Gaelic and hostile to Roman Catholicism, who disliked bloodshed and stories about bloodshed, there was no way of appreciating the more positive side of seventeenth-century Highland culture. Though the old inheritance of Celtic art was by now moribund there was real life in the poetry and music of the day. This can be recognized in the *Carmina Gadelica*, the collection of religious poetry with its elaborate use of traditional imagery. It was in the seventeenth century that the Pibroch, the 'great music' of the pipes, based on the formal structure of air and variations, was built up. The Scottish government never came to appreciate this side of Highland life, and indeed by encouraging law and order in the Lowlands, did much to cut off the two parts of Scottish civilization from each other.

At the end of James's reign some parts of the Highlands had received the geographic clan pattern they still retain. The far north was dominated by the house of Sutherland, a branch of the Gordons. Its power, and that of the McKays of Strathnaver, the north-west of the present county of Sutherland, were supporters of monarchic policy. South of these lay the expanding power of the MacKenzies, holding Kintail and now Lewis too, and with various cadet branches that stretched right across the country to Easter Ross and Cromarty. The MacKenzies and the Campbells were the two imperialist clans of the century but the great Campbell expansion had only just begun. Between their two empires lay a number of lesser clans, struggling to survive by force and guile – Macleods in Skye and Harris, MacLeans, Camerons, and the broken branches of the old Macdonald power. In the centre lay a variety of Stewart branches and the rising family of Murray: Murray and the great block of Gordons in the east were to show how clanship could shade off into the more settled landownership of the lowlands. A clan chief on the edge of the Highlands, particularly on the eastern edge, was also a landowner and enjoyed the advantages of dual status, as did all chiefs in the eighteenth century. He ruled his clan, but he also had a possible career in law or in the king's service available for those sons he chose to educate for it. In this dual position stood the Campbells, the Gordons, the Monroes, the Rosses, the Colquhouns, and some of the MacKenzies. At this upper level the two cultures of Scotland could merge, but we do not have the opinions of the ordinary clansmen on this. Merging of cultures did not yet mean that these areas could as yet live peaceably together. A chief had to be ready to show and use his armed force, and a landowner was glad of a tower house in which to defend himself.

James did better by the northern isles than by the Highlands. There the problem was not lawlessness but misgovernment. In spite of the promise of 1472 that the earldom there should not be given away except to 'ane of the Kingis sonnis of lachtfull bed' Mary had allowed her half-brother Robert, a bastard in every sense of the word, to gather together the rights and lands of the earldom and add to them those of the bishopric and the Crown. This process was complete by 1581 and Robert and his son Earl Patrick were able to rule as independent princes, combining the advantages of Norse or Scottish law as it suited their interests. James found an efficient and loyal administrator in James Law, whom he made bishop, and in 1608 was able to use him against Earl Patrick when the earl appeared to be negotiating with the King of Denmark as a ruler on his own. After an armed rebellion, which gave James the opportunity to execute the earl, the bishop was installed as sheriff and commissioner, and the central government at last had someone to activate their wishes. This lightened an oppressive dictatorship for the islanders, but dictatorship reappeared in the economic form of a stranglehold by the lesser landowners which did not lessen till the end of the eighteenth century. This kept standards of living for the majority at little more than subsistence level. The history of the islands is a reminder that British imperialism has not been an English monopoly.

The connection with English-ruled Ireland after 1603 made possible an enduring change there in the early seventeenth century, the colonization of Ulster after 1606 with lowland Scots. Ulster had been the most recalcitrant province of Ireland under Elizabeth: as a result there were forfeitures to exploit and frequent war had reduced the population. Scots went in and settled, sometimes on their own initiative, more often in organized groups whose leaders competed for grants from the forfeitures. This sort of colonization did not call for large amounts of capital: supplies could be sent in driblets across the narrow gap of the Irish channel as required. Kin would gradually follow a leader across. Slowly through the first half of the century the Scottish settlement grew: probably by mid-century the Scots in Ireland numbered 50,000, perhaps more. This again was a threat to

Gaelic society, separating its two sections. It made it certain that events in Ireland would be closely felt in Scotland.

More ambitious colonial schemes foundered. There was the idea of Nova Scotia, a Scottish colony in America in an area with the climate of a somewhat harsher Scotland. In 1621 Sir William Alexander got a charter to settle this vast district. James created the Nova Scotia baronetcies, which were to be sold to finance an expedition there. But not enough men or money were available for a serious settlement. People did not want to go, though sometimes they were ready to pay for others to do so. Those prepared for dangerous excursions could find ones nearer at hand. Probably the country just could not raise capital on the scale needed. Overseas adventures to the mainland of Europe, soldiering in the Thirty Years War or in Ireland, took the men instead. In the end Nova Scotia became little more than a name on the map and some dirty business in the honours system with a substantial rake-off for the hangers on at court. It has been frequently said that colonization failed because Scotland was not master of her own foreign affairs, but it seems more likely that the country, like England in the sixteenth century, could not raise the funds. But James in the 1620s was slackening in his efforts, deliberately load-shedding to his son and heir, Charles, as his health failed, and Charles had no special interest in the Scots.

It is typical and right that the great preacher Donne should have commemorated James in his funeral sermon first for his generosity. 'When you shall find that hand that had signed to one of you a Patent for Title, to another for Pension, to another for Pardon, to another for Dispensation, Dead: That hand that settled Possessions by his Seale, in the Keeper, and rectified Honours by the Sword in his Marshall, and distributed relief to the Poore, in his Almoner, and Health to the Diseased, by his immediate Touch, Dead. . . .' This is not just rhetoric or panegyric. It was the personal touch of James that had mattered, his gifts, his interventions, his known affection for his nobility, that had made acceptable the transformation of Scotland that he had worked. Charles, twenty-four years old at succession, the first monarch to inherit as an adult for over 200 years, born in Scotland but reared in England, had none of James's gift for giving affection, and so received little of it. It was more obvious that the king was over 300 miles away than that he was a Stewart. The qualities of

Charles that led to respect, his liking for order and seemliness, for beauty and the acceptance of authority, his real sense of religion, cut him off from his Scottish past, and his determination made it difficult for him to recognize facts or change his ways. Charles also reacted against James's personality: he disliked exuberance and was cold to men who grabbed at life, who knew where they were going and set about getting there. Where James conceived of government as the art of managing men, Charles thought of it as the creation of institutions and marking out of principles. It is true that in the long run the first attitude is not enough: but the second is not enough even in the short run.

NOTES ON DRAMATIS PERSONAE

Argyll. Archibald Campbell, seventh Earl (1575–1638), Justice General. He married Agnes Douglas in 1592 and Anne Cornwallis in 1610. In 1618 he became a Roman Catholic. James VI never liked him. His first son by Agnes was the Argyll of Chapters 12, 13, and 14, the Great Marquis. His oldest son by Anne was James Campbell, Lord of Kintyre.

Buckingham. George Villiers (1592–1628), Earl 1617 and Duke 1623 of Buckingham, favourite of James VI and close friend of Charles I, responsible for escalating the level of corruption and inefficiency in the royal court.

Carr. Robert Carr or Ker, one of the Kers of Ferniehurst (*c.* 1587–1645). Described as a new favourite of the king's in 1603; in 1611 Viscount Rochester, 1613 Earl of Somerset. Married, with much scandal, in 1613 to Frances, Countess of Essex.

Huntly. As in Chapter 9.

Bishop Knox. Andrew Knox (1559–1633), whose career illustrates the complicated mixture of functions of James's episcopate. In 1606 bishop to the Isles, and later moderator of this presbytery, responsible for the statutes of Icolmkill 1609, in 1611 bishop also of Raphoe in Ireland, 1614 active unsuccessfully at the siege of Dunnyveg, and in general deeply involved in the policy against the Macdonalds. He held both bishoprics until 1619 when the Isles passed to his son.

Bishop Law. James Law (died 1632), another semi-political churchman. 1601 royal chaplain, 1605 bishop of Orkney, 1610 Archbishop of St

Andrews and 1615 of Glasgow. It was he who separated off the lands and jurisdiction of the bishopric of Orkney from the earldom and so weakened the dictatorship of the earl.

Earl Patrick (*c.* 1585–1615). Succeeded his father as Earl of Orkney 1593. From 1599 complaints about his rule were frequent, and included accusation of piracy. Executed for treason 1615.

Earl Robert. Lord Robert Stewart (1533–93), illegitimate son of James V, married a Kennedy, in 1564 he began collecting the Crown's lands in Orkney and Shetland, in 1568 those of the bishop of Orkney. In 1581 he was made Earl of Orkney.

Chapter 11

Charles I

Brechin: reading the liturgy

A MONARCH WHO COMES gradually to the exercise of full power
never presents his subjects with the feeling of a fresh start. Charles
took over James's court and James's favourite Buckingham: the
latter fouled his relations with his English Parliaments; the former,
even when cleaned up in its more ostentatious forms of corruption,
made contact with his Scottish subjects difficult. The cleavage
between the in-group and the out-group remained severe: court life
was too expensive a gamble for any but great lords or those assured of
favour. Only a very few were sure. Charles offered real friendship to
his cousin, the Duke of Lennox, but this young man, married to
Buckingham's only daughter, settled down in the home counties and

looked on life as the son-in-law of Buckingham, a peer of the Garter, not as the representative and leader of the men of the Lennox, a vital march with the Highlands. He took his wife, his Church, his pension, and his interests from England. The Duke of Hamilton, though also married into Buckingham's kindred, was one of the few noblemen to be aware of English, Scottish, and royal issues. He was a younger man than Charles, always valued by the king and never fully trusted by anyone. Buchan has said of him, 'This was no man to ride the ford with.' The two centuries of hesitation that the house of Hamilton was to show in critical moments are personified in his great portrait by Van Dyck. There he stands in armour, to remind the public that he had taken 6,000 Scots to serve under Gustavus Adolphus, and there is the look that also reminds us that he lost most of them by inefficiency. Hamilton was to show throughout his life a magic touch that turned all to mud, a gift of invariable failure at the crucial instance. His house stood near to the Scottish throne but had no claim to that of England. Accusations that he planned treason were always at hand and probably unfounded, but his concept of loyalty was not what the king expected. Like the other great nobles of Scotland, he conceived his loyalty as first to his own house and then to the person of the king. The king's policy was another matter, to be supported where it served the interests of the house of Hamilton.

If the house of Hamilton was indecisive, the house of Huntly was wayward. It kept one foot in Catholicism. James's contemporary, whom he had tried so hard to reconcile with the Kirk, died a Roman Catholic in 1636, on his way home from a period of imprisonment in Edinburgh castle, an old venue of his, for double-dealing with the Privy Council over the Frendraught feud. His son, wild-eyed and indecisive, lacked the economic drive to make much of his great estates, the personal ability to get on with his followers, or the political talent to see the main issue of his day and decide on a coherent policy. The family had been deprived of two sheriffdoms by James, and had seen the hereditary rival, the Earl of Moray, given a lieutenancy in the north which it felt should only go to Huntly. Rothes was later to remark that 'two Fife lairds' could keep Huntly from crossing the Cairn o' Mount: 'three parts of his name is decayed'. Economic weakness and personal unreliability were the keys to Huntly. Some part of this sprang from the slow economic decline of the north-east and its general failure to make a mark in politics that emanated from south of the Border; some from Catholicism. Membership of the Catholic Church was illegal in Scotland, which it was not in England, but there was no formal system of recusancy fines to put financial pressure on Catholic houses. Still, it debarred from advancement in the state. The king could not use or benefit his Catholic lords without causing trouble with the Kirk which made such a policy unwise. Catholicism ran in the background of several important families and was a drag on their advancement. All the younger children of the first Marquis of Huntly were Catholic, and Lord Lorne had four half-sisters growing up in a convent in the Spanish Netherlands. The Catholic families did not practise the *apartheid* of the English Catholic nobility, but intermarried with Protestants. They seem to have regarded the church settlement as still open, the situation plastic. Until it changed in their favour though, they were bound to be dissatisfied and unreliable.

Below the great houses Protestantism was more definite. There was a fierce religion, held by many, which was Calvinist, anti-Catholic, and ready to see the popery it knew little of in reality in any 'novation'. These families were often linked with the Kirk: younger sons might become ministers, or daughters be married to the parish clergy. Bishoprics were now of little value, so there was no particular effort to secure them. The Kirk provided the only suitable professional middle-class career except for the few families with strong links with crown service. Its bishops were not members of great houses but useful members of the gentry. The other middle-class base was the merchant class – the families that provided the governing part of Scotland's diminutive burghs. Some of these people would be reckoned rich by any standards. There was George Heriot, hereditary goldsmith in Edinburgh, royal creditor who could lend James's queen eighteen thousand pounds at a time, at 10 per cent, and who put his money into founding Heriot's hospital. Many of the loveliest houses near Edinburgh are built on estates bought in the seventeenth century on the proceeds of trade and money lending – Mellerstain, Prestonfield, Penicuik. There was even the tycoon Nathaniel Udward who negotiated a monopoly in soap for several years. These people lived well, if in cramped space. They would have houses or flats among the huddled 'lands' and 'wynds' of the towns, having their luxuries in the form of feather beds, big stocks of linen, carpets on the tables, silver and glassware, and sometimes even glass in the windows. It was a way of life with commercial standards, valuing money rather than display, but not refusing opportunities of display when they also meant comfort. Merchants would be reproved for trading in grain when it was short, or trading with Catholic powers, and sumptuary laws were repeated against them with a frequency which suggests ineffectiveness. These men might still know the states of northern Europe at first hand, from travelling in person with their goods, and were more sensitive to foreign politics than even the much travelled aristocracy. Religion was of invading importance. When in the 1690s Sir John Clerk of Penicuik filled the back of his rental with commentary on the minor prophets he was showing the mixed interests of his trading parentage in profit and religion. This religion, Calvinist, was not always Presbyterian. In the north-east episcopacy was valued, and rightly, for there was there a succession of distinguished bishops, as well as the foremost university of Scotland. St Machar's in Aberdeen still kept its portrait of the Virgin and Child 'in curious work', there was the crucifix on the Old Town cross, and others set in private glass windows through the town. In the south, especially the south-west, it was more common for any form of ceremony or ornament to be equated with popery, and episcopacy was accepted grudgingly – but even so it was valued in Glasgow. That it was not valued in Edinburgh partly came from the long-standing reputation of the town's ministers for quarrelsome Presbyterianism, and also from the fact that the new bishopric of Edinburgh, created by Charles, involved heavy local expense in adapting St Giles to become a Cathedral.

Below the middling classes of Scotland, things were not prosperous. The small urban working class had seen its real income fall in the inflation of the mid-sixteenth century. The lesser tenantry of Scotland farmed by archaic methods and had no hope of gathering the reserves necessary to make a change, to break a vicious circle. All sections of society benefited by the relative peace of James's later years, but famine was always on the cards. It had occurred in 1587, and again from 1594–8, which were years of famine and epidemic throughout Europe. At least once every decade in the first half of the seventeenth century corn prices in the Lothians went up so sharply that one must deduce famine. In the 1630s they did so twice. There was little aid for the starving. The Poor Law passed by Parliament in 1579 was advisory and permissive only. It acknowledged that the infirm had a right to relief, and left it to the magistrates to do something about this. The great emigration of the seventeenth century is a commentary on the failure of the Scottish economy to expand as fast as the population. If Ireland received 50,000 Scots or even more,[1] perhaps as many or more went to Europe. Hamilton took his 6,000: in all Gustavus Adolphus received into civil and military service at least 20,000, perhaps 30,000. There was the Scots Brigade in the Netherlands. Over 6,000 Scots are known to have been raised for service in Denmark in 1626 and 1627. Over 11,000 went to France. Others went to Germany, to Poland, and to Russia. All this might add up to 100,000, but this figure might still be much too low.[2] Perhaps a tenth of the total population left Scotland, and not many of this number came back with a fortune made. If they survived the wars they went to serve they would settle where they were, leaving miscellaneous Scottish surnames in the upper echelons of eastern Europe, and families without surnames in the lower classes.

By going abroad they were relieved of the growing discipline and pressures of life in Scotland. The kirk sessions and the presbytery increased their hold on the daily life. Sabbatarianism came in. In the first generation after the establishment of the reformed Church, all that Sunday observance had meant was the cutting down of tavern hours and markets to prevent these amusements competing with sermons. At the end of the sixteenth century Aberdeen was still maintaining this degree of regulation, but then Aberdeen was a town which still kept the feasting of the old Christian year; enormous blowouts at Yule and Pasch went on till 1641. The far north still had its pleasures – it was said to keep Christmas till Shrove Tuesday, and Shrove Tuesday (Fastern's Even) was a binge everywhere. But in the rest of the year in southern Scotland the Protestant abandonment of saints' days meant that Sunday alone was the great break in the working life, the day when religious practice took over. So it was

1. Wentworth for instance put the Ulster Scots not at 50,000 but at 100,000.
2. As a comparison, the great exodus from Castile that began the settlement of Spanish America in the first half of the sixteenth century is estimated at 150,000 from a population of 6½ million.

G

natural to emphasize it further. By the end of the sixteenth century, Sunday markets were being legislated against in many towns, and bans were out against the overflow of activities from Saturday or Monday markets. Perth, in 1599, objected to carriers using the Sunday to walk home. Kirk sessions everywhere pressed steadily on the riotous, disorderly, and licentious, and though the reading of their records does not convey the impression that this discipline was effective, it shows the current of godly opinion. Down came censure on brawling and fornication, over-eating at banquets, and drinking orgies at weddings. The violent and exuberant outlets of a people hemmed in by poverty and overcrowded living, in small, mean houses with uncertain food supplies, were all under attack by Charles I's reign. In return for this discipline the new Kirk offered the sense of being one of God's elect, and a deep familiarity with the thought and imagery of the Bible. Men heard the Bible regularly: all heads of families who could were expected to read from it to their households. Most still could not, but the Kirk knew its duty lay in teaching them. It had not forgotten the plan of the *First Book of Discipline* for schools. In 1633 an Act of Parliament allowed the bishops and parishioners to rate the parish for a school – this was later to be made compulsory though without much increasing its force.[1] Godly landowners in the Lowlands were often willing to pay for a parish school, either voluntarily or by assessment, but it is likely that reading remained a minority skill throughout the seventeenth century. The towns were ambitious for their young, and took pride in grammar schools, the grammar being Latin. Beyond these, Scotland was over-supplied with universities: it was rare for all four to be in a state of numerical and intellectual health in the seventeenth century. St Andrews drew the nobility: Aberdeen was intellectually the leader: Edinburgh, only founded in 1582, was the junior partner.

It is fortunate that Scotland was not yet fully literate. At the upper end of study she was not producing intellectual figures of European renown. Her doctors were old-fashioned in opinion, her theology was sterile. Napier of Merchiston was a shining light but no first-class mathematician followed him. Buchanan's latinity was a thing of the

1. Whereas the English rating system stems from the Poor Law, the Scottish came from attempts to support the parish school. The contrast is a significant example of different values.

past, and though he had advanced exciting constitutional ideas on a bogus historical framework in his *History*, James VI had seen where these were tending and had taken care to ban this book as soon as he was in control. The great achievement of Scottish literature in the seventeenth century is the body of popular ballads. These came from a tradition of entertainment that did not rely on the written word, and had not been suppressed by the reformed Kirk. The tunes and some of the themes were often old, but the living nature of the art is shown in the number of seventeenth-century events embodied in the words. In particular the last manifestations of old Border society, with its feuds and violence, its background of magic and ritual, live on in an unequalled cultural achievement. The Border eventually succumbed to law and order, but it went down with song.

Law and order, even in the relative achievement of the late sixteenth century,[1] had unattractive elements. Government had to be paid for: the servants of the Crown were more numerous than in the past, could not be supported by ecclesiastical appointments, and were acquiring a taste for luxuries from English and French acquaintances. Charles had a better business head than his father, and saw that he could not live from hand to mouth. Taxation, still conceived of as an exceptional item in government finance, had occurred four times in James's reign since 1603. With Charles it became almost annual, and hit not only the landowners but *rentiers* too. The customs were revised to a more realistic level. The machinery of royal control of Parliament did not make it easy effectively to oppose the king's demands. Charles did not care to listen to complaints. He had his new body of financial servants, the New Octavians, and unlike James he stuck to them.

Charles had other demands to make. He saw, both in England and in Scotland, that something must be done to secure to the reformed Church a bigger and a more reliable share of the wealth of the old Church. In England this problem rumbled on throughout the reign. In Scotland it was dealt with briskly, as quickly as its vast nature could allow. A Scottish king was expected to make an Act of Revocation at the age of twenty-five, calling back the grants of his minority,

1. How relative it was can be seen by comparing the suppression of the Essex rebellion in England in 1601 with the mild treatment James had to offer to equally outrageous movements by Scottish nobles in the 1590s.

and in Charles's case this meant at once. Charles's Act was unusually wide, and cancelled all grants of crown property since 1540, and all temporal lordships made out of ecclesiastical land. The next year the king showed that this second section was not to be merely the means of minor adjustment. Clarification went on: the church property was not to be resumed by the Crown but would be held by present owners 'upon reasonable conditions'. The settlement was worked out in detail. For the most part the old monastic temporalities stayed in lay hands, but teinds were returned to the farmer and composition arranged for. Stipends for the clergy would nominally be no larger than of old, but would be more secure and drawn without the intervention of the lords of erection: the method of collecting them would give no opportunity for these lords to oppress the heritors and tenants, to 'thrall' them. The feudal superiorities over other people's lands were to be bought back for the Crown. All this was settled finally by Acts in 1633 – not a long period considering the complexity of the question, but far too long for the goodwill of those noblemen whose estates and incomes were involved and who had had eight years of insecurity and rumour to live through.

The new settlement gave the Church security and prevented teind being a drag on agricultural development later (England had to wait till the nineteenth century for a commutation Act for tithe). Gardiner has called it 'the one successful action of Charles's reign' and added that the nobles had no real ground for dissatisfaction. Others have said that the settlement took nothing from the nobles that they ought to have had. But if the Scottish nobility had not in practice often possessed powers and property that it ought not to have had there would never have been a problem in governing it. What evidence we have shows that the nobles had not been handing on to the Church her true share of stipend; besides financial loss they now had to do without the widespread power that they had enjoyed through feudal superiorities and the control of teind. The people who gained from the settlement were the ordinary heritors, the gentry: these were not yet a class whose opinion mattered in state affairs, for they could not stand up to the great lords politically. The story of the Crichtons of Frendraught reminds us of what happened to families that opposed their local magnates.

'The ground stone of all the mischief that followed after' is a contemporary's description of the Revocation. This brings up sharply the problem of the breakdown of James's achievements in government under his son. What was the basic reason for the storm that, starting in Scotland, destroyed the old monarchy in England, Scotland, and Ireland in the mid-seventeenth century? How far were the tensions in the three kingdoms similar? How much can be learnt from a study of other European disorders (and there were many of them) in the century? These questions are raised by the attempt of various recent writings to postulate a common crisis for European governments in that century.

Leaving aside the problem in semantics of a 'crisis' that extends over a whole century, a theory would be attractive if it could weld together all elements of discontent and connect them to a single line of development. One important element is said to be economic decline: that after a period of rapid economic growth, rising population and new trades and industries, there was a long term recession, a reduction or a halt in population expansion, a shrinkage in trade, perhaps a drop in production, and certainly a failure to take the next step forward into more capitalized production. Perhaps the end of the great European price rise could mark this change. The end of expansion makes the overweighty court and expense of government intolerable: both in structure and in theory it is repudiated, and the breakdown follows.

Apart from the inherent difficulties of a theory that thinks of the step into capitalized production as a single matter in differing countries, it is difficult to slip Scotland into this picture. Yet if the picture is to be convincing for Britain as a whole, Scotland, where the Great Rebellion of the seventeenth century began, must be part of it. In Scotland the economic growth of the period before had been slow: probably the population stopped increasing in the 1590s; at any rate further expansion was not reflected in rising food prices (in terms of silver), as it appears to have been in England. There were new economic developments but they were not transforming in their effects. Coal and salt were now commodities for export, as well as hides and fish, and coarse fabrics went overseas to most northern markets. But the main element in increased prosperity seems to have been peace. The country had certainly not outgrown an immediate dependence on peace at home and abroad and tolerable harvest weather for security. A bad harvest would send food prices soaring in individual years: with better weather, once the seed corn that had been eaten had been replaced, they would be back to the same level as thirty years before. There is no indication of a long-term recession, nor of a previous period of sharp economic growth.

The other aspect of a seventeenth-century crisis fits Scotland a little better, the picture of an overloaded government machine, an expensive court, the exclusion of some restless elements from profit or employment. For the first time in her history the country had something that could be called a bureaucracy, men from lesser ranks of the nobility and from the gentry, who served the Crown for most of their lives in the Exchequer, the courts, in troublesome areas such as the Border. This had to be paid for, and Scotland had also to pay her share in military expenses and preparations for defence, in a time when the cost of war had soared. But the vital element in government was still personal confidence in the king. The authority of the machinery of government was dependent on acceptance of its methods by the great lords, and even by lesser ones. If they did not accept them there was very little to be done about it.

So the Scottish breakdown goes back to the older theme of politics, to policy and methods. The one thing a Scottish king could not afford to lose was confidence. When the nobles of Scotland saw their power curtailed by the loss of teinds, and their finances too in all probability, they were filled with mistrust. They may have had an inkling that Charles's advisers in England, particularly Archbishop Laud, were trying to build a financial basis for the Church there, a Church they knew as more ceremonial than their own, and regarded as dangerously near to 'popery'. More serious was Ireland. If we have only recently discovered what Charles's government was up to in Ireland,[1] our seventeenth-century ancestors were under no disability of ignorance. Contact between England and Scotland was slight, but between both countries and Ireland was constant and considerable, because of the new settlements there. Nothing travels faster than suspicion: new planter classes are insecure and intolerant and alert to danger; the Ulster Scots were loathed by Wentworth, later the Earl of Strafford, the Lord Deputy of Ireland. Wentworth was enforcing the royal authority, raising unusually large sums in taxation and riding over the

1. As for instance in H. F. Kearney, *Strafford in Ireland* (1959).

interests of both old and new occupants of land. All landowners must have felt their estates in danger of sharp judicial practice. The policy in England and Ireland was nicknamed 'thorough', and in the seventeenth century the word thorough was the same as through. It meant a policy of steam-rolling of opposition, of making a decision and carrying it out in spite of all efforts at bargain and negotiation by those affected. Part of this policy was aimed at the establishment of funds for a Church using methods of worship distasteful to 'puritan' feeling in either England or Scotland. The leading figure of this Church, Laud, probably had more influence with Charles than had any other man. Charles's delayed coronation in Scotland in 1633 enabled his nobility to see that the king had a personal reverence for bishops. There had already been a row at James's funeral, when Archbishop Spottiswoode had turned up in the approved apparel of the Scottish Kirk and, finding himself expected to put on lawn sleeves (which were not part of it), had refused and left the procession. In 1626 Charles had tried to give the Scottish archbishops precedence over his lay officials. The Chancellor, Hay, had refused and threatened resignation: 'never a ston'd priest in Scotland should sett a foote befor him so long as his blood was hotte'. Charles gave way grumbling, calling the Chancellor privately, but not privately enough, an 'olde canckered goottische man, at whose handes ther is nothing to be gained bot soure words'.[1] In a mood for tidiness, Charles had re-moved the judges of the Court of Session from the Privy Council, probably an error from the point of view of the law, since the Council still carried a lot of decisions, and certainly one from the point of view of the efficiency of government, for these men, always at hand in Edinburgh, were the most reliable attenders and the most efficient part of the Council. In their place, several bishops were installed, and bishops, like the lawyers, were professional men who could be expected to turn up for meetings. If they did not, the Council was in danger of frustration since Charles had increased its quorum. Eventually the quorum was brought back to James's figure of seven, but the Council still felt the lack of the large body of the judges. The nobility grudged the bishops power. Except as officers of state they themselves were not prepared to put in the work Council needed, but they disliked seeing this done by bishops, and by bishops who were

1. The spelling is not the king's but the Lord Lyon's.

not members of the great houses as they had been before the Reformation. Charles went on to make Archbishop Spottiswoode Chancellor on the death of Hay, Lord Kinnoull, in 1634, a sharp reminder to the nobility that it was men outside their order who had the king's confidence.

There was a subtle danger in Charles's system. James had known his nobles intimately and liked the official class among them. He could jest in broad Scots about 'Tam o' the Cowgate', as he called the first Earl of Haddington. In a country where attachments and loyalties ran in the mould of families, he knew which kin had served him well and would do so again. Charles's touch was more distant and the bond of kinship escaped him. He was capable of ignoring a young and able member of an official family, such as the Earl of Montrose. Forgetting generations of service, he did not find a place for the earl, who consequently moved towards the group of opposition nobles.

This group is the most significant political feature of the early years of Charles's reign. It started with the nobles disturbed by the Act of Revocation. The Earl of Rothes, Lord Loudoun, and Lord Linlithgow had gone to London to protest at this. Loudon and Rothes were marked out again by Charles's disfavour when the king came to Scotland, but Rothes was a brash and forceful figure and Charles such a cold fish anyway that Clarendon was later to complain that the disfavour was not as obvious as it should have been. Charles's presence in Scotland showed the Scots how their king liked his church services conducted, and a lot of heat was engendered when he altered the vestment of ministers. There was an Act of 1609 conferring this power on the king, and Charles demanded surplices. He also listened to the English prayer book.

The Parliament held then was not an occasion of goodwill. 'Of 31 Acts and Statuts concludid ... not thre of them bot wer most hurtefull to the liberty of the subiecte,' reports the Lord Lyon, Sir James Balfour. Opposition was so open that Charles took a note of those who voted against his measures. Opposition failed to defeat the ratification of past church statutes but Rothes claimed that the division result had been faked. An opposition petition against church innovations and high taxation was refused by the king. Charles went on to have one of its compilers, Lord Balmerino, tried for 'leasing treason', which we today would call sedition, and the long-drawn-out case went to conviction, but only by the President's casting vote. After a considerable delay the death sentence was changed to a royal pardon. Charles saw Scotland as a country where irregular services were held in mean churches by ministers who prayed and exhorted their flocks at enormous length *ad lib*. The Church needed money and regulation and should get them. Because he could frustrate political and religious opposition, he ignored it.

The story of the origins of the Scottish rebellion has marked resemblances to the Catalan revolt of 1640: a slowly developing policy that systematically annoyed the upper classes and filled them with suspicion, and then a particular action that enraged the mass of the common people. In 1635 Charles issued a collection of canons for the Kirk without bothering to consult or call a General Assembly. These canons had certain features unpopular with the more puritan section of the Kirk – the communion table was to be at the east end of the church, and extempore prayer was forbidden – but their main significance was that they seemed to assume that the machinery of government of kirk session, presbytery, and General Assembly did not exist. Charles was already getting work done on a new liturgy: the *Book of Common Order*, which as a whole the Kirk used, was felt by many to be inadequate, especially in the form of its communion service. James had begun work on a liturgy, but it had been suspended to allow feeling to cool down after the affair of the Articles of Perth. This was now scrapped, and the whole task begun again.

The new liturgy of 1637 has been a much maligned document: it is commonly and untruthfully described as Laud's Liturgy or the English Prayer Book. It is customary to talk about it in Scotland today as if any liturgy was a sign of popery, and as if the present Kirk did without one. The new book was created on Charles's order by the bishops of the Scottish church, and vetted by the king, but no General Assembly had passed it. In several places it paid particular attention to traditional Scottish forms and preferences. But Charles himself, brought up on the Anglican Prayer Book, and sharing with Laud a vision of a Church docile, seemly, and uniform, extending to all his people, was not prepared to allow that his two kingdoms should worship the same God in conspicuously different manners. King and peoples alike held the opinion that there was a right and a wrong way of doing things, and that the right way should extend to both countries. Both countries contained a large body of vocal puritanism; in England this had welded itself to political opposition, and for the king to license religious forms in Scotland which he did not permit in England would have been to encourage this opposition. For this reason he could not grant the demands of the Scottish puritans. An example of this was shown in the treatment of the Apocrypha. Protestantism had moved from the position of Calvin that the Scriptures are the sole authority of the Church, to the cruder belief that all Scripture is divinely inspired. This attitude made it impossible to allow to the books of the Apocrypha the position of partial canonical authority which was traditionally theirs: either they were the Word of God or they were not. As King James remarked, 'some of them are as like the ditement of the spirit of God as an Egge is to an Oyster'. On the other hand they contain passages of great beauty and force. Charles insisted on retaining portions from them in the liturgy, particularly sections from *Wisdom* and *Ecclesiasticus*, and because the lectionary could not be longer than the canonical year, this meant, as an opponent put it, that there were '120 chapters of Canonick Scripture, whilk, by the course of this new Bible, the people of God shall never hear in publick'. The difficulty of reconciling in practice a Church which gave authority to the Ecumenical Councils of the Early Church, and so to a source other than Scripture, with one which did not, does not seem to have occurred to Charles.

The new liturgy was to be the norm: it was to be read in all churches, and imposed on all a change in their habits of worship. This in itself was a policy which would only be successful if put over by a government sensitive to the various strands of contemporary opinion. Charles, who had already roused unprecedented opposition in his Scottish Parliament, which was not an organization in which opposition was easy, pushed on. Hitherto he had mainly come up against members of the nobility, but the new liturgy gave the opposition mass support, and Charles was opposed at all levels. In the High Kirk of St Giles riots broke out, or were organized, and the bishop of Edinburgh was mobbed: Bishop Whitford of Brechin read the new service through with a pair of loaded pistols on the desk in front of him and his servants armed at his side, and had no trouble. Answering the threat of force with force was effective but it was hardly the best way to encourage religious devotion. Most of Charles's governing class in Scotland was of a more equivocal attitude. It did not like the way things were going, and saw no need to help them on. The Lord Advocate, Sir Thomas Hope of Craighall, though he had prosecuted Balmerino, was an old man of strongly puritan temper: his diary gives little sense of surprise at the Edinburgh riots, and it is possible he knew they were coming. The Privy Council may well have thought that riots were the sort of fact that would force the king to change his line: it saw no reason to run risks in opposing them. Rioting in the capital was an effective, if expensive, way of bringing home to the king what he could not do. It was for Charles to make a rapid retreat – as Elizabeth of England had done in 1601 over monopolies – and later work out a compromise. The difficulty was that monopolies were a secular matter: neither Charles nor his subjects were prepared to compromise over how God should be worshipped.

Compromise would involve big surrenders. The opposition nobles seem to have been surprised by their popular success, but they were readier than the Privy Council to exploit the situation; they were more united, and they did not have to wait on orders from London. There are indications that even before the riots these men were in active alliance with some of the leading ministers of the Presbyterian faction; if not, they were soon after. The High Street of Edinburgh and the wynds off it swarmed with demonstrators, gentlemen, and ministers who came up to town to bring petitions or join in the protests against royal policy. Edinburgh, with all sections of society packed into tall houses with no segregation, the great ones on the first floors, the shops below and the craftsmen above, the single great steep street, with the tolbooth and court and Council all to be found in it, where everything went on; Edinburgh is a city perfectly designed for making riots and demonstrations effective. After a second major riot in October 1637 Charles tried the method of subduing the city so successfully worked by James: he ordered the Council and the Court of Session to remove. The capital is not a port; its business and prosperity depend on its political status. If the nobility had backed the Crown in opposition to clergy and citizens, this method would have worked, but this time the alliances were different. The only result of this royal proclamation was to bring about a formal supplication from the leaders of the nobility and clergy that the bishops should be removed from the Privy Council while the grievances of the Kingdom were considered. The bishops included the Chancellor. The protest was now openly against the machinery of Charles's government. The autumn days were shortening fast and petitioners could not indefinitely hold out in the city – like the Red Guards in Peking they created sanitary problems for which the city was not equipped. Many of them also needed to supervise the collection of their Martinmas rents, which were usually paid in grain. They set up a permanent representation in Edinburgh, elected representatives of the different 'estates', two gentlemen from each province, a minister from each presbytery, a burgess from each burgh, and a group of nobles, and departed. These representatives became known as 'the Tables'. They formed a revolutionary government in the capital, and since their followers could terrorize the Council, power and initiative lay with the forces of revolution. Charles in London, despising the ambivalence of his Council in Scotland, did not realize how divided was its loyalty, nor how paralysed its power of action. Even when the Duke of Lennox, in Edinburgh for a family funeral, reported back on these points, he could not make Charles understand the atmosphere in his northern capital.

It is interesting to stop for a moment and compare this revolution with the last successful one in Scotland, that of 1567. Both had been made possible by an alliance of nobility, ministers, and mob. But on this occasion the country was far more united. And it was considering more permanent political changes. In 1567 all that had been done was to bring in a child king: after a generation royal power had reasserted itself more emphatically than had been known before. The new revolution was aiming at formalized constitutional changes. It was harking back to a reaffirmation of the 'liberties' of the nobility in a medieval sense, but it was coupling these with the rights of the other Estates and of the General Assembly; and these demands were to be translated into law and enforced. Behind all this stood, not the negative opposition of 1567 to the private life of Mary, but an embattled puritanism which Charles I had never understood or allowed for.

The final aims of the revolutionary party have not been considered enough by historians. They were more than a harking back to the baronial free-for-all of the fifteenth century. Perhaps at the end something like the government by the nobility that Poland achieved at the end of the seventeenth century was in men's minds – a drastically weakened royal power, a Council and Parliament in which the nobility was supreme, and a highly disciplined Kirk working closely with this nobility. There was also a nationalistic aim, a reaction against English influence, particularly the influence of the English Church and its bishops. But the Revolutionaries were aware that the revolution could not be confined to Scotland. 'Whatever the Prince grants, I feare we presse more then he can grant; and when we are fully satisfied, it is likely England will begin where we have left off,' wrote the percipient minister Robert Baillie, who already fore-saw a 'bloudie Civill warr'.

At the end of February 1638 the revolutionaries made their next move, the drawing up of the famous National Covenant. The move for this came from Alexander Henderson, a leading minister, and Archibald Johnston of Wariston, a young and skilled advocate, a man with deep personal religion and ecstatic experiences, who had one foot in fanaticism. Wariston had already been involved in drawing up protestations against the royal proclamation. The legal mind looks for precedent: it was found in the old Negative Confession that James VI had subscribed in 1581. To this were added long lists of the Acts of Parliament either opposing Roman Catholic practices or establishing 'God's true and Christian Religion ... the liberty and freedom thereof' and the system of church government by presbyters and Assemblies that maintained it. Then came a General Band of the traditional Scottish sort, an agreement 'to be made and subscribed by his Majesty's subjects of all ranks' to defend the reformed religion, to support the king; and finally a declaration that the 'innovations' in religion would be 'subversion and ruine of the true Reformed Religion and of our Libertie, Law and Estates'.

The National Covenant was thus a lengthy and turgid document. It made no express attack on episcopacy, though it carefully left this item out of the description of the church government that was to be supported. A constitutional movement could hardly ignore the fact that the bishops were a legal part of the Church, and the Covenant was designed to seem as conservative as possible. It was expressly anti-Catholic, but it was possible for sincere supporters of the mixed church constitution of Scotland to subscribe. Part of the strength of the Covenant was its sheer unreadableness: subscription was to be demanded from many who had not read it, or could not read through its four thousand odd words and balance its long, involved legal clauses. But its final section, the promise of active resistance to innovation and support of the Law of the Kingdom, could be clearly understood as a demand for a free Parliament and General Assembly and the threat of total resistance until these were granted. At times its language became, like the Declaration of Arbroath, a trumpet call to unity and action. Through it all ran the Old Testament analogy, the concept of a nation binding itself in a special relationship to God.

Moderate and involved as many of its statements might seem to be to careful interpretation, they were not immediately acceptable all over Scotland. The agitators who had come back to Edinburgh thronged into the churchyard of Grey Friars to sign, and the citizens followed, for Edinburgh was a stronghold of puritanism. Copies were taken all through the country, but in Glasgow the university not only would not sign, but was inclined to argue, and Aberdeen was intransigent. Most nobles signed, though it was accepted that those on the Council could not. Lesser folk subscribed, perhaps less willingly. Subscription was difficult to evade, since it was done in church, 'publickly, with an uplifted hand'. As Baillie commented in April: 'Our country is at the poynt of breaking louse; our lawes this twelve moneth hes been silent; diverse misregards their creditors, our Highlands are making ready their armes, and some beginn to murder their neighbours.' King James's peace was over. The structure he had created to control and modify the use of force was gone. Take-over bids had to be accepted. Presbyteries deposed ministers who had approved the new Liturgy or were of known anti-Presbyterian temper. 'The ringleaders of the covenanters among the ministrie,' says Spalding from Aberdeenshire, 'left their own Kirks and went throw the countrie ... deposed whom they pleased, and admitted in their roomes others of the Covenant.' The Tables began buying arms and drilling supporters. In reply, the Treasurer, Traquair, ordered arms for Edinburgh castle, but because he could not install them there, garrisoned Dalkeith castle instead. Fighting was imminent, and for the present the Covenant ruled in most regions. As a hostile witness notes: 'Disputes bred no small trouble to the consciences of good christians ... not knowing whom to believe, for salvation of their sillie souls.' Most of the country, willingly or not, set its hand to the Band: 'We promise, and sweare by the Great Name of the Lord our God, to continue in the Profession and Obedience of the Foresaid Religion: That we shall defend the same and resist all these contrary errours and corruptions, according to our vocation, and to the uttermost of that power that God hath put in our hands, all the dayes of our life.'

What was King Charles to do to regain his rebellious kingdom?

NOTES ON DRAMATIS PERSONAE

Balmerino. John Elphinstone, second Lord (died 1649), son to one of James's new nobility with whom the king had quarrelled. He got his own back on the monarchy as President of the 1641 Parliament.

Hamilton. James Hamilton, third Marquess and first Duke (1606–49). Clarendon says of him he had 'more enemies and fewer friends in court or country than any other man'. He paid with his life for inheriting an English peerage. He had married at fourteen a sister of Buckingham's: all his children died young.

Henderson. Alexander Henderson (*c.* 1583–1646), minister of Leuchars. A long-faced elderly gentleman in his portraits, a leader in the resistance to the prayer book, proposer of the Covenant, one of the men of widest understanding and sympathies on the Covenanting side.

Sir Thomas Hope of Craighall (died 1646). Of merchant family, a lawyer of great reputation, Lord Advocate 1628, conducted the Balmerino trial for the Crown, but managed to keep a foot in both camps till 1638. Even then legalism kept him from being a whole-hearted Covenanter.

Johnston. Archibald Johnston of Wariston (1611–63). An advocate, helped compile the Covenant, Lord Clerk Register 1649, remonstrant leader. Carlyle has called him 'a man full of fire, of heavy energy and gloom'.

Kinnoul. George Hay (1570–1636), Chancellor 1622–36, Earl of Kinnoul 1633. His estate included church temporalities and some of the Gowrie lands given by James VI.

Lennox. James Stuart, fourth Duke (1624–55). Duke of Richmond 1641. A grandee of Spain, a Knight of the Garter, an international rather than a Scottish figure. The conspicuous consumption of the day was shown at his wedding party which involved sixty cooks.

Linlithgow. Alexander Livingston, second Earl (died 1648). He had Roman Catholic family connections, became a royalist and an engager.

Lorne. The Argyll of Chapter 12.

Loudon. Sir John Campbell of Lawers (1598–1662), first Earl of Loudon 1633 by marriage into the Campbells of Loudon of James's new nobility. Chancellor 1641, a leading Covenanter until 1653 when he went royalist, too late for Clarendon's approval. Clarendon says he was notoriously a loose liver.

Montrose. James Graham, fifth Earl and first Marquess (1612–50). A cultivated man of great pride, charm, and ability, a poet and a soldier.

Rothes. John Leslie, sixth Earl (1611–41). His career is marked by opposition to the Crown from the Articles of Perth to the second Bishops' War. Contemporaries agree that he was more concerned for his church temporalities than for religion. 'Very free and amorous,' says Clarendon.

Spottiswoode. John Spottiswoode (1565–1639); historian of the church, a pupil of Melville's, a new Octavian, Archbishop of St Andrews 1615, Chancellor 1636. Where possible he was a moderating force in policy, holding profanity as as great a danger to the Church as superstition.

Traquair. John Stewart, first Earl (died 1659), Treasurer 1636. Clarendon calls him 'a wise man' but 'not a man of interest and power with the people, but of some prejudice'. Balfour, Lord Lyon, is less generous: 'Fear of the Kinges and bischopes displeasure, one the one hand, and preferment on the other, did altogider extinguishe that professed zeall (if any was in him) to the peace of his native countrey.'

Chapter 12

The Great Rebellion

Argyll he has mustered a thousand o' his men
He has marched them oot richt early.
The Bonnie Hoose o' Airlie

THE MEANING OF THE Covenant that so many of the Scots had subscribed is worth a little attention. On the one hand it was a generalized
form of the old rebellious Band which Scottish nobles were accustomed to form when they planned a stroke for power. But the religious overtones of the word soon overshadowed this aspect: it was not
only a Band between men but an undertaking to God. By keeping it
the Scots would emulate the Jews as a chosen people. A generation of
men and women reared on biblical story, in which God had safe-
guarded and preserved his people against enormous odds, could
easily grow to see the Covenant as a means by which something special
lay in store for them. From this came two of the characteristics of the
later Covenanters, a narrow national conceit and a belief that the
normal needs of support for a movement – political backing and
military strength – could be ignored. God would secure the victory
of his own in his own cause against all odds; the cause would be made
known by those who claimed to have direct authority and guidance;
the generals and the politicians must do what ministers and mystics
decreed.

But this was still in the future. At first what the Covenant meant to
many was rebellion; rebellion led by the aristocracy and therefore
more against the civil than the religious establishment. The Scottish

aristocracy was reared in habits of war, even if not always efficiently. Within a month of the making of the Covenant it was raising funds – in the form of a 'voluntary' tax on rents. This was to be paid by supporters, but not all who took the Covenant were real supporters. In many areas it was unsafe to stand out. The concept of a compulsory and binding promise to God was incompatible with freedom of conscience, but so long as the Covenant was interpreted in its literal sense it was compatible with a reverence for episcopacy and so could be accepted by those who did not want Presbyterianism. Even so the north was resistant, and the doctors of Aberdeen refused to subscribe without royal authority. The young Earl of Montrose and various leading Covenanting ministers were sent north in July to persuade the resistant city. Aberdeen had just seen the ceremonies of bravery at the funeral of Lady Huntly, a lying in state, an enormous procession, the shooting off of the town's 'haill ordinance for ane good night', after which the Marquis had taken his vast household and ten children back to the country 'in high melancholie'. After such a display of the old attachments and way of life the city was in no mood for the new ideas. Wine and sweetmeats offered to the embassy were spurned so long as the Covenant was unsigned, so the provost and baillies, offended, gave the banquet to the poor. It was an unsuccessful visit. The issue of the adherence of the north was not to be settled by preaching but by force, and neither side was ready for this yet.

Charles always preferred negotiation to fighting, and at first he had to, for the English military machine was so rusty that it would take a year for it to be ready for action. That the smouldering discontent of his English kingdom, from two reigns of growing disagreement with the monarch over church and foreign affairs, and ten years of taxes and other governmental devices that many regarded as illegal, would make an English army almost useless, had not yet occurred to the king. The trouble was that, as with other famous negotiators, the words Charles might use did not necessarily carry his real adherence and consent. He had sent Hamilton north; there was really no one else he could use of great standing, uncommitted to his opponents. 'Flatter them with what hopes you please,' ran his instructions, but the Covenanters must not be declared traitors until the fleet could set sail. Hamilton brought two alternative proclamations: both played it cool about liturgy and canons; these were not to be pressed except in a 'fair and legal way'; in both the Covenant must be given up, but only in one was force clearly threatened. Enough information was leaked about both to make the more moderate one ineffective. There were public protests and secret haggles. The Tables demanded a total withdrawal of canons and liturgy and also a free General Assembly and a parliament. Charles had given Hamilton power to purge the Privy Council of the disloyal, but this he dared not use, even against the Lord Advocate whose refusal to call the Covenant illegal paralysed action against it. The king issued a rival 'King's Covenant', which did little more than denounce popery: so rabid had ecclesiastical opinion become that Johnston of Wariston called it 'atheism' to subscribe it.

A General Assembly had to be granted. The difficulty was that in the atmosphere of tension it would certainly not be 'free'. Men, never very far from the use of arms, were getting ready for trouble everywhere. Rothes's cousin, Field Marshal Alexander Leslie, 'an old, little, crooked souldier', the man who had frustrated Wallenstein's attack on Stralsund, had left the Swedish service and slipped back to Scotland in spite of Charles's attempt to blockade the coast, and Leslie, though only semi-literate, knew how to organize a war. There was, in many men's minds, an image of what a truly Presbyterian General Assembly should be, and now was the moment to carry it out. It would be a meeting of laymen and clergy, the only laymen 'ruling elders', sent by the presbyteries. Instructions went out from the Covenanters as to what kind of clerical and lay representatives should be chosen. Local groups of ministers and gentry packed the presbyteries, and if that did not get the right sort of members, the General Assembly was expected to disqualify all those who had cooperated in the church policy of the Crown. As a last resort there was simple terrorization. It was still in no way unusual for ministers to carry arms: it was inevitable for crowds to be dangerous. When the Assembly opened in Glasgow in November the episcopal party dared not attend, and as Hamilton said, it was for God to 'judge whether the Least shadow or footsteps of freedom can be discovered in this Assembly'.

Hamilton's words came when he was forced to recognize that he had lost control. He at least had not been terrorized. Glasgow lay in the heart of his own power. He had been frankly outmanoeuvred by the production by Wariston, elected clerk to the Assembly, of the old registers of the early Assemblies, those from the years before 1590 when James had been fighting for control of the country and the Assembly had experienced the first Presbyterian take-over bid. Though many denied the authenticity of these books, and the originals are now burnt, their copies fit in entirely with what we know of the opinions and language of the dominant party of the Church at that date. There was still an uncommitted body in the Assembly, even with these doctrinaire registers laying down Presbyterian principles and denouncing bishops, for Hamilton found considerable support when he attempted to get the returns of lay elders disallowed as not a normal part of a General Assembly. But he was defeated here, and this he saw ended his control. He called on Henderson, the elected Moderator, to dissolve the Assembly, but Henderson was shouted at to refuse. Hamilton walked out, and was followed by all but one of the Privy Councillors present. The sole exception was of immense importance for the future, the new Earl of Argyll. 'I take you for members of a lawful Assembly,' Argyll had said after Hamilton's protest against illegality. The compliment could not be returned since Argyll's own presence in it had now no legal justification by any system of law. He had been present as a Privy Councillor, not as an elder. But it was all-important. His open adherence gave the Covenanting party the support of one of the biggest magnates in the country. His estate might not be the wealthiest but it had the greatest military strength; 5,000 clansmen who could be put into the field, and on the edges of the Lowland zone. It also gave them the best political intellect in Scotland. The young earl, who had just succeeded his father, was a man of deep religious conviction, personal power, and the ability to hold his own counsel, daring in political decisions though unable to support these with military nerve; his reserve was enhanced by the disconcerting gaze that a slight squint gives.[1] Alone among the great feudatories of Scotland he had had no foreign education: he was even now seeing to it that his heir should be brought up speaking Gaelic as well as English, for language was a vital instrument for control of the clan. He had taken over his un-

1. The best-known portrait, as a middle-aged man in a skull cap, appears to exaggerate the squint: in the earlier ones it is no more than an ambivalent divergence. With the fashionable long hair, of typical Campbell light orange, and the pale skin that accompanies it, he must have been striking to look at.

stable father's estate and cleaned up the worst of its confusions, and even obtained Kintyre from his half-brother. In July Charles I had been considering enlisting the support of the Earl of Antrim, a Macdonnell ('a man of excessive pride and vanity, and of a very weak and narrow understanding', in Clarendon's judgement), by granting him Kintyre, and leaving him to take an army across from Ireland to renew Macdonald power in the peninsula. The plan, frowned on by Strafford and others, had remained no more secret than other plans in the great, disorganized, and only half-loyal court. It is the sort of scheme that gives the impression that Charles was taking a course in how to lose friends and make enemies. The resistance in Scotland had developed beyond Rothes's old opposition group and found leaders of greater spiritual and intellectual force than Rothes – Henderson, Wariston, Argyll, and the young Montrose.

The resistant Assembly, now openly illegal, held together by the determination of the nobility, went on to show how it interpreted the Covenant. The bishops were summoned and, in their absence, deposed and excommunicated on various charges – the evidence used on the tough old Bishop of Brechin illustrates the bogus nature of many of these: 'he was proven guilty of sundrie acts of most vile drunkenness: also a woman and child brought before us, that made his adulterie very probably; also his useing of massie crucifixes in his chamber'.[1] The Kirk was purged of ceremonies, of the five Articles, of the new liturgy, and half a dozen insufficiently Presbyterian Assemblies, those of the latter part of James's reign, were annulled. Most important of all, a permanent commission was set up to clean all divergent opinion out of the Church. As Spalding despairingly wrote:

> This was the first incomeing of committees that ever was heard of, in like fashion, within this Kingdome, and which bred thereafter meikell sorrow against the King and his subjects; for within the haill burrows of Scotland, the cheifest men of the covenant dwelling within ilk shire, barons, burgesses and ministers, had their committee . . . abuseing the King's leidges with greivous burdens, levie of men, money, horse, arms, taxation. . . . If any subject minted

---

1. Perhaps it is from this period that the Scotch name for the plant the English call 'ground elder' was coined, as 'bishops' weed'.

to arise to defend the King's authority, in any part within Scotland, advertisement ran frae committee to committee. . . .

Kirk and state now had each their revolutionary executive.

War came, as foreseen, in the spring. Montrose first showed a skill at manoeuvre by slipping into Aberdeen with a small force and collecting the anti-Gordon elements of the north. While the internal royalist element was thus neutralized, the main army of the Covenant took the royal castles – Edinburgh, Dalkeith, and Dumbarton – almost without fighting, and marched on Berwick. It was furnished by levies on the citizens, by loans from the greater merchants, and equipped with ministers to keep up the crusading spirit. Against it, Charles's troops from a disaffected country, unwilling to pay taxations regarded as illegal, were clearly not going to fight well. Wisely the king decided that negotiation was better than defeat. At Berwick in June he promised his rebellious subjects a Parliament and an Assembly. Both sides were prepared to evade definitions of these institutions and to look as if they trusted each other. The first Bishops' War was over. The most dangerous legacy it left was the Scots' belief in their own invincibility. Faced with a retreat by Englishmen who did not wish to fight, they believed that the English never would or could. It is true that the Scots had an army, the English a collection of troops, and that organization was more important than numbers in seventeenth-century war. But organization could be quickly created, given the will, and numbers would then tell.

The two main infantry weapons of the day, musket and pike, did not call for eighteenth-century standards of drill, but they were useless except in the hands of men accustomed to acting together and accepting discipline. Compared to the highly trained individualist fighter of the Middle Ages the troops of the mid-seventeenth century seem a bunch of amateurs, but there is all the difference in the world between amateurs with some practice at co-operation and those with none. One of the most heinous crimes of poorly trained troops was throwing away their weapons when in flight, and when we look at the weapons we can see why they would do this.

The old match-lock musket was a heavy instrument.[1] Its barrel was

1. Surviving examples in the armoury of the Tower of London weigh between $11\frac{1}{2}$ and 15 pounds.

four feet long and troops often supported it with a rest when firing. It had heavy appurtenances – it fired a bullet of an ounce or more. It took twenty-nine orders to pass from 'Unshoulder your musket' to 'Give fire'. Carelessness by musketeers might mean either that men let their match out when they should not, or let their left hand, carrying the double end of lighted match, get too near the bandolier of their neighbour which hung at his right side with twelve powder charges inside it. It is not surprising that the Highlanders, who knew something about fighting, still often preferred bows and arrows: they were safer and had a faster rate of fire.

The nearest equivalent to the pike is a sixteen-foot punt pole, though many commanders held out for eighteen feet, and anyway a punt pole is lighter. A little practice with one will bring home to any-one that the pike was not a weapon capable of rapid movement, nor one that could be redirected by massed infantry without co-ordina-tion. Undisciplined troops might saw a foot or two off their pikes to use as firewood and to lighten their burden, and this might be dis-covered only in battle when the planted rows of pikes were not long enough to cope with charging cavalry, or when infantry met 'at push of pike' and one side could push farther than the other.

The ability of any state in warfare was not necessarily related to population or wealth (any more than it is today), as the great achieve-ments of Sweden had shown, but to a government's ability to deploy its resources. But, as Sweden had also shown, someone had to pay for all the fighting, and a small country would do much better if it could pass on this burden. It was the Scottish achievement in the inevitable second Bishops' War to make the English pay for the privilege of being invaded.

The second war came because what had stopped the first was more a distaste for war than an active wish for settlement. The Scots were more open in their breach of agreement than the king: they failed to disarm. Charles disarmed willy-nilly because he could not afford to keep troops together. But at bottom he never meant anything that the Scots would have accepted as a free parliament or Assembly. Dis-trusting the Scots, he did not wait in the north for these meetings. The Assembly of 1639, sitting at Edinburgh, was even more in-transigent than that at Glasgow, and decreed that episcopacy was contrary to the law of God. Since neither Englishmen, nor Scots, nor king, had yet attained to a sophistication that would allow the law of God to differ in the two realms, this was an attack on Charles's position in England which he could not allow. The Parliament, freed from the mechanism of royal control by the absence of an Estate of bishops, fell into the hands of the revolutionaries. The new Committee of the Articles was elected by each Estate for itself, nobility, barons, and burgesses. This committee confirmed the Acts of the Assembly and made the Covenant compulsory. When prorogued by the hesitant Traquair, it reassembled illegally and appointed a standing Committee of Estates to take control of the revolution.

So the Scots were asking for war again. Charles called the 'Short' Parliament in England to raise funds, the first parliament after eleven years of mounting mistrust and discontent. Strafford, who had had experience of coercing parliaments in Ireland, had assured him that this one could be managed, but Strafford was half-crippled with gout and none of the other advisers of the king had skill at parliamentary tactics (this had not been needed in the king's service of late). Against them emerged Pym as a leader who had learnt opposition in the 1628 Parliament and not forgotten it. The Parliament, faced by an unprecedented demand for funds, dug in its heels and demanded redress of grievances first. There was reason to think some members were already intriguing with the Covenanters, so Charles hurriedly dissolved it without getting any money, and had to manage the war on what he already had.

There was a bit more fighting this time. Montrose led the Scots across the Tweed in August 1640 in a sweep round Berwick, turned the English army back at Newburn on the Tyne, and occupied Newcastle. Here he controlled London's vital coal supply. The forces of England, says the churchman Baillie, 'fayled like summer brooks'. Peace was made at Ripon with the Scots openly master. They were to be paid £850 a day in pay, which they took from the northern counties of England until Parliament should raise it. Thus they forced Charles to meet and keep his new Parliament, the 'Long' Parliament of the Civil War. It was the high moment of Scottish power and unity. The Long Parliament, meeting at the end of 1640, was to take the initiative from the Scots and face the king with the prospect of the destruction of his principal servant Strafford and the systematic reversal of his policy, until agreement with his intransigent Scottish subjects seemed easier than with it.

The unity of the Scots was not so absolute as it seemed. There was, however, as yet no effective leadership for those who wished to stand out against the Covenant. Churchmen would gulp at each new revolutionary morsel in Church or state, and then swallow it, and regard their previous position as incredible. Behind acceptance of the Covenant was more than a hint of violence. Non-Covenanters were a good source of supplies of confiscated grain for the army. Some felt that Montrose had shown 'too great lenitie in spareing the enemies houses' in Aberdeen. Argyll did not suffer from this fault and worked for the purification of the Kirk and the aggrandizement of clan Campbell. In the summer of 1640 he swept through the southern Highlands, as a terror to 'newtralists', with a commission of fire and sword from the committee of Estates. Highlanders disciplining each other were not apt to be gentle. Old scores were paid off against the Murrays of Atholl and the Ogilvys of Airlie, in spite of the fact that Montrose had given protection to the Ogilvys, who were his kinsmen. Argyll looted and burnt their two chief houses of Forther and Airlie.

> It fell on a day, on a bonnie summer's day
> When green grow oats and barley
> That there fell oot a great dispute
> 'Atween Argylle and Airlie.

Rivalry was incipient between the Covenanting leaders, Argyll and Montrose. Argyll had shown it with force, which was not his *métier*; Montrose was to retort with political scheming, which was not his. Two months after the burning of 'the bonnie hoose of Airlie' Montrose formed the 'Cumbernauld Bond', a pledge with a score of other nobles who were also disturbed by the political advantage of Argyll, to promote the public ends of the Covenant against private advantage. This did not stop Montrose leading the army into England, but he wanted more than fighting, and during the peace negotiations started to correspond with the king. Charles was not particularly interested, but the correspondence got Montrose and his immediate adherents gaoled for the summer of 1641.

By then the political revolution in Scotland had gone even farther The Parliament of 1640, meeting without royal permission, passed a

Triennial Act, laying down that 'a full and frie parliament' must meet at least 'every thrie yeir', and established full control over its own committee. It was half of a claim to parliamentary sovereignty, and it was enforcing that sovereignty as no government had before.

We need not feel that the heavy hand of discipline on the Scots was unwelcome or new. The Scotch peasant or townsman was used to close and arbitrary control, and the criminal law could be both savage and immediate. The town of Edinburgh was quite capable of decreeing hanging for people found guilty of concealing the plague. Kirk sessions everywhere went through a seemingly endless series of disciplinary cases of fornication and sabbath breaking (and in the case of fornicators with remarkably little effect it seems: the same people would be under judgement a year or two later for a similar offence). In tough cases the sessions' spiritual discipline was backed up secularly – town councils would put the recalcitrant in 'the jougs'[1] or 'douk' or banish them. Landowners would also fine and banish in their baron courts. The death penalty would be enforced for misinterpretation of the Church's law on consanguinity. What is striking about the new level of kirk discipline achieved by the revolution is its intrusive nature and its extension to the upper classes. The Dowager Lady Huntly is forced to go abroad to die to avoid subscribing the Covenant: otherwise she would risk confiscation of her lands. Lesser gentry, to whom this way out was not open, had to perjure themselves if of Catholic or episcopal sympathies. We find the new intruded Covenanting minister in Aberdeen claiming that none of his flock could be ready to take Communion for two years. The presbytery of Strathbogie could order the Lady Frendraught to Communion, and at least force her to church. Prison was available for the recalcitrant Catholics of lower status. So long as political and religious revolution went hand in hand, the Scottish lairds and nobles would submit to the same discipline that they gave their lesser folk and families: only when the two movements diverged would it seem irksome, and even then many would be unwilling to oppose the enlarged claims of the organized Church to control behaviour and intent. So it was eventually from the theocratic government of the later revolution, and not from a secular state, that the nobility were to learn discipline and the submission of private to national interest.

1. An iron collar which acted as a pillory.

Meanwhile apparent unity was helped by the creation of a new nomenclature. The advisers of Charles I were 'incendiaries', and it was the aim of the Covenanted party to pull them down, whether Scottish or English.

Charles had made some progress in learning how to use friendliness. He detached Rothes from the rest of the party. But Rothes, now a dying man, had not the brains to hold the leadership. A more realistic sign of the location of power was the contrary movement of Hamilton: rather than be classified as an incendiary he would come to terms with the Covenanters. Charles partly approved of this new alignment: Hamilton might act as a valuable intermediary with Argyll. The king did not realize that Hamilton was treating and manoeuvring not as his servant but as a great magnate on his own.

The negotiations about paying off the Scottish army ran on into 1641. The Covenanters sent Commissioners to London. Baillie, the minister, was one of them and has left us a picture of the excursion. In a new lace waistcoat, bought for the trip, he rode down through England marvelling at the palaces that served as inns, and wincing at the cost of everything. They came as ambassadors to both Parliament and king, and as missionaries to an unenlightened Church. They planned to show the English how to overthrow episcopacy and erect instead the full machinery of Presbyterianism, except for a General Assembly. The Scots, looking at the English Church in much the same way that imperial politicians look at the parliamentary achievements of colonies, considered a General Assembly would have to wait until parliamentary committees had purged the English Church, for 'the far most of their clergie being verie corrupt'. Schemes floated before the minds of the Commission of reforming other parts of Christendom, France, or Italy. Meanwhile they hoped to destroy the English 'incendiaries', and they wondered at the sluggishness of the English in accepting Presbyterian discipline.

If religious change was slow in England, the political change went as far as the Scots dared hope. The king could not evade having a parliament, nor could he get rid of it until the Scots were paid, and in this parliament was to be fought out the shadow play of coming Civil War, the duel between Pym and Strafford. Pym was backed by a large body of the parliamentary classes, an opposition that Charles had created which held a puritan distrust of royal religion and of the bishops as its instruments, a feeling resembling in a minor way that already shown in Scotland. There was also anger at the insignificant position of England in continental affairs, and a refusal to pay the money that might enable her to play a greater part; to some degree there was a distrust of the part she might play. These elements had been inherited by Charles in the country left to him by his father, and in a few years he had embarked upon the interpretation of his rights that led to governing without Parliament, raising money by methods many thought illegal for policies they loathed and pushing the uncertainties of the law as hard in his own favour as had Edward I. Now at last the opposition had its chance to shackle the king, and Pym would do this as soon as he could get Strafford out of the way. The duel between these two bold men took all winter and in the end Pym won. Under him the Long Parliament destroyed Strafford, imprisoned Archbishop Laud, borrowed the idea of a Triennial Act from the Scottish commissioners, wiped out the king's prerogative courts (the teeth of his administration), and went on to force the king to accept that this Parliament could not be dissolved without its own consent. This final victory, only achieved in the last days of the struggle for Strafford's life, when the king's perceptions were clouded by personal guilt and grief, was a seizure of sovereignty and went well beyond the demands that revolutionary Scotland had as yet made. Charles would now look on Scotland as the less recalcitrant of his two kingdoms. Perhaps he could negotiate there and gain support against the rising and organized opposition in England. So in August 1641 Charles was on the road to Edinburgh to seek terms and friendship and support in Scotland.

The visit was not a success. Charles was never to let himself negotiate freely with a real intention to abide by the agreement reached. He had not yet seen where support might lie in Scotland, and would probably not have known how to ally with it if he had seen it. He failed to enlarge the crack that had opened between Argyll and Montrose. Argyll was not to be won over and Montrose was in prison throughout the king's visit, lucky indeed to be no worse off – one of his lesser supporters whom he had cited as evidence against Argyll's plans had been executed for 'leasing making', spreading disaffection between the king and his subjects, and it is not clear who the king was in the minds of those who passed the sentence. Argyll, Leslie, and

Hamilton constructed, or took part in, what was either a plot or a counter-plot, an obscure episode nicknamed the 'Incident', in which Hamilton and his brother and Argyll fled in the night from Parliament and left it to the king to assert ineffectively that there had never been a threat against them. The Scottish Parliament demanded from Charles even more than his English one, the right to control appointments to office. It is possible that, in the stress of grief over betraying Strafford, Charles did not see what he had given to the Long Parliament. But he certainly knew what he was about in Scotland, and cannot have meant to let the essence of royal power go for good. As a French envoy was to remark a couple of years later, 'this country is a republic in all but name'. Charles had given way, but no one could believe that the surrender would be permanent. He also distributed honours and titles, not very wisely, under coercion from the Parliament, and put his chief opponents in office: Loudon in the Chancellorship, Argyll as one of the Commissioners of the Treasury. In the middle of these tussles over power the dreadful news came through of rebellion in Ireland.

The Irish revolt was not only the opening of tragedy for Ireland, the end of the hope of any settlement there that could combine the older Irish civilization with the new plantations, but it was also the source of passionate ill-will among many of the king's subjects in his native island. English and Scots were kith and kin with men whose lives and fortunes were now in danger, and that danger, if not caused, as they sometimes thought, by deliberate engineering on the king's part, was at least the direct outcome of a policy supported with unprecedented royal consistency. The Irish rebellion was caused more by fear that the growing power of the English Parliament would lead to further land confiscations in Ireland than by actions of the king, and the rebels nominally revered the authority of the king. In practice they would accept it only so far as it suited the old Catholic interest. If the king wished again really to rule in Ireland he would have to regain control there by force, yet at once this fact brought up the issue of who was to exercise the powers that Pym and his party were removing from the king's grasp. It showed that there was no way now open for moderates, for either the army was the king's, and the shackling of the king had failed, or it was the Parliament's. This is why the Irish revolt was followed at once by the developments in the House of Commons that split the country openly: the Grand Remonstrance (a general attack on the king's religious and political policy) and the Militia Bill which claimed for Parliament the control of the army. Because the Grand Remonstrance was as much an attack on Church as on king, the king found himself with a large share of the moderates on his side in the struggle over the Militia Bill. But in practice moderation was over, and this was shown by the king's unsuccessful attempt to arrest his enemies in January 1642, his flight from London, and in the summer of 1642 the start of Civil War all over England.

Scotland remained strangely inactive as her neighbour moved into Civil War, and for a year after the day the king set up his standard at Nottingham in August 1642. The Scots sent General Monro to fight against Catholic Irish in Ulster, but Ulster was a direct Scottish interest, and the Earl of Antrim, with whom Charles had been intriguing about Kintyre, made it a particularly close interest of Argyll's. There was a minor flurry of paper activity at the end of 1642 when both sides in England asked for help. The Privy Council leaned, by a narrow majority, to the king if he would promise to guarantee Presbyterianism. This was Hamilton's scheme for keeping Scotland loyal. Two rival petitions were sent in to the Council, and the General Assembly threw the whole of its authority against the royalist one, the 'cross petition' as it was called, which asked that the peace of Scotland and the king's honour be maintained. Presbyteries were ordered to act against all who signed it: sermons were preached against the 'malignant petition'. 'Malignant' was the new jargon for all who disagreed with Presbyterian dominance. A rift between the Church and the nobility in the Council had begun. Charles was refused aid, but Hamilton was still optimistic that he could keep the Scots at peace for another year. He miscalculated: they were waiting in a posture of biased neutrality, to see what Parliament would ask and offer.

In spite of having on his side the most brilliant professional commander in the country, his nephew Rupert, who had learnt his fighting early in Germany and had had time to study the theory in prison, Charles failed to win the war in the first summer when he failed to press through to London. This repulse probably decided the eventual defeat of the king, since it left him without the population and wealth of the chief port, and the cards for long-term war were in Parliament's hands: Parliament had the greater resources in taxation and armaments. But this was not apparent in 1643, and things looked bad from the Parliamentary side. The Parliamentary forces were knocked to pieces in the north of England, and were already weak in the west and south-west. Parliament could not retain Bristol or Exeter, and Hull, which was on its side, was under siege. By the late summer Pym, who was dying, saw outside help as vital to his cause, and was prepared to give away a lot to get it. He looked to Scotland, and after a long diplomatic silence events now moved fast. The Scots demanded a religious commitment, and threw the very shape of the agreement into a religious form. The English Commissioners, led by Sir Harry Vane, who was Independent in his religion, obtained a little latitude in the possible interpretation of this, and then accepted. So, in September 1643, was created the preposterous undertaking of the Solemn League and Covenant.

The Solemn League and Covenant was an agreement to work together to reform the Churches in England and Ireland in doctrine and discipline 'according to the Word of God and the example of the best Reformed Churches'; to preserve the reformed religion in Scotland; to extirpate popery and episcopacy; and to bring the three kingdoms to uniformity in religion, peace, and union. Those who opposed or resisted were to be brought to trial and punishment.

It is difficult not to wonder at the mentality of the Scots who insisted on the religious form of this bargain and the ecclesiastical nature of its terms. Since Flodden they had recognized that they could not defeat the English in a war on English soil. They knew not only that a fair half of England wanted the episcopal Church to continue – it was on this issue that Charles had been able to create the royalist party at the end of 1641 – but that a substantial segment of the other side wished for Independency, for self-governing local sects. They were aware that the insertion of the words 'the Word of God' was to keep a small door open for Independency. It is true that the door was small and only just ajar: the insistence on preserving the Scottish system, and on uniformity in religion, left little real room for Independency; and the Scots were sure that a literal use of the text of the Bible could be made that would convince all sincere listeners of the intellectual soundness of their claim that Presbyterianism was the only system in conformity with the Word of God. (Whatever the Word of God might mean to ecstatics like Johnston in their private devotions, in general parlance it now meant the collection together of chunks of biblical quotation torn from their context and used with total disregard of history.) The effective stifling of religious disagreement in Scotland itself may have been taken by the Covenanters for agreement. God would move with their army and his victories would turn this into active co-operation. Yet the bald fact of the bargain remains almost incredible: the dominant party in Scotland committed the nation in an oath to force a minority religion on two larger and more populous countries. To cover up the preposterous nature of this decision, it was asserted that the taking of the original Covenant implied all this. From now on the Covenants were one.

Yet what practical alternative had the 'malignant' party been able to offer in 1643? It was all very well for Montrose to claim that the king had freely given what his Scottish subjects asked, and it was for them to be loyal in return. Charles never meant to leave the settlement as it had stood in 1641. No one who regarded monarchy as more than a name would have acquiesced in it. And Charles did not feel bound in agreements he made with his subjects. 'A subject and a Sovereign are clear different things,' was his tenet. The trouble was that the Scottish nobles had been too greedy in 1641: they had asked and got too much. To defend one error in judgement they had to make another. They had to commit themselves to the impossible or they would be attacked. The greatest power in Scotland, the Marquis of Argyll, was particularly sensitive to the form the attack might take, for Charles was again airing the scheme of an Irish invasion in the west of Scotland, and an Irish invasion in 1642 was a threat of a very different order from one in 1638, for the Irish were impassioned and backed by the Crown. Argyll's own position was at risk now, but in a successful war he might secure it permanently. After all, he now held, or dominated, much of the area that had made up the old Lordship of the Isles. Even if monarchy was effectively recreated for Scotland as a whole it might never be more than nominal in this great Lordship, if Campbell rule were once well established.

The English attitude to the bargain was simpler. They would swallow commitments for the future for immediate help. In November the military agreement was worked out. The Scots would send a vast army, 20,000 men, of which 2,000 would be cavalry. The English would pay for it and control its use. Whatever the terms of the League, the Scots were not coming to the war as an independent political force. But they were represented in the controlling body, the Committee of both kingdoms, set up by the English Parliament, which had 21 English members to 4 Scots and a quorum of 2. They also sent observers or speakers, but not full members, to the Westminster Assembly, which was discussing the reform of the English church. Johnston of Wariston, and a young and driving politician, Lord Maitland, soon to be Earl of Lauderdale, attended as elders, and Baillie, present as a minister, has left us a detailed picture of its meetings. We can see it warmed by one of the few good fires to be found in a London bereft of its Newcastle coal. The few Scots among a hundred English expected to carry enormous weight as the exponents of Presbyterianism in practice. They had no intention of modifying anything in their church practice, and it was up to the English to realize that sincere Presbyterianism meant copying Scotland. So we find them resolutely staying away from Pym's funeral (there should be no exception to the disuse of such worldly pomps); urging the Assembly to ignore the Christmas holiday; pressing for the system of presbyteries and ruling elders and shaking their heads over the English inclination to 'bot a lame Erastian presbyterie'. The Scots, used to no single repository of sovereignty, were dismayed to find that the English would not allow the Assembly to legislate: in England law could come only from Parliament, and between Assembly and Parliament there was room for the growing minority of Independents to manoeuvre and work for toleration in church government experiments. The Scots had no use for toleration at home or abroad, and unwisely behaved as if it were for them to decide whether it should exist in England. In the end the Assembly produced, and the Scots accepted from it, the Confession of faith by which the Kirk today is bound, a splendid piece of seventeenth-century theology and language, crudely supported by the miscellaneous quotations from the Bible which were regarded as proofs of its truth, and the catechisms that explain it. It also approved a metrical version of the psalms which has lain like a wet blanket on Scottish poetical talent ever since. But it did not and could not establish Presbyterianism on the Scottish model in England. The Scots had got something from

H

their endeavour, but it was not to seek catechisms and Confession that the Scottish army crossed into England in January 1644. Leslie, now Lord Leven, who had sworn not to bear arms against the king again, led the troops, explaining that the hazard to his religion justified oath-breaking. The Scots expected a walk-over like those of 1639 and 1640. They were surprised to be repulsed at Newcastle, and settled down for a long and grinding siege of the town. Leslie's position might be doubtful but his army could attack the king with perfect legality, for it was commissioned under powers surrendered by the king in 1641. It was a conscript army, but discipline in the army was not necessarily much more severe than discipline at home. It carried with it a regular quota of ministers, armed, and was well supplied from a good harvest.

The Scottish politicians had hoped that Montrose would lead the army, and flushed with relief at evidence that he had opposed the plan to use the Earl of Antrim as invader, had shown their hand to him. Montrose's objection had been to an invasion led by Antrim: not to the service of the king or the use of Irishmen in Scotland. He was determined that if he was to fight he must do so in alliance with the resistance in the north and act with the full authority of the king. This was not secured till three months too late. Before Montrose had royal authority the north flared up in the spring of 1644: Sir John Gordon of Haddo had tried to force Huntly into open resistance. But the movement had collapsed, and the government of Scotland had dealt with Haddo and his supporters as had been forecast in the Solemn League, the first systematic executions of the Covenanting struggle. Whereas the Civil War in England only began to rouse bitterness, to lead to executions of prisoners and reprisals at the very end, in Scotland the demands of the Church and the acquiescence of the government led to slaughter from the beginning of the fighting.

Too late to support the rebellion in the north, the Irish actually did come: not the unstable Earl of Antrim with his penchant for being captured, but a young chief of gigantic size, Alastair Macdonald, son to Coll the left-handed, or Coll Ciotach, of Colonsay, who landed with his men in Ardnamurchan. There were well over 1,000 of them, Macdonalds and allies, and with them their families and cattle, a tribe on the march.

Argyll got ready to deal with the invasion when it should reach a more central and settled area. There were enough troops left in Scotland for a band of marauding Gaels. Not all the main army was locked in the siege of Newcastle. Leven and some of his subordinates, William Baillie, a routinely conscientious professional soldier, and David Leslie, who was something more and perhaps the ablest of the Covenanting generals, went south to join in besieging the king's northern army in York with the Parliamentary armies. There, at first outwitted by Prince Rupert, they met him on 2 July 1644, in the battle of Marston Moor, just outside the city. The battle was a close thing and a muddle: half the Parliamentary army fled the field and with them old Leven, who fetched up at Wetherby. But cavalry charges by David Leslie and Oliver Cromwell, and a determined stand by Baillie with the Scotch infantry, turned the battle into a victory and the capture of York. Perhaps it was natural for Cromwell, Parliamentarian and Independent, with a real belief in the active support of God, to claim in his first report that the Lord had given this great victory to Parliament, and to play down the Scottish part. The Scots in London felt that their army had shown its value, but the Independents made out Cromwell as sole victor, because they could not afford to enhance the political power of the Scottish Presbyterians. Wetherby, after all, is a fair way from York. While grumblings in England could be heard at the high cost of the Scottish army, and the disappointingly small contribution it had made, the Scots were horrified to hear of a real menace in the heart of their own disciplined kingdom. Montrose had crossed the border in disguise, and walked into Blair Atholl to meet the Macdonalds and the local clansmen whom Argyll had called up to throw them out. A first-class general, carrying the king's commission, had joined up with an army anxious to fight, and in territory where his own power lay. In the next few weeks of the fine autumn of 1644, the best season in the year in central and eastern Scotland, Montrose led his army to victory outside Perth, to the sack of Aberdeen, and then looping through the Highlands exhausted Argyll on a fantastic chase. At Christmas he took his Irish through the passes of the southern Highlands to loot the Campbell headquarters of Inveraray and sent the Campbell chief scuttling for safety down Loch Fyne. Pinned by his enemies in the Great Glen, Montrose swerved back through high and snowbound glens that no one thought an army could take, and smashed Argyll's army at Inverlochy in the New Year. Campbell military strength would never be the same again. The Estates took away Montrose's title and declared his life forfeit, but this was small compensation for a brilliant campaign. Montrose had used the rapid marching power of Highlanders and Irish and the effectiveness of their charge, in a day when the musket was a slow and inefficient weapon and the fixed bayonet still not thought of. But it was three months too late to win Scotland for the king. All the campaign did was to demoralize and embitter the Scots in their political struggle with the English. Just when they had finished off the siege of Newcastle and might have been free to join in the main campaign the Scots were weakened by the need to send troops home for defence. If, as Robert Baillie had commented in 1644, 'all things are expected from God and the Scotts' in English eyes, neither were now playing true to form. The Covenanting technique for dealing with the failure of a policy considered divinely inspired was to go through an agonizing re-think and tighten up the policy on the existing lines. It was not possible that there could have been a mistake about God's will. The more Montrose revealed the existence of anti-Covenanting opinion, the less the government of Scotland was prepared to placate this real and important element.

Montrose's campaigns have an attraction that is perhaps misleading. Partly this springs from the character of Montrose himself: with the immediate group round him he presents a standard of honesty, generosity, and decent dealing which is conspicuously absent otherwise in seventeenth-century Scottish politics. The military performance was outstanding, and is only slightly diminished in today's imagination by the fact that many main roads now follow the lines that he and his men took among the hills, 'thryce around from Spey to Athole', or through the broad glacial Glendochart to Dalmally, marching the hundreds of miles that confused their opponents and showed they could not be overtaken. The only time they were nearly caught, by William Baillie sent north from the English campaign, showed Montrose's ability and personal ascendancy at its greatest; he got his men away from looting Dundee and out of one gate as Baillie came in at another, and then cast back to shake off the pursuit in the night in the race for the hills. The difficulty of assessing all this lies in the negative quality of his ultimate aim – a sincere

adherence to the Covenant of 1638, and yet to monarchical government. Not for nothing did he come of a family that traditionally
served the Crown. Montrose could write;

> My dear and only love I pray,
> Be governed by no other sway
> Than purest monarchie.

Even without the complications produced by the adaption of the
term 'Covenant' to the Solemn League and Covenant, the refusal of
the king to accept the decisions of 1638 meant that Montrose could
never have a positive programme to offer. His was an appeal to those
who disliked the political and religious tyranny of Argyll and the
Covenanters. Charles had broken with Hamilton at the end of 1643
and imprisoned him for double dealing – Hamilton's younger brother
Lanark had escaped and was fighting with the Covenanters. Huntly
was back on the fence, and Montrose's marches in and out of Aberdeenshire were aimed at drawing him in. There was no leader except
Montrose in Scotland for those who opposed Argyll.

The only long-term effect of Montrose's campaigns was the weakening of the Scots in relation to England just at the time when the
anti-Presbyterian party on the Parliamentary side came to the fore.
'The greatest hurt our poore land gott these fourscore years, and the
greatest disgrace befell us these thousand,' Baillie had written in
alarm in October. 'If we get not the life of these wormes chirted
out . . . the reproach will stick in us for ever.' By April 1645 everyone
in Scotland was fearing Montrose at their gates. Messengers went out
from frightened towns to learn where he had last been seen. Plague
had broken out in several towns. Robert Baillie was puzzling over the
aims of God, who seemed resolved to humble the Scots by 'fifteen
hundred naked Scots Irishes' (James VI had not been alone in regarding Highlanders as barbarians). As the sects gained in political and
military power in England the English began to be dilatory about
paying for the Scottish army, and then condemned it for being ill-
provided and inefficient: having assigned it a largely holding job in
the north they then noticed that it had not been present at the decisive
victory of Naseby in June 1645 which shattered the king's army, lost
him his equipment, prevented him from breaking through to join
with Montrose, and established the Independent Cromwell as the

military master of England.[1] After Naseby the effort of the war went into negotiation instead of fighting. Messages, terms, offers, went back and forth, but the king would not surrender so long as things looked bright in Scotland. Montrose had collected an army with Gordon cavalry to enable it to engage with the Covenanters in a pitched battle. He came south, fooled General Baillie by crossing the Forth where he was not expected to, and then, when Baillie came floundering after him, met him in a chosen and entrenched position at Kilsyth on the edge of the Campsies. It was that rare thing for Scotland, a sweltering hot day in August. Baillie was handicapped by an advisory committee appointed by the Estates, which had not learnt caution in dealing with Montrose, as he had, and over-ruled his judgement. Montrose was not at all put out by some of the Highlanders starting the battle before he intended. The Highlanders fought unplaided in the heat in their saffron shirts and on ground which was nothing to men used to running barefoot over peat hags, but which prevented Baillie from using his cavalry adequately. Montrose swept the Covenanting army down the hill in flight, and Scotland was at his feet. Kilsyth lay on the most important road in Scotland, that between the upper Forth and the Clyde, the vital cross-communication of the country. The government of Scotland was toppling. Argyll and the Committee of Estates fled to England. Montrose, as King's Lieutenant, called a parliament. Noblemen and burghs made their peace with him and paid for it in cash to his army. Charles received the news that Scotland was won for him, and then came silence. While Montrose's army was expected in England, rumoured to be there already, most of it had melted away. The Gordons had gone off in a typical huff, and most of the Irish, not interested in the problem of governing lowland Scotland, or in the English war, and unwilling to enter a long campaign, had left to pay off a few more scores with the Campbells. What remained was caught off guard by David Leslie at Philiphaugh in the Borders in the early morning September mists. Montrose rode away defeated along the old track over Minchmuir to refuge in the Highlands.

Montrose had shown the extent of the opposition in Scotland. The Covenanters, regaining power, had no intention of meeting any of this half-way. The weeks after Philiphaugh were a time of penalty and

1. Clarendon's phrase is that at Naseby 'the King and the Kingdom were lost'.

punishment. The captured soldiers were slaughtered, and their camp-followers. Town councillors, who had recognized the fact of victory at Kilsyth, were deposed and imprisoned. Meanwhile the Scottish army tried to extract seven months back pay from the English. A flurry of negotiation took place. The French sent an envoy to try to reconcile Charles and the Scots. The king's last English army surrendered in March 1646, but the Prince of Wales was got out of the country and Charles disappeared from his Oxford headquarters. On 5 May he rode into the camp of the Scottish army outside Newark and surrendered.

NOTES ON DRAMATIS PERSONAE

References are freely made to the three most obvious contemporary sources. These are:

Baillie. Robert Baillie (1599–1662), minister of Kilwinning, professor of divinity 1642, and Principal, Glasgow University, 1660. His historical value comes from a relatively conservative point of view, and from the series of newsletters which he sent to his kinsman, the minister to the Scottish congregation at Campvere.

Clarendon. Edward Hyde, first Earl (1609–74), Charles II's chief political adviser in exile, who wrote his *History of the Great Rebellion* in his second period of exile, after his fall from the Chancellorship in 1667.

Spalding. John Spalding, clerk to the consistory court of the diocese of Aberdeen, and author of a *History of the Troubles*, which, as its name implies, deplores the whole Covenanting period.

Argyll. Archibald Campbell, eighth Earl, first Marquess (*c.* 1606–61), the Lord Lorne of Chapter 11, the strongest political intelligence in seventeenth-century Scotland.

Baillie. General William Baillie, illegitimate son of Sir William Baillie of Lamington, a professional soldier under Gustavus Adolphus, and of some competence.

Cromwell. Oliver Cromwell (1599–1658), the most effective organizer and general of the Civil War, unwilling architect of Britain's only period of military dictatorship.

Hamilton. James Hamilton, first Duke, as in Chapter 6.

Huntly. George Gordon, seventh Earl and second Marquess, inherited 1636, executed 1649. Contemporary accounts and his portrait show his 'peacock head', his suspicious glance, and his total indecisiveness.

Johnston. Archibald Johnston of Wariston, as in Chapter 11.

Lanark. Hamilton's brother and heir, William Hamilton, second Duke, Earl of Lanark 1639, born 1616 and killed at Worcester 1651.

Leslie ; Leven. Alexander Leslie (*c.* 1580–1661), 1st Earl of Leven, 1641. Born out of wedlock to a 'wench in Rannoch', an 'old, little, crooked souldier' of high professional standing.

Leslie. David Leslie (died 1682), professional cavalry officer under Gustavus Adolphus, after 1643 major-general in Scotland, in command 1650. Victor of Philiphaugh and loser of Dunbar.

Alastair Macdonald. Often given his father's combined name and nickname, Collkitto, killed in Ireland 1647. His father had been turned out of Colonsay by Campbells, was a Macdonald of Dunnyveg and close kin to the Earl of Antrim.

Maitland. John Maitland, second Earl and first Duke of Lauderdale, as in Chapters 13, 14, and 15.

Montrose. James Graham, fifth Earl and first Marquess as in Chapter 11.

Pym. John Pym (1584–December 1643), a solid-faced man with a professional approach to opposition politics, 'the principal architect of the constitutional revolution,' says Miss C. V. Wedgwood, 'King Pym', says J. H. Hexter.

Rothes. John Leslie, sixth Earl, as in Chapter 11.

Rupert. Prince Rupert of the Rhine (1619–82), third son of Charles I's sister, Elizabeth, Queen of Bohemia, an able general on both land and sea.

Strafford. Thomas Wentworth, first Earl (1593–1641), the chief instrument of Charles I's policy, Lord-deputy of Ireland, nicknamed 'Black Tom Tyrant'.

Vane. Sir Harry Vane the younger (1613–62), an independent, disapproving of all set forms of religion, of great sincerity and subtlety of mind, and consequently fairly unscrupulous in politics. Executed 1662.

Chapter 13

The Interregnum

Whether it is better to have war in the bowels of another country or
in your own.   CROMWELL

IN JANUARY 1647 THE Scots sold their king to the Parliament of
England: they accepted payment of £200,000, half of what was due
to them, handed Charles over, and marched home. The state of politics
in the two countries had left them no alternative. They were aware of
the divided sections of Parliamentary England: the so-called Presbyterians predominant in London and in Parliament; the Independents
dominant in the New Model Army and owning the leading soldier of
the day, Oliver Cromwell; and the raising radicalism to be found in
part of the army, the Levellers. Possession of the king had given the
Scots power among these groups so long as it had looked as if they
could make a real agreement with him. They had worked hard enough
at this. Before surrendering to them Charles had agreed to 'be
instructed concerning the Presbyterian government'; consequently
he had spent several months at Newcastle being argued with by
Henderson. As Baillie wrote to Henderson, it was essential that 'the
great God help you to soften that man's heart, lest he ruin himselfe,
and us with him'. 'We will be put to a fearful perplexitie' he was sure,
if Charles did not give way. But Charles had never yet in his life given
way in time. In return for this opportunity for persuasion the Scots
had agreed not to force the king's conscience, and to restore him to
his rights, and there was the implication in the confused wording of
the bargain that this might mean war against Parliament. The
bargainers failed to notice that the main force against the king in
England was not Parliament but the army. In any case whatever the
Scotch leaders had promised, they were still bent on the policy of the
Solemn League and Covenant. Gradually it dawned on them that it

was possible for Presbyterianism to be explained to a man by the ablest exponents, for its 'proofs' to be fully displayed, and yet intellectual assent to be denied. This presented a serious problem. They could not fight against the English for an uncovenanted king. Nor could they take him back to Scotland to be a focus for the anti-covenanting opinion which Montrose's campaign had revealed lying outside the brittle façade of unity. Argyll had been able to make statesmanlike demands for unity and co-operation when addressing the English, but he had no intention of compromise within Scotland. Montrose was still in the Highlands trying to raise another army. The king was persuaded to call on him to lay down his arms and go overseas, but the wayward Huntly remained in arms. It would not be possible, in the social opinion of the day, to guard the king so closely that he could not intrigue with persons outside his prison: if he was going to do this he had better do it in England. So they sold him and went home.

Charles did not remain long in the hands of Parliament. The removal of the Scottish army from England shifted the balance of power in politics and religion. As Baillie had noticed with dismay it was 'neither reason nor religion that stayes some men's rage, but a strong armie bridleing them with fear'. This realistic assessment was beyond the power of the English Parliamentary party, who tried to disband their own army without paying for it. Financial and religious protest combined and was effective. To the alarm of the Scots, the English army seized the king in June 1647, and in July it dealt with a Presbyterian demand from London by marching on the city. But Charles was no more cowed by this than by defeat. At the end of the year he made the Engagement – an alliance with envoys from Scotland, Loudoun, the young Lauderdale, and Lanark. The king would not take the Covenant, but he was to declare for Presbyterianism as the settlement in England for the next three years, and the Scots were to back him up by fighting for the vestiges of his prerogative there, the veto, and the control of appointments to office and the army. The Engagers had committed their country to fighting the trained army of England for a religious settlement there that would be without political guarantees.

Hamilton, who had been in eclipse, now worked his way to the front. He had been imprisoned by the king during most of the war, for rather too marked an appearance of running with both hare and hounds, and was eventually released by the royal defeat. He had tried to push through a compromise in the autumn of 1646 – an agreement between Parliament, king, and Scots, very like the subsequent Engagement. Now he came to Scotland to organize the country for its share, and came up against the realization that the Parliament of Scotland was only part, and perhaps the weaker part, of the forces organizing the country. The Engagement did not commit either the Scots or the king to the policy of the Solemn League and Covenant. As such it was unacceptable to the organized leadership of the Church. Argyll and the Commission of the Church argued against it; in March they found themselves in a minority against it in the Parliament. The standing Commission of the Church threw its organization, and the opportunities it made for propaganda, against the raising of a new army. Ministers who did not preach against the Engagement were to be reported by their presbyteries to the next Assembly. It was the end, and a poor end, to the unity of the Covenanting movement that had started in a demand for law and liberties. Levies for the army were opposed by preaching and excommunication, and in Fife and in the south-west resistance was strong. It culminated in a skirmish at Mauchline Moor in June 1648 where a massed communion of over 2,000 armed peasantry staged a rising and were dispersed with force. Both old Alexander Leslie and the younger David Leslie[1] refused to lead the new army, but professionals were still available to organize it, General Baillie, Middleton, and Sir James Turner. Turner had fought in Germany and helped to disperse the 'slashing communicants' of Mauchline, as he called them. Unfortunately the main command went to Hamilton: his military experience excluded the recent war, which he had passed mostly in prison, and was not enough anyway to compensate for his natural indecision. The army, already late for co-operation with risings in England, came in a disorganized trail into north-west England, was caught without supplies, and beaten in August by Cromwell and Lambert in a week

1. David Leslie was back from exterminating the remains of Montrose's Irish army in a massacre, after the surrender of the fortress of Dunaverty near the Mull of Kintyre. The massacre is laid on the ministers who advised him, but it was Leslie's weakness, now and later, that he listened to the ministry on military matters.

of running fight on muddy roads and in pouring rain between Preston and Warrington. Hamilton and Middleton at least fought hard before capture; hard enough for Preston to be thought of as a battle. It was not courage they lacked but organizing intelligence against a military leader who was prepared to move fast and take calculated risks. Hamilton was to be executed by the English for treason, as a peer of England: a dirty trick, but the Scots had already set an even more bloodthirsty level of penalties for failure.

Cromwell and the opponents of the Engagement were now dominant in the north of England and mopping up the remaining centres of this second Civil War. This gave the opportunity for the out-and-out Covenanters in Scotland to make their coup. The south-west, scarcely repressed by Mauchline, rose in force and rode on Edinburgh. The lay government, the Committee of Estates, fled, and effective power was in the hands of the Kirk militant. This was the famous 'Whiggamore raid' (Whiggamores or Whigs were the Galwegians when they came eastward annually to trade cattle for corn). The situation was confirmed by a treaty made at Stirling: the Engagers surrendered in return for a promise of their lives and property, and were to give up office. Cromwell came north to see settled in Scotland a kirk dominance that he would not have allowed for a moment in England, and lent it troops to safeguard itself.

A normal lay régime, conscious of being a minority and not even able to defend itself, would now have settled for conciliation, and tried to win support at large. But this was not the Covenanting way of thought. God being with them, his people needed no other help. This was interpreted as meaning that any support from those that the dominant minority considered sinful would be unattractive to God and might deprive the régime of his help. Opposition to Whig rule could only come from those not of the elect. So failings, political or moral, called for total censure. This philosophy led to three characteristics of Whig rule in Scotland,[1] which were to ensure that the country could not stomach it for long: the exclusion of all other

1. 'Whig' in Scotland never in this century carried the implications of liberalism it was to acquire in England, and though the Whigs in both countries held it as a principle that they alone ought to be in office, in Scotland this was regarded as of divine origin, not merely a secular concept. For this reason Whiggery never stood for Parliamentary authority.

elements from power in Church or state; the direct management of the army by the godly whether with any appreciation of military matters or not; and the use of execution for opponents or backsliders.

The state was purged in the famous Act of Classes of January 1649, passed in a Parliament with very few nobles present (for the nobility had mostly supported the Engagement) and with the other orders elected on a restricted basis. This Act, in wide sweeps of language, disqualified for office not merely all who had supported Montrose or the Engagement, but also all who had not protested against this agreement, as well as all guilty of the more obvious sins of the flesh. Those who were not leaders in the Engagement might hope for restoration after varying periods, but only after satisfaction had been accepted by the Kirk. The only great nobles now in the government were Argyll and the Earl of Cassillis. Johnston of Wariston was with them, and among the clergy the dominant figure was James Guthrie, minister of Stirling. These were not men who saw any virtue in compromise, and their greatest hatred was for their political rivals, the Engagers. A drastic purge was carried on in the Kirk. Already since the Covenant had first been signed, over a hundred ministers, as well as all the bishops, had been deposed for leanings to episcopal government or for co-operation with Montrose. More than another hundred went now, out of a parish ministry of less than a thousand, even though in some places the process of ejection was difficult – in areas such as East Lothian where the general clerical opinion was royalist it was difficult to force the presbytery to act. Clerical ascendancy over the upper classes was emphasized by abolishing lay patronage in the Church. Ministers were to be appointed by kirk sessions, and kirk sessions were to be filled by ministers, and one view would prevail. In practice the Act of Classes had to remain an ideal policy, not an actual one, though it was followed by Argyll and the Whigs whenever possible. It tied the ideal of the Covenant to a policy of exclusion and made it the property of a single party.

For moral and political offences the Covenanters were very ready with the death sentence. We have from Nicoll's diary a picture of life in 1650 in Edinburgh:

Much falsit and scheitting at this tyme wes daylie detectit by the Lordis of Sessioun; for the quhilk their wes daylie hanging, skurging, nailling of luggis, and binding of pepill to the Trone, and boring of tounges; so that it was ane fatall year for fals notaris and wirneses, as daylie experience did witnes. And as for adulterie, fornicatioun, incest, bigamie, and uther uncleanes and filthynes, it did never abound moir nor at this tyme.

A contrasting description comes from the Covenanter Kirkton. Scotland, he says,

> seemed to be in her flower . . . there was no case nor question in the meanest family in Scotland, but it might become the object of the deliberation of the General Assembly, for the congregational session's book was tried by the presbyterie, and the presbyterie's book by the synod, and the synod's book by the General Assembly . . . no error was so much as named, the people were not only sound in the faith, but innocently ignorant of unsound doctrine; no scandalous person could live, no scandal could be concealed in all Scotland, so strict a correspondence there betwixt ministers and congregation . . . The only complaint of prophane people was . . . they hade not liberty enough to sine. . . .

But Kirkton, not a particularly truthful man anyhow, was writing this happy picture of a police state a good while later. In fact Nicoll's picture should be no surprise to us: a time of war and revolution, with the consequent food shortages and profiteering opportunities, is not usually a time when crime is scarce. The penalties that he lists may have had a deterrent effect on delinquents, but no curative one.

So long as the régime openly adhered to the Solemn League and Covenant, peace with a non-Presbyterian England could not be secure. Typically enough the Act of Classes required that pardon for those excluded must come from 'both kingdoms'. It was still thinking in terms of religious unity, and it was not the Scotch settlement that was to adjust to create this. But Cromwell also did not always think constructively. The second Civil War seemed to him a needless bloodletting: the remedy, the execution of the king. This was pushed through at the end of January 1649, overriding legality, sentiment, and the majority opinion of the English Parliament. This marked the Independent and army dominance in English politics and the end of any hope of a negotiated settlement. It also made the breach with the

Scots open. Through centuries of defiance of royal authority, the Scots had almost always respected the king's person. However much they might oppose or ignore royal authority it was not for the English to kill their king. Moreover, to the Scots, Charles had surrendered the reality of power in 1641 (which he would never have done in England): it was difficult for them, who had been given what they wanted, to appreciate the *impasse* Charles's obstinacy had created in England. Immediately on the news of Charles I's death, the new King Charles II was proclaimed in Edinburgh, but this was followed at once by an Act of Parliament postponing the grant of authority to him until he should accept and promise to implement the Solemn League and Covenant.

Given the reality of monarchist feeling in Scotland, the obvious thing was to come at once to terms with the young king. It is true that it would make war with England certain, but adherence to the Solemn League in itself made this highly probable. The junction was delayed by clumsiness and brutality. Behind the back of the commission sent to persuade Charles, the government of Scotland executed the old and probably dying Huntly for his royalist misadventures, and this made terms unattractive. Charles would try other things first: an excursion to link up with monarchists in Ireland, which occupied the latter part of the year, and which failed; an attempt to see what Montrose could again do, which took the early part of 1650. Montrose had not got his Irishmen now; he landed in Orkney and moved south, but he could collect few followers on the mainland. His Orkneyers were unskilled soldiers, without the speed or experience of the Irish, and they, poor lads, got cut off from support by David Leslie and mowed down by cavalry by Colonel Strachan at Carbisdale at the end of Loch Shin, a great diagonal of water cutting across the far north. Already by then Charles II had come to terms with the Covenant. The Whigs were not in the habit of showing mercy, so Montrose, captured shortly after, could expect none. It is the unfortunate thing about his career that not only was it dedicated to an idea of monarchy which would no longer work, but its main achievement was to reveal the disunity of Scotland and to detract from her weight in her dealings with England. Charles, disowning his dealings with Montrose, had to let him and his officers be executed. He himself landed in the north in June 1650, swallowed the Covenant and a series of formal humiliations, and learnt a lasting repugnance for the theology and terminology of Covenanting thought. At the end of his processing he is said to have added to his penitence, repentance that he had ever been born.

Cromwell had tried to persuade the Scots to change their policy, or rather what they conceived of as God's policy. His most famous appeal is often and deservedly quoted: 'Is it therefore infallibly agreeable to the Word of God all that you say? I beseech you in the bowels of Christ think it possible that you may be mistaken. . . . There may be a Covenant made with death and hell.' Now he would not sit and wait for another Scottish invasion. He came north with a fleet to force action, by the east coast route, the easiest way into Scotland. His was a big army, 16,000 strong, but the Scottish army was also potentially large, and defences had been built around the capital. With the English at hand on the Braid hills, in what is now suburban Edinburgh, the Scots indulged in the typically Covenanting pleasure of 'purging'. The army was assembled on Leith shore and vetted again and again. 'The half of thame wer sent back, aftir a long space apoynted for purging of the airmy, to the discontenent of much pepill, and of gentillmen voluntiris quha haid freilie cum in to feght for the defence of the Kingdom,' says Nicoll. We do not know how many were sent away: Nicoll's estimate of a half is probably exaggerated. More serious than mere numbers was that the more professional element, the sergeants and officers, were by Covenanting standards the most likely to have compromised themselves at some point by supporting a less godly cause. Even so, David Leslie still had a bigger army than the English, and knew how to handle it. He evaded action and forced Cromwell back to the coast. He had deprived him of supplies by burning the corn stocks on the narrow, fertile East Lothian plain, and no stores could be landed from the fleet in bad weather. To use a harbour, Cromwell fell back on Dunbar, advanced again, and a month later was again forced back. The Scotch lay above him on Doon hill, an outlier of Lothian Edge, which follows the line of fault of the Southern Uplands. At this last point, in a skilled campaign, the Scots threw it all away. David Leslie's control was vitiated by an advisory committee of ministers who were anxious that the English should not escape punishment and had little interest in the 'carnal' problems of military strategy and technique. The troops came down off the hill and were caught with most of their match not lit and divided by a stream by an opponent who was always ready to watch for the hand of God in a change in the material circumstances of a battle. The English were more experienced than the Scots and better officered and, in the resulting hard fighting which began with the first light, the Scots lost more men than in any engagement since Pinkie. Many more were captured and, of those fit enough, some were exported by the English to the colonies ('Barbadoed' was the slang word), a monstrous infringement of the normal conventions of war.

Dunbar, 3 September 1650, was a disaster in a disastrous period. It came in the middle of food shortages and the total disruption of the country's economy. But at least it slackened the hold of the extreme Covenanting party. No one was prepared to take it as decisive, and passionate dispute broke out. The Covenanters of Fife broke away from their Western Association and urged moderation to opposition and Engagers. Charles had no desire to be the king of a minority only, yet only extreme Covenanting opinion could be heard in Church or state. The Westerners put forward a paper to the Committee of Estates, the 'Remonstrance', which showed openly that their concept of monarchy was a conditional one: the king was to be owned only 'so farre as he owns and prosecuttes the cause'. Doubting, probably with reason, the sincerity of Charles II's adherence to the Covenant, they demanded his removal from power, more purges, a tighter enforcement of the Act of Classes, and exclusion of all who had even suggested alliance with Engagers. This document marks the final laicization of the Covenanting spirit: from now on, Covenanting policy was a refusal to accept any authority in Church or state not chosen by the self-appointed minority of the south-west and an indifference to established law unless it suited this group. The original Covenant had been for the laws and liberties of Scotland: in 1643 this had changed to the enforcement of Presbyterianism on England and Ireland: now the Covenanting movement meant the dictatorship by a minority. The tragedy is that this entirely political aim should have been so successfully dressed up in religious verbiage that men were prepared to be martyred for it.

The Remonstrance ended with a threat of force that was not to be overlooked, for the Committee of Estates, unable to ignore the argument of patriotism, had allowed the westerners their own army, under

Colonel Strachan, the victor of Carbisdale. Charles, nervous of an anti-monarchical army, had run away to his own royalist friends in the north. Lauderdale had forced him to come back and join with the Committee of Estates. This episode, coinciding with the Remonstrance, produced a move for toleration and patriotism. Argyll added his weight to the moderates. The royalists under Middleton were granted indemnity, and the Remonstrance was repudiated as scandalous to the king. Almost immediately afterwards the Remonstrants were wiped out as a military force by the English general Lambert at Hamilton. Perhaps the divine will did not favour exclusion. At any rate it became possible to put patriotism above purity and modify the Act of Classes. It was a half-hearted move, but at least it lent the nation the services of her most experienced soldiers. Charles was crowned at Scone. Militarily everything was too late: the English held the south, including Edinburgh and the south-west, a valuable source of recruits, and were advancing up the east coast: the country was starving. The troops gathered round the centre of government in Stirling, entrenched and frozen through the winter, were ragged and hungry. A General Assembly at St Andrews in the summer of 1651 was dispersed by the English advance, but not before it had shown that there was a moderate party in Church as well as state. The parties now had their names, the Remonstrants, later often called the Protesters, on the one hand, and the Resolutioners, who had supported resolutions in favour of co-operation with Engagers, on the other.

It says something for the perception of the nation that the Resolutioners were the larger party. Baillie was not alone in seeing that the claim to minority rule in the Remonstrance would go on, as it did, to a similar claim for the Church: 'where a State and Militarie separation is necessare, there a Church separation is much more necessare'. It would also lead to control by smaller and smaller minorities. No army could be officered with the whole of the nobility cashiered: letting in Engagers confirmed the political schism and the Remonstrants added religious schism by disowning the General Assembly of St Andrews because they had not had a majority in it. In spite of poverty and disunity, a third army was got ready to take on the English. It marched out from Stirling and down the west coast to recruit the royalist support of western England. At last Charles was marching with his countrymen. But little support came in in England, and Cromwell, glad that the war was one of movement again, followed fast. His subordinate Monck completed the conquest of Scotland: Stirling and Dundee fell, and the Committee of Estates was captured before Cromwell caught Charles, on 3 September at Worcester, and defeated him totally in a fight through the town. Charles escaped abroad; Lauderdale and many others began a long captivity. Cromwell called it 'the crowning mercy'; he was master of the three kingdoms.

Scotland now had no government and no army, and no generally accepted leadership in the Church. Her economy was desperate. Trade had stopped, shipping had been wiped out, the towns were starving, and many country areas had been devastated. Round Stirling, Lieutenant-General Monck had destroyed 'the whole cornes'. In Nairn, they spoke of the 'lamentable conditioune of this wasted land': in Lanarkshire and Dunbartonshire, 'the ground wholly ruinated', 'great devastation and universall Losses' and the seed corn gone. The Border had lapsed into banditry. For the first time since the early fourteenth century Scotland had been conquered, and Cromwell meant to make this conquest total. In turn he had had to fight the royalists, the fanatics, and finally the whole nation: there was no adequate group he could install in power to keep the country safe as a satellite. He would incorporate Scotland into England. Plans for the Union went into action at once. Commissioners from Cromwell's purged and submissive 'Rump' Parliament came north early in 1652 and asked for the consent of Scotland in the only units of expression Cromwell would allow, the shires and burghs. They asked for assent to incorporation in the English Parliament, and co-operation with English government. This meant co-operation with the English policy of toleration for the sects.

For all that Scotland had now no leadership (Argyll had retired to his estates and was lying quiet and inaccessible), and that many of the burghs were ruled by councils of yes-men put in by the Remonstrants, there was a good deal of national spirit in the answers to Cromwell's proposals. Toleration raised indignation: as the representatives of Moray said, this was 'no freedom or favour but more bitter than . . . death itself'. If Union was wanted, Kirkcudbrightshire pointed out, it should have been on the basis of the Solemn League. But it was national dignity that spoke most effectively. Glasgow showed that the separate units could not give national assent. Kirkcudbrightshire protested with real feeling: 'the Lord for our transgressions has been pleased to bring us in thraldome to you, of whom we may say wee have meritted better things, we haveing been at much expence of Blood and estates for England's Releife in the day of her Adversity'. Only in Orkney was there a note of enthusiasm for the English as liberators from an oppression which had overtaxed the isles and thrown out their native clergy. Elsewhere, the most that Cromwell could get was grudging assent, and sometimes only by conducting his own purges of councils. Eventually even Argyll stopped behaving like an independent prince and gave way. Conquest was a fact which had to be accepted. Cromwell did not try to stifle the main outlet for expression, the pulpit. Sermons were exclusively political in Covenanting areas. Even during his invasion in 1651 he had put up no more than mild protest at denunciations by the Glasgow ministers, but he did try to persuade the Church to stop praying for the king by name. The parliamentary form of the Union was not settled until Cromwell had quarrelled with the Rump and tried his hand at constitution making. Under the Instrument of Government at the end of 1653 Scotland was to have thirty members (the same number as Ireland) to sit with 400 English. Not even this bare allowance came to the first Parliament, and those that did were largely hand-picked, but through them and other lines of contact some sort of attention was paid to Scottish opinion.

Cromwell's government had some real benefits to offer. He sent judges to Scotland, of whom the main complaint was that they had little attention for the tie of kin in Scottish society – a suggestion that they were less corruptible than their predecessors. The feudal courts, the heritable jurisdictions, and the baron courts ceased. The English made it difficult for the national sport of witch burning, but did not exorcize the local animosities that led to it, so that old scores were saved up. Since a heavy share of the cost of the army of occupation lay upon the country, the excise and customs system had to be overhauled. A Mr Thomas Tucker was sent up to survey and reform the system, and has left us a vivid picture of the country's primitive economy. Even Tucker could not get much money out of the Highlands. He sent in a Gaelic-speaking collector, a kinsman of clan Campbell; but after collecting £30 the man was knifed in Islay, in spite of the Campbell connection – or perhaps, since old feuds live long, because of it.

For the first time in history the central government of Scotland had a large army to back it. This meant that law and order could be maintained, eventually even in the Highlands. For a time royalist forces held out there, under the Earl of Glencairn, and later under Middleton, but Monck reduced them in an encounter on the bleak pass of Dalnaspidal in 1654. After that, forts were built at key points, including one in the Great Glen at Inverlochy, where a Colonel Hill learnt to like and deal with the clans. The Cromwellian government made the chiefs stand surety for their clans or their neighbours' and held the peace. But it was expensive. The Scottish contribution to its army of occupation was eventually settled at £6,000 a month. Perhaps with full prosperity this payment would not have been hard. Indeed, compared with 1650, the Cromwellian peace was not uncomfortable. There was enough to eat and to spare. Corn prices stayed low. But these were the low prices of depression. Trade was dead, the money that could have made it live had gone in the wars, for towns and noblemen alike had contributed; the ships that might have carried it were destroyed, and a régime concentrating on English economic interests completed the forces of adversity. Scottish exports of wool and hides were forbidden because it suited England to keep the commodities at home, and her best customer was cut off by the Dutch war of 1652–4, a war arising out of Anglo-Dutch rivalry. Fines and forfeitures of the nobility completed the loss of capital. Baillie wrote of the noblemen as 'wracked or going to wrack', Hamilton and Lennox largely sold up, Huntly with 'more debt on the House than the land can pay', and Argyll 'almost drowned with debt'.

Money shortages did not prevent the chief occupation of these times, church wrangles. The rift between Remonstrant and Resolutioner remained open because the former, who numbered perhaps 20 per cent of the ministry, would not accept any church court in which they were not in a majority, and because Cromwell, fearing the strength of united Presbyterianism, deliberately favoured the minority. The Remonstrants would rather co-operate with English than with Engagers. So Cromwell intruded the compiler of the Western Remonstrance, Patrick Gillespie, as principal of Glasgow university. The first care of the English, complained Baillie, was 'to plant our Universities with their own', and wisely too, for the universities bred the ministers of the future. Gillespie in return was the first to pray publicly for the Protector, Oliver, and worked with him on a scheme for the rapid enlargement and enrichment of the university. But this co-operation removed him largely to London: he became the prototype of the modern educational head who 'pops up to London' and does little actually to carry out policy. Because the Remonstrants' allegiance to Charles II had all along been notional rather than real (some of them would favour any government so long as it disliked Engagers), Cromwell could get more support from this party than from the Resolutioners, and his preference and promotions kept the schism open. Remonstrant and Resolutioner hated and opposed each other with far greater bitterness than either side would show to Roman Catholic or Episcopal, and fought their battles out on lay as well as religious ground. The schism was at base political and the complexion of the town council was as much an issue as the principalship of the university.

That Cromwell had to rely on the minority party brings home his failure to get a wide-based support. Even in England the régime was a minority one, resting on force. In Scotland it rested on alien force. But it was administered by men for whom any country might have been grateful: Lord Broghill as President of the Scottish Council, and Monck as Commander-in-Chief, both won over from royalism and caring first for good government. Gradually, Cromwell won the support of some Scots – Johnston of Wariston for instance took up his old job as Lord Clerk Register in 1657, and later went on the English Council of State. Some young and impecunious members of James VI's new aristocracy, for instance the young Earl of Tweeddale, were prepared to work for his government, and some of the families that were tied to the law. Support became a bit wider when Broghill started giving some share of favour to the Resolutioners. But the bulk of Scottish opinion was no more than acquiescent in the settlement. The clergy had been persuaded not to pray openly for the king, but they did not cease to think of him. The Resolutioners found an intelligent negotiator in their dealings with Cromwell, James Sharp, a young and far-seeing cleric who had initially opposed the Covenant. Cromwell, in one of his rare jokes, referred to him as 'Sharp of that ilk', a perceptive phrase.

It was a dictatorship, but it had some of the advantages of one. Never before had Scotland had so much government at such a cost: passes were necessary even to move about the country. But there was a freedom of religious expression, though, to the convinced Whig, expression without political dominance was useless. Both political groups in Scotland viewed with horror the spread of new non-Presbyterian opinion. Quakers were found in Aberdeen, Independents were allowed to give voice. What made life tolerable for most was the conviction expressed by Cromwell of the Scots: 'God hath a people here fearing His name, though deceived.' Most Scots would have echoed this of the English. It had not been for nothing that the army that defeated the Scots at Dunbar had answered the Scottish battle-cry of 'the Covenant' with 'the Lord of Hosts'.

NOTES ON DRAMATIS PERSONAE

Most of the names in this chapter are for the same individuals as in Chapter 12. This includes Argyll, Montrose, Huntly, Lanark, Hamilton, Johnston of Wariston, and most of the generals. There remain:

Gillespie. Patrick Gillespie (1617–75), Covenanting minister, Remonstrant, supporter of Cromwell, principal of Glasgow university 1653.

Glencairn. William Cunningham, ninth Earl (*c.* 1610–64). Royalist in the Civil War, Engager, and leader of Charles II's forces in the Highlands 1653–4.

Guthrie. James Guthrie (*c.* 1612–61). Minister, leading opponent of the Engagement, aider of Cromwell. He was less pliable than Gillespie, and was one of the victims demanded at the Restoration.

Lauderdale. The same as in Chapter 14. At this period an Engager.

Middleton. John Middleton, first Earl (*c.* 1608–74). Served as a pikeman in France, fought for the Parliamentary side, and against Montrose at Philiphaugh. Subsequently a consistent royalist, fought against Monck in the Highlands. A man of great height and too big a nose.

Turner. Sir James Turner (1615–86). A bookish professional soldier whose memoirs are a valuable source, and whose *Pallas Armata*, a treatise on the art of war, made a reasoned plea for the use of bows and arrows. He fought in Germany in the '30s, in Ireland in the '40s, at Preston, and at Worcester.

NOTES ON POLITICAL LABELS
IN CHAPTER 13 AND AFTER

Engagers. Adherents of the Engagement of 1647 by which Scots agreed to support Charles I and the king agreed to impose Presbyterian Church government, with the help of Parliament, on England for three years.

Resolutioners. These took their name from the public resolutions passed in the winter 1650–1 by the General Assembly effectively suspending the Act of Classes.

Remonstrants. These were adherents to the Western Remonstrance, October 1650, which objected to recognition of Charles II as King of Scots and demanded enforcement of the Act of Classes.

Protesters. These were effectively the same group. They are labelled from protests in the General Assembly of 1651–2 against association in an Assembly in which the 'plurality' was 'corrupt'. Though this objection was ecclesiastical in its occasion and the Remonstrance political in its demand, the aim was the same, government by a minority, and the terms are used interchangeably.

Chapter 14

Restoration

1660 : the salute

DICTATORSHIPS GO VERY FAST when they begin to crumble:
Cromwell's was no exception. At his death in 1658, on the anniver-
sary of Dunbar and Worcester, power passed to his son Richard,
possessor of about a quarter of his personality. Richard was too idle
to hold together army and Parliament and too gentlemanlike to rule
by army alone. Within a few months he had passed into gentlemanlike and idle retirement. In his place the English army leaders broke
apart and quarrelled among themselves, and with the 'Rump' of the
old Long Parliament, which they had brought back, and all forgot that
even army rule rested ultimately on acquiescence, if not consent.
In Scotland Monck kept aloof from this. He held his own army

together, removing the men whose politics he suspected, and waited enigmatically. Much of the enigma remains today. His portrait shows a round face in a full-bottomed wig, confident and uncommunicative. His reputation was for decent dealing and loyalty to those whose authority he had accepted. Faced with the collapse of any authority to be loyal to, he seems to have decided to declare for basic legality.

Legalism in England by 1659 could only mean two things, the old Long Parliament in its entirety, and the king. Monck decided to throw his army into the scale for the Parliament and see what happened. This meant a march south, a slow, considering march, with plenty of time for consultations. But these consultations were with Englishmen, who counted in politics, not with Scots, who did not. All that Monck would say to the Scots, when he called a representative meeting of nobles and townsmen before his departure, was that he would do what he could for a reduction in taxation. Meanwhile the Scots were to keep the peace, and the counties edging the Highland line could have enough arms to keep down cattle stealing. He would not take Scots into his army: the English had grown to dislike Scotch soldiers cruising about their country. In London he used his army to recreate the Long Parliament, to get it to recall the monarchy, and finally to dissolve itself. And so, in May 1660, there was a king in London, a man of thirty, over-worldly-wise, and done with travelling.

Charles II had been called back by English opinion and an English Parliament and on promises made to England. To his 'ancient kingdom' he was under no bonds. The decisive control by English politics over Scottish events had begun, and was to stay. In all the stages of the change the Scots had had no say. They had been unrepresented in the army, the Rump, or the Long Parliament, except for the lonely figure of Wariston, half mad and wholly hated, who had for a short time presided over the Rump's executive council. The reaction into legalism kept the Scots out of the Parliament; no one was going to let them have their own army; they would have to take what was offered.

What was offered was not abhorrent to large sections of the kingdom. Charles II was a Stewart; he knew Scotland; he was intelligent and active, and he had appeared as a supporter of the Covenant. As a

king, Charles appeals to the modern world, perhaps disproportionately, because of his dislike for the stuffed-shirt side of monarchy in
which his cousin Louis XIV excelled. He liked doing things for himself, walking, sailing ships, experimenting in the company of scientific
friends. He had a real flair for the possible in politics, a rare quality
in his family. His first-hand knowledge of Scotland was not entirely
a benefit, for he had seen the country in 1650, a fact which had
strengthened his natural distaste for fanaticism of all kinds, and made
him particularly impatient of Calvinist phraseology. His brother
James, now Duke of York, had little of his quality, except his physical
courage and his dislike of pomp. For both of them the Catholic
influence of successive royal marriages had worn allegiance to
Protestantism thin. James was soon to declare his conversion to
Roman Catholicism, but Charles was intelligent enough to disguise
his inclinations until his deathbed.

The country wanted a king, and would have accepted worse. So
when the Edinburgh diarist Nicoll records drily 'the two Houses of
Parliament had proclaimed King Charles the Second to be King of
the three Kingdoms', it was still with real enthusiasm that the cannon
of the castle were fired to mark the occasion. That a cannoneer of
known republican leanings managed to get himself fired off too could
be a judgement of God. The spouts of Edinburgh Cross ran with
claret, the town council stood around drinking healths and breaking
glasses, and enough citizens followed their example to leave three
hundred dozen broken glasses in the street.

But it took some time for it to be clear what all this excitement was
going to lead to in terms of government. The return of the king must
in some sort mean the return of the nobility: the end of army rule
would mean the restoration of Scottish courts and law. There seemed
a general likelihood that the Presbyterian majority of the Long
Parliament which had brought back the king would be strong enough
to settle some sort of Presbyterianism as the joint church of the two
countries, a view encouraged by the fact that it had already declared
for the Westminster Confession, though, in typical English fashion,
without the section on church discipline. To join in the in-fighting
for the new settlement, various self-appointed groups of ministers
sent down representatives. Some of the nobility found their way to
court; Lauderdale and Crawford, liberated from prison in England,

were there already, and Argyll came south to pay the respect of one princely ruler to another, only to find himself first cold-shouldered, and then arrested for treason. As far as Charles was concerned, Scottish affairs could wait till the more urgent English ones were settled. He put back in charge the only available executive body that was both legal and experienced, the old Committee of Estates that Monck had captured in 1651. He sent Middleton north as Commissioner to Scotland and kept Lauderdale as companion and Secretary of State in London, thus dividing office between a leading royalist and an old Presbyterian. The next few years saw a duel between the two for the control of Scottish policy.

The most immediate issue was the relationship between the two countries. If the Protector's Union was to be dissolved, then, Lauderdale insisted, there could be no return to the Commonwealth position with Scotland as a conquered country. Scotland must be freed from English rule, English law, and English troops. This was a straightforward issue of patriotism. The really difficult questions were the balance of power between the two countries, their divergent demands on the king, their economic rivalries and disputes; and these remained.

Parliament opened in the New Year of 1661 with traditional but unfamiliar pomp. In the general emphasis on the good old days and royalty it was easy to put back the Committee of the Articles. The next important point was to decide how far back to set things. The royal surrender of 1641 was already being overlooked in practice: no king who meant anything by his kingship could have consented to a total loss of the right to choose his servants. But if the Parliament of 1641 was to be scrapped, then also that of 1640 should go; it was in this one that, against the wishes of the Crown, episcopacy had been abolished. This line of thought made it easy to go back farther, and 1633 became the next date to look at. In the Act Rescissory all legislation after 1633 was annulled. Scotland was legally back where she had been before the Great Rebellion, as if nothing had happened. With twenty-eight years of legislation to make good somehow, the rest of this Parliament was fully occupied, and Acts flowed out. The normal needs of changing law and interest had to be met, the returned monarchy must be buttressed and its restoration legalized. In all this business, the Act of Indemnity, the pardon for those of his subjects who at various times had opposed him or settled under other governments, was postponed.

At Breda Charles had promised England an indemnity that would exclude only those picked on by Parliament. In this way he could arrange for the deaths of the regicides with an appearance of general benevolence. He could hardly insist on more severe punishment for the kingdom that had fought for him through the starving winter of 1650, and in any case he had issued a general indemnity in Scotland in 1651 as an appeal to unity. Yet there were men he could never be expected to forgive. Two prime troublemakers, Argyll and Wariston, drowned, as Baillie had commented, in universal hatred, were early marked out for revenge, though the real reasons could not be used against them. They were killed because of their destructive policies as Remonstrant leaders, and the hostility they had shown to Charles himself as well as to his father; but they were tried and condemned on their co-operation with the Cromwellian régime. Other co-operators among the Remonstrants were marked down. Gillespie made his peace with the government, but Guthrie was executed, unbowed, and with him a minor figure thought to have been involved in the execution of Charles I. These deaths were impossible to justify in any spirit of fairness or law; yet in the three main cases they could have a patriotic look because the victims were men who had pursued a policy destructive not only to the monarchy but to Scotland as a whole. Unfortunately even with them out of the way the Act of Indemnity hung fire.

The king was not the only person with scores to pay off. At the lower end of the social scale this was shown by a great outbreak of witch-burning. But mostly it was not in lives that scores were settled: it was by fines and forfeitures that many a house had been wrecked, a family reduced by its rivals. The royalist nobility that came back in 1660 had suffered heavily in defeat. Some had spent years in prison or exile: all had grievances about land. Estates had been confiscated, and, even before this, the direct expenses of war and civil war had put a burden on many patrimonies. At the height of his rivalry with Middleton, Lauderdale was to exclaim in the king's presence that he had been 'six times excepted' in the troubles, 'twice for life and estate', 'twice for estate', and twice prohibited from office; he was here voicing a general bitterness and insecurity. He and others hoped that the restoration would lead to reimbursement, and quickly. But the hard-pressed Crown had no money to give. Help to royalists could come only from the salaries and perquisites of government office, which could not extend to more than a few; from political weight in private lawsuits, and from fines and forfeitures on their old opponents, a sure way to maintain bitterness.

Even with royal help the nobility would not get back its old position after twelve years of exclusion from power. There were to be no more 'bands'. Even at its weakest and most distracted, the central government from now on would exercise more authority than James VI or Charles I had ever hoped for. Partly this was the achievement of Cromwell, who had given the country a taste for government, for law and order enforced sharply, for justice independent of the ties of kin. But it came also from the Remonstrants who had ruled tumultuously for a short time with hardly any great names on their side. They had used presbyteries and kirk sessions to discipline the nobility. Lauderdale had done penance in the parish church of Largo for his politics. Huntly had been executed, and the Gordons would never again run their blood-feuds and private wars across Aberdeenshire. The game of power from now on had to be played on the central government's terms, and within the fairly elastic bounds of law, even though some great estates, notably that of Argyll, were still very independent.

A nobleman faced with a mortgaged or broken estate from the wars did not find this a good time to salvage it. Corn prices were low, steadily low, reaching as low as men could remember in 1664, but returning to this same level again in the late 1670s. There was only one year of high prices, that of 1674–5, in all the next thirty years. This meant a country free of famine, but it also meant low rents, since these were still mainly paid direct in corn. The nobility did not easily make up its losses. And slowly, as a result of this shift of power, it was to become possible for the lairds and gentry to assert themselves too as a political force. They did not immediately take an active part in Parliament; the Committee of the Articles still meant that the Crown had control there. In any case the gentry were held back by habits of practical subservience to the nobility which continued long after these were necessary for safety, and of intellectual subservience to the clergy. The form of expression of this class was to be the law and the lawyers. It is in these years of the restored monarchy that the gentry begin to move forward. Unfortunately for the peace of the country others moved also, and there developed in the south-west the first important movement in Scotland that did not look to the upper classes for leadership.

On the whole in secular matters the Scots managed to adjust their expectations with a certain realism. But in ecclesiastical affairs many ministers failed to keep a foot on the ground. The Protesting clergy can have had little reason to expect royal support, but they were used to suing for government help and could not keep up their position in Scotland without it. They sent a delegation to meet Charles in London, and were apparently surprised as well as pained when the first act of the restored Committee of Estates was to arrest their leaders. Charles shelved any further decisions on the church settlement by a smooth letter in which he promised to maintain the legal religion. The Resolutioners of Edinburgh had also sent a delegate to London, the able and fluent James Sharp, and peppered him with instructions that showed they were paying no attention to the reports he sent back, in particular to his warnings that it looked as if episcopacy would be restored in England. Sharp, brought up in the north-east where the episcopal Church was valued, an anti-covenanter in his youth, probably did not really view this with dismay. In any case he was not the man to sacrifice himself for other people's pigheaded-ness, and he seems to have decided to make his own adjustments to the situation. There is no evidence that he was responsible for the Crown's decision against Presbytery, but his adjustment was so smooth and speedy that it was easy for Presbyterians in Scotland to accuse him of treachery, far easier than looking coolly at the facts of the situation. Presbytery, rightly or wrongly, was tied up in the eyes of the court with the Covenant, and the Covenant since 1643 meant the Solemn League. For the first time for many years Scots who disliked this were free to say so, and there are reports of a considerable number doing so. Yet ardent Presbyterians had used and were still accepting language about the Covenant which made it impossible for any government to accept it. Here is part of Argyll's speech from the scaffold: 'God hath laid engagements on Scotland: we are tyed by covenants to religion and reformation; those who were then unborn are engaged to it, in our baptism we are engag'd to it; and it passeth the power of all Magistrates under heaven to absolve a man from the oath of God.' So long as Presbyterians used these terms about an agreement to force their church structure on the other two kingdoms they seemed a menace to an episcopal Church in England, and gradually it became clear that in England the battle was going to episcopacy. In reality, in spite of their language, both kirk parties in Scotland had largely abandoned the main feature of the Solemn League since the failure of 1651, and were prepared to live peaceably with England whatever her religion.

The other difficulty in the way of a Presbyterian church settlement was that the Remonstrants had successfully broken its machinery of government by refusing to accept the decisions of any Assembly or synod in which they were not a majority, and Presbyterianism without its courts would have been a mockery. Influential in practice also was the fact that Charles had a distaste for it. He had taken Presbyterianism on the chin years ago, and now told Lauderdale that it was 'no religion for a gentleman'. A modified episcopacy would prevent the kingdoms threatening each other, and mistakes that had given an opening to rebellion could be avoided. This might even be popular. Very few ministers had had much difficulty in accepting James VI's changes in the Church, and these few had been in the south. There was no doubt that episcopacy was popular in the north.

An episcopal church settlement, in fact any church settlement tolerable to the nobility, was bound to meet difficulties with many high-stomached individuals, for, as Sharp wrote to Lauderdale, 'the truth is we have been so many years out of the channell of subjection and obedience to the magistrat as we know not how to returne to it'. The line had to be to stress the habits of the past and the law of the past. But since Parliament had met, the law of the past was now that of 1633: the royal letter on the church settlement was found to carry a new meaning.

So it was not surprising to find bishops coming back to Scotland: four were consecrated in London at the end of 1661 and appeared in Scotland soon after. The two leading figures among them were the adaptable James Sharp as Archbishop of St Andrews and Robert Leighton as bishop of Dunblane. In May they consecrated another six, including Alexander Burnet as Archbishop of Glasgow, and were restored to their jurisdiction, property, and place in Parliament. Next year their use to the government was shown in the return to the old method of electing the Lords of the Articles, by which the bishops kept the choice of this committee to royal nominees.

This was legal and ecclesiastical reaction, but it was not a simple return to the past. The bishops were to work hand in hand with their synods, though these synods would not include elders. Charles II's government did not dare face the disturbance of a General Assembly in a divided Kirk, so none was held. No high claims were made for the episcopal order. The Act of Parliament acknowledging their jurisdiction spoke of their usefulness to the Crown and their preservation of public order and the liberty of the subject, which was fair enough and roughly true. There was no general re-ordination of Presbyterian ministers, though Leighton, protesting slightly, had been re-ordained. No ceremonies were introduced, no altars, no liturgy prescribed beyond the use of the Lord's Prayer, the Creed, and the Gloria. Only the two archbishops were to go on the Privy Council. Charles was not going to make his father's mistake and annoy the nobility by governing through the Church. It was a settlement that would disappoint the north, with bare churches, and must have left the less articulate of ministers at a loss in public praying, but it might pacify the more moderate adherents of the Westminster Confession.

In a settlement as cautious as this, it is not surprising to find the bishops a mediocre lot. There was Leighton who would have made his mark in any religious community, and Wishart at Edinburgh, who carried with him the standards of humanity and decency that marked the group of close followers of Montrose, but otherwise they are typical of a Church on the defensive, adequate administrators doing a job properly, but uninspired. They reflect on the limitations of the two archbishops who had a large say in choosing them. Archbishop Burnet at Glasgow, nicknamed 'Longifacius' by Lauderdale and his cronies, was not the man to meet the more Presbyterian of his clergy half-way: he had nothing of the spirit, for instance, of the second Vatican Council; he stood, whenever he could, conscientiously and narrowly, on the rights and law of the Church. Sharp was a more subtle man, a skilled negotiator, keenly aware where power lay and anxious to make up to those in authority and share in it, liking order, obedience, and efficiency in those under him and not prepared to bother about much else.

I

As soon as the Act Rescissory again gave the king the right to choose his servants, the Privy Council was restored, not so much from deliberate conservatism as through the lack of alternatives. To mark the return of the nobility, it was well filled with Engagers. The fact that it had Glencairn, by training a soldier, as Chancellor, Middleton, also a soldier, as Commissioner, and was presided over by the semi-literate Lord Rothes, brings home one of the difficulties this aristocratic structure created. There was not a large body of trained executive ability in the nobility of a small nation: when part of what there was was kept out of power because politically suspect, the king had to choose his servants from a narrow range of names and a small pool of talent. No effort was made to widen the Council and make it the debating place for policy. The Oath of Supremacy was exacted from all Councillors, and the Earl of Tweeddale was reminded that loyalty meant unanimity or silence by a short stretch in prison for voicing sympathy in Parliament for Guthrie. Lauderdale found that 'guilt by association' was being attributed to him for interceding on behalf of Argyll's son. Since, with the Articles, Parliament also became muzzled, opposition to royal policy had only two weapons open to it; intrigue and resistance.

The Privy Council was trying in an amateur way to do a great deal. It had to hold down the Highlands, almost without troops, which it did by making the chiefs stand surety for one another. It was desperately trying to boost Scottish trade and industry. It was supervising the courts, and in particular trying to insist on decent standards of legality in the trials of witches. It was also hearing a lot of miscellaneous cases itself – a job for which it was totally unsuited. There were only a few lawyers on the Council and even though they were very regular attenders they could not make it a proper court. Much argument went on as to how to speed the departure of the English troops. The central government did not dare to leave empty fortresses which could be occupied by troublemakers, but it did not have troops of its own to fill them. So the English army could not be got rid of until the fortresses were down. As there were still outstanding debts from the building of them, money had somehow to be found to hurry things up before scraps between soldiers and citizens became frequent. The Council had to see that the magistrates and councillors of the burghs were of the right political flavour. It had to decide whether

Kirkwall was or was not independent of the earldom of Orkney; and
what was to be done with the bankrupt Royal Burgh of Anstruther
Easter? And it had to do everything on very little money because
little money was circulating. Parliament, in royalist enthusiasm, had
promised taxes of £40,000 sterling a year to the king, but this was
more than the kingdom could bear, particularly since, with the end of
Union, customs barriers in England had been raised again. It is not
surprising that the Privy Council had to extract taxation by the old
and unpleasant method of quartering soldiers on those behind hand
with their share.

The Scottish Council must not again lose touch with the king's
wishes. Special arrangements were made for fast posts to London, and
Lauderdale, as an intimate of the king, knew how to catch his attention. Lauderdale had chosen the position that proved the strongest,
but it was some years before he could oust Middleton, and not till
1667 was he in full control of Scotland. His first step forward came
when Middleton attempted to get him and his friends excluded from
power as part of an exception to the Act of Indemnity of 1662.
Getting wind of the move in time, though Middleton attempted to
stop the posts, he was able to present it to Charles II as not only a
personal affront on his choice of servants but an infringement of the
royal policy of pardoning. With Charles behind him, Lauderdale
could afford to be scornful of Middleton: the king 'will not let me be
bitt to death by a Duck,' he said. 'He hath no interest in any of the
nobility by blood or allegiance.' Middleton went off to govern
Tangiers and Rothes took his place as Commissioner.

It was natural that, looking back at all the turbulent water that had
flowed under the bridge since 1637, men should feel that security for
the future must lie in an exaggerated royalism. In particular, the
nobility showed an entirely new loyalty; it knew that Crown and
aristocracy stood together. The settlement of 1661 was therefore one
that would have well suited an earlier age. Charles II was careful to
keep his English and Scottish affairs separate, and hoped to keep
oppositions in the two countries equally separate. One of the few
occasions on which he was ever known to have lost his temper
completely was over the attempt of the English Parliament to bring
down Lauderdale in 1678. English and Scottish archbishops could
write each other letters of good advice, but no English churchman

was allowed to provide Scotland with a liturgy. The red-headed and intelligent Lauderdale would have made a superb minister for Charles I if that king could have stood his robust conversation: he was as learned in religion as most Scottish divines, forceful and courageous, and both completely loyal to the king and strongly patriotic for Scotland, if elastic in his religious convictions. He knew how to build up and keep a party by cajoling, threats, and favours.

It is this administration that has had the label 'drunken' pinned on it by hostile historians. The comment was taken from criticism by Gilbert Burnet, then a pious youth in his late teens, inclined to criticize his superiors. 'Drunkenness' was a convenient accusation by seventeenth-century ecclesiastics, brought forward almost exclusively in periods of political stress. Our ancestors at this time all consumed a lot of ale or wine whenever they could afford it; the total lack of indoor heating obliged them to warm themselves up for work in this way. Rothes drank heavily, even by the standards of his day, but could still claim proudly that no one had ever seen him incapable in office through drink. This is perhaps not the best of boasts for a President of the Privy Council, King's Commissioner, and later Chancellor, but it is not enough as a basis for condemning the Privy Council and its policy. The Council's weakness lay in limited ability, the private acquisitiveness of its members, and general clumsiness.

This clumsiness showed in two important matters. The first was the 'fines', the list of over 700 exceptions to the Act of Indemnity of 1662, the men who had to buy their way back into favour. The fines were to be used to compensate royalists who had suffered confiscations. They were not much as compensation, only a little over a million pounds Scots, but this would be enough to hurt those who had to pay. If this way of settling old scores was to be taken, then, to make it tolerable, great care should have been used in carrying it out. But the lists seem to have been at fault, and the officials who tried to extract the fines were corrupt. The deadlines for payment had repeatedly to be put off till, at the end of 1665, the Council was promising that if half were paid and the offender took the Declaration against the Covenants, he would be let off the other half. This was a sure way to annoy both sides.

The other example of clumsiness comes from the handling of the

Presbyterian ministers. Parliament had insisted on the Oath of Allegiance on presentation to a parish. Then, along with the bishops, it restored lay patronage, and insisted that all ministers appointed since 1649, when patronage had been abolished, should obtain formal presentation to the bishop and collation from him. This meant that many men opposed both to episcopacy and to the terms of the Oath had either to leave their parishes or conform. There was something to be said for clearing up the confusion that the Remonstrants had caused by disputing the election of ministers not of their party, and a great deal for restoring to the impoverished nobility something they regarded as their property, but this action contradicts the policy of letting sleeping dogs lie. On 1 October in a Council attended by neither of the archbishops, Middleton gave the ministers a month to comply or get out. Two hundred and sixty-two ministers left. In about 60 cases there were other claimants to the parish, but the Church found herself with 200 vacancies and with 262 discontented and unemployed clergy. The 'outed' included all but one of the ministers in the presbytery of Edinburgh, and every one of those in the presbyteries of Kirkcudbright, Wigtown, Stranraer, and Paisley. The vacancies were not a problem. The clergy was always, as Adam Smith pointed out a hundred years later, an oversupplied profession, with many qualified ordinands obliged to work as clerks or school teachers. But there was now a solid block of vocal opposition outside the Church exercising an enormous influence on her more Presbyterian wing. The centres of this 'Covenanting' opposition were Fife and Galloway, but it had a sizeable body of sympathizers elsewhere, particularly in Edinburgh. The situation was particularly serious in the south-west, a district much more cut off from the rest of Scotland than it is easy to envisage today. Here, faced with a new body of episcopal ministers, many people refused to accept their services at all and set out to make life unendurable for them. Religion was a matter of state, particularly in this area where the basic motives were largely political, and the government could not ignore this situation. In 1663 an Act of Parliament laid down fines for non-attendance at the parish kirk, and Sharp revived the Court of High Commission the next year. Rothes's comment is fair enough. 'Vie in this cingdum ar will ffull, proud, and nesiesitus eivin to begarie,' he wrote in his inimitable spelling, but 'a verie litill taym will randir bothe oposiers and with drawiers verie in significant.' But only a little time of peace was allowed for the settlement.

NOTES ON DRAMATIS PERSONAE

Argyll. As in Chapters 12 and 13.

Glencairn; Middleton. As in Chapter 13.

Burnet. Alexander Burnet (1614–84), Archbishop of Glasgow. No apparent kin to

Burnet. Gilbert Burnet (1643–1715), the 'Burnet' of Chapter 16, made bishop of Salisbury by William III. His *History of my own Time* is a much used, vivid, and unreliable historical source for this period.

Hamilton. William Douglas, third Duke (1635–94), as in Chapter 16. He was given the dukedom because of his marriage to the heiress of the first Duke (that of Chapters 12 and 13).

Lauderdale. As in Chapter 15. At this period, a politician of royalist emphasis, suppressing his Presbyterian inclinations and abandoning his Covenanting past.

Rothes. John Leslie, seventh Earl and first Duke (1630–81), son to the Rothes of Chapter 11. The worst speller of Scottish history and one of the heaviest drinkers.

Sharp. James Sharp (1613–79), Archbishop of St Andrews. Before that an anti-covenanter, then a Resolutioner negotiator.

Tweeddale. John Hay, second Earl (1627–97), as in Chapter 15.

1665–85

> It will not be unfit for your Lordships of the Clergie to endeavor to moderate Severities as much as may Consist with the Peace and Order of the Church.　　　　　LAUDERDALE to SHARP

THE DUTCH WAR OF 1665–7 brought the first serious strain on the new system, a war purely in the English interest: no Scot would have recommended fighting Scotland's best customer. War dried up the Scottish customs just when the demand for money was at its greatest. The government decided to use the 'fines' to help pay for its share of troops, which annoyed those who had to pay. The disaffected in the south-west took to holding large prayer meetings, 'conventicles', out of doors, with the 'outed' ministers in charge. Most of the landowners dissociated themselves from these meetings, but the Privy Council had spasms of nervousness that, even without leadership from the upper classes, a rising might link up with a Dutch invasion. It forbade the conventicles and demanded that landowners repress non-conformity on their estates. Still, nobody can have been very apprehensive, for when the rising did occur in November 1666, too late in the year for Dutch help, the government forces in the area consisted of Sir James Turner (in Dumfries collecting fines and probably embezzling them) and only seventy soldiers, mostly quartered on the disaffected in the countryside.

Taking the easy-going Turner along with them, the rebels marched east along the muddy tracks of Lanarkshire, expecting support. But none came and, in bad weather and despair, men seeped away. Perhaps at their strongest they had numbered 3,000 ill-armed peasants, with no one much above the status of farmer to lead them. Finding Edinburgh ready and defended, they turned back, hoping to break up and disperse in safety; but they were caught in the short mid-winter afternoon at Rullion Green in the Pentland Hills by General Dalyell, and totally defeated. The dominant party in the Privy Council, Rothes and Sharp, had been unreasonably frightened and now, nervous that any leniency would be taken as a sign of disloyalty, hanged more captured rebels than the danger had warranted; over thirty suffered. The 'Pentland rising' achieved a real benefit for Scotland, for it, together with the impeachment of Clarendon in England, made a change of power necessary. Royalism was no longer the only recommendation for office. Rothes was pushed upstairs into the Chancellorship, an amnesty was granted, and Lauderdale began his period of real control.

Lauderdale carried with him into power a group of intelligent, decent-minded men who, until he quarrelled with them, gave his administration support from moderates. These were the earls of Tweeddale and Kincardine, and Sir Robert Moray; with Lauderdale they show a high level of intellect and education, a pleasant change after Rothes. Moray was one of the original members of the Royal Society. Tweeddale and Kincardine were, like Lauderdale, Presbyterian in preference, and had opposed the return of episcopacy. With these men dominant in the Privy Council, Scotland was to experience a decade of fairly efficient government, full of important developments.

It was under this group that Scotland's economic life broke through the bonds of old monopolies. Markets and fairs were licensed outside the old burghs, so that for the first time rural Scotland could provide opportunities for buying and selling its own produce. Upstart new towns, such as Falkirk and Bo'ness, which were not royal burghs, entered foreign trade and an Act of 1672 allowed anyone to trade abroad in the main trade goods of the day: henceforth the royal burghs could reserve for themselves only the old list of luxuries; wines, silk, spices, and dyes. The future did not lie with these, but with salt and coal, corn and hides, and the imports from the Americas. The old staple system was nominally kept on, and even renewed at Campvere after the Dutch wars, but it was moribund, and with the cargoes of coal to Rotterdam went parcel after parcel of staple goods that should by law have gone to Campvere.

The members of the Privy Council were not disinterested in insist-

ing on these changes. Lauderdale owned the unfree burgh of Musselburgh. Kincardine came of the family that built the great coal and
salt works at Culross, always geared to export. What matters is that,
disinterested or not, they were right. They were less successful in
other patriotic efforts to widen the economy. Nothing the Scottish
government could do could get better terms with England. The
Navigation Acts remained law, though in practice, with a few forged
documents and a spare pot of paint, Scottish ships could trade illegally
with the English colonies. It was impossible for the English to supervise the whole coast line of Jamaica and the northern colonies. Glasgow started and developed her colonial trade in this period, as fast as
her shortage of capital would allow, and was regularly bringing over
tobacco cargoes in the 1670s. It was the English protective tariff on
salt and on cattle fattened in Scotland that hurt the important parts of
Scottish activity, and Charles could not get the English to relax this.

Scotland's answer was the obvious one, a protective system of her
own. But she had little to protect, and the whole object of her barriers
was to get concessions from the English. Concessions did not come,
and while the Scots waited for them they also faced the growing
protectionism of another market, France under Colbert. The world
where they could sell was narrowing, and Scotland was not important
enough for either England or France to wish to offer terms in their
trade war. She had not the skills or the special commodities which
would make her valuable to others in a competitive world.

Faced by these walls, the Privy Council tried to widen the economic
basis of Scotland in other ways, unsuccessfully. Its efforts were based
on trying to build up the same sort of minor luxury industries as
England had. Cloth mills, soap works, sugar boiling houses were
encouraged. Gunpowder and paper works had government help.
Joint-stock companies sprang up, and carried these on, with remarkably little success. Typical of these was the cloth factory at Haddington, which in spite of privileges, never managed to produce enough
cloth even to clothe the troops in Scotland, and which could use
Scottish wool only as a blend, and only for the coarsest quality of
cloth made there. There was an expensive attempt at a 'Royal
Fishery Company' in 1670, which was given a monopoly to imitate
the Dutch and develop the Scottish fishing grounds. But it all remained a top-dressing too rich for the poverty of the soil of Scotland.

A sound economic foundation in markets or in the sources of raw materials and a tradition of technical skill were both lacking. Yet here again was recognition that the economic future of Scotland was not to be strangled by the royal burghs.

The value of the Lauderdale régime was also shown in the founding of modern Scottish law. This was the Age of Stair, and lawyers today talk of pre- and post-Stair law as economists talk of post-Keynesian economics. At this point the modern world reaches out and touches the Scotland of the seventeenth century. James Dalrymple, later first Viscount Stair, produced his great *Institutions* in 1681; but it was not written in a hurry. It is a fine book, imbued with philosophy and written in a simple but elegant eighteenth-century prose, foreshadowing the style of Adam Smith. Here the statues and decisions of Scotch law are woven into a logical pattern permeated by the spirit of Roman law. It is not an accident that the reign of Lauderdale produced the Age of Stair. Law can only be refounded when the society of the day is ready for it, and a glance at Stair's contemporaries in the legal fraternity shows that Scotland was. There was Sir George Mackenzie of Rosehaugh, who became Lord Advocate in 1677, and who also wrote an *Institutions*; though this is a slight book. Mackenzie's book that matters is his treatise on Scottish Criminal Law which was to be the standard work for the next 130 years. Here we can see a good legal mind struggling to bring order to a law confused in origin, and confused still further by religious prejudice and the interventions of the Privy Council acting as a court. Mackenzie's intellectual difficulties explain the gradual disappearance of witchcraft trials in Scotland. True there is that awkward text in Exodus about not suffering a witch to live, but this is merely evidence that witchcraft exists and must be punished. It is no evidence in any particular case, and to Mackenzie no excuse for the 'cheat' of pricking for evidence or other illegal processes. Mackenzie knew well that hardly anyone once accused of witchcraft got off; if the judges insisted on real evidence, the trials did not get passed to them. But steadily and unpopularly the Privy Council and the lawyers went on pressing for legality in this beastly business, in the end with effect.

Mackenzie's collection of criminal law coincides with the creation in 1672 of the Court of Justiciary – a central criminal court strong enough to hear cases involving even great men, and able by its example and its travels on circuit, to keep some standards before the holders of heritable jurisdictions. Mackenzie is also honoured as the founder of the Advocates' Library – he left his own books, 1,500 in number, to his colleagues as a start for it. This is a sign that the advocates were becoming a coherent professional body – they were even able to stage a splendid quarrel with the Crown in 1674, a complicated affair in which they claimed the right to appeal from the Court of Session to the Scottish Parliament. They were wrong in law, but they held on in opposition to Charles II's instructions, and a great many of them were disbarred for several months. In the end the 'lockout' technique worked and they gave way; but it had been a demonstration of professional solidarity as well as a significant show of opposition.

Scotland was thus able to end the seventeenth century with a legal fraternity conscious of its unity, with the legal treatises that saw her through the next century, and with effective courts.[1] By the eighteenth century the lawyers were the most effective group in her society. They were closely tied up in the economic advances and the intellectual excitement of the day, and their social position as the intelligent and professionalized section of the landed gentry kept Scotland together as a unity. The Court of Session became the great bargaining centre of Scottish life. Its rules allowed almost indefinite appeals, and the nature of cases could be changed from day to day. The judges were not yet renowned for impartiality. The unsuccessful Royal Fishery Company took care to include some of them, to make sure that it was not embarrassed by the effects of bankruptcies among its debtors. They were more like umpires of the points in a game of tennis than final deciders of victory. By the end of the eighteenth century this was creating chaos both inside the courts and in society at large: dilatory and reversible justice was always unsuited to the affairs of merchants and businessmen. But in the seventeenth century, when lawsuits provided a substitute for family feuds and warfare, the slowness and uncertainty of the Court of Session was an advantage. For the rule of law to be effective it had first to be attractive to the country at large; it had also to provide the material for legal action,

---

1. We must not overestimate the modern character of the law: the Court of Justiciary handicapped itself for some time by a belief that only males, and physically complete ones at that, could b e witnesses.

and finally something of the continuing excitement and entertainment that in the bad old days had lain in illegality.[1] All this it did.

But this was not achieved in a day, and for some time the rising demands for good law and justice could conflict, sometimes ostentatiously, with autocratic features of the régime. Members of the government too often managed to be judges in their own cases. There was dirty work at various levels. Cases could still be heard in the Privy Council and then again in the courts, leading to undermined defences or double punishments; by contrast heavy fines placed on people who opposed the régime would be remitted when they conformed – and who knew what had passed between such men and Lauderdale to bring about this happy relationship. Lauderdale became a rich man, and not only by means of his official salary. Here was more fuel for opposition.

So it was not only the advocates who learnt to oppose. Middleton had attempted to carry on Parliament in the old way, with the main body only a rubber stamp for the decisions of the Articles. But growing interests in Scotland were too strong for this. When the young Duke of Hamilton had settled some of his family's debts he led a party in steady opposition to Lauderdale. Disputed elections became so frequent that in 1678 a parliamentary committee had to be appointed to settle them. The abortive attempt of Charles and Lauderdale to carry through a parliamentary union with England in 1669–70 had given the first big chance for opposition to develop. It was a policy that Lauderdale had known would be unpopular, and would call for all his skill and force. 'You cannot imagine what aversion is generally in this kingdome,' he told Charles. The memory of Cromwell and his fortresses was green, and England had done nothing since his time to appease Scotch feeling. But Lauderdale's group saw the inevitability of adherence to England: as Tweeddale put it, gloomily, 'all we doe or can is bot fending over to put off ane evil time that must com unless that be doun'. They would risk unpopularity for necessity. Lauderdale carried out his part and got the right to nominate the Scottish commissioners, but the whole thing broke down when the Scots claimed seats in the future Parliament for every member of the

---

1. This same point has been independently and much more vividly made for England in the early seventeenth century by Lawrence Stone, *The Crisis of the Aristocracy, 1558–1641*, pp. 241–2.

Scotch Parliament. Opposition passed on from this to the grievance of monopolies. Members of Lauderdale's party were doing themselves well in these matters at public expense. In 1673 a big attack by the opposition Lords in Parliament forced Lauderdale to give way on his financial policy and dissolve the Parliament. As Lauderdale's party began to break up at the end of the 1670s Charles II steadily found himself facing an 'ancient kingdom' in which royal policy might meet real opposition in a Parliament no longer subservient.

If in the long run it was this growth of parliamentary independence that proved important, the eyes of contemporaries were more taken up by the illegal and unconstructive opposition of the Covenanting wing of the Kirk. Intelligent observers bewailed the continuing of schism after the occasion for it had ceased, and in fact this continuance shows that the motive had always been political. The Remonstrants had demanded that the government of Scotland in Church and state be confined to those they thought godly, in other words to themselves, as a self-chosen group. They had been able to insist on this only in the vacuum of power after Preston, but they had not forgotten the claim. There had been quiet for some months after Rullion Green, but when the troops were dismissed at the end of the war, the extremists began to make trouble again in the south-west. As Mackenzie commented, 'they thought that all injuries done to Episcopal Ministers were so many acceptable services done to God'. Government by a group with marked Presbyterian sympathies may have encouraged demonstrations. At any rate large outdoor meetings were soon being staged in Fife and the west country, with no attempt at secrecy. Compared to the strong political meat these would offer in their sermons and denunciations, the preaching of the established clergy seemed tame. Some who had made Scotland too hot to hold them had taken refuge in Holland and were sending over subversive books and pamphlets. This underground literature, clothed in the most violent metaphors of the Old Testament, attacked the established clergy and pointed out to the faithful the dreadful fates, in both this world and the next, that had been waiting for all prelates. For the most part it did not expressly attack Charles himself, but it commended the days of the Covenant, and illogically called for a total separation of civil and religious authority. (Lay intervention, when it did not back the Covenanting wing, could always be criticized as erastian.) With this stuff coming into the country in quantities it is not surprising that there was an attempt to murder Archbishop Sharp. According to the would-be assassin, James Mitchell, God put it in his head to shoot Sharp when he saw him near at hand in his coach, but evidence showed that he had been following Sharp about with a pistol for several days. Sharp was unhurt, but Bishop Honeyman of Orkney, who had been sitting by him, carried the wound till he died. In spite of the fright produced by this, Lauderdale, who cared very little for Sharp personally, pushed on with an attempt to compromise with the 'outed' ministers.

His main instrument in this was Robert Leighton, bishop of Dunblane. Leighton represented a temper not often found in the Kirk of Scotland. He was an undoubted saint, one of those rare individuals with their own form of private contact with God who can afford to be indifferent on many points of theology or discipline because they have the heart of the matter. It was thought that he had chosen the bishopric of Dunblane as the poorest of the Scottish sees, but Gilbert Burnet, who knew him well and loved him, thought that it was more likely that it became his choice because it carried with it the deanery of the royal chapel, where he could hold common prayer with proper seemliness. Before this he had been Principal of Edinburgh University for seven years, so that he had had time and opportunity to pass on his own attitude to the young men he was teaching, and now he had a following in the Kirk, if not a big one. He wore the Calvinism of the day not so much lightly as unconsideringly, on the grounds that predestination was 'too great an abyss' to be probed. His description of the whole situation is characteristic: 'a poor church doing its utmost to destroy both itself and religion in furious zeale and endless debates about the empty name and shadow of a difference in government, and in the meanwhile not having of solemn and orderly publick worship so much as a shadow'. He held to a form of non-resistance in both Church and state because concern over government got in the way of man's chief duty and pleasure, which was worship. The time was ripe, Leighton felt, for the Church to offer generous terms to those still outside, and he was prepared to take on the job.

The strength and narrowness of the opposing attitude in religion is best shown not by recourse to the writing of the Covenanting wing, since their attitude was basically dictated by political opposition, but in the religious exercises of those of Presbyterian preference who tried to conform to episcopacy but could feel the pull of Covenanting propaganda. The strength of the Covenant lay in the fact that it had been taken: it was a bond with God, by which the Scots were mortgaged to extremism. To legal-minded eyes it could not be broken unilaterally any more than a family settlement could. There is a scene in the diary of Alexander Brodie of Brodie which shows this outlook. In the short days of January 1654 the whole Brodie family, in all its branches, held a day of humiliation, and after confessions and a sermon, the men solemnly one by one renewed their personal covenants with God, surrendering (in this order) their souls, bodies, estates, lands, rents, houses, families, wives, children, and servants to Him. After that their womenfolk pledged themselves too. The agreement has the force of religion, but the language is that of the family lawyer and the clauses of a mortgage. Covenanting speech always harked back to the question of what was lawful, what bonds were on the Scots. Could this bargain with God be ignored and cast off for the sake of unity and peace?

In their attempts at compromise Leighton and Lauderdale were bound to annoy the right wing of the episcopal party. They planned a conference with the leading Presbyterians of the old Resolutioner party to see if there were any acceptable terms on which they would re-enter the Church. Protest at the existence of bishops would be allowed, and at the synods, bishops, though presiding, would have no powers. Hutcheson, for the Presbyterians, went into conference with Leighton, but resisted the compromise. All the same Lauderdale put out his Indulgence, an offer to the more peaceable of the 'outed' ministers, which would give them a living and a flock, provided they kept sedition out of their sermons. Forty-two preachers were temporarily regained, but at the cost of extreme annoyance among the higher wing of the Church. Sharp sulked, but the main issue belonged to the south-west, not to his province, and it was in the Glasgow synod under Archbishop Burnet, that complaint was voiced. The government was unreasonably enraged by opposition from this quarter, and accused the clergy of imitating the Remonstrants, of subversion, of interference with the rights of monarchy. Unfortunately for the government, the clergy were right in law, for the Act of 1662 which recognized episcopacy gave the right of licensing preachers only to the bishops. Lauderdale had hastily to push an Act through Parliament endowing the king with 'supreme authority over all persons and in all cases ecclesiastical', a drastic assertion of a royal supremacy that Scotland had never before allowed.[1] On the strength of this authority Burnet was forced to resign and Leighton was put in his place to carry on the policy of compromise.

To please a minority who were unlikely to accept the compromise anyhow – Tweeddale commented of the Covenanters that 'som of that gang will not subscribe to the Lord's prayer, if asked' – Lauderdale had insisted on a clumsy piece of legislation which annoyed and frightened all kinds of opinion inside the Church. Under the pressure of this and of his own increasingly imperious temper, and the ostentatious lining of the family nest by himself and his near relatives, his party began to disintegrate. Leighton started up the conference again, but found that Hutcheson had never intended to make any bargain at all. In spite of this, another 90 non-conforming ministers were won back for the Church, but the hard core remained outside and had no intention of any compromise. Against them Lauderdale passed in 1671 what he himself called 'a clanking Act against conventicles', making field preaching a capital offence. The Act may have clanked: it did nothing more. Nothing is more striking in this period than the physical immunity of the extremist preachers. In spite of punitive legislation, unless they engaged in active rebellion or openly refused to acknowledge Charles II as king, the conventicle preachers moved about Scotland with impunity and were sure to die in their beds. The worst that would happen to them was a spell in prison on the Bass Rock, chilly but not fatal.

Lauderdale's régime looked authoritative on paper; the Act of Supremacy and the Conventicle Act gave the Crown enormous theoretical powers. Lauderdale had also taken great pains over a militia Act which could be used to offer an army to Charles if he should be faced with trouble in England. But the material resources of the Scottish government in reality were still too slender for the job it had to do. It had not got the troops to protect conforming ministers from being beaten up in the south-west. The 'indulged' ministers, obliged to keep off politics in their sermons, were often so narrowly

1. The 'Act of Supremacy' of 1669.

trained that they had very little else to preach about. Their flocks soon left them for conventicles. Leighton, despairing of doing good, asked for leave to retire from what he called 'a drunken scuffle in the dark' and went off to England where he could pray in peace. Lauderdale had a final attempt at leniency, a proclamation relaxing penalties on dissent, and the conventicles began again, armed. As the months passed, these meetings got larger and bolder, till the government found itself faced with the menace of armed bands of over 10,000 staying out on the hills and moving round the country like an army. It put into action the strongest legal weapons it had, making land-owners responsible for the behaviour of their tenants, fining those known to attend conventicles, and using the fines to reward their local enemies. These techniques were fairly effective in areas where the movement was a minority one, but were useless in the south-west.

Charles was determined not to allow Scotch and English opposition movements to get together: he was well aware that it was in this way the Great Rebellion had started. There does not seem to have been actual liaison between the Covenanters and Shaftesbury's English Country party at this time, but the relative immunity of non-conformists in England after 1672 was well known in Scotland, and so was the unrest which came into the open in the attack of the 1678 Parliament on Charles's ministers, and on Lauderdale in particular. Lauderdale was fighting on both the English and Scotch fronts. He was familiar with the irrational nature of Covenanting decisions – after several hours of prayer the true Covenanter would 'get clearance from God' and know His will from the first text that entered his head, though it might need some rather forced interpretation. Rebellion could not be counted on to come at the rational moment, but with disturbance growing in England it would come some time. He abandoned conciliation altogether and attempted to cow the south-west by inviting Highland chiefs to send troops there to live 'at free quarter'. This meant an invasion of some 8,000 Highlanders with an open invitation to loot; there was also a substantial body of Lowland militia doing itself well in the same way. Arms were re-moved from the area, and even the nobility saw their horses con-fiscated.

These actions raised the cry against him very loud indeed. The use of free quarter was in fact legal; it was a regular instrument of the

Privy Council for extracting overdue taxation. But the confiscation of horses and arms and the insistence on surety from landowners for their tenants were less clear in law. We may regard the quartering as the oppressive part of the policy but the protests that went to court, led by Hamilton and supported there by Charles's illegitimate son, the Duke of Monmouth, concentrated on the actions against the landowners. Charles openly stood by Lauderdale, but he quietly advised him to see that the duke had some of his horses left him. After two months, Lauderdale withdrew the Highlanders, and hoped the south-west had had its lesson. But he had been right that it was impossible to calculate when the rebellion would come. It came next year.

It began with a nasty business in May 1679 – the hacking to death of Sharp by a group of armed horsemen outside St Andrews. These men had been out looking for the Sheriff-depute to pay off some old scores, when Sharp drove up in his coach. After murdering him and searching the body for evidence of witchcraft, they rode to the west and gathered forces. In a confused way the rebellion snowballed. When the young soldier, John Graham of Claverhouse, tried to disperse a large conventicle at Drumclog in the moors he found it had become an organized army. Claverhouse and his dragoons were repulsed with loss, fell back on Glasgow, but soon had to leave the city to the rebels. The rebellion was defeated at Bothwell Brig in June 1679 in some real fighting by Monmouth with troops from England. It had already split on the standard Covenanting issue of whether to accept support from those not entirely 'godly', in particular from those who had accepted the Indulgences. By the end of August, Monmouth had secured pardon for most of the prisoners (for all who would agree to keep the peace, but over 200 refused, were shipped off for the Barbadoes and wrecked in Orkney, where many drowned). There were a few executions, and one minister was tortured for information, but it was clear that the main rebellion had collapsed. The pull of the extremists on the more moderate of the Presbyterian party had been destroyed by the brief period of trying to co-operate. It had been just feasible to keep a party together pledged against the Engagement of over thirty years back, but when it came to one dedicated to opposition to Lauderdale's Indulgences, common sense lifted its head. The sending of Monmouth was a sign of Charles's recognition that, with the Popish Plot rampant in England, gentleness must be shown to all manifestations of Whiggism. Monmouth was deliberately generous. Conventicles were for a time allowed, within doors, except in the main cities, on the sensible grounds that architectural limitations would make these a lot smaller than the armed crowds frequenting the hillsides.

Bothwell Brig was the end of Lauderdale's power, as Rullion Green was the end of the earlier ministry. Charles kept him on nominally for a while out of affection. His colleagues had already left him – Moray and he had split shortly before Moray's death in 1672 and Lauderdale had shrugged off the friendship with the alliance. Tweeddale and Kincardine had passed to opposition. Lauderdale was failing, though it was not till August 1682 that Lauder of Fountainhall records the death, signalled by a comet, of 'the learnedest and powerfullest Minister in his age'.[1]

In place of Lauderdale, Scotland was sent James, Duke of York, brother and heir to the king, as Commissioner. This was to get him out of the way of the scare over the Popish Plot – for James wore his Catholicism with gloomy ostentation. Conventicles were again put down: James saw no reason to meet Whiggery half-way. The Presbyterians by conviction were in an awkward position. The Covenanting movement was openly political in aim, and clearly a minority affair. It could exercise little influence on the country in general, but could and did make it very uncomfortable for anyone in Galloway or Dumfriesshire. It was deteriorating, and sliding into the hands of younger men like Richard Cameron, of strong passions and little education; 'men that were not counsellable' as Law says of them. It was Cameron who was to give the name of 'Cameronians' to this faction. These men started up field preaching again and produced a series of extremist documents – the *Queensferry Paper* and Cameron's *Sanquhar Declaration* in 1680 and James Renwick's *Apologetical Declaration* in 1684.[2] The *Apologetical Declaration* is the most

1. As an obituary, here is a comment on him by the conventicle minister Robert Law: 'truly a man of great spirit, great parts, great will, a most daring man, and a man of great success, and did more without the sword than Oliver Cromwell did with it, was a man very national, and truly the honour of our Scots nation for wit and parts'.

2. The hard core of these papers can be read in *The Source Book of Scottish History* (1961), III, pp. 175–82.

obstinately bloodthirsty of these – declaring the intention of the Covenanters to make war on all officials, soldiers, judges, conformist ministers, and all who gave information about the extremists as 'enemies to God and the covenanted work of reformation'. But the *Queensferry Paper* probably did most harm to their aims, because it made it impossible for most Presbyterians to accept their lead. This paper declared for a Church and state to be ruled only by the Covenanters and their associates, and governed 'not after a carnal manner by the plurality of votes ... but according to the word of God', in other words by a small group of self-appointed theocrats. As Robert Law sadly commented: 'they disowned the Presbyterian Church of Scotland' by breaking up the 'standing fixed ministrie in the land which is the ordinance of Jesus Christ'. The party had also discarded the Westminster Confession, for this accepted the civil power and the royal choice of ministers and bishops, and had also discarded a part of Calvin's own doctrine in denouncing prayers for the king. The subtleties of doctrine and the realities of Christian living were pushed aside for the sake of war.

In accepting the challenge, the government also discarded its principles. In 1681 the Scottish Parliament accepted the Test Act, a crude weapon which was to dismay many. It demanded from all office holders other than the immediate royal family,[1] adherence to the old Knoxian Confession of 1560, acceptance of the king as supreme governor of the Church, allegiance to him and his heirs, and the renunciation of all intention to attempt changes in Church or state.

This bears a likeness to the desperate attempts of apartheid legislation in South Africa to prevent revolution by making illegal all intention for change. Both create intellectual difficulties for the more honest and intelligent of the supporters of the régime. It was difficult to reconcile the Confession of 1560 with royal supremacy, or this supremacy with the prospect of James as governor of the Church. Leighton's following in the Church, those who wanted a liturgy and more reverent forms of worship, could hardly be expected to repudiate all change. A sizeable body of ministers of this opinion refused the Test: efforts were made which kept a few within the Church, but sixty-three left. Some found cures in England or the colonies, but they were lost to Scotland.

1. An exception put in because of James's Catholicism.

The main political victim of the Test was Archibald, ninth Earl of Argyll. He had made his peace in the 1660s and, with Lauderdale's help, had regained his father's estates. Safe as one of Lauderdale's party he had made himself hated in the Highlands by repudiating his own and his father's debts while he pursued his creditors in his own court. After building up their obligations by compound interest he had foreclosed on the lands of the Macleans of Duart, and backed his court with the usual Highland addition of commissions from the Privy Council for action by fire and sword. The Campbell empire now included Mull, Morvern, and Tiree, and there were many discontented chieftains ready to fall upon Argyll when Lauderdale's protection died. Argyll gave these their chance when he found he could only take the Test with qualifications – in particular he accepted it 'so far as it was consistent with itself'. Argyll's words in Parliament on this occasion were taken as coming under the head of 'leasing making' or verbal sedition. The Crown of Scotland had developed weapons in its long battle with the nobility which it had rarely been strong enough to use, but which were to prove intolerable when it gained in strength, and this was one of them. Argyll was condemned for treason; it was made easy for him to escape abroad, and he went.

The government had made itself a crude weapon in the Test, which enabled it, however unwisely, to investigate men's opinions. The indulged ministers were turned out again and leading figures of known Presbyterian inclinations felt it wise to get out of the way, among them the President of the Court of Session, the great legist Stair. Another resignation enabled the Privy Council to send the young soldier and courtier, Claverhouse, to Galloway as sheriff of Wigtown, with troops to back him. Claverhouse showed what vigour and a show of force could do by rounding up the delinquents of Galloway, showing them the list of fines they were liable for, and getting most of them back into church on Sundays with astonishing speed. This did nothing to affect the religious and political opinions of the region: Claverhouse himself remarked 'there were as many elephants and crocodiles in Galloway as loyal or regular persons', but it prevented forcible demonstrations and made life safer for the conforming clergy. The mixture of rigorous investigation and force might, if allowed time, have calmed the issue, for it would have obliged a fairly ignorant peasantry to have heard another point of

view. Events outside, particularly in England, prevented this and
pushed the government to still more drastic action.

In the early months of 1683 there was brewed in England the confused series of intrigues known as the Rye House plot. It involved
at least two levels of conspiracy, part being aimed at the kidnapping
of Charles and his brother on their way home from Newmarket, and
part at murdering them. Kidnapping the king was an old Scottish
habit, but in this context it could not be separated from plans to do
without him altogether, and it is difficult to see how anyone could
have engaged in one part of the plot without being sympathetic to the
intention of the other. This English conspiracy had a Scottish branch.
This was organized by Argyll and other refugees, and supported in
Scotland not by the wild men of the south-west, but by sober
gentlemen of Whiggish and Presbyterian leanings. Charles stamped
hard on the intrigues. Twelve or thirteen Scottish prisoners found in
the unravelling of the plot were sent north for trial, because the
Scottish law of treason was more flexible than that of England, and a
particular attack was launched on the landowners who had links with
the plot – Baillie of Jerviswood, Gordon of Earlston, and a Presbyterian minister, William Carstares. Against some of the prisoners the
Privy Council used its old power of torturing to extract information.
In spite of the scare, and the body of evidence, there were not many
executions, but many gentlemen felt unsafe, and rightly.

Fighting went on in the south-west, small but bloodthirsty actions.
Cameron was killed in a cavalry encounter in Ayrshire in the summer
of 1680. In August 1684, there was a short battle in the green cleft
of the Enterkin pass when Covenanters ambushed some of Claverhouse's troopers in the hope of rescuing prisoners on their way to
trial at Edinburgh, and two or three troopers were killed. Such affrays
would lead to local reprisals and the execution on inadequate
evidence of any armed men found near at hand, and bitterness would
spread. After the *Apologetical Declaration* the Covenanters began to
fulfil their promise of systematic murder, and in reply the government
insisted that anyone not abjuring the more bloodthirsty sections of the
Declaration when asked, should be shot out of hand. Suspects, even
if they passed this test, should be sent up to Edinburgh for trial. This
was the start of the period known in Covenanting mythology as the
'killing time'. Seventy-eight people are known to have been killed

without trial during it, either in scuffles, escapes, or in refusing to abjure, and others were executed after trial.[1]

Scottish historiography of this era and later cannot be properly understood without the realization that a vast amount of nonsense has been talked about this short and disturbed period. After the establishment of Presbyterianism, various members of the Kirk, while repudiating the Covenanters' concept of church government, accepted the leaders of the sect into the martyrology. Robert Wodrow, who was a small child at the time of the struggle, spent a large part of his adult life in collectiong written and oral material on it which was published in 1721 as *The History of the Sufferings of the Church*, a semi-official account. As he included in it large sections of the papers of the Privy Council, historians have found it a useful work, without always noticing that much of the rest of his material is hearsay which does not even bear the name of the teller. Also, in the renewed emphasis on evangelical Calvinism in the nineteenth century, many documents from this period were published in handsome and useful editions, often with low or uncritical editorial standards. Though there have been protests at times, a great deal of garbage has been inserted into the received edition of Scottish history. Scotland's folk memory, as unreliable and synthetic as most folk memories in modern societies, recalls the Covenanters as defenceless saints who were slaughtered for religious reasons, defending the cause of liberty against a ruthless and persecuting government. Nicknames such as 'the Bluidy Mackenzie' for Mackenzie, the Lord Advocate and chief prosecutor in the trials of the period, have become established. The Privy Council is accused of using torture frequently. To support the story there has been a selective use of materials, sometimes by historians who were not only biased but dishonest. The Privy Council of this period was certainly repressive in its policies and clumsy in their execution. It had legal powers that weighted the scale against its opponents, and the right, or rather duty, to use torture when it thought information could be obtained vital for the safety of the state. Its main weapons were fines and confiscations, and these were sometimes used to drive families into penury. It was a rough age, and the treatment of prisoners was

1. As a comparison, in eighteen months of disturbances in the ex-kingdom of Naples (1861–3), recently liberated by Garibaldi, there were 1,038 summary shootings. See Denis Mack Smith, *Italy: a modern history* (1959), p. 73.

not gentle.[1] Penalties indirectly fell on the innocent as well as the guilty and produced bitterness. But the Council was unwilling to pursue men on religious grounds, and would grant pardons wherever good reason could be urged, preferring threats to action. The members of the Council clearly disliked the duty of torturing: they had to be ordered to attend these grisly sessions, and would do all they could to find excuses to end them. When they were finally instructed to put Alexander Gordon of Earlston to the torture he got off by feigning madness: 'he roared like a bull and cryed and struck about him' and finally produced a tale that the rising of the fanatics was to be led by General Dalyell. Not all the Council were taken in, but they accepted the excuse. In all the twenty-eight years of the restored monarchy the number of cases of torture before the Privy Council was fifteen, all of them connected with the likelihood of plots. Torture is always disgusting, but this is not an excessive list for a time of disorder. If we are to have a 'killing time' in Scottish history the name would much more appropriately belong to the period immediately after the Restoration, when the English and their courts were got rid of, and several hundred old and unpopular women were put into prison, tortured, tried, and condemned for witchcraft.[2]

NOTES ON DRAMATIS PERSONAE

Argyll. Archibald Campbell, ninth Earl (1629–85). Executed under James VII. He pursued an uncertain course in politics, partly because of his bad relations with his father, the great Marquess, but there was nothing uncertain about his enlargement of the family estates.

1. Some idea of the roughness of the age can be gleaned from the fact that the 'thumbykins' or thumbscrew, the new instrument of torture that was used by the Council on three of the Rye House plot conspirators, was already in use by landowners as a means of disciplining troublesome miners.
2. In the first six months of 1662, when the backlog of old scores was already largely paid off, there were commissions granted for the trial of 125 witches, most of whom had confessed and had no likelihood of acquittal. In the rare cases of a woman getting off, her prospects were still black, for she faced ostracism, unemployment, and starvation.

Richard Cameron (died 1680), schoolmaster and preacher, leading Covenanter with a price of 5,000 merks on his head, which was eventually won.

General Tam Dalyell or *Dalziel* (*c.* 1599–1685), professional soldier of gentry origin, who served in Ireland, at Worcester, and in Russia. He is credited with introducing the thumbscrew from Russia.

Claverhouse. John Graham of Claverhouse (*c.* 1649–89), Viscount Dundee 1688. A newer style of professional soldier, with a political commitment to royalism.

Hamilton. William Douglas, third Duke (1634–94). He received the dukedom via his wife, the daughter of the first Duke. Political leader 1688–9. Gilbert Burnet complains of his boisterous temper and lack of polish.

Hutcheson. George Hutcheson (died 1674), a leading Resolutioner minister, outed in 1662, a great preacher.

Kincardine. Alexander Bruce, second Earl (*c.* 1629–80), of royalist and Presbyterian sympathies, scientific talent, and wide business interests.

Lauderdale. John Maitland, second Earl and Duke 1672 (1612–82). As a young man a leading Covenanter, later companion to Charles II, a large-faced man with a speech impediment, intelligent and passionate. After one suitable marriage had ended in estrangement he shocked his contemporaries by choosing his second wife for her brains and personality.

Leighton. Robert Leighton (1611–84). One of the few clergy sympathetic to the Engagers, 1653 Principal of Edinburgh University, 1661 bishop of Dunblane, 1670 Archbishop of Glasgow.

Rothes. As in Chapter 14.

Sharp. James Sharp (1613–79), Archbishop of St Andrews. An early anti-Covenanter, from Banff, he became a Resolutioner, and eventually a politically-minded bishop with a sharp eye for the main chance.

Stair. Sir James Dalrymple, first Viscount Stair (1619–95), founder of one of Scotland's legal dynasties. He was made a judge by Cromwell and was kept on by Charles II in spite of refusing to renounce the Covenant. Father of the Master of Stair of Chapter 16.

Tweeddale. John Hay, second Earl, and first Marquess (1625–97). His family, connected to much of the wealth of lowland Scotland, was at first Covenanting, but gained a peerage and joined the Engagement. He was probably the most able man it has produced, widely trusted in politics. His son married Lauderdale's daughter and heir.

Mackenzie. Sir George Mackenzie of Rosehaugh, see Chapter 16.

Chapter 16

The Revolution Settlement

Siege of the Bass

WHEN CHARLES II COLLAPSED with a stroke in February 1685, it looked as if he had achieved his main aim as king, to make sure that the monarch never again had to go on his travels. He went away with his Catholicism still a secret, shared only between him, one or two others, and the priest who gave him his last unction. His openly Catholic brother James could reign supreme because the English Whig opposition had overreached itself. In Scotland the government was still fighting the vestiges of the extremist party and looked like winning. The government's power was greater than it had ever been. The Privy Council was still checking on several hundred people thought to have been at Bothwell Brig, or to have encouraged others to be there. The Test and the Oath of Allegiance were being imposed to distinguish the accommodating from the disloyal. It looked as if even James could not undo the tight lock of his position. If Scotland had been alone this might well have been true.

Parliaments in both kingdoms were royalist and generous. James was the first king for over 150 years to be secured in an income adequate to his needs. Royalism was further heartened by incompetent risings against him – in May Argyll landed in his own country with 300 men after a well-advertised, lethargic journey round the north coast, and in June, when this rebellion was already on the run, Monmouth opened his disastrous campaign in the south-west of England. These two attempts to put Monmouth on a throne, for which he was obviously unfitted both by birth and character, received poor support. Even Galloway was held so firmly for the Crown that little help came in, and in any case Argyll was too moderate and Monmouth too lax to get the support of the extremists. Argyll was guillotined under his old sentence of 1681, with a speech from the scaffold composed almost entirely of biblical quotations, and Monmouth was axed. Argyll's swing to Presbyterianism against a government which had long favoured him had been too late to carry much conviction. The Privy Council in Scotland found itself with several hundred prisoners who refused to acknowledge James, and did the only safe and humane thing possible in shipping them off to the Barbadoes. That their handling before they were sent off was at best rough and ready, at worst systematically brutal, is a commentary on the prisons and prison-keepers of the day.[1] There was a good deal of devastation of the country round Inveraray, but no parallel in Scotland to the Bloody Assizes and executions in England.

The main result of these inadequate demonstrations was the simplification of the issue of the monarchy. Those who felt that a Catholic monarch was unacceptable had now no choice but William of Orange, Stadtholder of the Netherlands, nephew and son-in-law to James. At first only a few in either kingdom were ready for such a choice. It was James's work to increase both the British refugee

1. The toughest treatment was that of those already in prison for refusal of allegiance before the rebellions. These were hustled off to Dunnottar castle and kept short of food and water for a month. There has been a certain amount of escalation about this story.

population at the Hague and the readiness of his English subjects to look abroad for a king, by the methods he adopted to obtain toleration and privilege for Roman Catholics. In Scotland James's policy involved a struggle between king and Parliament. James, never a good judge of men, started badly by sacking his Commissioner, the Duke of Queensberry, who would not change his religion to suit James, and employing instead the Earl of Perth. Perth had already changed sides from Lauderdale to opposition: now he changed his party, and his own and his wife's religion. His brother, Lord Melfort, became one of the two Secretaries of State and also decided for conversion. However desirable it might have been to acquaint Calvinists with the real practices and beliefs of Roman Catholicism, about which most of them knew as little as they did of Buddhism, this was not a way in which experience of Catholicism would lead to better relations between the Churches. The Countess of Perth was mobbed after mass by the Edinburgh apprentices, and this led to a night-long riot up and down the narrow wynds of the town. At the second session of his Parliament James asked for the repeal of the penal laws against the Catholics; as a bribe there was a vague offer of royal help towards free trade with England, a thing Scots felt they were entitled to anyhow. This attempt at a Toleration Act gave a plentiful opportunity to members of Parliament to give their views on the Roman Catholic Church, and the reply was so nearly a direct negative that James had to prevent its publication. His legal adviser, Mackenzie of Tarbat, Lord Clerk Register, had thought that Parliament would acquiesce in James's policy, and indeed it probably would have but for James's own actions. There had been too open a manipulation of burgh elections, including acceptance of votes by councillors who had refused the Test; army officers in opposition had been brusquely sent back to their units and an attempt had been made to convict Bishop Ramsay of Ross for libel after a parliamentary sermon of intemperate Protestantism. The historian must particularly regret one arbitrary action, which, though it shows the climate of the time, silenced one of the liveliest chroniclers of the day, Sir John Lauder of Fountainhall, a leading lawyer. He closes his account thus: 'In April 1686, my two servants being imprisoned, and I threatened therewith, as also that they would seize upon my papers, and search if they contained anything offensive to the party then prevailing, I was necessitat to hide this Manuscript and many others, and intermit my Historick Remarks till the Revolution in the end of 1688.' Life under James had become difficult and dangerous for those who did not think like him.

Not all James's servants were convinced, or time-serving, Catholics. He used two men whose long association with different governments marks the rise of professional politicians with purely secular interests, Sir George Mackenzie of Tarbat and Sir John Dalrymple, Master of Stair, son to the great legist. With their help he went on to show that he could do most of what he liked without the aid of Parliament. The laws against Catholics depended on the executive for action, and it did not act. In February 1687 James offered toleration to Roman Catholics and Quakers: they could hold meetings in private houses under ministers who would accept this Indulgence. In June 1688 this was extended to Presbyterians. All that was still forbidden and prosecuted was field preaching.

This was the same policy as that pursued by James in England, toleration by decree and a general selection of office holders in favour of either Catholics or yes-men. Burgh officials were soon all royal nominees: the Privy Council gradually took on a Catholic flavour. The effects of this on the Church in Scotland was, however, much more drastic than in England. The Presbyterian Church could now organize itself openly, and it gathered strength. The government captured the leading Covenanter, James Renwick, and executed him. The rest of the Covenanting ministry merged with the more moderate Presbyterians, gaining thereby the advantages of the toleration. Presbyterianism at last had a united front. The whole basis of security for the Episcopal Church was shaken. Without liturgy or ceremony, and without even security for purely episcopal ordination, the Episcopal Church in Scotland had had little to cling to beyond royal support, and this had now been withdrawn. There was no longer any attempt to make the established Church comprehend the bulk of the nation. The Archbishop of Glasgow and the bishop of Dunblane were deprived of their sees for opposition, and the bishops were shooed off the Council. The whole political and administrative system of Scotland had been based on the alliance of Church and king. This alliance was now ended.

Unrest and unease were accentuated by news from Ireland, which showed that there James was undoing the Protestant ascendancy. Seventeenth-century Scotland was always sensitive to Irish events: the two countries were only separated by a narrow strip of water, across which small trading boats moved constantly. In Ireland there was a large body of Scots whose position depended on Protestant dominance over the native Roman Catholics. With this dominance apparently being destroyed it began to look as if the Protestants in Ireland would be lucky if they could pull out with their lives and a residue of property. Yet in this tense and urgent situation James's government could still hold Scotland, and did; it was England alone that made the Revolution of 1688.

On 5 November William of Orange landed in the south-west of England in answer to an invitation from several leading English figures. By the end of the year he was provisionally installed in London, and James and his baby son had taken refuge in France. The Scots had not moved during the crisis, even though James had brought his Scottish troops south for a battle that never happened. The year 1660 had shown that if the Scots waited for royal decisions they would be at the end of the line. So the high road to London thronged with people.

William, 'Dutch William', soon to be William III, was not totally ignorant of Scotch affairs. He had collected at the Hague a scatter of influential men, and so was able to bring with him refugee Scots as well as refugee English. These included William Carstares, who had already been involved in the Rye House Plot, and tortured for it in the Privy Council in spite of the sympathy of the Councillors; George Melville, fresh from the Monmouth rising; and the voluble and active Gilbert Burnet. Between them these three represented the main strands of Scottish religion; Burnet was a Whiggish supporter of moderate episcopacy who went on to show the Anglican Church what an active and conscientious bishop could do. Carstares was a moderate Presbyterian, the son of an ardent Remonstrant. Both the men wished to see the Kirk as comprehensive as possible. Melville was a narrower and more extreme Presbyterian. The big element in Scotland, with which William was as yet unfamiliar, was the nobility, but the speed with which they travelled to meet him soon amended this.

James's flight had left his supporters high and dry, and even before it he had denuded Scotland of troops. Chaos was near at hand. The Covenanters of the south-west appeared in large numbers in Edinburgh, and the Highlands were restive. William called a Convention of the Scottish Estates: it could not be a parliament until he had become king, and it had to be elected on an irregular and wide basis to shift power away from the burgh councils that James had been manipulating. With the royalist party in confusion it was natural that this Parliament should strongly represent the dominant flavour of the day, Whiggish and Presbyterian. Its first trial of strength showed this, a vote on whether communication from William or James should be received first, which the 'Williamites' won: the 'Jacobites', as they were later to be called, were not only defeated but intimidated. Since Edinburgh for them was a danger spot, with every cellar holding a western Covenanter anxious to do a godly murder,[1] they left the Convention altogether. Claverhouse, now Viscount Dundee, rode north to his craggy and embattled house of Claypots with a troop of horse. Sir George Mackenzie, the Lord Advocate, took refuge in Yorkshire. The Earl of Balcarres fled abroad. Melfort and Perth set out for France, but Perth was caught on the way and ended up in the town gaol of Kirkcaldy.

The path of events in England soon made it clear that William would become king; the important question was on what terms. The disappearance of the opposition in Scotland made it certain that these would be drastically Whiggish. The settlement in Scotland had none of the moderation produced in England by the necessity of compromise within a parliament predominantly Tory. Yet the Whigs in Scotland were more markedly a minority than they were in England. Parliament drew up the famous and long-winded Claim of Right – the statement of the offences of James, which contained three elements vital for the future. James had forfeited the Crown:[2] no 'Papist' could be king, queen, or officer of state in Scotland: and 'Prelacy and the superiority of any office in the Church above Presbyters, is, and hath been a great and insupportable grievance and trouble to this Nation'. The much greater range and wordiness of the Claim of Right, when compared with the English Bill of Rights, reflect the

1. Scott, in his song *Bonnie Dundee*, says, 'With sourfaced Whigs the Grass-market was crammed.'
2. 'Forefaulted' is the word used.

fact that in Scotland the monarchy had legally more autocratic powers, and on the rare occasions when it felt strong enough to use them, could govern more dictatorially. This was now to change.

William III had none of the ready charm of so many of the Stewarts. He was blunt, and made contact with his court for business not amusement: his pleasure came from gardens and strenuous hunting. He had behind him a lonely childhood of chronic illness and political obscurity. From this background he had learnt his tenacious courage. He had come to England not to benefit that country but to bring her wealth and power to his side in the grand European alliance he had made against French aggression. His greatest asset to his new kingdoms was his talent for men – his ability to choose the best men as servants, his knowledge of how far to back them, and his will to do so. He had also learnt, in a hard school, the virtues of tolerance. A Calvinist himself, he did not want to coerce men against their consciences, or to pry into the reasons for spiritual and worldly allegiance. He would not provoke a crisis on spiritual loyalty if he could help it, and where political loyalty failed him he would be ready with pardon. When he insisted that, before he could accept the Crown of Scotland, the oath of office that bound him to root out heresy must be understood not to mean persecution, he was not merely publicizing his attitude, or getting out of an awkward position, but simply stating something that was fundamental to his idea of statecraft. The climate of opinion as to the righteousness of coercion in religious causes was modifying, and William looked at the subject with the eyes of the eighteenth century rather than of the seventeenth. As a result, the apparatus of government in Scotland, as far as the king could secure it, was to be used in a new way.

But neither William, nor his wife and co-ruler, Mary, had much time for Scotland. In March 1689 James landed in Ireland to turn the fighting that was already going on there into the full bitterness of religious and civil war. William had to follow him. Meanwhile, he had learnt that his supporters in Scotland were a minority. The 'Jacobites' may have left Parliament to intransigent Presbyterianism, but they were predominant north of the Tay, and the great majority of the existing ministry in the Church would never readily support William. However rational and convenient it would be to have a similar church settlement in both countries, the Scottish bishops'

K

refusal to acknowledge William as king forced him to accept that episcopacy must go. Perhaps he still hoped that the bishops would later give way: at any rate he did not want the future of the Kirk settled by a parliament of the complexion of 1689.

Parliament had given the throne to William, sending the new Earl of Argyll, the young Master of Stair, and Sir James Montgomery of Skelmorlie, to make the offer. William had at once seen in young Stair a man he could use. Stair was the new phenomenon in Scotland, a 'man of state'. He would serve the Crown and the law without much regard to religion, a man of tremendous talent, witty and good company, clever, with a fine understanding for both political and military issues and a lack of scruple. As a recent servant of James's, his entry into William's service committed his family absolutely to the Revolution, a valuable point in a time of uncertainty and treachery. William took as his other servants in Scotland, Melville as Secretary of State (where he proved neither efficient nor politic), and the only ardently Presbyterian figure among the older nobility, the Earl of Crawford, as President of the Privy Council. Hamilton was put in as Commissioner, for though he did not like Presbytery he had led the Williamites at the Revolution.

Parliament, deprived of a normal opposition, was extremist, and somehow must be kept from infuriating the half-hearted. The more the dominant Presbyterian group asserted itself as the only victors of the Revolution, the more uncertain became William's support among the nobility, the northern half of the kingdom, and in particular the Highlands. As Mackenzie of Tarbat said, in remonstrance to Melville over his Presbyterian preferences, 'The Presbyterians are the more zealous and hotter; the other more numerous and powerful.' It was William's hope to attract both to his government, and Presbyterian intransigence made this difficult.

The English have called the Revolution of 1688–9 'Glorious' because of the absence of bloodshed. This is strictly an English point of view. From the first there was fighting in Ireland, and in Scotland it looked unlikely that Dundee would sit quietly at home and dismiss his troops. Soon he had slipped into the Highlands and was writing to the chiefs in James's name. Several were ready to help him, for the victory of William and Presbyterianism would mean the restoration of the power of Argyll, and the return to him of the lands and superiorities his father had grabbed by dubious means in the 1670s. As before, the political and religious settlement of Scotland was bound up with the territorial aggrandizement of the Campbells. Dundee had the talent to keep his Highland chiefs together in his army with their private disputes temporarily shelved. The sixty-year-old Sir Ewen Cameron of Lochiel, who came out in person with his clan, was of enormous help in this. The government sent General Hugh Mackay of Scourie to police the north, and this poor man, with half-trained troops, was tramping the glens of Badenoch and Atholl, rightly distrusting the allegiance of the population of the whole of the north of Scotland,[1] suspicious, with reason, of some of his own officers who were in league with the elusive Dundee, and indignant at the ambiguous behaviour of the Murrays of Atholl. (Highlanders who live on a main through-route learn a double-faced technique if they are to survive.) Only in June was the Jacobite garrison got out of Edinburgh castle, and there was still another, besieged ineffectually on the Bass Rock, off North Berwick, in league with foreign pirates and endangering the corn supplies of the capital.[2] It was in this setting that the Parliament chose to fight out the issue of royal authority.

The fact of successful revolution, even if only marginally successful, had naturally increased the power of the landed classes in Scotland and weakened that of the central government. William had to rule with the approval of those who had brought him in. No single group of great men comparable to the Revolution aristocracy in England rose to the top in Scotland, a fact which is understandable since it was England and not Scotland that had made the Revolution; but several leading houses were inflated in importance, notably the Hamiltons and Argyll. In addition, several lesser families reached the peerage in the new reign, notably Melville and the Primroses of Rosebery. One of the reasons why William trusted Stair was that his family stood apart from the great houses, and backed his authority more wholeheartedly than they did. It is a sign of the revived power of the aristocracy that Stair was continually under fire in Parliament. William had had to fill the Privy Council largely from the aristocracy

1. His own moderate comment was that the people of the north had 'no true sense of the deliverance which God had sent them'.
2. These were Jacobite prisoners, put there for safe keeping, who had proved too much for the gaolers: in the end they left the Bass with full honours of war.

with the result that this body was irresolute in the face of Parliament and often at odds with the Secretary in London. Also, under Crawford's guidance, it was unlikely to play fair over William's church policy of moderation.

The members of the opposition group in Parliament gave themselves the misleadingly bonhomous title of 'the Club'. This was led by the unstable Montgomery of Skelmorlie, disappointed at not being Secretary of State. It is often thought of as simply an extreme Presbyterian grouping but its willingness to ally with the Jacobites when convenient makes it more easily understood as a fairly unscrupulous political opposition. The Club was out to break the machinery of royal 'absolutism'. Its most positive achievement was the destruction of the Committee of the Lords of the Articles, the machinery by which the Crown traditionally controlled Parliament. While the ministers bumbled about, trying to find a substitute method of getting what they needed in legislation through the Parliament, the government was nearly paralysed. The Club asserted that William's kingship did not entitle him to appoint judges and re-open the courts, and it was some months before the ministers dared take these steps. Meanwhile the Parliament restored to their parishes the surviving remnants of the 'outed' ministers of 1662, but refused to do the same for those 'outed' over the Test in 1681: 'some animals are more equal than others'. The sixty now put back were the only ministers absolutely secure, for they had never accepted bishops: the Church was in their hands. Many of the official clergy in the southwest had already been manhandled and driven from their parishes at Christmas, 'rabbled' by one or more armed gangs going from village to village. Many more were to go as the sixty 'purged' the Church. The surviving ministers of the Covenanters rejoined the Kirk, which left the outposts of fanaticism leaderless. Things were working for a demarcation between Church and state, Parliament and General Assembly, but for the present the Church had got hold of more than most of the laity were prepared to allow.

Into this divided scene came news of catastrophe in the Highlands. Dundee had defeated Mackay in Atholl, just beyond the pass of Killiecrankie. The Highlanders had swept down the hillside in a barefoot charge, their long line wrapping round Mackay's shorter formation, and giving no time for his clumsy musketeers to get their plug bayonets in. It was a supreme example of what Highlanders could do in war, all over in a few minutes in the late afternoon. Mackay collected those troops who had not scattered and used the short midsummer darkness to cross the mountains and take up position south of the Highland line: the Privy Council got ready to retreat to England if Dundee should reach Stirling, the key to the Lowlands. But a few days later the emergency was over: the High-landers had followed up their victory by showing what they could not do: provide the organization for a sustained campaign. Dundee had received a bullet between his raised arm and his armour in the charge, and died on the field. His personality had held the army together, and now it disintegrated. There was a tiff and Lochiel went home. Enough men kept on for an attack on Dunkeld, where they came up against a regiment of Covenanters recently recruited. These 'Cameronians' fought with the ferocity of their creed and broke the impetus of the clans. The Highlanders dispersed, having failed to break through to the Lowlands, and went home. They were neither pacified nor settled, but they were no longer in arms. William's government would probably have survived even defeat and with-drawal, for there was England to fall back on, but it was spared this loss of prestige, and now it had a chance to establish itself. But there was still the war in Ireland, and the Scottish clans had still to be reconciled. Mackay pushed through to the Great Glen, and at Inver-lochy began to build the fort which he named Fort William – a key point for holding the Highlands because it could be supplied by sea. The old Cromwellian soldier, Colonel Hill, who had long ago helped to hold the Highlands under Monck, was put there again and told to fortify it.

William, who had now learnt a certain amount about managing Scotland, was able to make things go more smoothly. He would not now allow his Scottish and English Parliaments to meet at the same time. When he next let his Scottish Parliament meet, in the autumn of 1689, the Club was breaking up – its leader Montgomery of Skel-morlie was soon to be plotting with the Jacobites. The courts were re-established, and William began to look for his servants beyond the extreme Presbyterians. Stair came more to the fore, with another of the same secular outlook, Mackenzie of Tarbat. Tarbat had had a long career in law and politics, moving from fighting for the cavaliers in the 1650s to the detached view of an elder statesman at the end of the century. His own preference, as a Highlander, was for episcopacy and if that was not feasible he worked to limit the violence of the Presbyterian dominance. He was reputed to be corrupt, almost certainly with good reason. He was valuable because he understood the chiefs. In 1690 he proposed that the king should settle the basic unrest in the western Highlands by buying up the disputed superiorities that gave rise to it – for example Argyll's claims over land occupied by Camerons and Macleans – and holding them in the Crown. He suggested that some machinery of civil government could be started up in these areas, a shire and burgh based on Inverlochy, so that the representation of authority was not simply military. Then with a few small payments made to the clans to compensate them for the cessation of cattle raiding, the Highlands would be peaceful at small cost. That put the price at £5,000, a good deal cheaper than fighting. Unfortunately, when the scheme was seriously considered, a sea-change had come over it.

William gradually gained the upper hand in secular matters, but he had lost to the extreme Presbyterians in church ones. He had had to admit that he must govern the Church through the Williamites, and that meant establishing Presbyterianism. The 1669 Act of Supremacy was abolished and Melville as Commissioner gave the touch of assent with the sceptre which passed an Act abolishing patronage. The Presbyterians who had held out under James had established their Kirk on elected ministers, and this had now become to them a necessary feature of Presbyterianism. Melville's instructions allowed for this, but it marked the breach between him and William. The king felt that this was an unnecessary surrender to the sixty. Appointments in the Church now lay with heritors and elders, but the ministry, by swamping the kirk sessions with elders, could always ensure that only ministers of strong Presbyterian preferences were appointed.

In other ways William tried unsuccessfully to modify the new settlement. He wanted it to be called 'the government of the Church . . . established by Law' instead of 'the only Government of Christ's Church'. Officially at least the settlement was to be moderate and there was no rehabilitation of the Covenants. The practical workings were very different. He could not prevail upon the General Assembly to leave the conformist ministers alone. This Assembly was a body drawn entirely from the south of Scotland, and resolutely refused to let anyone in who had accepted episcopacy. It announced that it would confine censure to cases of 'error, scandal, insufficiencie and negligence', and having made this bland announcement proceeded to carry through the most drastic purge the Church has ever known. In all, over 650 ministers were turned out in the years following the Revolution: the purge was most complete south of Perth, where all except twenty-four ministers were forced out. In the north, the Assembly had to proceed more cautiously, if only because in many cases the foundation of a Presbyterian Church did not yet exist. In the synod of Aberdeen, for instance, all the ministers were episcopal in loyalty and it took some time to intrude others, to create Presbyterian presbyteries, and to give them power. In 1695 things were made a little easier for those episcopal ministers still in occupation and prepared to conform. In that year William secured that if they took the oaths of allegiance and assurance to him, and accepted the Confession of faith and Presbyterian government, they could stay, but in practice the Assembly continued to persecute ministers of the other side for 'drunkenness' or 'insufficiencie' whenever it could get local support for this. Eventually nearly 200 ministers remained because the Presbyterians could not force them out, and among these was one significant group. In 1692 Charteris, the pupil of Leighton, was accepted, bringing back into the Church the best traditions of episcopacy. For all this, a large and organized body of what now gets the name of 'episcopalianism' lay outside the Church, a constant source of political unrest. On the other side, in 1690 the remaining ministers of the Cameronians, the extreme Covenanters, had come in. This left the remnant of extremists outside leaderless. It also encouraged the Church to start the long process of fabricating seventeenth-century history in an attempt to sanctify the Covenanting past and weld it on to the Church.

In the summer of 1691 it became clear that the war in Ireland was effectively won, and that it was now time to complete the settling of the north. The clans which had gone home after Killiecrankie had sworn to meet again in the cause. Lochiel held them surprisingly steady in this, never attempting more influence than he really had. French help was hoped for and constantly talked about. Some

French ships actually reached Skye. The chiefs in Skye, Duart, the Lochaber region, and a central block beyond the Great Glen refrained from taking the Oath of Allegiance, and it was known that Macdonald of Glengarry was systematically fortifying his house. The lowland north was more passive in its disaffection, but it suffered under an unwanted Church, heavy taxation, and free quarters for the troops. The unrest there was for the most part straightforwardly political and religious and could only be appeased by time, peace, and firm government. In the Highlands the scene was complicated by personal and legal interest. Religion disturbed those of the Macdonalds who were Catholic, but they, Lochiel, and the Macleans had also very real grievances against the means by which overlordship and actual possession had been gained by the Campbells over land they regarded as theirs. It would be hard to reconcile them with the re-establishment of Argyll. To them, the Protestant succession was by no means a closed issue. The Privy Council had neither troops nor money to spare for a campaign in the mountains, but so long as Argyll was a leading figure on the Council, conciliation was not likely. Stair, in London, in the confidence of the king, wanted to see what negotiation would do. He took over Tarbat's scheme, but did not know or understand Highland issues – he was impatient with the attitude of the chiefs to William's sovereignty and did not appreciate their values and way of life. (The landowners of the south-west had been particularly unsympathetic to these ever since the stationing of the Highland Host on their properties in 1678.) To negotiate with the chiefs he rightly chose a Highlander who could go among them, but unwisely chose a man whom nobody could ever begin to trust. The Earl of Breadalbane had never been known to do anything straightforwardly: though a Campbell he had the advantage of standing apart from Argyll's hegemony, and he did not attune his politics to Lowland themes. William thought of him as a useful bridge-head in the Highlands. But Breadalbane had his own schemes and feuds to follow. At any rate, in the summer of 1691 Stair offered him the job of negotiating with the chiefs on Tarbat's plan earlier of buying up Argyll's superiorities, with a prospect of £12,000 (sterling) to make the necessary payments. The Privy Council disliked the plan and Colonel Hill spoke of it as an instance of setting the fox to keep the geese. It was held up because Stair never got round to obtaining

Argyll's agreement to the purchase of his superiorities for the Crown, and because the chiefs refused to take the Oath of Allegiance to William without James's express permission. James's consent to the Oath only came through late in December 1691 and the question of buying the superiorities had been silently dropped. The chiefs had been given till 1 January to take the oath. Some still held out, Glengarry and Clanranald for instance, and Lochiel himself only made it on the last day. Macdonald of Glencoe was late, having gone to the wrong place and got caught in a blizzard. He took the oath on 6 January at Inveraray.

Tarbat's plan had miscarried because Stair was not the right man to carry it out, but the unity of the band of chiefs had gone. Stair was piqued, and the Privy Council anxious for some sort of disciplinary showdown. With Breadalbane as a key figure in the negotiations there was an obvious victim. Stair was soon writing of the Macdonalds, or MacIans as they were often called, of Glencoe as 'that set of thieves' and 'the worst in the Highlands' – and if the Glencoe men went thieving it was obvious where they would do it, in Breadalbane's lands around the river Orchy, across the moor of Rannoch. They were a small clan, and could safely be picked on by their greater neighbours. Some very underhand dealings by the clerks of the Privy Council meant that the Council had not been officially informed that Glencoe had taken the oath; and Stair, who had been informed, stuck to it that all that mattered was that the time limit had been passed. Discipline was planned, and when a seventeenth-century government felt strong enough to act in the Highlands it acted by fire and sword and indiscriminate slaughter.

The story of the massacre of Glencoe, of the slaughter of thirty-eight out of a clan numbering over 140 in February 1692, by a Campbell regiment to which they had given hospitality, is well known and frequently told. It was a botched affair – the passes were to have been closed by Argyll's followers and by troops from Fort William, but many of the victims got through in spite of the bad weather that the high mountains bring down upon the narrow glen. As Highland slaughters go it was not a particularly bloodthirsty one, but it was unusually underhand, and when the news slowly filtered through to the outside world, the broadening humanity of the age showed in a desire to repudiate it. This coalesced with a much more effective political move; that of the upper classes of Scotland to get rid of Stair. William managed to stave off attack in the 1693 Parliament, but in the next one in 1695 a commission of investigation was set up, and its report made it difficult to retain Stair – some six months later he was shelved. Breadalbane, who had not Stair's scorn of public opinion, had covered his traces too well to be got at, so well that to this day nobody knows whether the much-talked of £12,000 did pass through his hands, and if it did, how much came out the other side. Opinion now put it on record that whatever individuals might do, a certain standard in dealing even with Highlanders was expected from the Crown: the government was condemned for having 'barbarously killed men under trust'. More seriously, but less explicitly, it had been shown as having failed to win the support of the clans. In its immediate object terrorism succeeded, as it usually does. The resistant chiefs made their peace at once. Within a fortnight of the slaughter Colonel Hill had occupied Glengarry and Castle Eilean Donan, and was expecting the submission even of McNeill of Barra. But though the clans yielded to the threat of force the basic cause of discontent in the growth of Campbell power remained.

William's government to the end of his reign rested on uncertain foundations. Jacobitism remained an open, or openable, question far longer in his northern kingdom than in England. It was attractive to all who disliked the supremacy of Presbyterianism, and the Kirk did nothing to meet this feeling half-way. Though his ministers kept on the old usage and spoke of Scotland as William's 'ancient kingdom', he knew little of it and did not have enough time or attention to keep up with its politics. Partly from necessity and more from deliberate intent William's rule was lighter than his predecessors. Executions for treason were rare, though imprisonment was not. The Claim of Right had stated that torture was not to be used without evidence, or in ordinary crimes. In fact it continued to be used, but decreasingly, in the same sort of cases as before, where there was reason to suspect a conspiracy behind the crimes known; the change lay in that an occasional resort to it became even rarer. The social discipline of the kirk sessions continued unabated. The ministry had been drastically purged, but the government refused to interest itself in the religious inclinations of the individual layman. Going to church was still the only passport to a tranquil life in many districts, but it was no longer the seal of political reliability. New branches of intellectual and artistic achievement reveal the benefits of the relaxation of political discipline, even if they were no surety for peace.

NOTES ON DRAMATIS PERSONAE

Argyll. Archibald Campbell, tenth Earl and first Duke 1701 (died 1703), son to the Argyll of Chapters 12, 13, and 14, and father both to that of Chapter 18 and that of Chapters 19 and 20.

Breadalbane. John Campbell of Glenorchy (1635–1716), first Earl: a Highland politician. Only in his last and failing years did he commit himself to a losing political side.

Crawford. William Lindsay, eighteenth Earl (died 1698).

Dundee. As in Chapter 15, John Graham of Claverhouse, Viscount Dundee.

Hamilton. William Douglas, third Duke (1637–95), as in Chapter 14, son-in-law to the Duke of Charles I's reign, Chapters 12 and 13, and father to that of Chapter 18.

Mackenzie. Sir George Mackenzie of Rosehaugh (1636–91), king's advocate, the Mackenzie of Chapter 15, to be distinguished from

Tarbat. George Mackenzie of Tarbat (1630–1714), lord of Session under the name of Lord Tarbat and (1703) Earl of Cromarty.

Melville. George Melville, fourth baron and first Earl (1634–1707), a refugee at the Hague after the Rye House Plot. Secretary of State for Scotland, 1689.

Montgomery of Skelmorlie. Sir James Montgomery, tenth baronet (died 1694), an enthusiastic Williamite in 1689, and in 1694 plotting with the Jacobites.

Perth. James Drummond (1648–1716), fourth Earl and first Duke (this title conveyed by James VII in exile). Lord Chancellor 1684. Released from his Scottish prison in 1693 he joined the refugee court at St Germain.

Queensberry. William Douglas, third Earl and first Duke 1684 (1637–95), father to the Duke in Chapter 18.

Stair. Sir John Dalrymple of Stair (1648–1707), 'Master of Stair'. Second Viscount 1695 and first Earl 1703. Eldest son to the great legist, the Stair of Chapter 15.

William III (1650–1702). The son of Charles I's eldest daughter and William II of the Netherlands, nephew and son-in-law to James VII. He had no children, so the conjunction with the Netherlands ended with his death. The succession in Scotland and England then went to his sister-in-law, Anne, the younger daughter of James VII.

Chapter 17

The late seventeenth century

The Scots in Darien

FROM MILITARY AND POLITICAL crisis Scotland moved to famine –
the 'ill years' of the 1690s. In 1695, 1696, and worst of all, in 1698–9,
the harvests failed to meet the country's needs. The long season of
tolerable autumn weather necessary for the clumsy, late harvest of
corn was lost in wind and rain. Even in 1697 though the weather made
a harvest of normal proportions possible, the shortage of seed corn
from the last bad year meant that food never became plentiful and
again in 1699 seed corn was short and much of the harvest failed. In
the first two bad years some help came from the north of Scotland,
where things were not so bad, but for the final two years there was no

outside source of food except some cargoes from Ireland. It was a famine that involved most of northern Europe. We do not know how many starved and died, but the accounts show us the full horror of the old-fashioned famine, sustained so long that the very young, the old, and the weak, who might have got through a single bad year, could not hope to last out.[1] 'Everyone may see Death in the Face of the Poor,' wrote Sir Robert Sibbald. Families begged, people died of hunger in the streets, and the epidemics that follow shortage finished off still more.

This disaster caught the imagination of the eighteenth century and lives to this day, with all the inaccuracy of biblical analogy, as the 'Seven Ill Years of King William's reign'. It is not the inflation of four bad years to seven which is of note in this phrase, but the deep impression the famine made on contemporaries. Scotland had known many famines in the past: there were four periods of famine prices between 1620 and 1645, and the high prices of the 1690s were not as bad as those of the years of the Cromwellian war, when the destruction of crops and towns broke the whole marketing system of the country. What is striking about the disaster of the 1690s is that it was the last general famine in Scotland,[2] and that it occurred at a time when in forty years there had been only one year of dearth (1674). The men of the 1680s could believe that Scottish farming had outgrown such failures and learnt to produce enough. The men of the 1690s saw the final manifestation of the spectre of want.

The men of the 1680s would not have been far wrong. All in all, the Scotland of their day was a more prosperous country than it had been sixty or eighty years before. A modern historian has written 'had the Union of the Parliaments come to pass in 1689 instead of 1707 history would unquestionably have given the verdict that the period

1. In Finland where crops were even more chancy, there is good reason for thinking that a third of the population died: but there the seriousness was made worse by unsympathetic government action: see *Scandinavian Economic History Review*, 1955. E. Jutikkala, 'The Great Finnish Famine in 1696–7'. This proportion of deaths gives some credence to Fletcher of Saltoun's guess that one in five in Scotland died.
2. There were shortages in 1709, 1740, 1782, 1796, and 1800–1 all over Scotland, but only in the potato failure of 1846 was there famine, and then only in the Highlands.

of the Union of the Crowns had been favourable to Scottish economic advance'.[1] Farming was more skilled: some new ideas were coming in, and in the south-east men were learning to lime their land. More land was under the plough, and cattle stocks were probably bigger too. There is a lot of evidence to show that more food was produced, and it was moved about more easily. The old local markets were widening; not only could grain be moved by ship but it could go across the country – the two paved roads of Scotland of this period brought together the estuaries of Forth and Clyde and gave Edinburgh contact with the Leadhills area in the south-west. We have no material on which to base estimates for the growth of Scottish population in the seventeenth century, but the emigration of the earlier part of the century had largely stopped and it is likely that the loss then of some 10 per cent of the population to Ireland and Europe was now made good. In spite of the famine of the 1690s our ancestors were right to feel that the repeated disasters of the past were not going to recur.

Another sign of increasing prosperity, of more reliable resources, comes from the beginnings of the 'domestic revolution' in Scotland. This phrase is the name given to the changes that can be tracked across England in the sixteenth and seventeenth centuries, the transformation of standards of comfort and space inside the home. It records the moment when the substantial farmer, or the minister in a rich parish, begins to take some part of his wealth from the field and put it into living with the beginnings of comfort. He doubles or trebles the size of his single-roomed house: he builds with better and more lasting materials; he begins to have furniture of seasoned hardwood, carefully put together with real joinery; he collects enough linen to enjoy the luxury of occasional clean sheets and clothes, even in winter; his food has variety; he uses silver instead of horn for spoons, pottery instead of wood for plates. This change is not just a subject for antiquarian or architectural interest, but a vital stage in economic growth. The space and cleanliness it allows are a step to an increased expectation of life: the demands it creates are the springboard of the industrial revolution.

Signs of this change can be found in the Lothians in the 1680s and 1690s. There are some farmhouses with three or four rooms, some

1. T. C. Smout, *Scottish Trade on the Eve of Union*, p. 244.

even with staircases to an upper floor, with all that that implies in structural changes. One or two rooms may even have window-glass, though this is not to be taken for granted even in the houses of the gentry. The richer merchants begin to build up linen stocks. It is not till the eighteenth century that these changes get to the north or west, but already the beginnings of domestic comfort are there in the south-east.

The towns can show another side of this increasing economic activity. The most prosperous and growing part of Scotland's trade was now in the Clyde. Glasgow was becoming a real city growing at a phenomenal rate; more than doubling her size in the seventeenth century; trading with the English western ports, with Ireland and the Highlands, and even forcing her ships illegally into American business; developing her industries – soap, sugar, paper, and beer. By contrast, the Solway had slumped and those Fife burghs that relied on fishing were in decline. A milder decline afflicted the north: fewer ships used the Tay or Aberdeen, and Aberdeen's wool plaiding exports were doing badly. But the silence of all areas of Scotland about bad times in the 1670s and early '80s makes it likely that most parts of the country found things pretty good. The Royal Burghs were not the only towns doing well, and some places benefited that were not towns at all. Coal went out from the small ports of the Forth, linen was a largely rural industry, and the great cattle trade to England moved slowly every autumn over the broad drove roads on the hillsides with little attention to towns. Even so, many burghs expanded in the seventeenth century, and Edinburgh fulfilled the duties of a capital city – politics, gossip, theology, and litigation all centred there, though not to everyone's pleasure. Mackenzie of Rosehaugh delivered a backhanded swipe at both Edinburgh and the climate when he complained about the summer sessions of the courts filling June and July; that 'the only pleasant months and the only months wherein gardens and land could be improven, were spent in the most unwholesome and unpleasant town of Scotland'. But foreign visitors were glad to find themselves in a city with modern amenities such as coffee houses, and with the feel of a capital. There were still nasty habits. Lauder of Fountainhall describes the accidental death of an Edinburgh woman who threw herself, along with a pailful of noisome liquid, from an unbarred upper window one night. A good deal of violence was acquiesced in, even if not exactly tolerated, both in the capital and outside.

Scotland was also learning to apply her resources to her own affairs. Taxation had developed rapidly, not merely in the devising of new types of tax, but in the actual extraction of the cash. Excise stayed on after the Cromwellian period as a tax on rents and became fixed as the 'cess' – landowners in every shire who allotted it were known as the 'commissioners of supply' and these provided the basis of county government until late in the nineteenth century. Poll taxes were experimented with, and on one occasion, in 1691, a hearth tax was levied, to help find money for William's French war, but these were eventually dropped, perhaps because they were too hard on the poor, perhaps because they were unenforceable.

Looking around the remnants of seventeenth-century building which still stand today it is easy to feel that standards of living for the upper classes were going up. As a simple contrast, there is the difference in type between the old tower houses of the countryside (which can be seen elegantly at Craigievar and crudely at Scotstarvit), and the country house on which the later Georgian mansions were modelled. These later houses had a central block and linked side wings, all in conscious, and restrained proportions. Their charm can be seen in Auchendinny and in the other houses Sir William Bruce was building for those lucky enough to be able to afford his services. Luxuries provided a good proportion of Scottish imports – silks and dyestuffs, pictures, raisins and oranges, fruit trees, and garden seeds for those anxious to spend June and July improving their grounds. The poorer classes also had their luxury imports, and the spread of the tobacco habit suggests there was money to spare. The 'riding' of the parliaments was splendid with velvet, but in 1690, when it was expected that William would attend, the Master of Stair warned his colleagues in the government that the court would have to revive and enforce the old sumptuary laws, or the expense of keeping up with the English Joneses would eat up any subsidy the Crown could hope to get. Herein lay the rub. Scotland grew richer in the seventeenth century, but so much more slowly than her neighbour. The Scottish Privy Council could look at the profits of the English cloth industry, at the variety of small, well-made consumer goods that the English produced, and feel envy. Some of these goods the Scots would import from Holland or England – pots and pans, cheap earthenware, good quality linen, woollen cloth, pins, needles, and drinking glasses – but there was all along the feeling that Scotland could and should make these herself.

But Scotland offered advantages to some they could not get in England. The landed gentleman had a position in the countryside nearer to the built-in privilege of the French upper classes than to that of the English squire. His legal privilege was considerable; his tenants were closely under his authority. A Scotch 'barony' or small estate still carried its own baron court for disciplinary actions, and the pages of the surviving court books show the effectiveness of the baron's authority. He would try minor criminal offences himself: more serious ones could either be dealt with by handing the whole thing over to the sheriff, or more simply by exiling the culprit from the estate. This was a drastic penalty. Most tenancies were at will and could be broken at short notice, and the tenant sent away, and he would find it difficult to rent another farm without a certificate of good behaviour from his kirk sessions. Charles II, who had seen something of Europe, remarked that 'there was no natione or king-dome in the world, where the tenants had to great a dependance upon the gentlemen, as in Scotland'.[1] The gentry might seem lacking in independence when faced with the intransigence of nobility or clergy, but they had an authority at home from which no appeal lay. They gained in independence and opportunity during the century; they profited by economic development if they had coal or cattle to sell; their sons went into trade or into the Church as of old, but more and more the wealthier landed society built up its connection with the rising profession of the law. This was the place for the eldest son of a good family, and the names of the great lawyers of the end of the century are tied to sizeable estates. The intellectual experiment and growth of the '80s and '90s goes hand in hand with the rise of the lawyers and the relative depression of the divines in society, and shows itself most markedly in the great direct achievement of the lawyers; the creation by Stair of modern Scottish law. This must not be thought of as the fluke of a lonely genius. In the first half of the seventeenth century only one intellectual discoverer in Scotland makes the world class, Napier of Merchiston. In the 1660s several

1. Charles's knowledge did not extend to eastern Europe.

leading figures in the Royal Society were Scots. In the 1680s the intellectual flowering was not confined to the lawyers. There was Sir William Bruce, anticipating the Georgian style with his sturdy but exquisite houses. There was the charming Sir Robert Sibbald, originating both the Edinburgh Botanical Garden and the Royal College of Physicians, and spending his spare time in research into local history. Between them they foreshadow the eighteenth-century achievements in architecture, history, and medical education. The ecclesiastical intellectual dominance of the earlier generation was shifting, and higher standards of critical and creative thought emerging. Symptomatic of this is the decline of interest in witchcraft. Cases of witchcraft get rarer, though they go on till the 1720s, and the diaries of the gentry reveal less in the way of morbid and uncritical accounts of the manifestations and mal-practices of their local witches. In 1684 Lauder of Fountainhall records the death of an accused witch in prison 'of cold and poverty' because the King's Advocate gave 'no great notice' to such accusa-tions now. This also reminds us that the shift of interest of the legal and upper classes did not immediately benefit those accused by their neighbours. But growth in critical and intellectual life became poss-ible only as gentry ceased to believe that neighbours of theirs whom they disliked spent the dark hours in bed with the devil or using obscene techniques to bewitch other people and their cattle. In so far as these beliefs persisted, their survival was most marked among those of Covenanting sympathy. Wodrow's history is full of tall stories of this kind which have not prevented historians accepting his use of other evidence, a reflection on the critical powers of others than Wodrow.

A little, not much, of the intellectual development of this period got through to the labouring classes, but the vital steps were taken which were to enlarge the scope and content of education in the next century. In 1696 the Parliament passed the famous 'Act for Settling of Schools' by which every parish was ordered to have a schoolhouse, and schoolmaster with a salary paid by the landowners. Even though only partially observed it was the beginning of a great Scottish achievement; the system of education of the eighteenth century through which it was possible for a boy of ability to start at school in his parish, and go on to the university where he would get further education with an emphasis on the new and exciting subjects of the day. The Commission set up in 1690 by Parliament to clean the last vestiges of episcopal teaching out of the universities began the process of adapting these institutions for the modern world, though the first marked signs of change did not happen till Carstares became Principal of Edinburgh in 1708. The intellectual achievements of the Scotch universities, and the opportunities of social mobility that the whole educational structure made possible were to be enormously important. Here it is necessary to record their restrictions and limitations. Parish schools were rare outside the Lowlands until the second half of the eighteenth century, and a parish school in a big parish might from sheer distance be inaccessible to many. The school was held in the single room where the schoolmaster and his family lived, since this was all the heritors were obliged to provide. The education was not free: fees had to be paid, and were needed, for the statutory salary of the schoolmaster gave him a wage which, as the value of money dropped in the later eighteenth century, fell below that of the agricultural labourer. Only with an unusually good or conscientious teacher could a boy make the university at the age appropriate to the upper class student, his early 'teens. In most cases he would be held back by inadequate Latin, and till 1727 all university teaching was in Latin. The great names of the Scottish intellectual renaissance of the eighteenth century do not come from the parish schools, but from the upper classes or the towns. All the same, the door to a different life had been opened, though narrowly, for the peasantry.

In other matters the door was still firmly shut: the social categories were clear and distinct. Power and freedom went with landholding. The social discipline of kirk sessions fell on everyone, and discipline in this age was conceived as simply punitive and repressive. A study of kirk session records does not give the impression that it was effective in reforming character. Churchgoing on Sunday involved two long sermons, and in the stretch of time between them people were forbidden to walk about or gossip, or even sit at their house-doors; children were kept inside and forbidden to play. When we remember that the normal peasant house, usually a single room without the amenities of chimney or window-glass, measuring perhaps fourteen foot by twenty, was shared with pigs and hens, we can visualize Sunday as almost literally stifling in its oppressiveness. Now and again the Kirk would decree a day of fasting, and this would be backed by a royal proclamation and the powers of the civil government. Family structure was authoritarian. The practice of Scotch Calvinism was built on the concept of family prayers conducted by the father: it was because of this that the churches remained locked on week-days. These prayers would be limited in scope except in cases where there was natural oratorical ability, for the Kirk allowed no service books and most families did not possess the Bible, and indeed many had no dry place where any book could safely be kept.

If life was severe for those within the Kirk's fold, there were large groups of the population outside the civilized nation. Miners and salt-workers were bound into the occupation at birth, and until almost the end of the eighteenth century this form of serfdom was accepted without protest. These people could be pursued by legal process if they left their work, or their employer. Women worked at the coal face with men occasionally, and went down the mines in large numbers to do almost all the carrying of the coal. Perhaps because of this the houses of mining families were notably lacking in minimal furniture and comfort throughout the eighteenth century, and the miners formed a caste on their own. There were other outcasts. Since the Poor Law offered help only to the infirm, and then only in voluntary and inadequate amounts in most parishes, the country had a lot of beggars – in times of famine it swarmed with them. Fletcher of Saltoun guessed that in the famine of the 1690s one person in six, which he summed at 200,000 altogether, was begging on the roads. This has often been taken as a serious estimate of Scotland's population, which it was not; its significance lies in the estimate of the ratio of those who begged to those who did not.[1] Other classes also lay outside respectability. The General Assembly, in an effort to get rid of the minister of Foveran, in Aberdeenshire, who had episcopal sympathies, used the plea that he had given communion to fishermen; it could be assumed by decent churchmen that they could not be worthy of it. To the Lowlander, the Highlander was an unchristian barbarian; a belief which justified barbaric pro-

1. As a commentary on the social thinking of the day it is worth noting that he recommended that the begging poor should be transported to found colonies.

ceedings against him. Indeed the Kirk had problems of discipline in the Highlands which reveal the continuation there of sub-Christian practices and beliefs. Most parishes in the late seventeenth century produced accusations of witchcraft, a fact that tells a lot about the atmosphere and suspicions of rural life. And there were the broken men, those without ties in allegiance or land, who moved about the country; there were people who had failed as farmers and been evicted; there were those who had backed the wrong side politically or ecclesiastically, and who could not conform to the standards of Calvinist discipline, or who had outcast themselves by volunteering for the army. To make an estimate as wild as Fletcher's on the beggars, probably a third of the population lived outside the community in one or another of these ways. When we look at the signs of improving prosperity and civilization we must not forget those it passed by altogether. At least for the Highlanders this was not entirely a loss. They had, and for another generation or so would continue to have, their own civilization, though not one with much material wealth in it.

Increasing prosperity was also bound up with a change in the materials and destination of Scottish trade. The incoming trade had many features that had not altered in the century: the great number of useful objects produced by Dutch and English manufacturers, the wines of Bordeaux, the metals of Sweden. But in addition there were now a few cargoes from America, and a large amount of wool from England was smuggled across the border, either for home use or for re-export, a fact that enraged English mercantilists. The exports of Scotland had changed much more drastically. These were still raw materials or the products of crude manufacture – salt, coal, herring, hides, cattle, grain, and rough textiles. But the dominant textile was now linen, not plaiding, and it mostly went to England, not to the continent. The cattle all went to England, and linen and cattle were the most rapidly expanding branches of Scotch exports. Personal and trading contacts with England had increased during the century and the Scots found themselves taking an attitude to their neighbours similar to that of an under-developed country today towards European or American technology. They envied the technical and economic achievements of their neighbour without realizing that these could not be simply imitated at the level they had obtained, and without realizing that imitation would change the whole structure of their society. So there were government-sponsored efforts at new industries and new trades, most of which were expensive flops. And all the time the bonds of the trade that did not need government help bound the two countries closer together. If Scotland were involved, as she had to be, in English wars, then it became steadily harder for her to maintain her own separate pattern of overseas trade. The three Dutch wars of the seventeenth century had been against her best customer; the two French wars of William III's reign and of Anne's drove a blow against her remaining privileges and contacts in France.

It was not as if the English would offer corresponding privileges. The late seventeenth century was a period of mercantilist thought and protectionist policy. The English had set up their Navigation and Staple Acts, mainly directed against the Dutch carrying trade, but including a general prohibition of foreigners taking part in the colonial trade. English industries were protected by duties or prohibitions – the tax on 'foreign' salt and the prohibition of the export of wool were typical of these. The French followed suit: Colbert's ministry, which began in the 1660s, was the start of an era of protection. The duty on imported coal was steadily stepped up after 1664; in 1689 the French forbade the import of herring altogether, and in 1690 of woollen cloth. Other branches of trade decayed for economic rather than state reasons. The skins sent to the Baltic got fewer as the cattle trade to England increased. The Dutch learnt drastic economies in their use of coal. Yet the Scots still needed the goods they bought abroad.

First signs of the tightening economic situation appeared soon after the Revolution. There was a bad slump in the French and the Baltic trades from 1689 to 1691, with repercussions on the whole level of Scottish economic activity. Then in the famine years money had to be used in a desperate search for grain. There followed the renewal of war with France in 1702, which resulted in a sharper slump, so that in 1704 the Scottish economy reached rock bottom.

It was during the stages of this economic decay, before its full severity showed, but while the closing in of the economic world could be felt, that Scotland made one last bid for a foothold in the New World and the golden treasure of colonial trade. In 1695 Scots in London and at home prepared the scheme for 'A Company of Scotland trading to Africa and the Indies', with approval of the Scottish Parliament, with a Court of Directors and an open subscription. As an idea, in its original form, it was not unsound. Africa might absorb Scotch textiles, leather, and salt fish. If a connection could be made with the East Indies, without causing political trouble with the powers already established there, it would provide luxuries that the Scottish home market could use. The capital forecast as necessary, £600,000 sterling, half from Scotland and half from England, would be enough to take the company through its teething troubles.[1]

But then came protest from the English East India Company, protest of sufficient force to threaten impeachment of the English directors in the English Parliament. The English forbade subscription in England, and secured pressure abroad by the government of William to prevent international subscription. The Scots, understandably angry at this, went on alone, and to some degree made up the lack of English funds by extra effort. Perhaps they lost more by the English prohibition than just the capital: certainly it was when the Company was surrendered entirely to Scotch leadership, in particular to that of William Paterson, that it parted with political and economic common sense. The undertaking became an effort to found a trading colony at Darien in the Panama area of Central America (a district notorious for heavy, unmapped jungle and for disease), against the will of the colonial power of that region, Spain, with whom at that moment friendship was vital to William's foreign policy. That the Scots could provide no suitable trading goods for such an entrepôt and that the English settlers and traders in Jamaica refused to help when disaster was imminent, were extra reasons for total failure, but not the basic causes of it. The result of all this was that by the summer of 1700 it was clear for all to see that Scotland had lost ships and men and money. The loss in men was not great but the money loss was over £150,000 sterling, which put an appalling strain on the Scottish commercial system. Little critical attention was paid to the fundamental causes of this overwhelming disaster, for anger concentrated on the English. The fantastic courage that the Scots had shown in this and other enterprises was now reinforced and turned in a collision course against her partner in the Union of the Crowns.

1. The only effort that the Company actually made to trade with Africa did produce a profit.

Chapter 18

Union

You micht hae ta'en her maidenhead
She would hae hired your hand, your hand,
She would hae hired your hand.

EPPIE MORRIE

AT THE END OF his life William saw England moving into the war of the Spanish Succession. This can be considered as the first of the colonial and trade wars of the eighteenth century, a struggle for commercial superiority between England and France, in which England finally eclipsed her old rival and new ally, the Dutch. It was also a struggle against French dominance in Europe, and for the continuance of the new Protestant succession in Britain. All these causes meant much more to the Englishman than to the Scot, to whom, indeed, the predominant issue of superiority meant nothing at all. It is not surprising that it was this war that brought relations between England and Scotland to a head.

The war was more William's than his servants' or his peoples', but at least some English ministers had had a share in the decisions that led to it. Since the days of Cromwell the foreign policy of Britain had been either an English or a purely royal one, carried out by the English servants of the Crown. At the peace of Ryswick in 1697 there had been a half-hearted attempt by these agents to get property and privileges in France restored to the Scots, and in 1701 an unofficial delegation went to France to discuss Scottish trade, but otherwise no attention had been paid to Scottish interests. The pressure put by William on the merchants of Hamburg to prevent subscriptions to the Darien company had brought this fact into high relief. This had been bad enough to Scottish feeling before the colonial scheme ran on disaster: now with the disaster plain to see, feeling raged uncontrollably.

The basic problem was that the Crown and its servants could not serve two masters unless the interests of these agreed. In an era of protectionist economic thinking, and with foreign policy at the mercy of such theories, it was impossible that they should agree. If they did not, then the stronger and richer country, the one more valuable to her king, would determine things. This situation had been causing trouble since the 1650s: in the world of narrowing economic opportunities at the end of the century it caused a crisis. The series of wars that started in 1689 sent up all forms of taxation, and transformed minor customs dues into a protective wall. Scottish trade and Scottish commodities were not important enough to any country for any ruler, least of all her own king, to see that special concessions were made. Scotland entered the biggest trade slump, the worst economic crisis, she had ever known, and nothing was done because, as the irascible Fletcher of Saltoun said, she was 'a farm managed by servants and not under the eye of the master'. Because of her bondage to English foreign policy, she had had to let slip her overseas connections. Her major branches of trade were now with England. Even the maintenance of her existing low level of economic activity depended on the English deciding that this was in their interests.

At the same time the Crown had increasing reason to be dissatisfied with the bonds that held the two countries together. It was no longer possible to conduct foreign or home policy against the direct wish of the English Parliament, yet since 1689 the Scottish Parliament had ceased to be the tool of the Committee of the Articles, and even before then the control of it by the Privy Council had been uncertain. William's Scotch Parliament had opposed him tooth and nail in its first sitting, had forced on him an ecclesiastical policy he disliked, and given its backing to the Darien scheme which had annoyed Spain. He had been able to express his disapproval by sacking the Commissioners who had given the touch of the royal sceptre to the unacceptable Acts, but this did not end the political problems produced by them. Anne was dominated by her English ministry, and through her it could order the Scottish ministers about, and expect them to obey, but there were limits to what these ministers could do when Parliament was insubordinate.

There was still one solution open to the Scots that the Crown would not readily accept, a political separation. Scotland could reverse the decision of 1689, which had not been made by her any-way, and go back to the main line of the Stewarts in the person of James VIII, James Edward, the child born in 1688. The large Jacobite party in Scotland would be delighted, and the country would have her own king again. She would still be poor. It would take at least two generations to build up a new pattern of export trade, but she would be independent. However, the price, either immediately or later, would be war with England, because the Stewarts would never drop their claim to the English throne. Since Flodden the Scots had known that the French were not an adequate ally in a war with England. But there was just a chance of a stretch of peace if the return to the Stewart dynasty was made now, quickly, while the English were deep in war with France.

In every way the war brought home the urgent need for a new settlement with England and the Crown. The Scottish Jacobites provided a solid block of opposition to the government in Parliament. In 1702 Anne was forced to dissolve the Parliament that had brought William to the throne and been kept on into her reign with dubious legality: a generous bunch of promotions in the peerage was given to those who had been useful and might be so again – Argyll for instance got a dukedom, and Seafield an earldom. The new Parliament, which met in May 1703, showed at once that it too was going to need a lot of useful helpers. The English desperately wanted the Scottish succession settled on the Protestant house of Hanover, as their own had been since the death of the last of Anne's children. Instead, the Parliament took up the English technique of withholding supply till grievances had been met. The 'cess' must wait on the 'Act of Security'. This proposed legislation was a vigorous demand for independence. The Scottish Crown, it said, was not to go to 'the successor to the crown of England unless that in this session of Parliament there be such conditions of government settled and enacted as may secure the honour and independence of the crown of this kingdom. . . ', fine and explicit words. There must either be immediate admission of Scottish sovereignty, or the whole connection with England would last only as long as Anne herself. The Commissioner, Queensberry, refused to 'touch' this Act, but he had to pass another claim in the 'Act anent Peace and War' which insisted that after Anne's death the consent of the Scottish Parliament would be necessary for waging war or making peace and alliances. Since much of Scotland's economic problem lay in her unwilling participation in English policy this Act went to the heart of discontent. In this session and the next equally vehement one, two less constructive Acts were also passed, mainly to annoy the English: the Wine Act and the Act allowing the exportation of wool, both arranging for trade with the enemy of England in commodities that would undoubtedly be smuggled over the Border in large quantities. Again in 1704 Parliament put forward the Act of Security in a modified form; this time the need for money made Queensberry give in. The royal touch was granted two days after Marlborough made the greatest single stroke of the war at Blenheim. If news had come a little faster, Queensberry might have held out. Finally, in 1705, the Scots did all they could to rouse the English to the same passionate anger as they themselves felt by carrying through the judicial murder of three members of the crew of the English ship *Worcester* on an unsubstantiated charge of piracy against a ship of the Darien company. The men were hanged on Leith shore with the Privy Council too frightened to intervene and insist on decent standards of evidence. The English would have to learn that the Scots were angry.

It was only in their anger that the Scots were united. There were deep divisions in Parliament and this elementary party structure created its own problems for the government. Just as the problem of the war redefined the parties in the English Parliament, so the problem of relations with England disturbed the crudely formulated allegiances in Scotland. There were three main parties – the Jacobites, the court group who formed the main core of office holders, and the 'Country party'. This last group was not as wedded to opposition as its name would suggest. It was responsible for the dissolution of William's Parliament, for it had forced this by practically going on strike. It was led by the Duke of Hamilton, who suffered from the vacillation chronic in his family. On the one hand he liked to pose as a leading patriot; on the other, he did not wish to endanger the Hamilton inheritance in any way and his will for action was weakened by the memory that that inheritance traditionally included a claim to the succession to the Scottish crown which had no bearing on the English succession. Another 'Country' figure was the much liked Andrew Fletcher of Saltoun, a useful pamphleteer, but an incompetent parliamentarian who had to rely on written speeches. His ideal constitution was an aristocratic republic, a Venetian dream. Since he had no family to promote, he was able to ignore the advantages of office, and ready to denounce those who were not. The Country party had been much reduced in the 1703 election, and part of it went into office, but the remnant managed to have a dominating influence on the anti-English legislation of the period. This was made possible because the Jacobites also took on a patriotic and anti-English posture; England had chosen to take her next monarch from Hanover so this was the obvious attitude for them. Behind Jacobitism lay the discontent of those who had appreciated the episcopal Church and resented Presbyterian dominance.

The English Parliament took up the glove and answered the Scottish Acts with the Alien Act. This was a method of putting the screw on the Scottish Parliament. It gave the Scots until Christmas 1705 to move towards negotiating a Union of Parliaments: after that the Scots would become aliens in England, unable to inherit property there, and the cattle and linen trade would be forbidden.

It was like a quarrel within a marriage. Each side had done the most they could to hurt the other, and for the same reason that quarrels within the bonds of marriage are worse than those outside, because the partners are fighting not only against each other but against the fact of the marriage that holds them together. Some historians have questioned the genuineness of the anti-English feeling of this last Scottish Parliament in the face of its subsequent conversion to Union, but there is no need to consider it insincere. When husband and wife have finished throwing insults and crockery at each other they can sometimes give real consideration to improving the basis of their relationship.

The violence of Scottish feeling forced both sides along the difficult path of reorganizing their ideas. The result was a negotiation for Union made by people really determined to find some better relationship. Charles II and Lauderdale had attempted this but the English had refused the Scottish claim for a representation in Parliament of something over a third of that of England. In 1689 William III had suggested Union without anything coming of it, and in 1702 the English had appointed Commissioners for it, but then allowed the meetings to fail. At this point the Scottish government was reinforced by the 'New Party', sometimes called the 'Squadrone volante', numbering eighteen members of Parliament and led by Tweeddale. It was a section of the Country party which accepted the idea of Union. With the help of the young Duke of Argyll as Commissioner, it managed to persuade the Parliament to leave the choice of Commissioners with the Crown, and give them leave to negotiate a Union provided they did not touch the church settlement. The English Parliament repealed the Alien Act, and thirty-one Commissioners from each side, the Scotch ones representing in some degree all parties, met in Whitehall.

The English had decided to insist on 'incorporating union' at all costs. The Scots had a preference for some sort of federation, but they had no very clear scheme for this, and the obvious foreign example of federation, the Netherlands, did not provide an encouraging model. In any case the Scots were not prepared to make a big fight on this point. There was not available in 1706 a formal study of political institutions, or a wealth of written constitutions to consider as examples. The Commissioners decided to do their main arguing apart and in private. Open disagreements openly arrived at were not considered essential to political health in that era, so we have only brief accounts of these discussions, but it is clear from these that the English rapidly forced the Scots on to the ground that suited England. After that, both sides had a fair idea, from the previous unsuccessful negotiations, of what the other would tolerate. The main difficulties came on the adjustments of two different systems and levels of taxation, and on the existence of an English national debt, funded and established as a means of fighting the last two wars, and consequently not a thing the Scots would want to pay for. The Scots, while objecting to paying towards this, glossed over the fact that their own government had salaries and army payments overdue for many years, going back behind the date when the English debt was funded, and adding altogether to over a quarter of a million sterling. In spite of these points the negotiations went smoothly and fast, for both sides were aware that the real struggle would take place in the Scottish Parliament.

The main features of the Treaty of Union, as the Commissioners constructed it, had a bold simplicity. The Hanoverian succession was accepted for both countries. The two Parliaments were to unite, but the Parliament of Great Britain which they were to form in fact met in Westminster and carried the more developed structure and procedure of the English Parliament, so that it has become common to think of the Union as a grafting of the Scottish Parliament into the English. There has been no break in parliamentary continuity for the English, such as the Scots have experienced, so this view has a good deal of truth in it. The Scots were to send sixteen peers and forty-five commoners to join the one hundred and ninety peers and five hundred and thirteen commoners already there. This was a mean representation when we consider the probable ratio of population at this date (estimated at one to five), which nobody could then know accurately, but a generous one when we look at the ratio of crown revenue (one to thirty-six) which the Scots knew only too well and which was rubbed in by English pamphleteers. Since Defoe tells us the Scots wanted an 'arithmetick mean' between population and revenue, it seems they got fairly near to what they asked. The Scottish peerage became a closed caste, electing its sixteen members for every Parliament: the representation in the Commons remained on the narrow, but not yet totally inadequate basis of tenancy-in-chief and the royal burghs. The two countries were to have freedom of trade with each other, and with the colonies; they were to use a common coinage, the English; and, theoretically at least, a single standard of weights and measures. They were to keep their civil laws and church settlements apart. The different church settlements were not expressly mentioned in the Act of Union but secured by separate Acts in the two Parliaments.

These were the main features. They were backed by small but important adjustments. The local privileges of burghs and nobles in Scotland were to remain. The Scottish 'cess' was accepted on a fixed ratio with the land tax, and temporary concessions were made about the malt and salt taxes – the two English taxes that bore most heavily on the ordinary peasant farmer. The Scots accepted the duty of paying for the English national debt in return for an elaborately calculated pair of 'Equivalents': one, a payment outright of almost £400,000 sterling which went partly on reimbursing the unlucky subscribers to the Darien scheme, but mostly on the unacknowledged Scottish public debt; the other would come off the Scottish revenue when it expanded in the more prosperous future that was axiomatic to all negotiators, and would be used to give Scottish industry a shot in the arm.[7] Scottish ships, wherever they had in fact been made, were to become 'British built' from the point of view of the Navigation Acts.

The voluminous and strongly worded pamphlet literature of the period gives every shade of opinion and argument over the Union. It shows that some sections of the country accepted Union as the only peaceful solution to the country's problems. Some of the court party were enthusiastic in their acceptance of this fact. Stair and Tarbat were both strong advocates; Tarbat, for as he said, 'I am old, and in long experience of slavery and now of poverty, and I wish to leave the nation free of the first, and at least in the road to leave the other . . .' In some cases there was a strong material interest driving men to Union. The Earl of Galloway sold his cattle in England and would be hurt if this market was cut off. The Duke of Argyll hoped to wield political influence on a wider field, though this did not stop him writing a painfully frank letter to the Secretary of State saying that he was not going to exert himself to help the Act get through without some sort of direct reward. The landed classes on the whole wanted Union, though they would stand to lose by it, if not in wealth, then in privilege and prestige, since inevitably the conventions and customs of the two countries would assimilate them more to the position of English landowners. Their motive may have been the economic opportunities that lay before them. The most important and growing branches of Scotch trade were ones in which they had a considerable share. Similarly the opposition of many of the royal burghs may be a sign of fear of competition to their privileges. But in neither case can economic hopes or fears adequately explain the line that men took. The most vocal opposition to Union came from the mobs in the larger towns; the most serious from the clergy who felt the old pull of the Solemn League and Covenant on them, and found it hard to acquiesce in a settlement which carried security for the episcopal Church in England. Neither of these elements of opposition were really foreseen when Queensberry as Commissioner, the most tactful and persuasive of Scottish politicians, and Mar as his follower and

1. The Equivalents, and the arrangements made to get the Scottish debt paid by them, survive today after a mixed history in two very different bodies, the National Gallery of Scotland and the Royal Bank.

Secretary of State, came to Edinburgh in September 1706 to put the treaty through Parliament.

Queensberry was a small, swarthy man, entirely committed to the Protestant line of kings. John Erskine, Earl of Mar, adhered less from principle and more from the usefulness of office to one who combined vast estates in a bad way with a strong family feeling. He was not a good speaker in Parliament, but skilled in private negotiations. He expected a Parliamentary majority of sixty-six, a lot in the Scottish Parliament, so though he was glad enough of the Squadrone's help, he did not feel it vital. But some of his majority peeled away as disturbances out of doors frightened people, and the Duke of Hamilton encouraged the troubles in a half-hearted way. The clergy joined in the disputes in their sermons; Defoe, sent to Edinburgh in a role of part-spy, part-advocate for the English government, called the Kirk 'a Refractory, Scrupulous and Positive' set of people. He was astonished at the influence of the ministers. But in fact they had little direct pull on the Parliament except in reinforcing the opposition of the burgh members. Riots at Dumfries, Glasgow, and in the capital itself looked ominous, but Mar did not dare have English troops to help him. The crucial debates were fought by gentlemen with hands at their sword hilts, late on into the night, with lighted candles burning under the painted timbers of the Parliament hall. The spectators who were allowed in carried the violent feeling into riots that ran up and down the royal mile. But the Act passed, clause by clause, if not with the help of all Mar's sixty-six, at least with adequate majorities, and only small amendments on the taxation clauses got by. It was through in January 1707, to become law in May. The Chancellor Seafield was able finally to sum up the end of Scottish separate independence in the last meeting of the last Scotch Parliament (28 April 1707) with the words: 'Now there's ane end of ane auld sang.'

It was a little more than fifty years since Scotland and England had mutually invaded each other and fought it out in the hard battles of Dunbar and Worcester. Bitterness and dismay at Union at worst, distaste at best, were the very understandable Scottish reactions. Yet it was the only practical solution to a deepening political and economic crisis. The Scots did not go into Union simply because they were poor and saw no other way of riches, but because they were poor and rapidly getting poorer. The English went in because the structure of politics in the two countries had changed and it was no longer possible to work the Stewart relationship. At the same time the party dominance in the English Parliament of one group, which could also exert great influence over the queen, made it possible for the English representatives to adapt their plans to Scottish needs.

As with all important changes, the Act of Union affected more things than people expected. It did not end the existence of Edinburgh as a capital, but it changed the way in which this was manifested. The splendid display of haberdashery that had made up the 'riding' of Parliament passed away; more seriously the Edinburgh mob no longer had a government within easy reach. But the law and the lawyers saw to it that Edinburgh never became a mere provincial backwater. It was always the centre for the most important of indoor sports, pursuing your neighbour at law, and on this was later built the cultural and intellectual developments of the later eighteenth century. But Union froze many Scottish institutions in the attitude, or stage of development, of 1707, and made it hard for them to adapt in the next hundred and twenty years. It was a period of British history when the process of legislation was tedious, and consequently rare. It needed between fourteen and eighteen separate motions in each house of Parliament for an enactment to get through, and as a result, only topics for which steady and deep feeling could be raised could get through to the statute book. The Law, the courts, the burghs, the electoral system, the schools, the universities, the Church could all adapt only within whatever legislation had already been passed. Even though the period immediately before the Union had been unusually prolific in legislation, Scotland was to suffer from under-government, and in particular from a lack of legislation, for a long time.

Where changes in the law did come, there was to be a normal tendency for the more powerful country to take the odd trick. Both countries borrowed unofficially from each other. Scots as Lord Chancellors were to rationalize the English common law, and the English majority in the House of Lords helped to fill in the gaps in Scottish law – the thinness of the section of Stair on mercantile law shows that there was plenty of room for this. But in official matters, in the work of Parliament, it was to be rare for a Scottish model to be preferred to an English one, even when, as for instance in the Scottish system of banking, it was a better one. The whole notion of statute law has followed the English concept.[1] It might have been logical to abolish the Scotch Privy Council immediately after the Union, but as this action was not accompanied by any arrangement for a Scot to be a leading figure in the Cabinet, the government of Scotland suffered from a lack of informed direction, except when the chances of party activity provided such a figure – as they did during the reigns of the dukes of Argyll and Henry Dundas. Another thing lost unperceived in 1707 was the Scots language; in practice since the middle of the nineteenth century, English usage has come to prevail almost entirely over Scots in educated and literary circles, and one of the results of this has been, and still is, an unwieldiness in Scottish expression, a clumsiness that comes from using one idiom in speech and another on paper.

But these unforeseen losses are not, on the whole, the aspects of the Union that raise the heat in Scottish opinion today. The questions asked now are also important in our assessment: these are, whether the Union was attained by bribery, and whether it was a wise decision. The two points are entirely distinct, and nothing is to be gained by thinking that an answer on one dictates the answer to the other.

The bribery issue was rather late in starting. It was not raised in the extensive controversial literature of 1706, except that at one point Mar hinted that someone in the opposition was paying the hostile Edinburgh mob (bribery has never been a government monopoly). Bribery is perhaps too crude a word for the mechanism of persuasion developed by eighteenth-century governments; for promises, promotions, and peerages, which hostile critics call corruption, and the eighteenth century called influence. In 1711 George Lockhart of Carnwath wrote his *Memoirs*, a vivid but biased account of the manoeuvres over the Union, which as a Commissioner he knew well, and which as a Jacobite he resented. These were published, ostensibly against his will, in 1714, and in the second edition there is a full account of a mysterious twenty thousand pounds that passed from the English Exchequer to Scotland during the Union debates. This money was a payment of part of the overdue salaries of past and

1. The Scottish principle, by which Acts still in the statute book could be disallowed for disuse, has been dropped for matters concerning both countries in favour of the English principle that a statute is a statute is a statute.

present office-holders. Over twelve thousand of it was owed to Queensberry, who as Commissioner had to live at vast expense. The money had to come from England because the Scottish Exchequer was empty: it came then because a sweetener was needed, and it came secretly because feeling was hot. If Lockhart is right we only know about it because later on, after the Union, some of these salaries were paid again, and we have evidence that Queensberry paid back his second allowance.

It is difficult to regard the payment of salaries as bribery, however long overdue. This is particularly difficult for the Commissioner, who got nothing directly from his – there survives a letter from Lauderdale to Charles II asking to be taken off his £70 a day allowance since Parliament had ended and he was tired of being 'mine host' to the whole of Scotland, a letter which shows where the Commissioner's salary went. In any case, since Queensberry paid his second payment back, there is only little under £8,000 – arriving, if it did, as a second bonus well after the Union – to puzzle the historian. One thousand pounds of this went to Atholl, who voted against Union throughout, the rest to people who show no signs of being new arrivals on the government side. There is a remark of Lord Melbourne's which seems applicable, made when it was suggested that he should give an available 'garter' to himself: 'What is the good of my taking it? I cannot bribe myself.' What does seem clear from the history of Scotland immediately after the Union is that politicians were intensely interested in securing government salaries and that the machinery of crown influence by means of 'jobs', pensions, honours, and other favours was already well developed. There seems no adequate reason for believing it had been unusually heavily used in 1706, but it was in full use very soon after.

Recently, the attack on the character of the Union Parliament has shifted from money to peerages as the means of corruption, and here we are among the imponderables. It is not good enough to say, as the late Professor Pryde has done, that 'it was a corrupt age'. Sheltered from risk today by a structure of fixed salaries and retirement pensions, and prevented by death duties from attempting to found a landed family – the ambition of our ancestors – we are in danger of ceasing altogether to understand why men in the eighteenth century undertook the risky and laborious task of serving the Crown. David

Hume has said of crown influence, 'we may . . . give to this influence what name we please . . . but some degree and some kind of it are inseparable from the very nature of the constitution and necessary to the preservation of our mixed government'. We have only got rid of it by getting rid of the 'mixed government'. Half a dozen promotions in the peerage are considered as evidence of corruption in 1706–7. But peerages and favours were always given out at the end of troublesome Parliaments to those who had proved helpful. At least seven can be found after the 1702–3 session,[1] a tricky one, but nowhere near so difficult as 1706. When Lauderdale came north to hold a troublesome Parliament he wrote to remind Charles II that there was a special favour he desired. It is really not the number of rewards that is exceptional in the period of the Union but the extremely crude way in which the Duke of Argyll made his request: 'When I have justice dun me here and am told what to expect for going to Scotland I shall be ready to obey.' Well, he was that sort of a man. Having already got to the top of the Scottish grades of honour, it was not a further step up he wanted, but a major-generalship and the means of promoting his followers. There is no evidence of any abnormal generosity by the Crown in the year of Union, but it remains impossible to draw a line between the corrupt and the uncorrupt use of favours of all sorts in the early eighteenth century.

Lockhart's accusation of bribery brings up indirectly the question of Scotland's practical need for Union. It reminds us that the Scottish Crown was heavily indebted, with no prospects of paying off accumulations of debt since the revenue was inadequate. It is difficult to regard a country that cannot pay its servants as viable. Other signs point the same way. The repeated difficulty of Scottish governments of providing enough troops to police the country, whether it were against Covenanters or Jacobites, and the place of foreign coins as the normal means of exchange; both emphasize the economic problem of the country. There was no answer to this problem except Union. Even at the height of mutual animosity between the two countries in 1705 there is no indication of a serious desire to fight. Enough contacts and friendships had been made in the previous fifty years to make war between them feel like civil war. In the modern Britain, which has teetered on the edge of economic union with Europe for

1. Argyll, Seafield, Lothian, Annandale, Carmichael, Glasgow and Stair.

several years without going in, there should be sympathy with the vocal distaste showed by so many Scots in 1706 for what they saw to be inevitable.

Union was a bold and decisive step, calling for courage on the part of the Scots and generosity on the part of the English. Within a remarkably short space of time, both nations changed this approach, the English to meanness and the Scots to regret; but the reasons for the rapid failure of the honeymoon spirit do not destroy the validity of the original decision. But there have been times since 1707 when the Union has come to mean things not only not foreseen but unforeseeable. It is understandable that in a world where sovereignty, government, and Parliament all mean very different things from what they did in 1707, many Scots should now think that some elements of the bond between the nations need recasting.

Defoe, that clever, bold man, the father of modern journalism, who gives us one of the most vivid pictures of Scotland that we have, has offered an answer ahead to those who argued about who got most out of the bargain. He spoke of the pamphleteers who opposed Union:

> They never dreamed, that to unite, was, in itself a full and general retribution for every step taken from one side to the other; that a new national interest was to be erected; and that giving or conceding rights, advantages and interests, whether in commerce or in privileges was losing nothing at all, but was like a man giving presents to a lady, whom he designs to make his wife.

We also, like our ancestors, tend to forget the new national interest.

NOTES ON DRAMATIS PERSONAE

Anne. Queen Anne (1665–1714). Queen 1702–14, younger daughter of James VII by his Protestant wife Anne Hyde, married 1683 to Prince George of Denmark. Many times a mother, but with no children who survived her.

Argyll. John Campbell, second Duke (1680–1743), as in Chapter 19, field marshal 1735. Clever, handsome, and ambitious, he gained distinction in his chosen profession, the army, in Marlborough's war.

Defoe. Daniel Defoe (1661–1731), journalist and novelist, with sympathies for nonconformity and for economic venturesomeness. He was in Scotland during the Union debates as a reporter for the English minister Harley, and later compiling his own *Tours*.

Fletcher of Saltoun. Andrew Fletcher (1655–1716), to whom the label 'patriot' is commonly applied: an uncorrupt, vehement, and hot-headed political figure, bad at public speaking, advocating an aristocratic and republican government.

Hamilton. James Douglas, fourth Duke (1658–1712), son to the duke in Chapter 16, made Duke of Brandon (G.B.) in 1711 but prevented from sitting in the House of Lords for this title. He was killed in a duel in the following year.

Lockhart. George Lockhart of Carnwath (1673–1731), a member of a distinguished legal family, put on the Commission for Union as a solitary representative of the Jacobite party, author of an unreliable set of *Memoirs* and originator of several quarrels within the Jacobites. He also was killed in a duel.

Mar. John Erskine, sixth Earl (1675–1732), head of what he himself called an old and not inconsiderable clan. In Chapter 19 he is shown as unsuccessful leader of a rebellion; he seems to have been more capable of decision in politics than in war.

Queensbury. James Douglas, fourth Earl and second Duke (1662–1711): he was the first to change allegiance from James VII to William, 'a compleat Courtier' says a contemporary, '. . . partly by art, and partly by nature', but he was also a consistent and forceful politician.

Stair ; Tarbat. As in Chapter 16.

Chapter 19

1707–45

We cannot reasonably expect, that a piece of woollen cloth will be brought to perfection in a nation, which is ignorant of astronomy, or where ethics are neglected.   DAVID HUME

THE UNION OF 1707 led at once to discontent. Some of this should have been foreseen. The feeling whipped up in Scotland against it would not go down quickly, especially since it was supported by an unusual and powerful partnership of Jacobitism and the Kirk. Of course there was a last-minute attempt to profit by entry into the new customs union: indignant English merchants were soon insisting on measures against undercutting by Scots, who had imported large quantities of French wine before the adoption of English duties for sale on the English markets. The extension to Scotland of the English customs and excise services involved a lot of uncomfortable adjustment, and should have involved a higher level of official probity, but did not. The raised level of duties was a Scottish grievance, and Scottish customs frauds an English one.

More serious were the deliberate acts of provocation from an English-dominated Parliament. Just when goodwill and tranquility were needed to enable the Scots to discover and get used to new channels of power and influence, English politics made them unattainable. The political hegemony which had sustained Marlborough's campaigns began to disintegrate and, in the rising party strife, Scottish affairs became a gambit.

There was enough change to make things uncomfortable, anyway. With surprising speed, the whole English machinery of rewards for the faithful was applied to Scotland. The most conspicuous example was the Commission of Police,[1] originally the Commission of

1. 'Police' here means government.

Chamberlainry. This started as an attempt to provide a channel for political control, but soon became simply a method of transferring a few thousand pounds a year to Scotch politicians of the right alliances. Even as a channel of power it would not have been needed if the English had not acquiesced in the abolition of the Scottish Privy Council in 1708 to suit the electoral advantages of the Squadrone party. This was an extreme example of political short-sightedness, for the Privy Council possessed the miscellaneous reserve powers of the Crown that enabled a Scottish government to act effectively in emergencies. Its abolition was potentially dangerous as well as unsettling. Less important, but still producing its own little pool of annoyance and indignant pride, was the disappearance of the Scottish mint a year later. Bigger items of injured national self-consciousness came after the completion of the political swing and the disturbances of the Sacheverell case in England. There was the case of James Greenshield, an Episcopalian minister prosecuted by the city of Edinburgh for disobedience to the orders of the Presbytery, who appealed to the House of Lords. This action showed the import of some careful wording in the Act of Union, by which Scottish appeals to the Lords were feasible. The decision in 1711 infuriated Presbyterian feeling by allowing worship in an Episcopalian meeting-house by a set liturgy. The liturgy in question was, of course, the Anglican prayer book. The case brought up an odd deviation of doctrine that had become popular since 1637, that the reading of a written prayer or 'set form' was against Calvinist theology: 'idolatrous' was one of the words thrown about. Behind this general prejudice lay deeper issues that tended to get masked in the controversy, but which gave it its political heat. Was the security of the established Kirk compatible with the right of anyone to differ in worship? How could two nations smoothly co-operate with different established Churches and the open admission by one of them that the joint Parliament could legislate for it? And of course in practice Episcopalianism in Scotland tended to go hand in hand with Jacobitism, and under the repression of the day was going to do so even more.

Greenshield's case was followed by parliamentary decisions which emphasized the first two of these issues further, and also showed the relative powerlessness of Scotland in the current political structure.

The 1710 Parliament, busy repressing the liberties of Presbyterians in England, not surprisingly had a crack at their privileges in Scotland too. In the Toleration Act of 1712 it extended free worship to Episcopalian ministers who would pray for the queen, and imposed a form of Oath on the Kirk antipathetic to the conscience of many. In spite of protests, it took seven years to get the Oath amended. In the Patronage Act Parliament recreated lay patronage, a direct affront to the existing power structure of the Kirk. Till 1784 the General Assembly regularly protested against it. In reality patronage ceased to be a conscious burden in the later eighteenth century because those exercising it, the aristocracy and gentry, learnt to work it smoothly, and were represented and active in the courts of the Church as elders, so keeping their control unobtrusive. But enough had been said against it in the years since 1689 for it to be an obvious target for any revival of the Covenanting spirit later on. In any case it was not only religious opinion that was outraged by this restoration. National feeling rightly saw it as destroying the effectiveness of the Act of Security, a precondition of the Union, which it had been thought would protect the Kirk from any alteration. That the new united Parliament was to be truly sovereign was to be tremendously important in the nineteenth century. Scotland could not for ever be left with only the institutions she had achieved by 1707, even though that year saw the end of an unusually creative period. But it was a black mark for the Union that this sovereignty should be established in a partisan attack on the most important of her institutions.

Affronts to the Kirk annoyed the nation at large. The political nation, the aristocracy and richer gentry, was also having a difficult time of adjustment. Incorporation in the larger, wealthier, and more law-abiding upper classes of England was bound to reduce the freedom of action and the political power of the Scottish nobility: if they foresaw this, they might feel that it would be compensated by wealth and careers. But there was considerable resistance in practice in the upper-crust world to opening dominant positions to Scots. That the young Duke of Argyll hoped to succeed Marlborough as Commander-in-Chief shows his political naivety, as well as his excessive sense of his own abilities. Ambassadorships and high military office were reasonably available and in one way or another well paid, as the treasures amassed in some great houses, such as Inveraray, or the vast plan of the Earl of Stair's gardens at Lochinch, show. But the top positions in politics and army were going to stay in English hands, and even with the Commission of Police there was not much of the political cake available for Scotch shares. It would have been prudent to arrange for more, since Jacobitism in Scotland had not faded from the position of a real alternative policy, as it had in England. In the Hamilton case in 1711 the House of Lords exacerbated the discontent of the Scottish nobility by refusing to allow the Duke of Hamilton to take a seat on an English peerage recently conferred. Peerages were, after all, the cheapest form of bonus that the ministry could distribute, and therefore of special political convenience. Where they brought a Scottish peer into the House of Lords they were not empty titles but links with the source of wealth and power. In practice, eighteenth-century governments could get round the ban of the House of Lords by ennobling heirs to Scottish peerages who had not yet inherited, but these actions did not cure the ill feeling of 1711. A government which would not or could not give prizes to its supporters was not going to be backed by many.

Irritation reached its peak over an attempt in 1713 to extend the English level of the malt tax to Scotland. Since the Union had laid down that this should not be done during the war, and technically the war was not yet over, the action was a breach of promise. It was also an issue bound to unite all classes. Malt and salt taxes were the duties pressing hardest on the poorer part of the population. The Scots in Parliament moved the repeal of the Union. Even those who had carried the articles of Union through their Parliament six years before, against great opposition, were now fed up. The movement for repeal failed and events moved swiftly to the readjustment of parties which accompanied the end of the queen's life and the succession of the Hanoverian, George I. The English Tories, whose dominance had produced the bad relations, were in disorder, and power was soon seen to lie with the Whigs. The prospects of the Union improved. But the Hanoverian succession also produced a flurry of Jacobite plotting. No shadow of Stewart legitimacy hung about this monarch. Spies and arms were ostentatiously entering northern Scotland; messengers crossed the narrow seas with little disguise. A complicated arrangement was created by which the various Jacobite areas of the

United Kingdom, northern England, the south-west, and Scotland, should all rise together.

The final event that started the rising of 1715 was a personal slight to the Earl of Mar. He left London in a buzz of rumours and went north with an appearance of secrecy, by collier to Newcastle and then on to Fife. At the end of August he had called an assembly, three hundred, it is said, ostensibly as a deer hunt in the hills above Braemar. The ministers and their aides in Scotland looked on at this last manifestation of the old style of life of the northern nobility, but lacking the powers of the old Privy Council did not dare to intervene until the earl had actually raised the standard of 'James VIII'.

Mar collected a big army, ten or twelve thousand, Highland and north-eastern in composition, most of it without formal training, and waited for his royal master, who showed no sense of urgency. The rest of Britain's Jacobitism showed itself half-hearted as well as inefficient. Argyll was restored to government favour and sent up with his brother the Earl of Islay to defend southern Scotland. However disagreeable he might be, the duke was a confident and efficient soldier. Heavily outnumbered, for he had less than four thousand men, he could at first do no more than hold the narrows of Scotland at Stirling: but that was enough to reduce Mar to a state of paralysis. The only general in the Jacobite army with an appreciation of the need to move and strike briskly was Brigadier Mackintosh of Borlum, who got a force of 600 men across the Forth only to find it penned in at Leith. Later he broke out again and, leaving a trail of Highland deserters across the Borders, tried to link up with the English Jacobites. These proved not worth the effort, and the joint force surrendered at Preston. Meanwhile, Argyll moved his army slowly north through a snowbound November, and met Mar in a bloody and disordered battle at Sheriffmuir, above Dunblane. The battle was a victory for Argyll against numerical odds, in spite of the fact that both right wings ran away. The rebels had needed to force their way south and had failed to do so. The Stewart claimant, James VIII, the 'Old Pretender', giving by his gloomy indecision, as a contemporary remarked, unmistakable evidence 'to show he is of the family', did not arrive till after the battle, hung around for a while, burnt a couple of villages in the Ochils, left money to pay for the damage, and took ship from Montrose. The rebellion in the north of England had already folded up, and in the south-west had not even started.

The '15 was not only an inefficient but a gentlemanly affair. At the height of the campaign Mar had written to Argyll to ask him to see that his gardens at Alloa were not damaged by government troops. Immediately after the main military threat all ranks in Scotland closed in an effort to ensure that no stern reprisals were taken. All families had kin who had committed themselves and lost. The judges, the politicians, and the soldiers together pressed for easy terms of surrender, for release of prisoners on promise of good behaviour, and for only token forfeitures. In February 1716 the Marquis of Huntly was released from captivity and once this leading Gordon rebel had his freedom little in the way of drastic measures could be taken against anybody else. This was a help militarily. No professional soldier wanted to campaign in the block of the southern Highlands that had provided, often under coercion from chiefs or neighbours, the Highland contingent to the rebel army. It was easier to take sub-missions and put through a few confiscations. The connivance of lawyers and judges meant that a Jacobite family was extremely unlucky if it did in fact lose its lands. In one way or another, by exag-gerating the claims of trustees, feudal superiors, or heirs of entail, it was easy to prove that very few rebels had such complete ownership of an estate that it could easily be forfeited. The whole settlement was mild. Nineteen peers lost their titles, and one, Viscount Kenmure, his head.

The uneasy division of political profit and power between the two Whig groups, the Squadrone and the followers of Argyll, continued. Scottish politics bred long term and major parties because the su-preme importance of the election of representative peers meant that any politician of aristocratic origin who wished to get to London had to belong to one of the groups that had a chance of winning some of these places. In London, too, the Scots tended to act in Parliament as an organized group: it was later said that those in the House of Commons liked to have a tall Lord Advocate, so that they could see which lobby he entered, and follow. This coherent development was at first halted by the difficulty of identifying the political leader. Through whom did power and influence flow now that the Privy Council was gone? Would it be the Secretary of State, the Lord

President of the Session, the Lord Advocate, or someone else? In practice, power for such administrative actions as eighteenth-century Britain allowed lay diffusely between politicians and the judges, who were not at all divorced from politics. Administrative action, if it were effective, would eventually have results which affected the judiciary; often it was totally masked in judicial form. The Scottish bench consisted of fifteen men administering a still immature law with wide discretionary elements, and representing important kinship groups. Appointment was by politicians for political reasons, and the judges, once appointed, knew who were their masters. But they held by life appointment, and had a real professional grounding. Capture of the bench by one group would only be achieved if it held the strings of political power completely and for a long time. Under normal circumstances this was not achieved: as a result, the judges valued their own professional reputation, and government in Scotland was weaker and less monolithic than in England.

English politicians might feel that Scotch members of Parliament weighted the scales in favour of the growing power of certain massive political groupings. In this way they added to the movement towards stability. The achievement of political stability naturally did not appear as beneficial to those left out in the cold as it did to those within the big groupings, though in the end it gave great benefits to both kingdoms. The economic complaints against the Scots had apparently even better grounding. It was notorious that the Scottish customs were more honoured in the breach than in the observance. Books were not made up, quantities were not checked nor inspections made; if an official was allowed to stay more than a few years in any one customs precinct he would become involved in systematic fraud, receiving fees for non-observance of his duties. All officers belonged to some great man's kin or following and could not easily be sacked. In the process of developing an efficient administration from the partisanship and corruption of the later seventeenth century, Scotland had farther to go than England. Used, before the Union, to low customs charges on only certain items of trade and the technique of farming out to men who were willing to compromise rather than make a loss, she had now to develop a real system of protection. This meant that control had to be maintained over the unremunerative north and west. The structure was burdensome and expensive. The Scots disliked paying and showed this dislike by violence. It was said that the officers in the south-west were afraid to be seen on the quays. The courts were openly on the side of the smugglers and against the officers.

The situation had two disadvantages: one was economic, the uncontrollable drain of specie abroad; the other political, the government of Scotland running at a loss. Even if some money was moving from Scotland to London, she was not bearing her share of the cost of government. The customs receipts were well below the amateur estimates made for the Union. The excise, which seems to have been less corrupt and more independent of political patronage, was doing better, but not well enough to compensate. The pre-Union calculators had ignored the problem created by the indebtedness of the Scottish Crown, because these debts were not funded. The obligation to take part in the English national debt had therefore primarily been set against the claims of those who had lost in the Darien venture, and it was to these that the Equivalent had first been made. The much more appropriate allocation, the paying off of the Scottish public debt, stood second, and by the time the distribution got to it the debt stood at a quarter of a million and there was some sixty thousand pounds of Equivalent left. The creditors would not get paid until the second Equivalent was created, the profit from the increased revenue forecast for Scotland. On this also hung the two thousand pounds a year that was to be devoted to encouraging the coarse woollen industry. Probity and a sort of patriotism were united in requiring an end to the systematic flouting of the revenue laws.

It was not the interests of Scottish creditors after all that accounted for the attempt by the Prime Minister, Walpole, in 1722 to clean up the Scottish customs, but the protests of English merchants at unfair competition. English tobacco sellers were being undercut by Scottish tobacco which had evaded duty: it was calculated that over a million pounds of duty-free tobacco was crossing the Border every year. Though Walpole tidied the system up as best he could, it looks from the level of customs receipts that the habit of not paying remained prevalent in Scotland up to the rule of Grenville in the 1760s. And here again was a sort of patriotism. The right of the Scots to engage in trade with the English overseas empire was in practice restricted by the difficulty of getting a foothold in it. It took two generations for

Scots to have a fair share in the East India Company, since that company was exclusive to London. If Glasgow merchants got a toe in by illegal undercutting the benefit eventually accrued to Scotland as a whole.

The great achievement of the Union was the creation of the biggest free trade area in the world. Yet within this area the Scottish part was to remain backward unless the country got economic help by fair or foul means. It is therefore representative of the real issues facing Scotland that the two big lowland disturbances of the first half of the eighteenth century rose out of revenue disputes: the famous Porteous riots in Edinburgh in 1736, in which the Captain of the Town Guard was lynched by a disciplined mob, and a conspiracy of silence at all levels made investigation fruitless; and the far more dangerous Shaw-field riots in 1725 in Glasgow over the enhanced malt tax. The tax was an attempt to get a more adequate Scottish contribution to the central government. Only Glasgow rioted, with the looting and burning of the house of a Whig member of Parliament, Campbell of Shawfield, but the towns all over Scotland were ready to join in and every sign points to this being a movement of national resistance. It was fomented by the judges and politicians of the Squadrone faction. The London government, aware of how little stood between riot and rebellion in the eighteenth century, woke up to Scottish problems. Walpole was at the height of his power and able to monopolize it within his own Cabinet. He sacked the Squadrone Secretary of State, the Duke of Roxburghe, and committed Scotland wholly to the Argyll faction. Islay, as Lord Justice General, was to dominate the judges; and Duncan Forbes, Lord Advocate, by arresting the inactive Provost and magistrates of Glasgow, was to show that executive authority still existed in the Scottish government.

This outbreak of government activity coincided with an attempt to reduce the menace of the Highlands. The Cabinet had already sent up General Wade to look into the problems of law and order there, and Wade, moving slowly as befitted his vast size, brought roads, a system of military policing, and relative security to the Jacobite block of the southern Highlands. At the same time Islay's influence gave coherence to the judicial bench without openly corrupting it, and Forbes was able to go on and extract the second Equivalent. In 1727 the intent of this section of the Act of Union was met by the founding of the Board of Trustees for Fisheries and Manufactures, a body of gentlemen, lawyers, and merchants, appointed by the Crown, meeting in Edinburgh and administering £6,000 a year, of which nearly a half was earmarked for the linen industry. The fund was of course tiny, and seemed even smaller in practice because the Board tried to do everything with it: promote research in technology (flax preparation, bleaching), found schools for spinning, encourage farmers in flax-growing, offer technical aids for spinning and weaving, and inspect the end product, the cloth, and stamp it for sale. It is easy to criticize it for over-extending its activities. Yet the linen industry already stretched over half Scotland, and was the one activity that could rely on a big home market as well as on demand in England and the colonies. The Board could see both the need for technical improvement and the openings to which it would lead, and did not see very clearly that partial fostering of a few growth centres might achieve its ends more quickly than dribbling out its small funds everywhere. Nor did it appreciate that importing flax of good quality from the Baltic was probably a sounder method of approach than trying to re-educate both the agriculture and the industry of Scotland at the same time.

Slowly, like a long distance express with its wheels slipping, the Scottish economy began to move forward. The Glasgow merchants, living in a more open and competitive society than that found in most burghs, showed the way to develop the tobacco trade. The city had natural advantages for this; the Clyde as a sheltered waterway, and the shortest route to the colonies of any major port; but some positive initiative was necessary if the existing course of trade was to be diverted from Whitehaven and London. The Scots built up a 'store system' in tidewater America, a system of depots where the planters could exchange tobacco for goods without waiting for its sale in the home country. This meant that the merchants had to provide all the working capital of the trade, which was a strain on an undeveloped economy, yet one which was met. Unusually forward looking and adventurous banking in the west of Scotland was one of the means: another may have been English capital. But for the most part, English capitalists were cautious about Scottish ventures: the delays and uncertainties of Scottish law made investment across the Border insecure. Yet the tobacco trade seems to have had no difficulty in getting money from somewhere. The reward of initiative came in the 1740s when, by readiness to respond to a tip passed on by a banking house, Glasgow picked up the great French contract for tobacco, the biggest single re-export available. After that expansion was steady. The trade was a self-contained matter of purchase and re-export, locking up a lot of money, and with little effect on industry and labour, but it was a well-deserved success story.

There were other developments a generation after the Union. At first the only part of Scottish agriculture which had responded to the openings with England had been the cattle trade. Late every summer the great herds converged on Crieff and began the slow walk on upland tracks to England. The money sent back for them raised the value of pasture land everywhere and, indirectly, the level of rents. It gave a motive for abandoning the standard vice of over-cropping which kept the arable lands on the verge of exhaustion, a reason for breaking out of the vicious circle of unproductive farming. In Galloway the rudimentary agricultural system was reorganized early to profit by the cattle trade, and enclosing and large scale specialization followed. Galloway was an area which had long reckoned on exchanging cattle for grain. New ideas on methods began to enter elsewhere. The York Buildings Company, a group of speculative financiers, had bought up the estates forfeited for the '15 and was trying to make easy money out of them. An even more corrupt offshoot of this corrupt organization, the so-called 'Charitable Corporation', grossly overstepped the lax financial standards of the eighteenth century, and as a result an ambitious and intelligent laird, Sir Archibald Grant of Monymusk in Aberdeenshire, found himself in 1734 cashiered from the House of Commons and on the verge of bankruptcy. Agricultural reform was already established in England as an outlet for frustrated politicians. Grant threw himself into making his estate pay on a transformed scale, and built in Aberdeenshire an oasis of intellectual interest in farming and forestry. Another contemporary, John Cockburn of Ormiston in East Lothian, was also forecasting the way things were to go. Here again the impulse was tied up with a political career, for Cockburn seems to have gathered his ideas on the long journeys to and from Parliament. The new techniques and crops had come to England from the Netherlands, a country frequently visited by the Scotch gentry, but the political and intellectual climate of Scotland was not receptive of these ideas until the 1730s. Cockburn saw 'improvement' as a whole; the growing of good crops, the making of sound commodities from them (good beer, quality linen), and the selling of these at low prices; an end, he wrote, to the 'foolish, narrow, low notions' that already obtained, high prices for poor products. Local trading and manufactures would promote local agriculture. They would encourage hard work and punctuality, produce a profit and a higher standard of living for all. Hence his new model village at Ormiston, where every child over seven worked, and the houses were well built, of two stories, the focus of an estate of enclosed fields, long leases, and new equipment. Ormiston was the kind of growth centre on which a new Scotland would be built, but this would involve more than a simple appreciation of the value of good beer, potatoes, and turnips. It meant a change in ambitions for the upper classes, no more concentration on 'thralling' men to themselves. Instead, their competitive impulses were to find an outlet in their standards as landlords, and their patriotism in collecting ideas from England and abroad, to spread at home.

The new ideas had been slow to take over. In 1727 Defoe's *Tour* shows a Scotland still appallingly unproductive and ruled by an upper-class which, in his middle-class eyes, seemed to give little impetus to development. But already a group within it had produced the 'Society for Improving in the Knowledge of Agriculture', the first sign of the new approach. In the 1730s this manifestation widened. Aberdeenshire had a local landowners' society for better farming, and Cockburn in East Lothian had his own little one at a lower level for the farmers themselves. Pamphlets and books on the new farming were coming out, and even though they kept their sights low – urging that not more than three successive grain crops be taken, and arguing that some sort of fencing or hedging of fields would eventually pay – they show that the most difficult step an undeveloped country has to take, the creation of a new attitude, was being made.

Better farming would yield higher rents, but it seems that only part of the increased gains from the land went to the landowners. At all levels there is evidence of more elegant or more comfortable living. At the upper end of things there is the arrival of the Palladian style in country houses, with new standards of space, elegance, and domestic care. Lower down the 'domestic revolution' affected all but the poorest. People indulged at last in comfort and cleanliness, made possible by having second or third rooms to the farmhouse, by building chimneys, slate roofs, and wooden or stone floors. The first signs of this change would be investment in linen stocks, and after that would come well-made furniture, glass in the windows, earthenware or tinplate dishes. There would also be new items of luxury, such as London porter to drink, soft blankets from England, coffee, sugar, and tea. In 1742 Duncan Forbes tried to curb the last of these in the interests of the profits of the excise on the older habit of beer drinking, for the excise supported his precious Board of Trustees. He proposed that no one with an income of less than fifty pounds a year should be allowed to drink that 'mischievous drug', tea, since those with lesser incomes were unlikely to afford any but smuggled tea. But he was too late: it was already established as a standard item for the middle classes, and the one luxury of the urban poor.

The beginnings of the characteristics that we associate with polite society, such as drawing rooms, cleanliness, and tea drinking, were linked up in Edinburgh with a more important development of clubs and societies. Edinburgh was the second city of the United Kingdom in size and provided the features of a capital. The law centred here, and this brought to the city for a large part of every year intelligent men of the landed families in an atmosphere of professional legal competition. Round the lawyers there gradually grew up an astonishing collection of clubs and societies, to meet and further every taste. The University was big and growing. It had accepted the new discoveries in anatomy and was applying them in the medical school. The upper classes came to Edinburgh when they could afford it, for business and social life, and the General Assembly in the summer brought not only ministers but also the gentry as elders. Church affairs were important, even if the Kirk no longer claimed to dominate politics. There was the need to assert its dominance over the surviving body of Episcopalianism; there were genuine problems of doctrinal definition, and there was the work of implementing the Act of 1696 that had decreed a school in every parish. The Kirk was a great self-governing body working, not entirely happily, in harness with lay society.

It was ostensibly over patronage that it suffered its first secession, that of Erskine and his followers in 1733. Behind this lay not only the question of church government, the relationship of presbyteries to the General Assembly, but also changes in the theological climate. Disputes which, as this one did, use the word 'erastian' are usually concerned with more than government: all parties in the Church were prepared to be erastian if the lay power would favour their side. Erskine wanted a Church militant as it had been in the 1640s, dominant over society and state, repressing all others, and made up of the assured elect. Its preaching would not be to expound or enforce morality but to assert and explain dogma to the faithful. This was incompatible, in his eyes, not only with patronage but with toleration and with the Union. The particular irritants that brought out the gulf between his followers and the majority was the Kirk's slowness in censuring John Simson, professor at Glasgow, who was thought to hold a qualified Arianism, and its readiness to condemn for antinomianism the reissue of an old seventeenth-century puritan text, *The Marrow of Modern Divinity*. There is always a strong chance that democratic or semi-democratic Assemblies will apply censorship without having properly read or understood the work they censure, and the charge of antinomianism was an easy one to use against the extreme Calvinist view of grace. The minority could be held within the Kirk until the Erskinites created their own presbytery. The Kirk, which had done exactly the same on a large scale in the north-east after 1689, could not brook this violation of the basic notion of Presbyterian government, and the offenders formed the 'Secession' Church. In their last broadside against the Kirk, Erskine and his supporters showed the basic gulf in opinion by protesting against the repeal of the laws against witchcraft.

These laws had been repealed in 1736, and even before that had slipped out of use. The last record of a witchcraft execution is for 1722 at Dornoch: this survives by a chance communication of some years later, and there may have been other cases of similar date. Certainly in 1726 the Reverend Robert Wodrow, who was credulous about such things, was recording 'some pretty odd accounts' of witches in Ross, as well as some tall stories of second-sight. But executions had declined since 1678, when the Privy Council asserted that it alone had the right to torture, and there had been few since the Union. This decline, and the repeal, were evidences of a change in outlook. The social and political tensions that had needed witches as scapegoats had eased, and the intellectual climate of the day was averse to the concepts involved.

For, at the same time that Wodrow was listening to tall stories, David Hume was beginning to work out the ideas of knowledge and causation which were eventually published anonymously in 1739 in his *Treatise of Human Nature*[1] Hume applied a splendid and critical intelligence which illuminated all it touched to the theory of knowledge and the whole concept of deductive thinking, and arrived at scepticism of dogma and of all knowledge not based on cumulative experience. He took further the cautious, experimental method of Newton, turning it from science to philosophy, and adding something approaching the modern idea of statistical probability as the basis of a scientific 'law'. As applied by Hume, this attitude left very little for Christian belief to stand on. Organized religious belief, in his opinion, was apt to end up with constructions resembling a 'sick man's dreams'. But since he dismissed causation altogether, except unseen in the inner working of men's minds, he was not prepared to settle for the eighteenth-century deistical compromise, and to talk about the 'prime cause' instead of God. Yet atheism was too dogmatic a position for him. Only gradually in the growing tolerance of the age did he allow his total scepticism to appear. But the Kirk had wit enough to see the tendency of his thinking, and firmly kept him out of university office, even though neither it nor anyone in the western world could begin to reshape philosophy to counter his extreme empiricism for another generation.

Hume was not alone in his ability to detach himself from the existing emphasis in religious matters. Francis Hutcheson, as professor of moral philosophy in Glasgow from 1730, though he fully accepted the Kirk's official dogma, was forming the coming generation in debate on natural religion, the instinct of benevolence, and the moral sense. The specialized leaders of Scottish intellectual life later in the century had almost all passed through his classes in their teens, and their personalities and intellects had developed under his persuasion, both in and out of class. The reforms of the Scottish universities of the generation before had, in most places, ended the old regent system. Under this system the university teachers had taught the whole of the

1. Revealingly subtitled *An attempt to introduce the experimental method of reasoning into moral subjects.*

university's curriculum. In the eighteenth century the university professor was a specialist, though often in a wide subject which had to be taught at a fairly low level.

Both intellectual and economic development depended on not going back to the sterile disputes of the previous century over secular or ecclesiastical power. If there were elements in the Church that were unwilling to abandon these, so also were there in the state. Jacobitism was still the political settlement many would have preferred, but the monolithic rule of Walpole in the late 1720s and early '30s had made it a less pressing issue. After 1733, Walpole's power was slowly crumbling inside his own Cabinet. It disintegrated faster in Scotland, for he quarrelled with the Duke of Argyll, and even though Walpole remained in alliance with Islay, the abler of the brothers, a lot of support was lost. The military structure was weaker than it appeared. Wade was too old and too massive to patrol the Highlands in person. In 1739 Walpole blundered into the war with Spain which gradually widened to involve a major attack by the expanding European powers on the boundaries of their neighbours, and in which England and France were bound to look for a show of strength against each other. It was an old-fashioned war, fought with grand and incompetent alliances. War blunders and war taxation weakened the government until in 1742 Walpole was replaced by a coalition. This gave renewed strength in Scotland to the Squadrone, who were rewarded with the revival of the Secretaryship of State in the person of the Marquis of Tweeddale. Infirm in person and purpose, Tweeddale's main qualification for office seems to have been that he was the new Prime Minister's son-in-law. The need for troops in Germany led the government to band together the Highland companies, which kept law and order of a partisan sort in the Highlands, into a regiment and sent it abroad. The regiment was not at first a success: understandably, men who had not enlisted to serve in north Germany mutinied when they found that that was where they were going. Its absence left a vacuum of power in the Highlands which could not easily be filled, because the disarming Acts, aimed at the rebel clans, had little effect on these but made it illegal for the Whig clans to carry arms. With the disappearance of the companies went the element of force that persuaded Highland chiefs to keep up the appearance of law-keeping. With the arrival in power of the Squadrone, Islay, who inherited his brother's dukedom in 1743, was weakened in his attempts to secure a share of government benefits and patronage for the Highlands. Jacobite intrigue began again, and on a scale which more than compensated for its incompetence. There was almost open recruitment for a Jacobite regiment under the exiled Duke of Perth in French service, and no hope of a military career under the government. Control of the Highlands in the interests of law and order and the Hanoverian succession had become a structure of straw.

'Jacobitism', so far as it meant real activity in favour of the Stewarts, had been weakening fast in the two generations of their exile. In particular, the episcopal Kirk had stood up to repression since 1689 much less successfully than had extreme Presbyterianism in the 1660s. This was partly because of the much more decisive and unscrupulous form of the repression, but it also suggests that episcopacy was a weaker structure at base level than presbytery. The bishops had an awkward problem in their relationship to the monarchy. If they insisted that new elections had to be ratified by the king in exile, they were laying stress on leadership by a man known to be of a different faith. Yet residual Episcopalian sentiment could link with discontent against the Union, or with discontent caused by the actions of members of the government, Scottish or English, to form a large body of potential Jacobitism.

Jacobitism lived on mostly in inactive form. Left to herself Scotland would never have made the Revolution of 1688. Because of this, all sorts of discontent naturally gathered under the label of Jacobitism, even if much Jacobitism was no more in practice than a refusal to take the Oath of Allegiance. From the point of view of the security of the Hanoverian régime, the word 'Jacobite' was rightly applied to all who would be prepared to settle down contentedly under Stewart rule. In this sense it can be applied to David Hume and some of his friends, to a lot of the landed society of the north-east, to all who were unenthusiastic for Presbyterianism, and to those who still either resented the Union or felt that it had not yet been profitable enough to Scotland. It could be applied with much more force to the unsettled clans of the southern Highlands, who associated Hanoverian rule with Whig power, the Whigs with the house of Argyll, and Argyll with the loss of their lands or superiorities. Since no Whig government had yet been strong enough to dispense with Campbell support, this chain of association was continually emphasized to the dis-affected clans.

The structure of eighteenth-century government, ramshackle everywhere, was even weaker in Scotland than in England. In the 1740s the fall of Walpole showed Whig power divided in both countries, but more deeply and persistently so in Scotland. The result was a vacuum of authority and power.

The gloomy inheritor of the Jacobite claim, James Edward, the Old Pretender, had a young and adventurous, though rather stupid, heir, the Prince Charles Edward. The Prince was ready to take a chance, and rightly saw that the Stewarts would not come back to Britain by waiting for other people to put them there. Jacobite intrigue was amateur and incompetent, but its revival in the 1740s was itself a symptom of government weakness.

It is appropriate that the attempt in 1745 to reverse the course of eighteenth-century development in Scotland and bring back the Stewarts should have had to push aside the main instrument of that development, the law and its courts. The autumn calendar of cases for the Court of Session in that year is interrupted by the words 'the court did not meet this session, the country being in arms'.

NOTES ON DRAMATIS PERSONAE

Mar ; Hamilton ; Argyll. As in Chapter 18.

The Old Pretender. James Edward (1688–1766), only son of James VII, 'Jacobite' claimant to the throne after his father's death in 1701, he lacked either the brains or the character to make a success of a difficult position.

The Young Pretender. Charles Edward (1720–88), elder son of James Edward. He possessed more dash than his father but not much more intelligence, and in his later life succumbed to depression.

Erskine. Ebenezer Erskine (1680–1754), founder of the Original Secession Church: before that minister at Stirling and a distinguished preacher. His brother Ralph (1685–1752) joined the secession in 1737.

Forbes. Duncan Forbes of Culloden (1685–1747), Lord Advocate 1725 and Lord President 1737: one of the best-loved of Scottish judges and politicians and the member of the government with the clearest understanding of opinions and the balance of power in the Highlands.

Hume. David Hume (1711–76). Philosopher and historian. In the former capacity his achievement is the highest attained in Britain.

Hutcheson. Francis Hutcheson (1694–1746), from northern Ireland, of Scottish extraction, professor of moral philosophy at Glasgow 1729, the initiator of the Scottish Enlightenment.

Islay. Archibald Campbell (1682–1761), third Duke of Argyll on his brother's death 1743. He was created Earl of Ilay or Islay 1706 as part of the bargain to secure his brother's adherence to the Union. Though he fought at Sheriffmuir his professional talents were legal. In 1710 he was made Lord Justice General for life.

Mackintosh of Borlum. William Mackintosh (1662–1743), Brigadier in the 1715. Imprisoned for many years in Edinburgh castle he wrote a patriotic treatise encouraging improved farming.

Tweeddale. John Hay, fourth Marquess (*c.* 1695–1762).

Wade. George Wade (1673–1748), field marshal 1743, Commander-in-Chief in Scotland 1725, and builder of the first important system of roads in the Highlands.

Wodrow. Robert Wodrow (1679–1734), antiquarian and church historian, minister of Eastwood 1704, collector and publisher of both the official documents of the Restoration period and of hearsay accounts of Covenanting sympathy.

Chapter 20

The later eighteenth century

The new landscape

ON 4 AUGUST 1745 the Reverend Lachlan Campbell, minister of
Ardnamurchan, said to one of his parishioners, 'I can take my oath
upon it that the Pretender is in my parish.' He was right. The landing
of Prince Charles Edward with ten thousand French troops some-
where in Britain had been planned for 1744 but frustrated. Now a
modified version had taken place. The prince with a characteristic
mixture of courage and ignorance had pressed for the expedition, but
the French had been unwilling to extend their military commitments.
On 25 July he had landed in Borrodale, near Arisaig, without soldiers.
The success of the move depended on whether his personality and
presence would persuade the leaders of the disaffected clans, already

under promise to join in with their men if French help came, to call out their men without this help. The gentlemen in Skye, getting word early, hesitated for several days, but eventually refused to join, and one of them, Norman Macleod of Macleod, passed the news to the Lord President, Duncan Forbes of Culloden, in Edinburgh. But Donald Cameron, heir to Locheil, allowed himself to be persuaded, and so did young Clanranald. The two together could bring out a thousand men, if necessary by coercion. Armed and ready to fight, these could and did do a lot to persuade their neighbours to join in too. On 20 August the Camerons joined the prince in strength and he unfurled his standard at Glenfinnan. His army was still small enough to move fast, and insecure enough to see the advantage of doing so. Six days later it was preparing to march by Wade's road over the Corriearrick pass from Fort Augustus in the Great Glen to Dalwhinnie in Atholl, where it would meet the main route south.

The '45 arrived to find a government disunited. George II was in Hanover, and only grudgingly returned. The Scottish allies of the two main groups that made the coalition government in London, the Duke of Argyll and the Secretary of State, were conducting a cold war with each other. The country's defences were in the hands of few and untrained troops, mostly commanded by aged generals. Sir John Cope, the youngest, had been an officer for thirty-eight years, and was probably only in his late fifties. With his 1,400 men he could have sat down and held the centre of Scotland at Stirling as his predecessor had done in 1715, but believing that it would be best to stamp out rebellion by a show of force before the clans mustered in strength he decided to go north. Forbes of Culloden left Edinburgh on 9 August, the day after the news arrived: a Highlander himself he knew that his presence would do a lot to fix loyalties in the farther Highlands. Cope could not follow till his unready troops had food and money. Baking biscuit, and waiting for cash from the south, kept him back for ten days, so that it was not till 26 August that he arrived at the southern end of the Corriearrick with a herd of bullocks, to learn that there were two or three thousand men in arms in the twisting passage through the hills in front. It is quite possible that if young Macleod could have made up his mind which side he was on a few days earlier the crucial battle of the rising would have been a small action in the Great Glen. As it was Cope knew he could not win on that terrain. Nor could he hold his position, for much of his precious biscuit had been stolen. It was his job to get his army back to defend Edinburgh, so he turned aside and hurried to the sea at Inverness. Swinging round the coast road he made Aberdeen, where he put his men on board ship, landing them at Dunbar on 17 September. But the capital, unfought for and unscarred, opened its gates to the Highland army that day. While Cope sat in camp at Prestonpans waiting for reinforcements, he was caught out in a dawn action, and in the rout of his men had the embarrassing distinction of bringing the news of his own defeat to the refugee Scottish administration in Berwick.

Scotland apparently lay at the prince's feet. There was no military force left to oppose him there except the small garrisons of the coastal castles and the forts in the Great Glen. The insistence on legalism in governing circles prevented the arming of the Whig clans. Forbes, besieged in his house at Culloden, was patiently writing long letters of persuasion to wavering chiefs and organizing the creation of new companies, and Argyll in London was urging that he be allowed to bring out the Campbells. But for the time being the 'Disarming Act', aimed at potential rebels but observed only by the well-affected, induced military paralysis. For all that, even though Charles Edward would not have got to Edinburgh if a lot of people, from the chiefs in Skye to the Lord Provost of the city, had not been prepared to think of a Jacobite régime as acceptable, not many men were prepared to fight for it. Not only were merely a minority of Highland clans Jacobite, but not even all those that had come 'out' in 1715 would do so now. Though Lovat, that arch intriguer, had this time decided that his safety and advantage lay on the Stewart side, a vestigial desire to hedge his bets had meant that only some of the Frasers were in open rebellion. The hard core of disaffected, Macdonalds, Camerons, Appin Stewarts, and MacLeans, were 'out', but only some of the Mackintoshes and MacKenzies. The Gordons were passive, and with them much of the north-east. Forbes's personality and the trust it inspired held the far north steady. A few hundred Lowlanders joined, enthusiastic and episcopal gentry. In Edinburgh we have a list of 137 names, which includes a few merchants, innkeepers, and several goldsmiths and watchmakers. The south-west was hostile, Glasgow and Ayrshire particularly so.

So the army in this rebellion was almost exclusively Highland in composition, and fought by Highland methods. It was also small. At no point could Charles Edward command an army of even half the strength of that which had fought for his father thirty years before. This meant that he could not have any administrative hold on the country. He could get supplies by confiscating the money collected for the payment of taxes, and distrain on the corn rents of hostile landowners. But he could not occupy and rule. Even in Edinburgh itself he had not gained the castle. The Royal Bank had taken refuge there with its gold reserves, but the Hanoverian commander did not prevent it paying these out for its notes, and so enabling the prince to pay his men – another example of the ambivalent attitude of the Scottish propertied classes to Jacobitism. The forts and castles held out with less ambivalence, supplied by sea. Only Fort George, near Inverness, succumbed before the rising ended. The prince had no artillery, and even if he had been able to obtain it it was not an arm to which his Highlanders were accustomed.

The ambiguity over Jacobite support continued over policy. Charles Edward's proclamations took care to stress that he intended to leave the Protestant Churches in Britain both free and in control of all the educational institutions they already had, but he did not do much to improve the prospects of his main Scottish support, the Episcopalians. He declared the Union at an end for Scotland, but was careful to show that this would not automatically mean cancelling Scottish participation in the national debt. It was likely that a Stewart return would, at least at first, mean a change in foreign policy and an alliance with France. But since the existing war with France sprang out of rivalry in trade and over colonies, it was unlikely that such an alliance would be permanent as far as England was concerned. It was known that his father wished to end the system of private jurisdictions that enhanced the power of some Scottish landowners and in particular supported the authority of some clan chiefs. But since the bulk of Charles Edward's supporters had been sent to his army by clan chiefs, this was unlikely to be done in a hurry. Even though the Highlanders in this campaign were giving little support to the Lowland opinion of them as barbarians, there were aspects of their society which were incompatible with the level of civilization of the rest of Scotland. This was shown after the battle of Falkirk when the prince was unable to stop the execution of one of Clanranald's men as an eye-for-an-eye payment for the accidental shooting of Glengarry's son. The alternative would have been blood feud.

The problem of relations between Scotland and England was not going to be solved by a Stewart restoration and legal separatism. There were two basic obstacles, one that the Stewarts would not peacefully surrender their claim to add the English throne to the Scottish, the other that the common interests of the two countries in economic matters and the mutual threat that they offered to each other when separate, the basic arguments that had created the Union, remained. There was enough discontent to account for ambivalence or passive Jacobitism, but not enough to bring in real support. Some of the support, as always in rebellions, came from those on the edge of bankruptcy. A popular move of the prince's was the promise of repeal of the malt tax. None of this added up to much.

Charles Edward could not therefore rest on his partial and uneasy control of Scotland. On 1 November he marched south, to cross the border with five thousand men at Carlisle. That his control lay solely where his army was, is shown by the return of the refugee Hanoverian government from Berwick to Edinburgh. Five weeks later, with practically no English support prepared to come forward, he was at Derby. His presence frightened London and the government there, but he himself was made nervous by the careful advance of an army, recently put under George II's son, William, Duke of Cumberland, at twenty-five a competent professional soldier: this was made up of trained troops brought over from the war on the continent. The Jacobite army had received no recruits south of Lancashire and was not likely to find them in the south of England. It was in danger of being cut off from Scotland. It turned back. If Mar could not win for James Edward by staying put in 1715 it was impossible to believe that the '45 would achieve anything once it had begun the long retreat. Back the army went across the Border, followed by Cumberland. It won a messy engagement at Falkirk which did not stop the retreat. Finally, when further retreat would have meant guerilla warfare in the mountains, a programme unacceptable to the prince's Irish friends, it turned and fought at Culloden Moor on 16 April 1746. At this point it faced, on terrain which gave no cover against gunfire, a force half as large again, of disciplined men, cheered by a long advance, backed by artillery, and trained against the special risks of the Highland charge. Neither Charles Edward nor his Irish companions (for he had quarrelled with his original general, Lord George Murray) seem to have appreciated the particular merits and defects of a Highland army. They allowed it to stand in ranks against artillery fire before attacking. The resulting slaughter and defeat were inescapable.

But the '45 did not end with the battle. Everyone knew that, this time, rebellion was serious, and the smallness of the section of Scotland involved in it meant that real punishment would follow. The fact that many groups of clansmen got away from the battle gave a particular motive for punitive search. It would be made clear to those who had chosen to fight for the prince rather than have their roofs burnt over their heads by Locheil and his men, that they were not better off in rebellion. Burning of houses and crops, the confiscation of cattle, the search for men who might have served, and the incidental violence done by angry troops in a harsh environment led to devastation of the southern Highlands through the summer, and must for many have been equivalent to a famine. Cumberland encouraged the toughness, and Forbes of Culloden and the rest of the civilian government were unable to prevent it. Prisoners, not treated gently, were taken to England for trial. Some died in the prison ships in the Thames, 120 were executed, nearly a thousand transported to America. Next year those still in prison were released, but many had died. Some of the severity is explained, though not justified, by memory of the leniency of 1716; some by the severe fright that the government had had. But most came from the rift between the two cultures, Highland and Lowland, and unwillingness to extend humanity across it. The prince wandered in the west for five months, preserved by Highland loyalty, in spite of a price of £30,000 on his head (loyalty to the ordinary clansman was a quality offered in absolute terms) to be rescued at last by French naval courage and persistence.

Meanwhile government prepared to deal with the apparent cause of the rising, the structure and paraphernalia of clanship. The London government was stronger now than in 1745, for it had ceased to be a coalition. It put Acts through Parliament buying out the private jurisdictions of Scotland, abolishing the military features of Scottish feudal law, and suppressing the outward signs of the Highland way of life, the bearing of arms and the Highland dress. The chiefs in exile had mostly to wait a generation before they could buy back their estates. These were put into the hands of a commission of Lowland gentry which attempted to turn them from debt-ridden little despotisms to modern and industrious units. The economic and social changes completed the transformation from chief to landowner, but already, whenever it suited the chief, he had been coupling his position as head of the clan with the advantages and territorial interests of landed gentry, even before 1745. In the same way, the transformation of the Lowland laird from a cowed subordinate of one of the greater houses into an independent country gentleman was symbolized by this legislation, but had already occurred. Jacobitism declined in its leadership. All courts in exile easily slip into bitterness and intrigue. Most Jacobites had never personally liked the Old Pretender. His older son, Charles Edward, took to drinking heavily. The younger one had taken Catholic orders. There was little to command private enthusiasm. By the 1780s Jacobitism was dead, and the Hanoverian government, for the sake of British prestige, was considering offering financial support to the exiled house.

The Scotch lawyers and politicians had kept out of passing the legislation after the rebellion. Even when they approved of its aim they had no desire to be associated with its punitive characteristics. But afterwards Scotland found a more stable political life. Partly this was a reflection of increased stability in London. Till 1761 control in Scotland was in the hands of the Duke of Argyll. His rival, Tweeddale, had disappeared with the coalition in 1746: the Secretaryship of State remained empty. Argyll played the part of an elder statesman in the Cabinet, and distributed Scottish patronage. His rule was a modified dictatorship. The duke, by then over sixty, had acquired a practical sense of his limitations, not only in relation to English politicians, but also in seeing that it was undesirable to have promotion to the Scottish bench entirely political. The people he selected were got into Parliament by persistence and persuasion rather than commands. It is in this period that the Scottish electoral system became distorted to fit the expanding political interests of the upper classes, though there are instances of distortion earlier. Collecting burgh votes became a regular occasion for bribery. County seats needed a different sort of manipulation, the far-sighted creation of fictitious 'freeholds', which would enable landed wealth to have a proportional say in political influence. The actual elections were not occasions for lavish

M

expenditure, as they might be in England, but it was no use indulging in local power politics unless at a pinch you could stand the tremendous expense of law-suits to protect either genuine or bogus votes. The system was demoralizing, since it involved defending these votes on oath if their genuineness was impugned. It wasted the time of the Court of Session, which fell behind in its business, and it separated the reality of practice from the statements and intentions of the law. In short it was a scandal. But it had certain advantages. Its legal complexities and long time-scale kept even the wealthiest Englishmen out of Scottish county seats. As the Scottish representation provided in the Act of Union proved inadequate for the rising wealth and political ambitions of the Scottish landed classes, they could look for further opportunities in England while preserving the home market. In this way stability, which was achieved, did not involve much frustration. And the pickings for the lawyers were generous: they were 'never so well paid as in election disputes' said an observer.

The system lost its manager when Argyll died in 1761: from then on his house put its intelligence to economic rather than political affairs. Scotland shared the general uncertainty and instability of politics in the 1760s. Then, in the 1770s, it settled down again under the rule of Henry Dundas, 'Henry the ninth'. Dundas came of a legal family which had given the country several Lords President. In that office his father had stood for good appointments to the bench, while co-operating with Argyll. Dundas came into politics with a genuine interest in improving the system, rose to power by being a 'man of business', discharging work agreeably and efficiently, and then in the 1780s built up a system of political alliances inside Scotland which gave him detailed control over Scottish elections. His allies and potential allies were rewarded by the patronage that, as a leading member of the younger Pitt's Cabinet, Dundas either controlled or influenced, particularly in the navy and the East India Company. It was, by modern standards, corrupt, but this was not the word that contemporaries would have offered, for the people Dundas put forward in India in this way were, in personal quality and family backing, a marked improvement on those that had got into the East India Company from Scotland before his day.

The close connection between Scotland and the East India Company of the later 1780s and 1790s was an indication of how much society and economy had changed since the earlier part of the century. Scotland packed into about thirty years of crowded development between 1750 and 1780 the economic growth that in England had spread itself over two centuries. This was the great age of 'improvement', a term which embraced the reorganization of the whole farming system of the country, the development of a fine linen industry in the areas near Glasgow, the creation of a large and modern ironworks at Carron, and the attack, slow at first, on the problem of communications. Turnpike trusts were set up by the gentry of the countryside to build and manage better roads. Improvement meant also the Forth and Clyde canal, which after twenty-two years' effort opened from sea to sea in 1790.[1] It meant the achievement of higher standards of living at all levels of society, from the peasant, whose diet became more varied and nearer to nutritional adequacy, the town worker, with better domestic equipment and more hope of cleanliness, to the comfortable, if cramped, and reasonably fastidious and clean life of the upper classes shown so openly in Boswell's journals. The two great portrait painters of Scotland, Allan Ramsay and Raeburn, reflect it. Raeburn, the later worker, shows his subjects as greater personages than Ramsay does; perhaps they were greater. But Ramsay was the finer painter, with a real appreciation of what paint and line can do to carry the texture of fine fabric or smooth skin. The expansion in living was manifest in the building of that splendid upper-class suburb, the new town of Edinburgh, and also in the dignified houses of Glasgow. An eighteenth-century historian of Glasgow wrote in 1777 of the last quarter century: 'luxury advanced with hasty strides every day; and yet from this aera we may date all the subsequent improvements which have taken place'. Today we are not so surprised at the connection between higher standards of consumption and economic growth. The eighteenth-century farmer was unlikely to produce tolerable cheese and butter for sale until he (and the cheese and butter) had more than one room to live in together. He was unlikely to break out of the hard circle of bad farming and ruinous overcropping without both a market for surplus production

---

1. It is a commentary on the means of communication before this improvement, that Perth, which lost its bridge in the flood of 1621 (an event attributed to divine irritation at the five Articles of Perth of a few years before), did not get a new one until Smeaton built the present one 150 years later.

and an iron industry capable of giving him better tools. No undeveloped country can progress without improving agriculture.
Though some Scottish craftsmen all through the eighteenth century
could turn out work of the highest standards, notably the silversmiths (a craft in which the technology had not changed since the
Middle Ages), the gentry, when furnishing their new town houses
were likely to want to buy well-made Wedgwood pottery rather than
Scotland's own deplorable products, and for them to be able to do so
there had to be saleable Scottish products on the English markets.
To exchange the two there had to be basic improvements in transport. The different aspects of 'improvement' hung together.

One of the great handicaps in development was the problem of
money. Scotland made the best of what little she had by rapid
development in banking. A system of large joint-stock banks with
several branches gave us much stability as was possible before the
days of limited liability, while competition between the banks of the
east and west coasts made for easy credit. But there was always the
risk of over-issue of notes, a risk accentuated by the habit of issuing
them for very small sums. These might be as small as a shilling, and
though a shilling in the eighteenth century could buy more of meat
or grain than ten shillings can today, this practice meant that right
through the nation notes were in use, and might, in times of insecurity, drive out coin. In the early 1760s the evidence suggests that
the issue of notes and credit ran Scotland into an inflation and a
balance of payments crisis. In an effort to prevent this the banks
agreed to have the smaller notes abolished and make all notes more
readily convertible to cash. But this threw the country into banking
conservatism and a shortage of risk capital. To help meet the needs
of expansion a new bank, Douglas, Heron and Company of Ayr,
started an easier policy; and its 'accommodation bills' at once became
the support of those busy raising credit without much in the way of
security. The balance between economic expansion and economic
security was difficult to maintain. The spectacular crash of the Ayr
bank in 1773 shook the confidence of the country, but as in the end it
paid in full, by calling up the promises of its guarantors among the
landed gentry, it was also the vehicle of transferring wealth from consumption by the upper classes to development. It is not surprising
that Adam Smith's great book, *The Wealth of Nations*, published a few

years later, which started the modern study of economics and economic history, should be able to provide an excellent account of the difficulties and hazards of raising capital by accommodation bills, which was the equivalent of paying double the normal rate of interest for it. The Carron ironworks, which was in one way a portent of the new industrial age, a big unit using the new technology of coal, not only suffered all the technological and managerial difficulties of breaking through in scale and methods but lived for years under the menace of this unfortunate method of capitalization.

The great surge forward in Scotland's economic development was made possible by three vital elements. The first, indubitably, was the English connection. Scotland came into her pre-industrial wealth and skills by means of English money, English examples, and the English free trade area, even though, as in the early 1760s, that money was not always forthcoming. Because of this mid-century expansion she was ready in the 1780s and later to share in the breakthrough we know as the Industrial Revolution. It was with English money and with English skill that Carron developed, and the enterprise did not reach security until 1778 when it obtained the Admiralty contract for its famous gun, the 'carronade'. The opening up of the West Indies gave Scotland a market for her coarser linens in clothing the slave population there, and for a certain amount of her food products. American trade gave her the material for the re-export trade in tobacco, and for the earliest stages of the cotton industry. During the quarrel and ensuing war with the American colonies, the imports of the Clyde turned instead to sugar and to the long-staple cotton of the West Indies. The carved elephant on the gate-post of the Dundas house of Arniston is a reminder of how much the big houses of south-east Scotland relied on the East India Company for careers and wealth. It was from England that the fashionable enthusiasm for better farming and higher profits got its inspiration.

It was the largeness of the great impost-free market that gave Scotland her opportunity and not any particular generosity on the part of the occupants of south Britain. If Scotland drew on English technical skills, the English also benefited from Scottish inventions and from the financial and engineering talents of Scots. Though Smeaton, who built the Forth and Clyde canal and several key bridges in Scotland, was English born and English educated, the man who made the biggest single contribution to civil engineering, Telford, was entirely Scottish in background. So was James Watt, whose improvements of the existing steam engine transformed into a machine for general industrial use one that had before been suitable only for pumping out coal mines. All the same it is conceivable that England would have become a modern industrial society at about the time she did without the Union: the same cannot be said of Scotland.

Another vital ingredient in development came from the growth of population. We are on insecure ground when we advance any population figures for dates before the first census of 1801: estimates with no sound statistical backing have put Scotland's population at the Union at eleven hundred thousand. An enterprising minister, Dr Alexander Webster, produced in the 1750s an age analysis and total estimate with some material backing, which gives a total of 1,265,000. What is more interesting is that his analysis suggests a population growing steadily at about 0·4 per cent a year, and we can be fairly certain that no long-term growth at this rate existed in the seventeenth century. Population pressure began to have a marked effect on food prices in the 1760s, and this at last gave a general incentive to improve farming. The steadily rising price of grain was an argument for increased production, particularly to the landlords who, receiving their rents in grain, were the first to benefit. It also eased the burden of capital development in land. The surplus agricultural population provided a fairly docile labour force for the new industry. The influence of population growth on an economy, like that of a bump on a ski slope, enormously helps the performance of those sufficiently skilled to take advantage of it but throws the beginner off balance. Seventeenth-century Scotland would have faced famine with a population growing at this rate. In the mid-eighteenth century the country could not have coped with the expanding population of the early nineteenth century, a growth rate four times that of the 1750s; but it was in a position to benefit by the rate it did experience.

At what point the expansion of population reached the rate indicated by Dr Webster is not clear. It may have been a sudden change, or it may have been a slow acceleration from an earlier and slower rate. But there is good reason to see an expansion in population happening in the whole of western Europe in the 1740s initiated by a spontaneous reduction in the frequency or severity of epidemics of infectious disease, and subsequently enabled to continue by the expansion of food supplies and perhaps by the spread of inoculation against smallpox. The growth of population seems to have been sharpest in the northern and western districts of Scotland, which, if it could be proved, would indicate that it was not caused by the development of minor industries and trade but happened spontaneously. A reduction of the impact of infectious disease would be likely to have its most striking effect on the survival of children, and this would eventually provide a population better supplied than before with young adults of working age. But until more work has been done on this vital subject we are left with only one figure of reasonable certainty, a population in 1801 of just over 1,600,000. The rise in corn prices, which on average went up over 160 per cent between the 1740s and the end of the century, shows us the general trend of expansion.[1]

The first impact of this rise in prices was of course on agriculture. Though there had been examples of 'improving' landlords earlier in the century it is in the 1760s and 1770s that all over Scotland landowners set out to take advantage of the new price structure and to persuade their tenants to more intensive land use. This meant the end of the old open run-rig fields and pressure to abandon over-stocking and over-cropping. The introduction of leases was a means of exercising pressure for improvement and encouraging good practices. Only with a longer interest in the soil could the peasant be prevented from abusing it. If he would allow it to recover between crops he could send his grain yield up from three to one (a common estimate on oat yields in the early eighteenth century) to five or six to one. At five to one he would need to sow only half as much land for the same yield to himself; the other half could be rested. The arithmetic was simple, but it involved crucial decisions: the readiness of the laird to give his tenant security; the readiness of the tenant to take a chance of a short crop. Improved farming, once begun, would enlarge to include a new structure of farms, larger and more coherent, separate units, specialized crops and breeds, the use on the lighter soils of the 'turnip husbandry' as it was called, of Norfolk, and eventually the freeing of the peasantry from services. No longer would the farmers of Colstoun in East Lothian have to provide fourteen horses and two carts in the

1. The prices of the late '90s were drastically affected by war-time inflation.

middle of hay-making to 'lead' home the new millstones for the old mill. No longer would the tenantry of Lasswade be available for carrying coals to Edinburgh at their laird's wish. The use of coal would replace peats cut by the peasantry in the middle of an over-burdened spring schedule of work. 'Peasant democracy', so often sentimentally attributed to the older Scotland, could only begin to exist when the average peasant had some control over his time and labour. It was now that this happened.

The farmers of south-east Scotland responded well to the new independence, and by the end of the century they were capable of passing back to England instruction in the best practices of the day. The improved farming was not yet mechanized, except for minor instruments such as turnip cutters, but it was intensive, particularly in its use of labour and its specialized production for a market. The amount of man-power needed on an estate was probably the same, used much more systematically, but the growing rural population left a surplus which had to look elsewhere for work.

The third element in Scotland's development was her intellectual life, and this was made possible by the structure of her educational system. The Act of 1696 prescribing a school in every parish was never entirely effective. Even the aim, a single parochial school, was unsuitable for some of Scotland's widespread parishes, particularly those in the Highlands, and even in the smaller ones the fact that the nucleated village is not a natural form of social organization in Scotland meant that many households might be far from a school. There were always people in Scotland who, like the Lady of Drum, were 'never pit to skule'. But in the later eighteenth century most of the population in the Lowlands was literate and in most parishes some form of cheap and nominally obligatory education was available, through which, with luck, a very intelligent boy might go beyond the rudimentary elements of literacy and numeracy to be able to pass to a university in his later teens. The burghs were proud of their more advanced and formal education by which a mediocre degree of latinity could be belted into children who would be ready for university at eleven, twelve, or thirteen. The Scottish universities had all, except King's College, Aberdeen, moved by the 1760s to specialized teachers, and except for St Andrews, which was in a decayed state, gave a good secondary education with a wide spread of the modern subjects. These were the core of contemporary intellectual advance, particularly moral and natural philosophy in which were comprehended political economy and the whole of science. A further polish might be provided by either medicine or divinity, and for the upper classes there were the law schools of Holland.

The important feature of all this was that it was a complete structure and closely geared to the filling of professions. The bright village boy could get a bursary to a university and thereby proceed to orders. Less successful ones would study for a few years and end up as schoolmasters. This opened two important, if not very remunerative, careers to all. The more influential and lucrative occupations, such as the law, remained the preserve of those of good family. The limits to social mobility were firm: the village boys came up too old to break through into the central current of intellectual life. It was from the burgh schools and not from the country that the great men of intellect came. David Hume was from a small landed family and studied at the High School of Edinburgh; Adam Smith came from the burgh school of Kirkcaldy; William Robertson, the best of the Scottish historians, from Dalkeith grammar school.

One result of the system was to reinforce the argumentative nature of Calvinist theology, offered in enormous sermons to all every Sunday. Another was to give the sense of direct participation in the government of the Church to many. The Scotch peasant, though he lacked the relative economic security of his English counterpart, was trained to read, write, and argue with his 'betters'. By no means every man would want to use his brains and tongue in this sort of activity, but the capacity to communicate across social barriers and the existence, sometimes, of books among the possessions of even very poor people indicate a democracy of speech. Equally important was the creation of the professoriate. University teaching was at secondary school level, but a lot of it was well done: it involved, at least for the teachers, independent thinking and organizing of ideas in subjects still new enough to profit by this. So though David Hume never occupied a university chair, Adam Smith's *Wealth of Nations* and Reid's philosophy of Common Sense[1] derived from courses of university lecturing. The group of university professors, particularly

1. In his philosophy the phrase means something much more worth serious consideration than in colloquial English.

those in Edinburgh, created the society out of which the new academic disciplines were to grow. Joseph Black, though he stopped research when he became a professor, was in the heart of intellectual society in Edinburgh and had already made a major breakthrough in physics with the discovery of latent heat. Adam Ferguson's lectures on moral philosophy in Glasgow provided him with the opportunity for exploration into the social nature of mankind, and the link between his interests and those of the Scottish historians was close. Although Hutton, the founder of geology, did not hold a chair, he worked and relaxed in close association with Black. His interest in chemistry not only gave him the key to interpretation of the phenomena around him, but also provided him with his main source of income (from an extractive process on the soot in Edinburgh's already polluted atmosphere). His follower Playfair, in the chair of natural philosophy at Edinburgh, expounded his concepts.

The Scottish Enlightenment was thus clearly tied to the system of Scottish education. But its origin came from the push to develop two particular professions, medicine and the law. The law was valuable because its bond with the landed gentry brought these into the universities and put them under the influence of active teachers. People in Scotland could on occasion drink as hard as anywhere, but a Scottish university provided an atmosphere very different from the 'dull and deep potations' of the English universities. Lawyers in Edinburgh for half the year provided clubs and a social life, and a close concern for politics. The 'Select Society', one of the most outstanding of these clubs, held lawyers, philosophers, and clergy in active argument. Medicine was even more crucial. The Edinburgh medical school developed out of the interest created by Sir Robert Sibbald's Royal College of Physicians when the first of the dynasty of Monros became professor of Anatomy in 1725. Anatomy was still a subject involving research. Although the three Monros, who held the chair for 120 years, were said to have used the same basic body of lecture notes, the first two made serious contributions to physiology and anatomy. A medical degree involved a thesis. The subject was closely linked to the growing knowledge of science, and it was one on which the city of Edinburgh was prepared to buy the best available talent for 'the toun's college', seeing in this specialization both prestige and profit for the city. Glasgow also built up a formidable professional reputation in medicine; but her contribution was more closely geared to chemistry and physics than to anatomy, and she was less successful in holding on to her brilliant men. Cullen and Black, the greatest names in mid-century chemistry, both deserted to Edinburgh, and the capital also managed to draw John Gregory, mathematician and physician, from Aberdeen.

The value of the Edinburgh medical school was to be shown in the public health movement of the next century. In the eighteenth century it is doubtful if academic medicine saved many lives. Some contemporary treatments suggest to the historian that it was better that medicine should devote itself to moving forward the frontier of knowledge than to practising its theories.[1] On the scientific side its contribution was immense. It was a link between science and society, and within the sciences between physics, chemistry, physiology, and geology. It brought together able and argumentative men in a society that was convinced of the social and economic value of their speculations. Even if, as seems to be the case, few of the technical advances in Scottish industry came directly from her own natural scientists, the society of these men provided the debate that rendered the whole country appreciative of new ideas. Pure research often does not pay direct dividends, but rewards the secondary society it creates. The group of men discussing chemistry, anatomy, and geology in Edinburgh gave the opportunity for others to appreciate new methods of applying steam power or bleaching linen.

The particular interest of the Scottish Enlightenment is thus not its immediate consequences but the special coherence of the intellectual society it created. There were two main sections to this, the scientific side and the philosophers; together they derived their initiation from the great names in moral and natural philosophy of the seventeenth century, Grotius, Newton, Shaftesbury, and Locke. In particular they used the habit of scientific observation of Newton and the solvent logic of Locke. The earlier leaders in thought in Scotland, Hutcheson and Hume, provided the guide-lines of much that held the body of Scottish philosophy together. There is, for

1. This is not to suggest that doctors did not give good advice, at least to those able to afford the expense of following it. But apart from the use of quinine in the treatment of malaria, few active treatments can have done more than weaken the patient.

instance, a foreshadowing of Adam Ferguson's concept of man in society in Hutcheson's work. In Playfair's exposition of Hutton's views there is an echo of the scepticism of Hume: 'In the continuation of the different species of animals and vegetables that inhabit the earth, we discern neither a beginning nor an end.'

That most of the leaders of the Scottish Enlightenment did not wish, as did Hume, to stand outside the Church, nor to quarrel, as did those in France, with the state, must be attributed to the particular qualities of the lay and ecclesiastical society of their day. The political system ensured stability without subservience; it might be of direct benefit to only a small section of the nation, but it was impossible for active investigators of history (and the Scottish historians were leaders in their field) not to see how much more tolerable was their own day than that of a hundred years before. The sterile disputes of the seventeenth century over power in Church and state had led to a society afflicted with insecurity and intellectually dead. In the later eighteenth century government, in Church and state, was unobtrusive and the country was prospering. There was no need for reasonable men to think that there had to be conflict between the claims of Church and state, or between those of natural or moral philosophy and revealed religion.

This attitude was made possible by the growth of 'Moderatism' in the Kirk, and in turn contributed to sustain the Moderates in their temporary and precarious predominance. Moderatism was a movement starting in the 1750s, which sought to co-operate with the *status quo* in politics, and to have done with the arguments of the theocrats of the past century. The Moderates were a body of churchmen who saw no advantage in fighting the political system of the day. They wished to deviate from the practice of exclusively theological sermons and introduce a more positive moral content, a 'practical' approach to the needs of society. While accepting the basis of Calvinist dogma they claimed a certain latitude in interpretation of its formulae, and were averse to hunting through men's works in search of heresy. They believed, turning their eyes away from Hume, that their religion could be supported by reason as well as held by faith. At its best, their position was a valuable contribution to the Church, redressing seventeenth-century unbalance with an insistence on tolerance and morality, neither qualities made much of by divines of the past.

Moderatism started as a movement to persuade the Kirk to accept and co-operate with the law of the land, to work for instance without complaint the unpopular law on patronage, and to do so coherently, with the General Assembly acting as a court of law. The party, though never numerically large, expected the government in return to realize that it was a valuable element in public tranquillity and give it favour.

The line between the early Moderate position and one of simply supporting the *status quo* of social and political conservatism was a fine one. By the early nineteenth century it had become blurred. But at first Moderate domination gave the Church an environment of intellectual tolerance and inquiry. It had also a tolerance of the ways of the world. Moderate ministers saw no reason why they should not regard various amusements as innocent; they appreciated good claret, would attend dances, and even in the 1750s argued in the Assembly the right of ministers to see plays. Without being a real majority, their interest in the structure of their society and their intellectual concerns gave them key positions. In particular they held many of the university chairs, and professors sat regularly in the General Assembly. Under the leadership of William Robertson, principal of Edinburgh University, they had the dominant interest in church affairs. In 1784 the Moderate influence even persuaded the General Assembly to cease its annual, formal protest against the Patronage Act. It was its highest point.

Moderatism was a tolerable and tolerant creed so long as the basic society with which it co-operated was not challenged. This society was open enough to have allowed later writers to think of it as democratic. There was the possibility of moving into substantial professional positions for those who did not come of landowning stock, and, among the landowners, of easy contact between small and great, though not much mobility. In the professions, landed and unlanded society overlapped. The leadership of great men still enrolled large sections of all classes under the concept of the surname, but the ties of kin involved less mutual hostility between different groups than in the past. To the lower end of the landowning class, society could appear very open, indeed much more so than that of England where the peasantry was less educated and unlikely to speak freely to its social superiors, and where wealth created important graduations within the scale of landowners. To the peasant, with only the beginnings of tenant right, with a kirk session of his betters investigating his private morals, and the baron court of his landowner enforcing the payment of rent and acting as a minor police court, it may not have seemed so open. David Hume, whose small private income came from land, found social barriers to his advancement in England; yet he was able to lionize polite society in Paris in a way that no Frenchman of similar background could have hoped to do. To him, France and Scotland appeared to have open societies. He complained of English snubs to his friend Gilbert Elliot of Minto, who answered with a phrase which well sets out the best of all sorts of dual worlds that the eighteenth-century landed gentleman in Scotland could enjoy: 'We are both Englishmen; that is, true British subjects, entitled to every emolument and advantage that our happy constitution can bestow.' Increasingly at the end of the century, as economic change strained this happy constitution, more and more would question this simple belief.

NOTES ON DRAMATIS PERSONAE

Charles Edward; Forbes; Argyll. As in Chapter 19.

Cope. Sir John Cope (died 1760), Commander-in-Chief in Scotland 1745. A conscientious general with routine competence, but uninspired. The Council of Officers who inquired into his defeat claimed that he had done his duty at Prestonpans but his men had not, and this was taken as acquittal.

Cumberland. William Augustus (1721–65), Duke of Cumberland, second surviving son of George II. Educated for the navy but turned to an army career, fought at Dettingen and took over an army of some eight thousand men in England at the end of November 1745. Like Cope he was competent but not brilliant.

Dundas. As in Chapter 21.

The Industrial Revolution

Oh, I'll go back to the Calton weaving,
I'll fairly mak' the shuttles fly:
I'll earn more at the Calton weaving
Than ever I did in a rovin' way.
    Whisky, Whisky, Nancy Whisky,
    Whisky, Whisky, Nancy Oh.
        THE CALTON WEAVER

OVER THE BROW OF the hill from the main street of the old town of Lanark, tightly tucked in to the twisting cleft carved by the upper Clyde, is the nexus of buildings we know as New Lanark, the cotton mills and battleship-like tenements, built from 1785 on, which mark the new industrial Scotland. It was made possible by the economic development of the previous generation, by the organization of capital in the banking system, by the skills built up in the fine linen industry of the west of Scotland and the markets it had created at home and overseas. Even the limited improvements of Scotland's transport system mattered. Though in the 1780s the canal system, such as it eventually was, was still only in construction, the roads were now capable of regular cart and carriage use and the Clyde had been deepened. West Indian cotton was available in increasing quantities. But a mill on the scale of the new big ones of the 1780s and '90s (in the latter decade New Lanark gave work to over 1,300) could not have been built without the new English invention, Crompton's spinning mule of 1779, which made possible mass production of really fine threads for the popular muslins of the day.

The Industrial Revolution, which arrived in Scotland in the 1780s, was a special variant of the tremendous changes taking place in England, starting with the breakthrough of the cotton and iron industries into rapid growth. In Scotland it was at first one-sided, confined to cotton. Though Scotland already had a single great modern ironworks at Carron, it would be over forty years before her iron industry followed cotton into general and steady growth, and growth is as important as industrialization in a definition of the Industrial Revolution. Even in cotton the change was for a long time confined to spinning: weaving continued to be a hand industry and a profitable skill for those who possessed it. So we have, for instance, in the description of Nielston parish in 1792 in the *Statistical Account*, a picture of the new and bustling cotton industry: two cotton mills already built employing together more than three hundred people, over half of them children, a bleachfield for the cloth and 152 hand-looms at work. The minister points out the results of all this; expensive habits such as tea and sugar for breakfast, the children working in the mill instead of going to school, their minds 'contracted', their lungs full of cotton fluff, and their skin impregnated with smelly machine oil. In New Lanark and in Nielston one could already see the shape of things to come. The Industrial Revolution was to concentrate the population in the central valley of lowland Scotland, particularly in the western half of it. The workers were the surplus labour of the countryside. We do not know how many of them were pushed out in the reorganization of farming, and how many more came for the higher income available in industry. Even though improved farming was labour intensive, many parishes in the *Statistical Account* in the 1790s report a slight drop in population and attribute it to the throwing together of holdings to make large farms. Scottish tenant right had been so lacking that eviction would not produce the clamour that enclosure sometimes did in England. The absence of protest is not entirely adequate as evidence for the belief that people left the land because they were drawn to the towns rather than because they were pushed out. In any case some of those who came 'voluntarily' may have done so from a pressing sense of economic necessity. There were areas in the Highlands in which the future prospects even in the 1790s were clearly not in proportion to the population expansion. The early population of one Bastille-like tenement in New Lanark was drawn from the poorhouses of Edinburgh and Glasgow and from a ship, taking emigrants from the Highlands to the New World, Which was forced in at Greenock. In this closely organized industrial village they would learn the new disciplines of factory life, the importance of regularity and time-keeping, of wages which came by the week instead of the annual system of farming, of food from the store instead of the field, of a life in which small children were profitable to their parents. The block of one-roomed family homes still preserved in the Livingstone memorial at Blantyre, lower down the Clyde, is evidence of the social discipline under which the early industrial workers and their families lived.

The industrial transformation of the country was taken a step farther in the early nineteenth century when steam replaced water as the main source of power, and still farther after 1828 with the development in the iron industry with Neilson's hot blast technique. This was a method of smelting the 'black-band' ironstone of Lanarkshire. This ironstone combined a low-grade iron ore with a low-grade coal. The new technique meant a transformation of the economics of iron-smelting, and put on the market a pig-iron far cheaper than anything yet available in Britain. It swung the industrial weight of Scotland still farther to the south-west of the central valley, where the cotton industry was already steadily developing the use of steam power. Behind all this was the exploitation of the Scottish coal-fields. Coal meant concentration. The old pattern of rural industry gave way to one using cheap and dirty fuel in big towns, and these towns grew rapidly. They were overhung with smoke and provided with no more in the way of sanitation than had sufficed for the villages they replaced. Even before this, the Scottish cities had a bad reputation for disposal of filth. Sydney Smith had complained of Edinburgh's total lack of 'excremental delicacy'. What was squalid in a village, and nasty in a town of thirty or forty thousand, became a general menace to health and an obstacle to civilized living in a city of one or two hundred thousand. The social problems that accumulated were not solved, or even tackled, in Scotland until the middle of the century, but we can get some estimate of them when we remember that the population of Glasgow, already in 1800 a thriving city, expanded by over 25 per cent between each of the first five censuses, by over 30 per cent in the first three intercensal periods, and that in the first thirty years of the nineteenth century the death rate in Edinburgh varied between twenty-five and twenty-nine per thousand.[1] What was most sinister was that in both Edinburgh and Glasgow the trend of mortality in the 1820s and 1830s was upwards.

The increased use of coal brought a direct benefit in status to one group, the miners. So long as mining remained tied to serfdom it was impossible to recruit the labour the mines needed, so with expansion serfdom had to go. It had already been reduced in severity by an Act of 1775, which prevented the binding in of children at birth, and made it possible, though difficult, for adult miners to obtain their freedom. In 1799 it was totally abolished. But the mining areas remained excluded from the main stream of Scottish society. Miners were already noted for the squalor of their homes in the eighteenth century, and this did not change. On the east of Scotland, where the industry was more primitive and inefficient than on the west, miners' wives went on labouring underground as bearers for their husbands until the 1840s. This, and the geographic isolation of many mining communities, were reasons for the acceptance of degrading standards in housing, of totally inadequate child care, of dirt, and of bare, unfurnished improvisation within doors.

One of the great debated questions of social history is the impact of industrialization on the standard of living of the labourer and peasant. In Scotland this has its own special problems. The still-surviving tradition of low standards in housing probably comes from the removal in this period to the towns of people used to rural overcrowding and rural hovels. The Clydeside 'single-end', disguised by the pompous phrase 'the one-apartment house' is merely the result of stacking up in blocks the one-roomed cottages people were already used to. The urban doss-house is an enlarged version of the 'bothy' in which many unmarried rural labourers had to live. The absence of an adequate poor law in eighteenth-century Scotland means that we have little information about the impact of insecurity and under-employment on wages, either before or during the Industrial Revolution. We cannot specify anyway at what point the industrial town in its growth became so unpleasant a place to live in that it outweighed the advantage of having left the rigours of low agricultural wages and uncertain food supply. In 1810 it was still possible to stroll by the river in

1. The crude death rate for Scotland in 1966 was 12·3.

Glasgow in pleasant surroundings. It seems probable that for the first decade of industrialization, that is up to the mid 1790s, the change was wholly gain. The towns were still moderate in size, the industry anxious for labour, and able to pay it well. The turn of the century was a hard and bitter time for all. The harvests were inadequate for three successive years, and oatmeal rose to the highest price ever recorded. Part of this rise in prices was wartime inflation. The war with the French republic had started in 1793, and after a short intermission was renewed with Napoleon in 1803. The second war involved the French attempt to exclude British exports from Europe. The cotton industry all along had been particularly geared to export, and the brunt of the insecurity and narrowed margins of profit resulting from French policy was borne by the workers. After the peace of 1815 industrial expansion began again and was rapid, but there were recurring periods of bad trade and unemployment from the fluctuations of the trade cycle.

In the 1820s the housing conditions of the big towns began to create new problems in epidemiology. Even before this, the towns were killing more people than they supplied by the birth of children: population in them was sustained and expanded by immigrants, from the areas near at hand, from the Highlands, and from Ireland. In the 1820s and 1830s began the increase in deaths from what contemporaries called 'fever', probably mostly typhus. This had been of minor impact in the 1790s and now accounted for nearly half the cases into the Glasgow Royal Infirmary. We can surmise that the early years of the Industrial Revolution were beneficial to all: we must remain uncertain as to how far improved employment and a more varied and secure diet were counteracted in the next twenty years by the strains that war and inflation placed on the economy. After 1820 it seems probable that for the poorest section of the working population, increasing squalor and disease enhanced the total insecurity of life. What we do not know is how big this section of the population was, or whether it was bigger or smaller than the hardest pressed element of the pre-industrial society. Throughout this period we must remember the strains of adjustment to a new way of life. A man moving from country to town had to build anew the bonds of his social world, to adjust to a different concept of time and space. He might, or he might not, regret the absence of the old immediate discipline placed on him by laird and kirk sessions, even if he had resented the inequalities it had enshrined.

One social experiment of more than immediate significance gave him something like the old discipline: Robert Owen's attempts, when he took over New Lanark in 1816, to show that moderate working hours and tolerable conditions and education were not incompatible with profits. The example impressed visitors perhaps more than it did workers. Not all workers liked compulsory dancing exercises, for instance, though there was general acceptance of the merits of close surveillance of the activities and health of the working children. But Owen was as ahead of his time in social standards as he was behind it in his views of discipline, and except in matters of schooling, did not have many followers.

It is in the 1790s that articulate and self-organizing Scottish radicalism emerges as a social force. Scotland had been relatively unaffected by the political unrest of the period of the war of American Independence, and had taken little part in the agitations that had won Ireland her independent legislature and put into action the economical reform movement in England. These movements had been predominantly of those with an 'independence', some secure economic standing which was usually the ownership of land. In Scotland the landowning and propertied classes had remained quiet, firmly under ministerial control, and nobody else counted for much in political life. But the 1780s had seen the appearance of a form of personal radicalism in the poetry of Robert Burns, and the immediate success of this, when published in 1786, shows that Burns was speaking for many. Burns liked to call himself a peasant: but he was one with a high degree of literacy and a formal education gained through the parish school system. He was also a conscious artist handling a dual language, the rhythm and wide vocabulary of colloquial Scots and, when he wanted it, the formal diction of eighteenth-century upper-class English. Fortunately, along with his English he had not accepted the deadening rules and classifications of contemporary style, which has ensured that only those of this time who were mad enough to disregard the rules, or too simple fully to understand them, have left us real poetry in England. Also fortunately, his native talent was strong enough to overcome an upbringing on the metrical version of the psalms. The appeal of Burns was that he voiced the basic views and the rebellious protest of much of Scotland's male population. It was shown in his hostility to Calvinism, his indignant recognition that, rank or no rank, he was a good deal better than the next man, and his rudimentary concept of the function of the female sex.

Events were also to prove Burns's fundamental devotion to Scottish culture. Patriotism to Burns meant devoting several years of his short life to the folk-song of Scotland, gathering, altering, and improving both words and music, modifying dance tunes into love songs and publishing them. His songs, he wrote, were 'either *above* or *below* price'. In other words, he accepted no payment for them. The price they took of him was an almost complete monopoly of his poetic talent. It is right that Burns should be the national poet of Scotland for it is almost impossible to sing a snatch of Scottish song without using a form enhanced by his work. In the nineteenth century various criticisms were made of his work, some of them from a tone-deaf belief that songs are separate from poetry and less literary, some because much of his work is unblushingly bawdy. But there had been a long tradition of outspoken lewdness in Scottish poetry from the days of Dunbar. Many of Burns's songs had been cruder in their earlier forms. A more serious criticism might be to the almost exclusively bucolic emphasis of much of his work. By the eighteenth century, Scots had ceased to be the language of a court or aristocracy, or of direct, deep religious experience, and this has narrowed his range.

The growing personal radicalism of which Burns spoke was enhanced by the effects of the French Revolution. This time, Scotland responded both to the movement abroad and to its repercussions in literature at home, particularly to Burke's horrified conservatism in his *Reflections on the French Revolution* and to Paine's *Rights of Man*. If the French could have clubs to debate the principles of government and representation, so could the British. So there were founded a host of societies, of which the most important in Scotland was the Society of the Friends of the People, created in 1792. This consisted in fact of several local societies in the growing towns, appealing to the skilled worker with a subscription of 3*d.* a quarter, holding meetings and debates, and conducting a correspondence with every organization that indiscretion could think of – with the Jacobins in France, the Corresponding Society in England, the United Irishmen in Ireland.

Governing classes were terrified by the fact that the breakdown of an organized structure of government in France had allowed the network of debating clubs to take over power and destroy the monarchy. As the French moved to Jacobin dictatorship under the Convention, the innocents in Scotland also decided to hold a 'Convention' and debate the principles on which British government should be founded. Worse still, semantically, they called each other 'citizen' and even talked of the 'sections', reminding everyone of the Parisian *sections* which had let loose the massacres in September 1792. No eighteenth-century government could afford to risk riot, since it had no civilian police, and as the government of Britain saw the country sliding towards war with France the problem of genuine subversion came to the fore. Early in 1793 the government arrested as many of the active political radicals as it could lay its hands on, and through that year and the next it staged a series of trials for sedition, of which the most famous was that of Thomas Muir, a Glasgow advocate of middle-class origin.

'Trials for sedition,' Lord Cockburn was later to point out, 'are the remedies of a somewhat orderly age.' They were therefore new in Scotland. In past times of trouble the gravamen had usually not been sedition but treason, and the dominant question whether the Crown was strong enough to do anything about it or not. For all the boasted logical system of Scots Law, this meant that the judges now practically created their own definitions of sedition, and Braxfield, presiding over Muir's trial as Lord Justice Clerk, was able to translate conservative prejudice of an extreme kind into principles of the constitution. It is often asserted that the juries of these state trials were packed and the witnesses browbeaten. But all Scottish juries were handpicked over and over again. It is true that one of Muir's witnesses spent three weeks in gaol for admitting to having received outside advice to tell the truth, but, as very little evidence was offered in this trial, the real enormity lies in the assumption that the postures of panicked conservatism taken up under the alarm from abroad had anything to do with the law and the constitution. Thus Braxfield allowed the assertion in the speech of the Lord Advocate, prosecuting, that Muir had gone about 'recommending that club government which in another country has produced so much anarchy', which was of course the essence of the scare, in spite of a total lack of evidence, and the absence of this charge in the indictment. Muir had visited

France while peace still obtained uneasily, as an envoy from the Friends to the Convention; this, being 'without proper authority', was 'a species of rebellion'. The government in Britain, said Braxfield, 'was made up of the landed interest, which alone has a right to be represented', and on this counter-factual absurdity it was obvious that any organization talking about the right of the masses to be represented was subversive. The extreme height of nonsense of the Lord Justice Clerk can be measured by one of his rhetorical assertions: 'does not every man sit safely under his own vine and his own fig tree?' The level of fantasy in this remark was not merely horticultural or climatic. Serfdom still survived in the mines: there were the problems of the new kinds of poverty and squalor consequent on the early Industrial Revolution. The judges passed sentences of transportation for fourteen years, though one of them held that no adequate punishment could be named 'now that torture is happily abolished'.

Thus began the period of panic repression. Radical thought and radical associations verged on the criminal. There were other trials, leading to the same sentence, and some outcry in Parliament at the severity of Scottish law. The Secretary of the English Corresponding Society, Thomas Hardy, tried in England for a part in the same Convention, but under the heading of treason, met a much greater respect for legal principles and got off. After that, the English trials became an open show of strength between government and opposition, and the juries would not convict. In Scotland there was also enough evidence in one trial, that of Watt and Downie, to make the charge treason, and here too the word treason had its sobering effect. The Dundases, managers of Scotland, took care to issue a special commission for the trial so that Braxfield should not preside, and it was conducted decently. But the fright of the propertied classes continued. It became an age when it was dangerous to criticize the political or social structure. Those in control of power and property had closed their ranks and looked with hostility on all proposals of change. Cockburn's comment, from the tranquillity of old age and a reformed constitution, was that it was 'the natural consequences of bad times operating on defective political institutions: the frightful thing was the personal bitterness'. But this was the voice of the upper class, articulate, and well-connected, whose opposition would not be confused with sedition. To others, and to the historian, the demoralizing thing had been the misuse of law, and the best thing that can be said for the government is that this did not continue.

The political machinery of the Dundas régime was almost totally effective in the 1790s. A biographer of Henry Dundas has calculated that in the 1796 election he controlled or influenced thirty-six out of the forty-five Scottish constituencies, and that among the elected peers only three were hostile to him. This could not last. Already there was a growing opposition in Edinburgh under the leadership of Erskine and other Whiggish lawyers. Dundas got Erskine deposed from the deanship of the Faculty of Advocates in 1796, but he could not prevent this party growing. Cockburn, his own nephew, belonged to it. Then in the early years of the nineteenth century Dundas's empire began to crumble. In 1805 came the publication of an investigation into navy funds. It was clear that Dundas, as Treasurer of the Navy, had been careless in control over money in a way that had passed without question forty years before but would not do now. His paymaster, Alexander Trotter of Dreghorn, had been in the habit of walking across the road from his office with a cheque for a hundred thousand pounds and storing this in his personal account in his cousin Coutts's bank. Before he returned the capital he had made considerable profits from its investment, and some of this he had lent to Dundas. This comfortable, gentlemanly procedure was taking place at a time when, as usual in war, the country was behind-hand in paying the wages of her ordinary seamen. Dundas was impeached and had to resign office. Though this last impeachment in British history led to an acquittal, it and his failing heart ended the Pitt–Dundas government.

In Scotland the system did not yet fall. Dundas's nephew and son remained in office to manage things. The upper classes indeed felt that there had been an unreasonable attack on someone whose failing had been casualness rather than acquisitiveness, and raised a monument to Dundas in Edinburgh. Political opposition was only slowly gathering momentum. It was the social unrest that led to trouble in the later years of the war. The cotton industry had not yet fully adopted the factory system, but the irregularity of exports during Napoleon's Continental System and the cheap labour coming in to Glasgow made hand-loom weaving, particularly the plain cloth section of the work, an occupation with a lot of redundancy. The weavers were declining from their position as aristocrats of the labour world. Eventually they were to become a cheap adjunct to machinery. In the years 1811–13 they were prevented from having a trade union organization on the grounds that wages were to be fixed by the courts. Yet when they obtained a decision settling these wages in the Court of Session, the manufacturers were allowed to defy it, and the law was subsequently changed. The losing battle was fought out with strikes and trials at a time of maximum economic strain and of very high food prices. Economic hardship and rank injustice brought a new element into the rumbling undercurrent of Scottish radicalism. The position of the hand-loom weavers sank, and yet their numbers increased. The problems of dislocation from technical advance were enhanced by the arrival in large numbers of poor Irish and Highlanders into the Clyde area. These people were capable of learning the skill of weaving by hand, were uneasy under factory discipline, and would accept low wages. They depressed the condition of other workers. As this pool of labour was gradually absorbed by the factories, it tended to be taken up at the wages these people would accept. The last years of the war also brought hardship to the rural labourers, with high prices. Then after the war came deflation and the end of the protection that war had given to farming. The Corn Laws of 1815 replaced the earlier protection, but their action tended to exacerbate price movements, and this meant that many knew real hunger.

This element of distress added force to the political unrest in the years after the war. Cockburn has called it 'radicalism of the stomach'. There are stray scraps of evidence that the various plots and disturbances of this time were in some way linked up with that known as the Cato Street Conspiracy in London in 1820, and we cannot expect more than scraps of evidence to exist. Conspirators, if they have any sense, do not go around leaving their visiting cards for the use of historians. At any rate, Scotland shared in the general unrest and discontent of the years 1817–22, and witnessed in 1820 the pathetic military excursion known as the Radical War, a set of demonstrations in Clydeside which included a certain amount of rapine and a minor skirmish at Bonnymuir, some casualties, and later three executions. The alarm it had caused left the establishment looking rather sheepish. By this time there was enough of an opposition press to bring home this situation. The most famous of Scotland's new publications is probably the *Edinburgh Review*, founded in 1802, but this, though Whiggish and irreverent, was for the intellectuals and upper class, and for Britain as a whole. Much more significant in Scotland was the creation of the *Scotsman* in 1817 as an independent and respectable voice in Edinburgh. That the new press was influential can be seen from the violence of the reactionary press created to oppose it, and the disputes that followed, some of which even led to duels. Behind all this quarrelling lay the major problem of the decay of Scotland's institutions.

The French Revolution had probably some influence on the growing religious radicalism of the early nineteenth century as well as the secular. There had always been a large element in the Kirk to which the name Evangelicalism is currently given, anxious to keep extreme Calvinist theology and to fight again the issues of the seventeenth century. But with the departure of the Erskine group this had lost the element most sympathetic to the new 'Evangelicalism' of the Wesleys and Whitfield. At the end of the eighteenth century the more Calvinist part of this movement in England began to spread in Scotland. The instruments of this were the Haldane brothers, Robert and James, who had at first felt an enthusiasm for the French Revolution. Even in 1794 when such an opinion had obviously become unpopular with landed society and dangerous outside it, Robert Haldane was prepared to raise his voice against the war and in favour of the reform of abuses, and he did so at a county meeting. The willingness to think independently in political matters was translated into religious terms soon after, and the brothers started organizing preaching tours, Sunday schools, and the publication of tracts. The Haldanes held a narrow interpretation of Calvinism and were aggressive in its advocacy. They were quite capable of holding a big outdoor meeting on a Sunday evening to explain that what had been heard in the sermons in the local church that day had not been the Gospel. By the Gospel they meant a message concentrating on the doctrines of election, assurance and salvation. They also mark the decline of the reliance of Calvin on Scripture as the only authority of the Church into the canonization of the literal text of the Bible. It was of divine origin, the Word of God. The Haldanes were not interested in the existing structure of Churches, and their organization followed

Congregationalist lines, and after 1808, Baptist opinions. They had by then shed their earlier interest in the Revolution and held instead an acquiescent conservatism in politics. Their importance at this period was as a focus for extremism in dogma and as an incitement to the Evangelical wing in the Kirk, and a vociferous hostility to Moderatism, which they regarded as simply pagan. Moderatism was in any case in a bad way in the early nineteenth century. Its general tendency to co-operate with the civil power had for some time been failing to yield much of a dividend, since the Dundases could not afford to channel much political patronage in the direction of a minority group. With the establishment on the defensive, the Moderates had moved to a position of uncritical support of the existing system. We can find the celebrated Alexander Carlyle, minister of Inveresk, refusing to accept the services of a 'missionary' who could preach to the Highland troops stationed in his parish in Gaelic. The year was 1795 and he wrote: 'these times of sedition and mutiny . . . require that every person in office should be left to do his own duty, and that strangers should be cautious of intermeddling with the religious tenets or principles of any set of people, especially those of the army'. Doubtless the young missionary's religious opinions lay on the Evangelical side (in politics, Carlyle was still a liberal, advocating burgh reform). If Moderatism could offer no better counter-argument than this it was in a bad way. In 1805 it lost the approval of the intellectuals in Scotland by attempting to keep John Leslie out of the Edinburgh chair of Mathematics because he had written approvingly of Hume's theory of causation, an episode which brought into the open the moderate habit of influencing appointments at the same time as it showed them in defeat.

Moderatism was not the only body showing signs of age. The trouble was that by the second decade of the nineteenth century all Scotland's institutions needed reform. Her courts were clogged with cases, and functioning badly, and the backlog of Scottish appeals was also clogging the House of Lords. Her law needed, not so much revision in content, as a brisker method of coming to decisions and sticking to them. Her school system was failing to cope with the changing distribution of population. Even though in 1802 the teachers had been awarded an increase in salary and a two-roomed house, the swelling parishes of the industrial towns required a great deal more to be spent on schooling if it was to meet the needs of the bulk of the urban population. In any case, when a parent could gain a shilling or two a week from the labour of his children he was unlikely to forgo this and pay to have them at school. The universities were needing to find some higher level of teaching to equip their young men. In those subjects where the level of instruction was advanced, the relation of the universities to the bodies of the professions they served, the Kirk, the law, medicine, needed redefining. Glasgow was putting its money into the wrong subjects, giving priority to those of oldest establishment, and failing to discipline her professors and make sure they really carried out their functions. Edinburgh was locked in quarrel with the city over the details of the curriculum in midwifery, and the Court of Session saw no reason to support the University's claim for academic independence. The relationship of the different studies within each university to one another and to other outside bodies had to be reconsidered. Macabre emphasis was added to this issue in 1828 when it was discovered that the determination of the Edinburgh College of Surgeons to provide experience of dissection for its students, who did not receive it at the University, had led to an enterprising murder system for the provision of fresh corpses.[1]

The most conspicuous examples of decaying institutions, and institutions of importance to the whole governing structure of the country, were the burghs. They were important because their self-perpetuating councils provided a third of the country's members of Parliament. For this reason any general proposal of reform was unacceptable until 1830 when at last there emerged in power a Whig ministry determined on reform and with a strong enough party behind it to put it into effect. But by then, Scottish burghs had in many cases passed beyond ordinary remedies that would retain and use their existing forms. 'Omnipotent, corrupt, impenetrable' had been Cockburn's description of the town council of Edinburgh, and the capital differed from other burghs only in the enormous scale of its bankruptcy and corruption, which by 1833 gave it a debt of over £400 thousand. The citizens had had wind of this insolvency as early as 1799, but the council had managed to cover things up for a further twenty years. Aberdeen had also been declared bankrupt early, and

1. The case of Burke and Hare.

investigation showed that Dundee and Dunfermline were in the same case. So was Paisley, for the dignity of insolvency was not confined to burghs with the title 'royal'. The forms of decay were similar. Provosts and councillors were feathering their own nests with the corporate property. Four times in four years had Renfrew, at the suggestion of its provost, sold him property cheaply. The point at which corruption merged with sheer inefficiency was obscure to the citizens, who were kept in the dark. Edinburgh published fallacious accounts, and Fortrose, run by the most outrageous of local bosses, kept none at all. In the case of Edinburgh and Aberdeen, bankruptcy had been hastened by the inefficient handling of developments that were, or could have been, of great importance to the future of the town. As there was no public control of the membership or actions of the councils, but an atmosphere of subservience to the governing party and a panic fear of democracy, it is not surprising that there was no standard of public responsibility, and local ties and local patriotism were not the forces they had been. Behind the corruption of the long Tory ascendancy lay bigger issues. The burghs had gone into decay because their old form, scale, nature, and powers were utterly un-suited to the needs of the new age. Social and geographic mobility, the new scale of enterprises, new geographic advantages, all sapped the basis of the old burghs. The situation was shown most clearly in Glasgow, which was a town with a relatively uncorrupt but utterly ineffective government. Though it had sold its property unwisely, its debt was a mere matter of £78,000 in 1833. The urban area was a network of separate organizations and assessments, because the only way in which effective action could be taken for the growing social needs was the obtaining of special 'Police Acts' by separate districts, which thus got minimal civic services.[1] This separatism confused the issue of general reform.

The decay of the burghs was echoed by the malversation of the county electorate, the systematic creation of fictitious freeholds. By the nineteenth century probably half the county votes would not have stood up to rigorous inspection. It was by this means that country gentlemen who were not tenants-in-chief could gain the appearance of a share in political life. Even so there were not many of these votes.

1. 'Police' here and elsewhere in Scottish legislation meant the general provision of public services.

The entire nominal voting power in 1788, burgh and county together, was counted at 2,624 for the nation, and as many voters held votes in more than one constituency, the real number participating was much lower. In 1830 the nominal county vote had risen to 3,227, and the actual voters were about two-thirds of this figure.

The state of the country's institutions shows that an overhaul was overdue. Most states in Europe reached the late eighteenth century with governing institutions that had been little modified since the late seventeenth century, and even then had usually been a patchwork. So everywhere there was a complicated pattern of local privileges, jurisdictions, exemptions, and local laws, often overlapping at different levels. The French Revolution had led to a movement to clean this up and rationalize government in France, though the work had had to wait for completion until Napoleon was in power. Napoleon's conquests had taken the new methods and ideas of government across Europe, and after his defeat the main core of the problem of government was the gradual assimilation of this reorganization by the dominant conservative political opinion of the day. As the century went on the benefits of coherent and uniform government were reabsorbed by the states of Europe. But two major powers had resisted Napoleon successfully and lain outside his Empire: they had not had the break in historic continuity made by conquest. These were Britain and Russia. These countries had to find their own way to reorganization during the nineteenth century: they could not indefinitely afford the luxury of government inefficiency in a competing world. Political conservatism and the concentration on economic development kept Britain from undertaking reform systematically until the 1830s, but then it was undertaken in the programme of parliamentary and local government reform. But before that the institutions of Scotland had already shown signs of disintegration.

This is why the question of burgh reform was the main political issue in Scotland in the fifteen years after the Napoleonic war. The problem came up innocently enough with a confused burgh election in Montrose in 1817. The Court of Session disallowed the election, and the Lord Advocate, in order to constitute a new Council, allowed the town a general burgess vote and some permanent element of direct election. This led at once to attempts in other decrepit burghs to secure similar disqualifications, and the government did not dare go on in the same way. Even in the case of the totally bankrupt Aberdeen, the existing self-electing oligarchy had to be kept to preserve the political hegemony. Every fresh burghal bankruptcy brought fuel to the reforming fire. Meanwhile the less decayed burghs, or groups of townsmen in them, recognizing the urgent need of minimal urban services, began obtaining 'Police Acts' to provide these outside the existing town council. Edinburgh's first Police Act, in 1817, with a small section of propertied men doing the electing, was the first form of public election the city had known, and as time went on the elective share in successive Police Acts grew. It was impossible to put a total block on the spread of representation.

In this way Scotland had already, from necessity, worked out a form of urban government before general reform arrived in the 1830s. The impact of the two measures, Parliamentary Reform and Municipal Reform, was therefore slight. The political franchise became a little wider, the wealthier country gentry could now vote without a risk of perjury, but the vote did not extend beyond the more substantial farmers, and as there was as yet no nonsense about secret ballot, these farmers were expected to vote as their landlords wanted. In the burghs the vote became available to the middle classes and shopkeepers, but in the more decayed towns there were few of these. It was also recognized that urban growth had made towns which might reasonably share in political representation, even though these were not royal burghs. Altogether Scotland got a slightly bigger share of the seats in Parliament, she lost the protection of the old system which had effectively kept the English out of her county seats.

The reform of town government suffered from an even greater paralysis from conservatism. The old functions were left to the old type of councils, which were adjured, but with little force, to keep proper accounts. The existing parallel police burghs were allowed to continue, and other towns, where there was enough popular demand, could get them too. These police burghs had a skeleton of the public health powers necessary in industrial society. The result of this was an illogical dual structure, which survived till the end of the century. The total achievement of the reform movement in Scotland in the 1830s is reminiscent of the movements of the country dance known as 'Scottish Reform', in which, to an attractive tune, a lot of individual movement goes on, but the basic pattern of the position of the dancers barely changes.

All the same, in one way, more important than the formal content of legislation, Scotland was changing her identity. Better transport and more wealth was sending her upper classes more easily and frequently to England, and they might come back with an English wife or an English education, or not come back at all. By 1830 there was a regular connection by steamship between Edinburgh and London. Now major legislation affecting both countries had been passed by the same Parliament. It was inevitable that with more of this the institutions of the two countries would move closer to each other. Even with strong reasons for respecting different national traditions, it would be impossible for the same group of men to go very far in a process of passing different types of measure on different basic principles for similar problems. Since much of the legislation needed in the nineteenth century was a response to the problems created by a common industrial development, similar solutions were bound to be offered. Where, as in the case of the Poor Law they were not, the different institutions created would, in practice, borrow from each other. It is in the 1830s that Scotland's conscious national separateness, already reduced by the enthusiastic borrowings by the gentry in the previous century, began to disappear.

This is perhaps the reason why the 1820s saw the end of a great period of Scotch literature. The works of Walter Scott in the period since the war had provided a new genre of historical novels deeply grounded in the real life of his own country. They had been widely successful: the vision might be of the past, but it was of a past understood with strong sympathies for different points of view and supported by the full repertoire of Scottish speech and wide historical knowledge. When Scott dropped anonymity (a frequent feature of Scottish writers), the real affection people felt for him added to the success of his writings. In the 1820s there had appeared another novel placed in the past, the extraordinary and powerful *Private Memoirs and Confessions of a Justified Sinner* by the self-educated James Hogg. This is the greatest novel of Scotland, a lonely, single work that is unique in English and must be classed among a half dozen only on the international scene, an inward-turned psychological exploration of the extreme horrors of Calvinist dogmatism. But no one of stature followed Scott and Hogg. When they ceased writing, a weaker exponent of Scotticism, John Galt, was producing cosy novels, and the tradition declined from him. It has never recovered its earlier vitality and standing.

One major part of Scotland remained outside the economic development of this period. In the Highlands the changing economy produced stress but not development. Law and order had come into this area gradually after the '45, and this had drastically changed the organization of a society hitherto grouped under its chiefs for cattle-raiding and war. Even before this last rebellion the chiefs were gaining advantages from the fact that by lowland law they were extensive landowners over the clan lands, though they had not abandoned their tribal position which made them judge and dictator over clan affairs. Some had gone further and had begun to try and exploit their territories, regardless of the bands of clanship. The leader in this process had been the house of Argyll, which had property or superiority in lands of which the tenants were members of clans hostile to Campbell political concepts. This hostility was based on the feuds and misdoings of the seventeenth century and was backward-looking. Co-operation with the economic realism and social strength of the Campbells, which was only gradually achieved, was in the end in the best interests of most of the west coast, because the Dukes of Argyll and their leading Campbell tacksmen[1] were doing their best to assimilate the area to a more modern economy without unnecessary hardship. The weakness of the new system of landowning rather than chieftainship was that it encouraged some chiefs to make the worst of both worlds, to keep up their pretensions as great men, which in a territorial sense they were, by living as rich men, which they were not. The Scottish gentry as a whole was feeling the pull of English landowning standards of living; whereas a lowland laird could respond to this by exploiting the resources of his estates better, sometimes to the advantage of all, there was very little in the Highlands for a landowner beneficially to exploit. The old way of life had not encouraged the habit of thinking carefully in terms of the profit motive. Chronic debt, inefficiency, and emergency expedients of a disastrous nature often lay ahead.

1. A tacksman was a member of the gentry who held a 'tack' or lease; usually, in the Highlands a member of a cadet branch of the landowner's family.

Some new sources of Highland income were opened up in the generation after Culloden. During the war of 1756–63 Chatham in his own phrase 'sought for merit and wherever it was to be found', and raised two Highland regiments. The use of the British army as extra employment for all classes in the Highlands spread. The Commissioners of Forfeited Estates set out to manage the lands under their care with efficiency and honesty. Gradually they cleared up the tremendous and confused burden of great and petty debts (Lord Lovat never seems to have paid in cash for as much as a handkerchief) and tried to introduce new sources of income and a 'spirit of industry'. Their main instrument was the linen industry, and in the area immediately edging the Highland line, especially in Perthshire, they eventually succeeded in establishing it. But except in little towns, such as Comrie, it remained women's work, an addition to a household's income, not its base. The cattle trade to England seems to have expanded and drawn more and more regularly from the Highlands, at least until 1770. After that a significant change occurs, the coming of specialized sheep farming (developing the Border breeds), which even in the 1760s was spreading across the Highland line, though it did not reach the far north-west until the 1790s. Improved agriculture in England and the Scottish lowlands also made it more difficult to find free pasture sites for the night stances for the great cattle herds. In the 1780s a serious attempt was made to develop a herring fishery in the Highlands. But altogether the new economic resources of the later part of the century simply did not match the population growth of the period. Highland population grew by over 30 per cent between 1755 and 1801: it grew even faster after that, adding 50 per cent in the next forty years, and all this in spite of considerable emigration. People left the Highlands for lowland industry or to go to America, in increasing numbers after 1770, and still the population grew. The basic resource of this mounting population remained a thin, poor soil, soured by cold and wet into peat on the hilltops, producing rough grass that would make good grazing only in summer. Only in the narrow valley bottoms was there land that could give arable crops in spite of high rainfall. Potatoes made more intensive and secure use of this land than cereals, but the increase in yield was not of the scale of that of the population.

The rudimentary nature of the chemical industry in the eighteenth century gave the Highlands one further resource, the manufacture of kelp. This meant the collection of seaweed on the Atlantic coast, the burning of it in vast quantities, and the marketing of the ash as a source of alkali. It was not a particularly rich source: whenever Britain was not at war with Spain, Spanish barilla would be preferred. Kelp, already a useful source of income from the 1760s, expanded enormously in production during the long wars with France. It had two great merits to a coastal landowner. It was a labour-intensive activity, and it was one in which the marketing, and therefore most of the profit, remained in his hands. Its main disadvantage was that it was obviously only temporary. Peace, technological change, or a reform of the salt tax, would knock the bottom out of the market. It also distracted labour from farming during the summer months, and encouraged the fragmentation of holdings.

Kelp looked more socially desirable than sheep farming, though it was economically more unsound. The new sheep farm meant a complete reorganization of the land, and eviction of tenants, since little labour was needed. Both new activities brought higher rents and the gradual squeezing out of the old tacksmen class which had organized the supply of men and the farming of the clan lands. By the early nineteenth century Highland society had been reduced to three elements: landowners, large sheep farmers, and small tenants farming and sometimes making kelp. Vast incomes had been made on the kelp shores, without being used to any real advantage, when in 1815 peace destroyed the market. From then on the issue in most Highland areas was emigration. It was bound to come: the question was how and when.

So came the 'clearances'. Highland landowners evicted small tenants to make more sheep farms, the source of good rents, and reduce the risks of having to support a starving peasantry in a year of crop failure. In some areas this was done with consideration and skill. In much of south Argyll, and in Caithness, the population found other activities than farming and little real hardship was caused. In others the change was brutal. The Macdonnells of Glengarry treated their tenants with systematic unkindness and the glen is empty today. The broad inland straths of Sutherland lay between the two methods. The intention of the Duke of Sutherland was to get the population on to the coasts to form fishing villages. The handling of this in

Strathnaver by an absentee landowner and a factor with a vested interest in haste was inept, and no attempt was made to help the new activity. Real hardship was caused, and more significantly, lasting bitterness, so that the Sutherland clearances have become a slogan focusing feeling against the landowning class in general.

Some of this feeling was justified. As a class the Highland landowners of this period did not measure up to the needs of a difficult situation. Some is unjustified. The word 'clearance' has been applied to many districts from which people moved of their own accord in search of a better and more secure standard of living. The expression of this particular regional grievance obscures the fact that life was tough for all those without property in early nineteenth-century Scotland – for none more than the slum dwellers of the big towns. It also leads to historical misconceptions about earlier Highland conditions. The density of population in some barely cultivable areas in the eighteenth century meant that the standard of living had been appallingly low. At what level, for instance, could the nearly two thousand inhabitants of Assynt hope to live? In all, probably some three times as many people left the Highlands voluntarily as from direct eviction. But these voluntary emigrants also went because their presence was opposed to the economic interests of the landowners. They may have been pushed to the decision by high rents, by overcrowding in the coastal strips, or by a recognition of the hopeless situation.

They did not go in time. Up to the 1840s many landowners had not decided that a cut in population was unavoidable. They kept their tenantry on in a sort of privileged destitution, forgoing rents and bringing in food in hard times. It was the catastrophe of the failure of the potato crop in 1846 that brought home reality. Tenants had to sell their remaining stock, relief had to come in from outside, landowners went even further into debt. From then on, emigration, voluntary or not, became the only answer.

NOTES ON DRAMATIS PERSONAE

Cockburn. Henry Thomas (1779–1854), Lord Cockburn, advocate and judge. He was an active Whig and a chronicler of the social changes of his life as well as of the State Trials.

Dundas. Henry Dundas (1742–1811), Treasurer of the Navy 1783–1800, Home Secretary 1791–4, President of the Board of Control 1793–1801. He ran the politics of Scotland first as Lord Advocate and then through his nephew in that office. Some of his power was retained by his son in later administrations. He was impeached in 1806.

Erskine. Henry Erskine (1746–1817), Whig politician and lawyer, dean of the Faculty of Advocates 1785–96.

Glengarry. Alexander Macdonnell of Glengarry (died 1828), an arrogant and self-seeking example of the excesses to which chieftainship in decay could lead.

Lovat. Simon Fraser (*c*. 1667–1746), Lord Lovat from 1730, executed for his part in the '45. His long life of intrigue and violence is a picture of the excesses which clanship could tolerate.

Muir. Thomas Muir (1765–98), advocate; victim of the State Trials of 1794; transported and died of the indirect effects of this sentence.

Chapter 22

The Victorian age

A gunboat for Skye

SCOTLAND'S INDUSTRY MOVED FROM cotton to iron, and then to ship-building, in the central decades of the nineteenth century. Cotton ceased to expand, and later declined. The new techniques of smelting the black band ironstone came just in time, in 1828, for the coming of railways in the 1830s would otherwise have submerged the Scottish iron industry with English products. But the new iron industry was a Lanarkshire possession, and the ship-building that followed was mainly based on the inventiveness of Clydeside in marine engineering. Together they brought to the fore on the Clyde the problems of modern Scotland. People flowed in to all the large towns of Scotland, overwhelming their rudimentary social administration. Population was growing fast on a national scale but the need for rural labour did not expand, so families moved to the towns, and it was on the Clyde that the concentration of human beings was densest. This was the land of industrial opportunity. It was also easily accessible to Ireland and to the Highlands, which manifestly had little opportunity to offer. The Irish would accept low wages rather than stay at home to starve. In the central decades of the nineteenth century several hundred thousand of them entered Scotland. They created a new phenomenon in Scotland, the secular expression of cultural and economic rivalry that picked on religious difference as its nominal cause. The Irish enhanced poverty and overcrowding and contributed to the social evils that arose from these features, drunkenness and crime, to such an extent that Protestant antagonism to this influx was able to disguise itself as a concern for law and order.

The masses of the new urban areas lived hemmed together in tall and crowded tenements put up with enormous solidity of masonry but with no regard for amenity, inside or out. A report on Edinburgh in 1838 describes the common stairs of these tenements as 'little streets carried perpendicularly upwards' and instanced one on which there were fifty-nine rooms, almost all separate 'houses' in the Scottish sense of separate dwellings, containing fifty-six families and two hundred and forty-eight people, without a water supply of any kind. By 1861 a third of Scotland's population of something over three million was living in one-roomed 'houses', and nearly 8,000 of these 'houses' were rooms with no window. Into these fortresses came a population from the country, from Ireland, or from elsewhere within the towns. The movement of the population and the big scale of the towns broke the bonds that hold a man into society, his local community, the widespread kinship, the religious congregation, even the band of regulars at an alehouse, and it was only slowly that these would be reformed.

On the whole the Kirk responded better and more quickly to the new needs than did civil government. This is understandable, for religion throughout the nineteenth century was to most people a more dominant issue than politics. But religion was thought of as divorced from material living. The Churches were prepared to do a great deal to make it possible for people to hear their message, but they did not see that physical squalor was bound to have effects in spiritual degradation, that the stunting of intellect, the compulsions of necessity, the absence of choice for the future prevented for many the growth of full moral stature. The growing Evangelical emphasis of the day held to an extreme Calvinism, and for all that Calvin himself had a lot to say about the nature and functioning of civil society, Calvinism's insistence on the absolute quality of saving faith encouraged this separation of spiritual and material. An individual was placed in his physical circumstances by God's will, and the same will had decided whether he was foreordained for salvation or not. It was easy to think, therefore, that salvation had nothing to do with whether a child grew up in a street which, like the Cowgate in Edinburgh, also served the function of sewer. Such conditions, indeed, provided a field for others in happier circumstances to show that they were of the elect by providing minimal food supplies in times of unusual hardship, organizing Sunday schools and building chapels, but they did not call for the radical reconstruction of political or economic forms. To do so would be to weaken the challenge offered by God to the individual.

The main emphasis of the Kirk was therefore on opportunities for worship and Bible study. 'Church extension' was the great theme; the building of new churches, the carving up of new parishes. It was of course impossible that the ancient pattern of parishes should be suited to the new distribution of population. The dissenting communities were the first to realize this, and the established Church lumbered after them. There was a strong element in the Kirk that felt that the state should endow new churches in overpopulated areas. This scheme failed to do more than collect a government grant for churches in the Highlands. The dissenting bodies were strengthened by their display of adaptability, and for most of the century agitated against the whole concept of a state-supported church, calling this the 'voluntary' principle. They were too important politically for the government to give open favour to the established Kirk, and the Church had to raise its own funds for new churches. In 1834 the General Assembly passed the Chapel Act, recognizing the new parishes as valid for ecclesiastical parishes, or *quoad sacra* in rather horrid latinity, and accepting their ministers as full members of the structure of church courts. In seven years Thomas Chalmers, as convener of the Church Extension Committee, gathered an endowment and saw to the building of over two hundred churches.

Thomas Chalmers was the leading figure on the Evangelical side of the Kirk and his activity in this field was typical of the Evangelicals. The new *quoad sacra* parishes were particularly likely to have extreme Evangelical ministers, but Evangelicalism was gaining a predominance in the Kirk as a whole. It was particularly the Evangelicals who objected to patronage. They mounted a new attack on this, beginning with an attempt to place a real meaning on the old idea of the 'call' for ministers, the insistence that as the *First Book of Discipline* had said, 'nane be admitted without the nomination of the people'. This should mean at least the appearance of a positive demand from some of the congregation. In 1833 this was put forward to the General Assembly in a demand for the right of a majority of parishioners to veto a nomination, and was defeated. Next year the Assembly, with a changed membership, allowed this by a narrow majority in the Veto Act. This was a formal requirement that on any presentation an absolute right of veto should lie in the majority of the male heads of families who were communicants. No place was left for the authority of the presbytery, which had in the past presided over such matters, and no reasons for objection were required.

Church law already required that all candidates for the ministry be educated for it, and subscribe to the full rigours of the Westminster Confession. The trouble was that vital differences in the Kirk lay inside the definitions of Calvinism. It was a question of the emphasis to be placed on the elements of this creed, in particular the place of instant conversion and assurance, a difference in flavour rather than content. It was exacerbated by the Evangelical habit of labelling as 'unchristian' any preaching that was not of exclusively Evangelical emphasis. Outside the Kirk, the dissenting bodies, predominantly Evangelical (the organization of the Haldanes for instance), faced no bar to the choice and control of their ministers. Why should their brethren, in congregations which accepted the idea of association with a Christian state, put up with one? The anti-intellectualism and popular nature of the Evangelical movement meant that it did not appeal to the landowners, who were usually the patrons. It was also this emphasis that the Veto Act tried to protect by not requiring reasons for objections. An Evangelical pastor might encourage his congregation to value the flavour of his discourse more than the fact that it took place inside the established Kirk. With a successor of a different stamp, the congregation might desert to a Baptist tabernacle.

Beyond the immediate aims of a particular group of churchmen anxious to perpetuate their own individualist form of Christianity lay a question troubling all state Churches in the nineteenth century, the enhanced power of civil authority. The new post-Napoleonic state was very different from the miscellaneous collections of privileges and exemptions which had constituted the political structures of the eighteenth century. In the same way that the enhanced monarchies of the sixteenth century had involved a crisis in the relations of Church and state, and that the communist claim to detailed control of economic and social life has meant clashes between Church and state in eastern Europe in this century, so did the new efficiency of the nineteenth century. Only a year before the Veto Act, Keble had been provoked by the parliamentary reorganization of the Irish Church to preach the Assize sermon on National Apostasy which triggered off the Oxford Movement. The old Gallicanism in France, a system of mutual defence of Church and king against claims by the papacy, had not come back with the Bourbon monarchy in 1814. Instead the French Church was looking across the Alps to authority in Rome. The Rhineland Catholics were proving resentful of rule by Prussia, and in the Netherlands a part of the Calvinist Church was breaking away from the National Church. The relations of all established Churches to the newly effective government power had to be defined and redefined as the governments increasingly accepted the principles of popular representation. Churches and states were both claiming increased authority on territory they had hitherto shared.

It was typical of the problems involved that the Veto Act required the redefinition of powers to take place in an area where private property 'rights' were involved. It was unfortunate that it also involved a shift in the basis of authority in the Kirk from the presbytery to the General Assembly. The result of these features was a series of lawsuits. Property rights showed lawyers and judges in the grip of conservatism, even when personally many of the Scottish judges were sympathetic to Evangelicalism. The two most important cases, which in the usual system of Scottish judgements, staggered on for years, were the Stewarton case and the dispute over the Strathbogie presbytery. In Stewarton part of a seceded Church which had come back into Communion with the Establishment had been set up as a *quoad sacra* parish, and this was opposed by the patron of the older parish and a majority of the original presbytery, who applied to the Court of Session for an interdict. The case led the court to declare the Chapel Act *ultra vires*. The implications were such as no effective religious body could be expected to accept; that the Church of Scotland was not in a position to put its own house in order and respond to the needs of the new pattern of society in the way a dissenting body could. The Strathbogie case was more complicated. It began over the nomination of a minister in Marnoch who was vetoed by the majority. When a second candidate was put up by the patron the former obtained a prohibition on his admission from the Court of Session. The seven ministers making up the majority of the presbytery, that of Strathbogie, who accepted this verdict, were deposed by the General Assembly and new ministers promoted to their cures. The result was war in the Church, the Court of Session forbidding the new ministers to function and the General Assembly forbidding the old. The picture has been complicated by the General Assembly describing the ministers it had thrown out as 'intrusionists' and the ones that it had forced in as 'non-intrusionist', a piece of double-talk reminiscent of old Covenanting semantics. The situation was deplorable enough without this sort of falsification. In the course of battle the Kirk had appealed to the House of Lords and the Lords had declared the Veto Act illegal. An effort had been made by Lord Aberdeen to get a Bill through Parliament in 1840 modifying this, but it had aimed at restoring authority to presbyteries and would not have allowed the Veto Act in its existing form. This would not satisfy the Evangelicals, to whom the Act had become a battle flag, and the proposal was dropped. Two years later the General Assembly put together a tremendous denunciation of patronage and of the actions of Parliament and the Court of Session: the 'Claim of Right', a title that harked back to the Revolution of 1688–9, demanded in effect that the General Assembly and not the civil courts be the arbiter of the terms on which the Kirk held her rights and property. Here was a claim as impossible to law as the Stewarton decision was to religion. Neither side would give way.

The result came to a head in the General Assembly of 1843, when it was discovered that if the Chapel Act was disallowed the Evangelicals did not have a majority. The 'non-intrusionists', as they called themselves, failing to get the reduced Assembly on their side, walked out. Over two hundred, led by the Moderator, they marched in sombre clothes over the ridge of the New Town of Edinburgh and down to Canonmills. Effective pageantry needs organization and planning: a hall had been hired for the accommodation of the new Assembly. In the end some two-fifths of the clergy were found to have broken away to form the Free Church.

The 'Disruption' of the Church was an act of tremendous courage at all levels. The new Church had to organize an entire parallel structure to the old, and create its own funds, its buildings, train its ministers, and all along its membership was weak in the propertied classes. In some cases there was great hardship. Hostile landowners would not allow a church to be built, ministers left comfortable posts for insecurity. The strength of the Free Church was that it started with an organized and large body of ministers and a clear scheme of how a Church should be run. Within a few years it had created a central financial organization of the type later adopted by all modern Churches, and a theological college for its students. The Free Church did not regard itself as a dissenting body, nor did it approve of dissent. It was the true established Church of Scotland which, for particular reasons, had severed connection with the state. It would undertake all that other established Churches did, notably schools and foreign missions; it even dressed its moderator in the same style of knee breeches as did the Kirk of Scotland, and held its General Assembly in the same form and at the same time as its sister Church. Yet in a negative sense 'voluntaryism' came in. If patronage had been a basic cause of the split, it was killed by the disruption. No Kirk of Scotland parish need accept the forcing in of an unwelcome minister. The congregation could desert to the Free Church. Within a generation patronage was extinct, and in 1874 the Kirk of Scotland was able to persuade Parliament to abolish it legally. But the Churches continued apart. Organization, politics, personal issues, minor elements of theology, kept alive till the twentieth century the division between two great bodies each claiming to be the true Church of Scotland.

The split brought to the front the problem of the local public services of Scotland. Till this date the Kirk had controlled both education and poor relief through the machinery of the kirk sessions. The system was already outdated, as the decline in both services showed. The slowness of the Kirk to adjust to the new industrial society had not simply been a matter of churches and parishes being in the wrong places. There was a need for a new social understanding. Chalmers had brought to the leadership of the Kirk views and standards on society that were perhaps appropriate to the rural community in which he had been bred but which did not fit in the Glasgow parish in which he served. He could write of the society he hoped to see established: 'the sobriety and economy of our people will at length conduct them each to the possession of his own little capital, when they shall stand on the vantage ground of treating independently with their employers and not as if standing on the brink of necessity . . . able to keep themselves off when wages would be low'. Put against the reality of weavers on six shillings a week, unemployed in depressions and with a Poor Law which, besides being more honoured in the breach than in the observance, offered no help to the merely destitute, one can see little validity in Chalmers's social thought. Yet he had been convinced that it was there. He had made a tremendous attempt in Glasgow in the 1820s to show that the existing Poor Law could still be worked in seventeenth-century terms, without resorting to assessment. He had divided up the vast parish of St Johns into sections under deacons and elders whose function was to find out what voluntary resources could be deployed against every claim for relief, turning to family, neighbours, or voluntary charity before the parish was called on. His claim was that it functioned: that with only a little time spent on the matter each week his deacons could manage their case load and keep parish relief at a minimal level. There was no need of a poor rate. But Glasgow parish boundaries had no longer a real meaning as a fixed location for their population. Denied help in St Johns the destitute would flow to others, and the time that Chalmers claimed his deacons spent on their work shows that denial was their main response. In any case he was concerned not with need but with applications for relief. Under Scottish law only the disabled were entitled to relief: the able-bodied destitute knew this and did not apply.

Even before the Disruption, serious criticism had been offered both of the Poor Law and of its administration. Parishes would do all they could to avoid assessment. The list of those accepted for relief would be kept down to correspond with the alms available, and since this was little, miserable quantities would be doled out. Highland parishes would give those unmistakably qualified half-a-crown a year and licence to beg. Edinburgh, which like the other big towns had had to accept assessment, insisted on a three years' residence qualification, and then would not normally grant more than a shilling a week. The total expenditure per head in Scotland was less than a fifth of that in England and there was no reason to believe that actual poverty distributed itself on such a ratio. In 1840 Dr W. P. Alison, a specialist in public health problems, wrote a long pamphlet criticizing the Scottish Poor Law, and comparing its treatment of destitution with that in other countries, culminating in the indictment: 'the higher ranks in Scotland do much less (and what they do they do less systematically and therefore less effectually) for the relief of poverty and sufferings resulting from it than those of any country in Europe which is well regulated, and much less than experience shows to be necessary'. A Royal Commission a few years later, while accepting the limitations in concept of the Scottish law, held that it was not being carried out, and that what was needed was a clear definition of obligation and a Board of Supervision, which would push the parishes into paying out adequate sums, even if the result was assessment. This was the burden of the Act of 1845. The immediate effect of the new Act was that the number of assessed parishes jumped from 230 to 420, and that at last something systematic was done to provide medical aid. All the same the Act was a failure, because it was vitiated by the old Scottish principle that the only qualification for relief must be disability added to destitution. This had been maintained partly out of a respect for a deep-rooted Scottish prejudice, and partly out of respect for the current Malthusian dislike of poor relief systems altogether. This was illogical because the parallel growth of Scottish and English populations gave little support for the claim of Malthus that there was a connection between relief of the destitute and the pressure of population on the means of subsistence.

The Board of Supervision, regulating medical relief, could not help being drawn into the question of epidemic disease, and inevitably noticed the connection of this with destitution. It began to encourage parishes to relieve the able-bodied, a policy which culminated in 1878 with the advice: 'It is obvious that if a person is *really destitute* no long period would elapse before he also became *disabled* from want of food': it might be cheaper to offer relief before the full qualification was achieved. This was to ride a coach and horses through the Act. Medical men, working for the Board, also destroyed the principle of the law by acting on the fact that, as one of them said: 'If you examine a man long enough you will find some trifle that you can get hold of.' At the end of the nineteenth century the law remained; but evasion of its requirements was systematic. Its main point of observance was its influence in breaking up families. Since wives of the unemployed were not accepted as qualified for relief for themselves and their children so long as their husbands remained with them, it became advantageous to be deserted.

The urgency of the problem of poverty and destitution diverted the attention of social reformers in Scotland from public health. The public health movement in England relied heavily on doctors produced by the Edinburgh medical school, and the needs of Scotland were at least as great as England's. An influential body of medical opinion in Scotland rightly disbelieved the basic concept on the spread of infectious disease that obtained in England, that it was the result of bad air. Still incorrectly, but with good statistics, they correlated it simply with poverty. It might have been more beneficial in practice to the country if they had been less critical, and forced a joint approach to the question of housing and sanitary control, to cleaning up the towns. Scotland did not get a general Public Health Act until 1867, but by then the towns had already begun a piecemeal attack on the major problems, the most important aspect of which was Glasgow's construction of a water supply, pure and in large quantities, from Loch Katrine.

In education the need for reorganization was not so obviously urgent as in Poor Law affairs, because it was only in the big towns that the parish school system had collapsed without being unofficially replaced. The main effective step was the Act of 1872 making schooling compulsory from five to thirteen and setting up a rating system to support schools under local boards and a central Board. Before that the run-down in the towns had meant that proportionately only a few more children in Scotland, a country which boasted a national system of education, were at school, than in England, a country which had no such system. Yet this comparison underrates elements in the Scottish system which bridge the period of collapse. It was never accepted in Scotland that there was a special, low-grade type of education suitable for manual workers, that anything beyond minimal literacy would encourage the spread of subversive ideas. And there has always been a professionalism about the teaching: in fact, the Educational Institute of Scotland, to organize the teachers, was founded in 1847 as proof of the existence of the profession; and teaching qualifications were early defined. These good qualities had, of course, their disadvantages. Education in Scotland has always had a strongly bookish flavour and an over-emphasis on the virtue of hard work at disagreeable tasks. In nineteenth-century schools it was common to meet children being taught deliberately to read stuff they could not hope to understand, so as to prove that they made their attainments virtuously by the difficult way. Teaching has usually been efficient, but this has been accompanied by the assessment of qualifications in separate subjects, which is a handicap to altering the structure of curricula.

The universities were even slower than the schools to adjust to new social needs. This was partly because they had special problems. On the one hand they needed to offer an education that would go as high as that of the English universities, specialized courses from which young men could go to the Civil Service, or compete in the nation's other affairs. On the other hand, so long as there was no general structure of secondary education they continued to supply this, keeping their entrance qualifications low so that bright children could come to them from parish schools as they had in the past. For many years the problem was shirked. In 1858 it was partly met by the creation of Honours courses, available after the general M.A. course. In 1889 this was changed to a system of parallel Honours and Ordinary degrees. This was probably as good a marriage as was possible between an education system geared to formal instruction in a wide range of subjects and the demand also for intensive and independent specialization. The rest of the issue had to wait till the spread of secondary schooling in the twentieth century.

The Education Act of 1872 was a landmark in the structure of government as well as in the schools. For the first time the country was provided with elected local boards which did not give a special position to landowners, even though the old system of owners' rates was continued. Local democracy became possible, and the hold of the more forward looking of the two political parties, the Liberals, already strong in Scotland, was accentuated. In the 1880s Lord Rosebery could speak of Scotland as 'the backbone of the Liberal party'. There is a surprising inconsistency in the relative developments in representation in Scotland and England. The latter country, with no tradition of rural literacy, and no stronger radical heritage, had a more open political franchise, and no special territory in local affairs preserved for landowners though of course landowners had great influence. The administrative system devised piecemeal for Scotland had produced parochial boards for the Poor Law on which all owners of land in the parish worth more than £4 a year were automatically placed, leading to the ultimate absurdity in one Aberdeen parish with a dispersed pattern of landownership, of a board of over 2,000 members. Though elected County Councils were created in 1889, the anomaly of power in the hands of landowners remained: the Commissioners of Supply still had governmental functions till the 1920s. Scotland in the late nineteenth century needed a more rational system of administration. She was, as Rosebery complained, 'mumbling the dry bones of political neglect'. The lack of a Cabinet member with specific Scottish duties had become serious once it was accepted, as it was in the late nineteenth century, that the Cabinet should produce a regular legislative programme of needed reforms for Parliament, and push these through. Major changes were unlikely to be put forward for Scotland, and if they were, it was easy for minority interests to frustrate them. In so far as one can see a centralized political history for Scotland at this time it consisted in two separate parts – a Liberal domination among the members of parliament,[1] who nevertheless lacked organization, and the activities of the Boards set up for government functions. The Education Board and its department had, like the Board of Supervision for the Poor Law, gone a lot further than had been in the mind of those who had set it up. It had forced the Highland parishes to pay sums they could not afford for schools in which their children were coerced in a foreign language.

1. Until more work has been done on the history of political parties between 1860 and 1880 it will not be possible to explain the Liberal hold in Scotland.

The use of Gaelic in school became legal in the 1870s in theory but not in practice. Compulsory schooling meant a sharp decline in the language's capacity to survive. At the end of the eighteenth century there had been a continuing and active tradition in Gaelic poetry. The decay and destruction of clanship and the destitution of the Highlands put an end to this. The voluntary societies which organized themselves to preserve the language and culture of Gaeldom envisaged culture as divorced from everyday life and business and made no attempt at the minimal provision of school textbooks. Gaelic for many became associated with folklore and song, not with school. The schools were unnecessarily spacious for a community otherwise living in 'black houses'. The Act had envisaged a maximum school rate of ninepence. But in the 1880s Lewis was carrying one of six and eightpence, which was ruinous to a burdened economy.

The Board, so said its opponents, was also 'anglicizing' in its general policy. Anglicizing is a word used in the nineteenth and twentieth centuries much as 'drunkenness' was in the seventeenth, to indicate a generalized disapproval for which little factual basis can be found. With the general need for new institutions for a new type of society, it was ridiculous to refuse to borrow new ideas from neighbours undergoing a similar experience. But in schooling England had little to offer: she had only unwillingly abandoned the view that no education was better than one of the wrong religion, to take up the equally unfortunate principle of 'payment by results'.

The most serious weakness of Scottish government was not so much the policies of the individual Boards as their separation from politics and politicians. Not unnaturally this separation, and the influence of Ireland, combined to produce a nationalist movement. Though the Scottish economy was growing well, if lopsidedly, there were discomforts involved. There was genuine under-representation in politics until the Reform Act of 1884 tied parliamentary seats to population as a general principle. There was also the cry that Scotland did not get her fair share of government expenditure. In 1888 this was partly met by the 'Goschen formula', a calculation that Scotland was entitled to share in grants in the ratio of 11 parts to England's 80, as recognition of her share in taxation. But this did not meet the feeling of unfairness about direct government installations, those of the army and navy for instance. In the 1870s and 1880s it had become clear that Irish nationalist agitation was a successful means of extracting government concessions. In the 1880s Rosebery began to press, from within the governing Liberal party, for a better political structure. This was grudgingly awarded by the creation of a Scottish Secretaryship in 1885, an office not for another forty years to carry the status of a Secretary of State, but which was gradually able to force the Treasury and Home Office to disgorge powers. It was during the initial stages of the debate over this measure that Sir William Harcourt produced, more from ignorance than ill will, the statement: 'Scotchmen do their own business so well that the questions that come up for solution by the Central Government are singularly few.' This was in June 1883, during the struggle exaggeratedly known as the 'Crofters' War'. The next year the government sent a gunboat to Skye. In 1886 the young Balfour was to argue in Cabinet that lawlessness in Scotland was worse than in Ireland. This overstatement came from equating a refusal to respect property rights or pay rents with cattle maiming, arson and assassination. But it is true that there was widespread disturbance in the Highlands in the 1880s.

Much of the immediate inspiration of unrest in the Highlands, like other nineteenth-century manifestations of Scottish nationalism, derived from Ireland. From the 1850s on, observers had commented on the presence of alien agitators, and the literature of protest bear all the signs of artificial encouragement from outside. But the hard core of misery and degradation was real enough, and it is a comment on the traditional submissiveness of the Highlander to civil and religious authority that it needed outside help to make it vocal. The changes of the nineteenth century had increased the pressures on the Highland economy. The potato famine had shown that the whole area was disastrously overpopulated. It had also shown the limitations of a Poor Law which gave no aid to mere destitution. The peasantry were kept alive in that crisis by their landowners, by voluntary subscriptions from the south, and by some special relief from the Board of Supervision. The relic of this period best known today is the 'road of desolation' made by relief work from Poolewe to Ullapool. Emigration and clearance went on the faster after that crisis, and the only new economic factor to enter the Highlands did nothing to prevent them. This was the use of an estate for sporting purposes, for grouse or deer or salmon fishing. These activities on a large scale were made by the new communications of the nineteenth century, first the 'Parliamentary' roads (subsidized by a grant), then steamships, and then the railways. They brought in landowners and tenants of a new type, who treated their Highland property as holiday homes for part of the year. The most famous example of this was the royal family at Balmoral. Sport did not need a large local population, and had little use for its skills. The labour employed on the hill, or in the great house, was often in origin non-local. Long-term sheep farming ran down the fertility of the soil and in the 1870s and 1880s, when the agricultural crisis of the whole country brought catastrophically low prices, first in grain and then in wool, much of the higher pastures, cleared of small tenants for sheep farms, could not be let as farms and became deer-forest instead. To the land-starved peasantry it looked as if they had been cleared out for deer: and this idea became one of the standard myths about the clearances. Those crofters that remained had holdings too small to be viable, and stock too small to enable them to hope to undertake a bigger unit, while the economic climate was against cereal farming. They lived in a crowded, semi-protected situation from which development was almost impossible. Most landowners protected their tenantry from being the casualties of the new civilization in the terms in which the urban poor had been in the 1840s and 1850s. But by the 1880s urban standards of living had risen markedly. The town dweller could expect very different things in income and housing than those attainable in the north-west. Clearances had mostly ceased. Voluntary emigration now took families to the higher wages of the towns. And once there some of them would join political activities, and looking back to their old homes, spread these agitations there too.

Another element in the division between landowner and crofter was the Free Church. This, far more than the established one, came to share the resentments and aspirations of the poor in the Highlands. It was not an entirely happy relationship. The various dissenting Churches and the Free Church in the Highlands held hard to the faith as it had been at the height of Evangelical fashion, and the leaders of the Free Church had occasion to complain of missionary activity 'fanaticizing the Highlands'. The extreme rigour of some of these tenets gave a narrow and joyless quality to life, which accentuated social isolation and economic hopelessness. But it is clear that in most matters the Free Church ministers, often coming from poor families, were felt to speak with and for the crofters, in a society which otherwise did not provide them with leaders.

The crisis of lawlessness of the 1880s owed much immediate inspiration to the Irish legislation of the Liberal ministry. If Ireland was to be granted tenant right and a protected level of rents, there was no logical reason why the similar small-holding tenants-at-will in the Highlands should be denied these advantages. The issue came to a head in 1882 with the refusal of some Skye crofters to accept the removal of their pasture rights. A Highland Land League was formed: there were riots of a fairly peaceful kind, and a refusal of rents. This was the 'Crofters' War'. The government, in which there was a large element of Scottish landowners, was unwilling to apply its Irish policy to Scotland, but after pressure agreed to a Royal Commission.

This Commission, under Lord Napier, served a useful function in allowing the protest to become fully articulate and publicized. On it served the Edinburgh professor of Gaelic, to make sure that all were understood. It treated its peasant witnesses with sympathy and dignity. In its report it recognized that much of the evidence produced had been 'erroneous as to time, to place, to persons, to extent, and misconstrued as to intention'. But all the same the stories had a generalized truth: they were the sort of thing that had happened. And they had happened to people whose predecessors had been prepared to enlist and fight at the request of their landowners, and who by doing so should have established that there was more in the relationship than economic agreements, that there was a claim to consideration and security.

It was one thing to take the heat out of the agitation by listening to it and publishing. It was another to make recommendations for the future well-being of both land and tenantry. The Commission held firmly 'that to grant at this moment fixity of tenure in their holdings ... uncontrolled management of these holdings and free sale of their tenant-right, goodwill and improvements, would be to perpetuate social evils of a dangerous character'. The best it could recommend on the main issue was the idea of an 'improving lease', which would give security to the stronger and more enterprising crofters, the *kulaks*. For the rest, however hard it tried to soften the hard impact of economic reality, it could only envisage emigration. In the sways and swings of parliamentary fortunes in the crisis years over Ireland which broke the Liberal party over Home Rule soon after this report, what in fact was embodied in the Crofters' Holdings Act of 1886 was exactly what had been declared against, absolute security of tenure, with compensation for improvements and a protected level of rent – the remedy as offered to Ireland.

The agitation died away with the Liberal break-up of 1886. The later nationalist feeling, more indigenous, that came through with the socialist movement of Keir Hardie, was not particularly interested in the Highlands. Economic insecurity had been transferred by the Act from the crofter to his landlord, who could better withstand it. The main victim of the change was the land itself, particularly after a legal decision which allowed non-resident crofting. More and more it suffered from partial farming by crofters who made their main income outside the area. The long-term significance of the Act was the recognition of the Highlands as a special area for government intervention, with its own land law and with a series of government bodies created to 'do something' about the special problems of the area. Over the years since 1886 these have been set up with economic and social aims, and with varying powers, from the 'Congested Districts Boards' of the 1890s to the Highland Development Board of the 1960s. None of them have solved the modern form of the Highland problem, the lack of native resources and a population falling steadily and reducing the capacity of communities to be economically or socially viable.

Developments within the Churches also came to leave the Highlands out on a limb at the end of the century. The various Presbyterian Churches were having difficulty with their Calvinism by mid-century. They subscribed to the splendid language and clear definitions of the Westminster Confession, but with increasing qualms from its very clarity. The unhistorical use of scriptural proof attached to the Confession made particular difficulties in a period when history as an intellectual exercise was becoming generally accepted. The special problem of the historical origins of the Bible, springing originally from the intense interest in its actual text, started by the Haldanite attack on what Robert Haldane called 'the accursed apocrypha', led to a crisis in the Free Church in 1881. This was resolved with a compromise of considerable political skill but doubtful intellectual honesty. The source of the trouble, William Robertson Smith, was accused of holding that God was not the author of the Bible. His view, that the revelation of divine will in Scripture came through human and therefore fallible interpretation but was still revelation, was too subtle for most of his Church. He was deposed from his chair in the Free Church's New College, but not censured for heresy. Subsequently most of the Free Church absorbed his opinions.

A greater problem was the nature of Calvinism as it had developed in Britain, with heavy emphasis on the necessity of assurance. This made it a faith which could give little pastoral aid. Furthermore, out and out Calvinism reduces the emphasis on the atonement and incarnation, on the specifically Christological element in Christianity. Within many of the Scottish Churches in the mid-nineteenth century, as within Calvinist Churches in both England and America, there were more and more people who could not swallow the full rigidity of the dogma, who could only subscribe the Confession in a very general way. In the biggest 'voluntary' body in Scotland, the Free Church, this had led to division. A group wishing to keep their dogma as it had been in the 1830s split away from the modernizing majority and formed the Free Presbyterians, a communion almost exclusively Highland in its location. The Free Presbyterians welcomed their economic and social isolation in the north-west, convinced that they alone had the truth and aware that only by rigid discipline and absence of alternatives could the future generation be kept in the narrow way. The Highlands also received the principal impact of another breach. In 1900 the United Presbyterians and the Free Church amalgamated. Doctrinally there was no real distinction between them, and they shared a common Presbyterian structure. The only important point was that by tradition the Free Church did not hold with voluntaryism. Its belief in civilly established religion sat rather anomalously on a large, independent body, and had weakened since 1843. A small portion of the Free Church refused to enter the amalgamation, and claimed to be the only true successor of the principles of 1843. As such it demanded the entire property of the Free Church. The 'Wee Frees' won their case (the early twentieth century saw several unfortunate decisions by the House of Lords), and Parliament had to intervene with an Act to settle the property in a more just and practicable manner.

The interest of these events lies partly in the repeated tendency of Scottish dissent to reunite. Sharing the same Confession, and often the same qualms about it, as well as the same structure, when the issue that created a split has been dead for a couple of generations, the communions find it possible to undertake reunion. That the issues do become dead is because they are so often not connected with theology but with the relationship of the Churches to civil society. The lawsuit over property was a salutary reminder to those who disapproved of the 'erastian' position of the established Kirk, that all organizations hold their funds under the civil law, expressed in the civil courts, and that the days were past when a great religious body could conduct its multifarious work in poverty. It was time to reconsider the relations of Church and state in this new light. The established Church by now, like the Free Churches, raised most of its funds not from its established position but from gifts and endowments. It persuaded the government to tack a declaration of its spiritual independence on to the Act secured by the United Free Church. From there reunion of the two main Churches took merely a quarter of a century. There is a certain relentless logic about the history of the Kirk's division and reunion, but this logic breaks down over the continued existence after 1929, in a voluntary position, of the 'Wee Frees' dedicated to opposing the principles of voluntaryism.

THE PRINCIPAL DIVISIONS OF PRESBYTERIANISM FROM 1843 ONWARDS

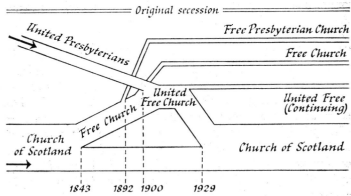

Chapter 23

The twentieth century

Clydeside

THERE WERE FOURTEEN HUNDRED THOUSAND more people in Scotland in 1901 than in 1861, in all nearly four and a half million, of whom the great majority lived in the towns of the central Lowland valley; almost half of these in the single conurbation on the Clyde. Yet in spite of this expansion the proportion of Scottish to English population had been declining. It was guessed at one to five in 1700, it was measured as one to six in 1801; in the early twentieth century it lay between one to eight and one to nine, and in the 1960s at slightly less than one to nine. This was not the result of lower fertility but of migration. Scotland in the nineteenth century lost more of her citizens by emigration than she gained by the influx of others. In the last decades of the nineteenth century approximately half the annual excess of births over deaths was neutralized by emigration. The main stream entering nineteenth-century Scotland was from Ireland, creating the Catholic areas of Lowland Scotland, the passions behind the rivalry of Glasgow's football clubs, and the cheap mythology and resentments of the Orange order. In the twentieth century the main stream became English, but the number of English arriving was markedly less than the number of Scots leaving. In one decade, the 1920s, the result of this was that though Scotland still had a birth rate well above replacement level, she actually lost population. Even in the 1960s emigration, to England or overseas, remained consistently higher than immigration.

The concentration of population on Clydeside was the result of the tremendous development of heavy industry in the late nineteenth century. The special emphasis was on ship-building. In the 1860s and 1870s the Scots already had a name for marine engineering, and were producing many of the great sailing clippers. These were the last splendid achievement of sail before the spread of coaling stations opened the distant ports of the world to steam, great iron ships of long lines that raced across the lower latitudes of the world, 'running their easting down'.[1] In the 1880s, iron was giving way to steel, sail to steam, and in the rebuilding of the merchants fleets of all the world the Scots took the lead. Starting with William Denny of Dumbarton, who launched the first steel steamer in 1879, the Scots moved ahead, specializing in the development of high-pressure engines. Their lead lasted till the early twentieth century when the creation of diesel engines, pioneered on the continent of Europe, showed that others were doing more than catch up. The reckoning came after the First World War, when ship-building was in chronic difficulties. But in the great days till 1914 it pulled the country into prosperity, with a supporting cast of the other heavy industries, coal, iron and steel, engineering.

It looks as if the result of this concentrated development was that for the first time in her history the income of the inhabitants of Scotland equalled that of the English, probably surpassing that of those in the northern English industrial towns. The industrial development of Scotland might be one-sided – in particular it lacked

1. Using the strong winds of the Roaring Forties to make their longitude.

jobs for women – but it needed and rewarded skill. The great names of the Clyde ship-building firms were associations of pride. It is not surprising that Scottish nationalism, that had been noticeable in the 1860s and 1870s in the negative form of a generalized disgruntlement, died down in the 1880s. It was replaced with Keir Hardie's image of Home Rule for both Scotland and Ireland: but this was put forward with what was felt to be a much more urgent need, more adequate representation of labour in Parliament. Hardie's main claim to fame is as the founder of the Independent Labour Party in 1888, for Hardie saw nothing incompatible in combining a labour organization for the whole of Britain with aspirations for Scottish self-government. The combination, while it lasted, gave Scottish nationalism the positive content it had previously lacked.

It is not difficult to see in this period why people entered the country from England and northern Ireland. Except in the case of the Highlanders, it is harder to understand why so many Scots left. Emigration does not seem to have been caused by the lack of opportunities in Scotland but by the draw of particular jobs, places, and the kin already overseas. It was a cumulative process, assisted by the information provided by the networks of Scottish kinfolk and friends. It is striking to this day not merely how many Scots have relatives overseas, but how many regard these as in some way nearer in culture than the English with whom they are politically associated.

The standard of living, in terms of money, might be as high in Scotland as in England, but in other ways it was beginning to fall behind. Scotland had benefited, as had England, from the drop in mortality rates after 1870 that resulted from the initial achievements of the public health movement and the beginnings of the basic concepts of modern medicine. But it is in the first decade of this century that the graphs of Scottish mortality, infant mortality, and expectation of life, cross those for England. In the later nineteenth century it was marginally easier at all ages to survive in Scotland than in England: it has not been so this century. Scotland lagged behind the improving standards of the developed nations. Some areas did still worse. One observer has written: 'in 1936 the infant mortality rate in Glasgow exceeded that for Chicago by 180 per cent, Oslo 270 per cent, and Stockholm by 290 per cent . . . it was in fact higher than the corresponding rates for Tokyo, Buenos Aires and Montevideo'.[1] But at least infant mortality, though undesirably high in the 1920s and 1930s, was falling. In some branches of public health the deterioration was not only relative but absolute. This was paradoxical, in view of the nineteenth-century achievement. Scotland had been the scene of work of the two great innovators in British medicine in the 1850s and 1860s, Sir James Young Simpson who brought anaesthetics into practical use, and Joseph Lister who advanced from Pasteur's study of fermentation to a realization of the material nature of infection and to the creation of antisepsis. These discoveries opened up modern surgery, and made hygiene a positive science. Yet maternal mortality in Scotland, calculated per 1,000 live births, had been under five when Lister started work, and was running at almost seven in 1929–30. The figures had shown a consistent increase since the turn of the century.

Some small proportion of these shocking statistics reflected the generally increased expectation of life. More women survived into the older age groups with a higher child-bearing risk. Other reasons are less creditable. A share was due to the absence of any comprehensive arrangements for ante-natal care and any system of hospital availability. A great deal of it seems to have been due to sheer bad doctoring. Heavy industry does not seem to have played much part. True, mines and furnaces fouled the air, and the houses near to them were small and crowded; but as the worst mortality was to be found in the Border counties, largely innocent of heavy industry, we can only feel that in the areas of heavy industry, fluctuations in activity and employment, by causing chronic malnutrition, added their bit to a bad situation.

If maternal mortality did not closely associate with bad housing, the same cannot be said of child deaths. The correlation here struck every dispassionate observer. The one-roomed 'house' had double the infant mortality of that of four rooms. It had three times the death rate from tuberculosis too. Not all of this correlation was directly causative. It was the poorer families, whose poverty often sprang from numbers or from illness, who crowded into the 'single-ends', instead of the much preferred two-roomed houses. Nearly half the population of Scotland in the period of the First World War

1. R. M. Titmuss, *Birth, Poverty and Wealth*, p. 90.

was living as families in one or two rooms. It was a degree of overcrowding that did not entirely spring from necessity: the acquiescence, even within this level, in general insanitariness, did.

We have a detailed picture of the horrors of Scottish housing in the early twentieth century from a Royal Commission on Scottish housing, which reported in 1917. It is a drastic condemnation of the single-roomed house. The Commission lamented that the earth-closet, widely used in rural England and France, appeared unknown in Scotland. It listed a collection of insanitary devices which served instead. The simple names of them are sufficient comment on their quality: the 'privy middens' of Dundee, the 'ashpits' of mining areas, the 'trough closets' of Fife. Whole streets in Perth were without any sanitary facilities and the children found necessary uses for the school playgrounds. Elsewhere the common stairs had this function. Then there were the problems involved in combining the Scottish tradition of wakes (the ceremonial visiting of a corpse in his own home), with the life of a whole family in one room. The Report is a grisly document. Overcrowding and squalor, though enhanced by the nature of the industrial specialization of the country, were general Scottish features.

The Commission did not inquire how far overcrowding was produced by an acceptance of deplorable standards, and an unwillingness to pay for anything better, but this feature is one of the main historical problems of Scottish housing. It is true that at various periods there had been real efforts for something better. Glasgow had been one of the first municipalities in Britain to try its hand at slum clearance and house-building, starting work on this before the end of the nineteenth century. In all British cities the nineteenth century had shown that there was always a section of the population prepared, if allowed, to live in rock-bottom conditions for the sake of low rents. The problem in Scotland is why this section was so large, even when wages were good. In spite of its early start, Glasgow's chief effort to regulate overcrowding had been by discipline. The smaller houses were 'ticketed', that is given an official maximum of human occupation based on the principle of 300 cubic foot per adult, and raids were made to see if the ticket was being kept to. These raids, with a thorough disregard of the comfort of the inhabitants, took place at dead of night, and the surplus population, hearing the police on the stair, would take refuge among the chimney stacks.

Acquiescence came partly because the structure of Scottish house-building was what the Scots liked: tall tenement blocks, set end on to the street and built of immense solidity, with little interest in fresh air. They felt safe and gave social cohesiveness. They were not structures into which water-pipes or closets could easily be introduced. Slum clearance could involve, and still can, hacking down stone walls several feet thick. All classes accepted the situation. Even upper-class housing had been backward in sanitary achievements. Smollett and Sydney Smith, in the eras of the Enlightenment and the Napoleonic War, and less outspokenly, Queen Victoria, in the mid-nineteenth century, had commented on the inelegancies of the features accepted in respectable housing. It was difficult for improving local authorities to win court actions against slum landlords. The sheriffs had their own interpretations of the laws on housing standards and an indifference to medical evidence, regarding water supplies and conveniences, recent innovations in their own houses, as luxuries for the working classes.

It was the Scottish housing situation and the Scottish insistence on low rents which forced the government in the First World War to produce Rent Restriction. This, and the war-time lag in house-building, meant that in the 1920s the problem of Scottish housing merged with the general British one of total shortage, and led to the main achievement of the first Labour government, Wheatley's Housing Act of 1924. John Wheatley was a Scot, the leader of the Clydeside group in Parliament, and felt deeply about living conditions. Yet his Act, which led to much subsidized building in England, was little used in Scotland. It offered houses too good and at too high a rent for Scottish habits. Instead, the Scottish authorities built more one-roomed and two-roomed houses. But standards of quality and acceptability were rising. Glasgow initiated her slum clearance programme in an area where people lived 1,116 to the acre. In the 1930s a further investigation into Scottish housing produced the Scottish Special Housing Authority, a direct-grant organization for building. Pressure by this body and successive governments has gradually raised the level of rent, but the habit of economizing on space and rent has continued. There were, in 1961, more people living in one- and two-roomed houses in Scotland than in the whole of England and Wales, and the average Scot spent about 15 per cent less on rent and rates than the average Englishman – much less if rent alone were looked at. But at least by then the Scottish houses were mostly adequately equipped.

Scotland has also gone a long way since the 1930s to make up her lag in mortality rates. The levels have become in some cases better than those in England and the others are not conspicuously worse, an achievement on which, if such an activity were ever safe in public health work, the Scottish authorities could congratulate themselves. The gap began to close even before the big welfare developments of the Second World War. The wartime determination not to allow social waste was as strong in Scotland as elsewhere, and the sense of national emergency overrode traditional distinctions and privileges. Some of the vital experiments that lay behind the creation of the National Health Service were done in Scotland. Scotland's education at its best provides an emphasis on professionalism which has proved valuable in this field. Yet in the 1960s there have been signs of the need for a new impulse. For instance, rickets, a disease which disappeared during the war, has shown again on Clydeside. Chest diseases of all kinds still kill more than they need to. A certain puritanical indifference to civic amenity has made the Scottish cities backward in smoke abatement, so that, though tuberculosis, once the scourge of Scotland, has largely gone, chronic bronchitis remains as a killer.

There was some connection in the early twentieth century between the gloomy mortality and morbidity statistics of Scotland and a specific push in the country for new political forms. Simple poverty had never made a major issue in politics, and by the early twentieth century Scotland had in practice, if not in theory, achieved a poor law which did a lot to relieve, though little to prevent, destitution. As this was mostly done by out-relief, it was at relatively low cost. But there were social evils that needed more radical treatment. There was also the effect of the general failure of real wages to rise in the years before 1914, a time when productivity as a whole was rising. The old Liberal party hold on Scotland had weakened. It had been given power by a strong anti-landowner feeling which, in the 1880s, had also produced the Scottish Land and Labour League, a socialist body. But land-reform slipped down in the Liberal programme. The whole

Liberal party too was slipping downwards in the 1890s, so much so that for the first time in 1900 a narrow majority of Scottish seats went Conservative. There was not much point in working-class organizations continuing to stay allied to the Liberal party when it lacked a programme that concerned them, and in any case had not enough centralized power to insist on constituency parties running a reasonable number of working-class candidates. Keir Hardie's Independent Labour party was one alternative, which had considerable support in northern England, and some in southern Scotland. There was also, after 1900, the Labour Representative League, to which the I.L.P. adhered in semi-independence, and for which it provided a lot of the theoretical basis. In the 1906 election this emerged as the Labour party, with a distinct parliamentary organization. There were other organizations of the left: Clydeside had a basketful of them, of various shades and types of socialism. The working-class vote, partially achieved in 1884, and the payment of members of Parliament in 1911, made working-class politics increasingly practicable, but things were not yet so advanced as to show clearly the split between radicalism and the immediate aims of the Trade Unions.

Hardie gave his blessing to the movement for women's rights, but this did not go far in Scotland. The combination of a dominance of heavy industry, a high birth rate, social conformity, and Knoxian theology was against it. The network of socialist organizations combined with the economic pressures of the First World War to produce a militant labour movement on the Clyde. This area had the biggest concentration in Britain of great engineering shops and shipyards, deeply involved in war-work and well aware of the pressures of wartime inflation and shortages on working-class life. It was here that unrest early in the war was at its highest, and in 1915 there was a crisis in the relationship of workers and government. This led to several important changes. The Rent Restriction legislation of 1915 heralded a policy which meant the assuaging of present hardship to tenants at the cost of drying up the future production of houses to rent. There was also born a tradition of trouble; of labour leaders put into gaol for non-co-operation, of shop stewards organizing labour 'dilution' and renewing, from a stronger position, the ideas about the control of industry by workers which had already been current before the war; of resistance within the ranks of labour to the organized leadership of the Labour party or the Trade Unions, and of interest in, and sometimes assimilation to, the Communist party in Russia.

At the end of the war, then, the political stage saw considerable divergence in the Clyde area from the currents of political opinion elsewhere. This did not show in Parliament until the 1922 election, when ten I.L.P. members came from the Clyde. By then some of the economic features of the inter-war years were showing. The old self-confident belief of British industry that the world needed its products was waning. Scotland shared in an extreme form the ills that were afflicting it, many of which should have been apparent before the war, but which had been accentuated by four and a half years in which much of the world had had to do without British exports. If British steelworks, by world standards, were small and unintegrated and therefore unable to get the full economics of scale, producing the wrong material and doing it in the wrong place, Scotland's were even smaller than England's. They were away from both the coast where the ore arrived and from the new markets of the south, and geared even more than the English ones to unsuitable end-products. Scottish coal, never of top quality, had become uneconomic to export. Ship-building suffered because it was the industry most sensitive to a decline in world trade. Nations which cannot fill the ships they have are slow to order new ones. Scotland shared very little in the newer industries which were the main recipients of the higher wages available since the war, but she had a disproportionate element of the old and now ailing staples.

The discomforts produced by all this are obvious. What is less obvious is why the situation had been allowed to become so threatening. One inescapable conclusion is a lack of entrepreneurial ability, but whether this occurred because Scotland was incapable of producing the ability, or because once produced it migrated to England or overseas, it is difficult to say. There can be situations in which the leadership of an industry may be aware that there is trouble ahead, yet for technological, financial, or structural reasons be unable to meet it. There is as yet no scale by which historians can measure entrepreneurship. The Scottish coal industry in the 1890s included one large mine in the west that was managed by the minister of a church in Ayr with the aid of a bicycle. This is not the sort of combi-

O

nation likely to produce striking results in either of the careers involved. But could even a ruthless efficiency have overcome in time the problems of an old industry, with an outdated structure of worked-out seams, which all the same was still finding a market overseas? Large-scale organization of industry, where it did affect Scotland, as in chemicals, meant organization from London, and this was unlikely to give a high priority to Scottish needs. Heavy industry in the inter-war period dithered between the policy of diversification within its existing framework, and the policy of cutting down. Either would be painful; so was doing neither. Probably both policies, harnessed together, were necessary for prosperity, and only then if carried out with vigour.

The particular difficulties Scotland experienced in the 1920s, when what appeared wrong with the world was the failure of international trade to recover to pre-war levels, became even more outstanding in the 1930s when what was obviously wrong was a world-wide depression. Scotland went into depression as fast and as far as the rest of Britain; but she stayed in much longer than did England. By the later 1930s her unemployment rates were markedly higher than those south of the Border.

Some reasons for this lack of buoyancy have already been suggested. There are others of a more complicated nature. At least part of the English recovery was caused by the housing boom of the 1930s, which drove along with it a host of consumer industries such as furniture, carpets, and cars. This was predominantly a private enterprise affair, though there was a fair output of council work too. There was almost no private building in Scotland, council building was still scanty, and the cramped and urban nature of what there was prevented it having much general effect. The uniformity of Scotland's depression, and the lack of housing stimulus, made it difficult to get started on the industries that proved so useful in the new English trading estates, the mass production of clothing, household goods, and minor luxuries. Scotland's poverty was generating its own continuance.

It had also generated a good deal of division inside the Labour party. It is conceivable that the I.L.P. group of Clydeside members of Parliament might have acted as a policy-making core for the Labour party as a whole. It had ideas and energy, and, since the I.L.P. effectively provided the constituency section of the Scottish Labour party, it had a useful form of backing in the electorate. In the first Labour government of 1924 it did something to fulfil expectations. The rift in method between elements on the left and the party as a whole, the question whether Labour should aim at being reformist or revolutionary, did not yet prevent co-operation, though the puritanical streak in some Clydesiders made it difficult. But in the second Labour government of 1929–31 there was a marked personal breach between Clydesiders and Cabinet. In the 1930s, after the death of John Wheatley, the remnant of his I.L.P. following came under the leadership of James Maxton who broke the I.L.P. away from Labour, to the loss of both parties and the eventual extinction of the I.L.P. It is a little difficult to conceive of the Clyde or the I.L.P. on its own carrying through a workers' revolution: the element of socialism in the inter-war Labour movement was not sufficiently well organized or ruthless enough in its philosophy to put such a programme into action. At a time when, intellectually and politically, Britain needed some new thinking – new concepts of the part to be played by the state in the economy, of the relationship between sovereign states and the world's political community, of the possibility of renovating a stagnant economy and reducing unemployment – there was a real place for an intelligent socialist group inside the Labour party. There was little function for one outside because the structure of British politics gives little opportunity for groups to influence affairs except from within a big national party. Failure to recognize this, and failure to do the new thinking needed, led to Maxton reducing the I.L.P. to impotence. In this period, 'the winter of our discontents', the remnant of the Clydesiders had little warmth to offer.

Economic recovery in Scotland, as far as it did come, came with the shadow of approaching war. Rearmament meant a need for ships after 1936, and so a renewed emphasis on heavy industry in its old form. The Second World War brought real recovery, and the creation of new factories, but this and other forms of wartime investment were not necessarily of long-term advantage. Some of it, such as the big airstrips on Tiree, could not be profitably used in peace. The whole nexus of protection round the battlefleet at Scapa was soon as obsolete as the ships it guarded. It might have been of advantage to Scottish slum clearance to have suffered heavy bombing; the single raid on the Clyde showed up, even more than most other initial air raids, the inadequacies of local provision, without putting continued pressure on authorities for improvement. It was obviously more immediately profitable to use the existing skills and facilities in any one industrial area than to create new ones, so wartime development re-emphasized the dominance of heavy industry in Scotland without diversifying much within the type.

At the same time Scotland benefited, as did the rest of Britain, from the most outstanding achievements of the war, the renewed sense of national unity, purpose, and success, the opportunity it gave, partly as a result of this feeling and partly by the greater share of national income that was taken for government spending, to tackle more radically the problems of health and welfare. She had a particular advantage here, for the regional structure of government set up during the war gave extra and needed strength to the Secretaryship of State. All war is tragic waste: but the Second World War also broke old bonds of habit, propertied rights, and hesitation that stood in the way of a better society. The world turmoil it caused also destroyed the old climate of economic thought and action. For reasons which are as yet only partially understood, western Europe emerged from the war into an exceptional period, combining social security aims successfully with rapid economic growth. It has been an age of innovation, positive government direction and investment, rising standards of living, high employment, and active trade. In this scheme of things, Britain, though doing much better in almost every way than before the war, did worse than the rest of western Europe, and Scotland was one of the parts of Britain that lagged behind the rest.

There was therefore considerable prosperity in Scotland after the war. People had incomes with increasing margins for comfort. New industries, in some form or other, at last arrived. The higher standard of living encouraged consumer industries. Under government pressure, car factories started. The chemical and oil-refining nexus at Grangemouth grew. Amalgamation in the 1930s had produced the vast firm of Colvilles in steel, which was to create an integrated works in 1957. Electronics, established during the war, enlarged and varied its products. But in the twenty years after the war Scottish unemployment was almost consistently double that for Britain as a whole. This meant that the country had to experience the periodic checks ad-

ministered by the government to expansion in the interests of international exchange, without having fully experienced the expansion
itself. She had to suffer the attempt by the Selective Employment Tax
to redirect scarce labour supplies although labour was not short in
Scotland. Some unwholesome features of her pre-war economic
climate remained. People left the country on such a scale that population growth was slow in the 1950s and appears actually to have fallen
in the 1960s. The impetus that an expanding population can give to
development has thus been lacking. Income from wages has remained
below that in England. Income from capital has been as high or
higher, but this form of wealth did not necessarily benefit the country
economically or socially. Scotland remains strikingly short of those
manifestations of local and intellectual enthusiasm that in England
can draw partly on inherited wealth. Trade Unions in ship-building,
remembering too well the hard times between the wars, have acted
on their fears in a way calculated to justify them, by greeting technological changes with battles over demarcation of jobs. The industry
was not radical enough in its approach to labour, nor quite skilful
enough in its costing, to hold its own in an unusually competitive
world. There were mistakes in the calculations for the building of big
ships when the margins would not allow these to be made in safety.
The industries entering Scotland have tended to be either government impelled or American in origin. Native enterprise has remained
poor. The closing down of Scotland's worked-out coal measures has
been uncomfortable because of mistakes in forecasting.

Some of Scotland's post-war weaknesses, as with those of northern
England, have been the obverse of the excessive concentration of
development in south-east England. The attempt to even things out
led in 1960 to the Local Employment Act, allowing government
encouragement to industrial development in the backward areas and,
in 1966, to the decision to offer heavy investment grants there.
Almost the whole of Scotland has been classified as a 'development
area' for these benefits, and there has been a powerful injection of
government capital. The signs are that most of the investment in
Scotland in the 1950s went on the necessary task of modernizing and
improving existing plants and industries, 'deepening' the economy
rather than 'widening' it. Investment now appears to be enlarging
employment and reducing the gap between English and Scottish

unemployment figures. But this will only continue if the country is prepared to adapt its social and educational systems. The Scottish upper classes of the seventeenth century expected the benefits of economic development without social reorganization: there is no law of society that restricts this attitude to the upper classes.

Political Epilogue, 1969

I ken, when we had a King, and a chancellor and Parliament-men o'
our ain, we could aye peeble them wi' stanes when they werena gude
bairns – But naebody's nails can reach the length o' Lunnon.'
                                    SCOTT, *The Heart of Midlothian*

IN THE LATER 1960s the Scottish people enjoyed a higher standard
of living than ever before: yet never in two centuries had the structure
of government received so much criticism. That the critics have had
very little positive to put forward is a result of the complexities and
difficulties of modern government as well as of the nature and structure of the political parties in Scotland.

Nationalism, in two of its senses, a pride and loyalty specifically to
Scotland itself, and an irritation at English assumptions, can be found
recurrently before the later nineteenth century. David Hume had
reason to indulge in the latter sentiment: Muir's defence at his trial
for sedition had a strong note of the former. None of it added up to
much in periods when the connection with England was either
obviously producing good new prospects or getting rid of old bad
features. But in the later nineteenth century a new strain of clamant
and aggressive nationalism arose here, as in various other parts of the
world. Some people came to believe that all development of a society,
except from forces within itself, was in some way an affront to national
dignity. There developed a special interest in the Celtic contribution
to Scotland, encouraged by the cultural revivals in Ireland and Wales.
A lot could be learnt about the organization of national pressure
groups from the Irish agitations during and after the 1860s: the
demands for church disestablishment and reform of the land law
were clearly derivative from Ireland. The radical content of nationalism was emphasized because this suited the main trend of Scotland's
politics. The country was a Liberal dominion, which made it natural
for nationalism to appeal to one of the boundary elements in the

framework of Liberal thought. Scottish nationalism has often had an element of simple accountancy, a demand for fair shares in any government issue of money or opportunities, but this was not to the fore in the radical period. Incipient or overt national feeling had a share in several government measures of the 1880s, the creation of the Scottish Secretaryship, the 'Goschen formula', and the Crofters' Holdings Act of 1886. But the Liberal fracture over Home Rule for Ireland in that year marked the end of the older radical domination in Liberal thought, and the weakening of the main themes within the national movement.

Perhaps because of this change, in the next forty years Scotland provided a large proportion of British prime ministers, but at the same time received very little government attention. Rosebery, Balfour, Campbell Bannerman, Bonar Law, and Ramsay Macdonald were all either Scots or men who had lived and worked in Scotland for most of their lives, and Asquith sat for a Scottish seat. They were enabled to maintain close Scottish contacts by the efficiency of the railway system and its provision of sleeper trains. They represented different social and economic aspects of Scotland, the industrial north-east, the comfortable country houses of the Lothians, the enterprise of Glasgow. Only Rosebery among them thought in terms of a specific policy for Scotland, and his wants were mainly administrative. That in his period of office, and in those of Balfour and Campbell Bannerman, there was little pressure by the government for the improvement of specific Scottish ills may be accounted for by the fact that both the methods and the theory of intervention by central power in local affairs were only gradually being worked out. The two main steps in this were the development of grants for education and the welfare agencies set up in the attack on destitution which, though mainly associated with the Liberal ministry of 1905–15, was initiated by Balfour's Royal Commission on the Poor Law. In both of these fields Scotland's position was distinct: in one she was still ahead of most English opinion, in the other behind. The main provisions of the welfare legislation were designed to ignore the separate national traditions: old age pensions and health insurance, for instance, were offered or enforced in accordance with personal status and needs, not local characteristics. There was, however, one specifically regional service created, the Highlands and Islands

Medical Service. This arose from the discovery by the Poor Law Commission that the Highlands and Islands were twenty years behind the rest of the country in medical provision. One of the revealing figures they brought out in these areas was the proportion of people dying with no doctor to sign their death certificates. In some places this was over 65 per cent. Because of poverty and bad communications, doctors were not available when they were needed. The new medical service was a forerunner of the National Health service of the third Labour government: it fixed a fairly low level of fees for hospital or doctor's attendance, and offered subsidized salaries to bring doctors into the area. Planned and started in 1913, it was not of real significance until the inter-war period.

Legislation did not, of course, ignore Scotland totally. The major social and administrative reforms included her. The changes in local government in the nineteenth century and after did not emerge from one specific theory of the relationship between different levels of government, but were the results of compromise between different ideas and interests. They were, as a result, littered with historic anomalies which only gradually disappeared. Since the pasts of England and Scotland differed, so did the compromises. The systems of local government of the two countries, though very similar in general, had basic continuing differences. Justices of the Peace were less important in Scotland than in England, and lacked the full range of English powers. The historic group of royal burghs, some of them too small for real urban life, or even effective village life, continued for a long time to clog the structure of government. The population distribution of Scotland's real urban areas had big gaps which made it difficult to devise a general type of structure, and the fact that the 1833 legislation enabled districts to classify themselves as an authority even if they had no real social, economic, or historic identity, left the map cluttered with unsuitable units. This structure was only slowly and partially tidied up in the twentieth century. It has left Scotland with a patchwork of small local authorities, unsuited to many of the main tasks of local government today. The sparseness of Highland population also means that local representation places a heavy burden on councillors in travel and time: island councillors in Inverness-shire may well spend three days in attending a meeting. The penny rate in Sutherland raises something over £600; in a reasonably prosperous county such as Ayrshire, it brings in sixteen times as much; in a city such as Edinburgh, over a hundred times. This is not a structure devised for remote and small communities, and it is not surprising that it works badly. More important in its effect on the problem of Scotland as a whole has been the increasing importance and frequency of Bills in Parliament that affect local government. The compilers of detailed enactments, concerned with features of British life as a whole, have increasingly forced functions on local authorities, or curbed the exercise of powers they already had. Since the actual authorities and their powers are different in the two countries this has meant either producing separate Bills for the two countries or clogging a single Bill with pages of separate schedules. Scottish national dignity has tended to demand the first solution. The pressures on parliamentary time have then meant that specific Scottish legislation has been often delayed or postponed indefinitely.

At the end of the nineteenth century the Conservative government created the Scottish Grand Committee, and the later Liberal government made it permanent. It became a standing parliamentary committee on which sat all Members of Parliament for Scottish seats: an allocation of a further fifteen seats were to enable the government of the day to balance the parties in its own interest. This mechanism has worked fairly well when the party representation of the two countries has not been very far out of phase. But when it has been beyond the redressing power of the spare fifteen seats, Scottish business has had to be brought back again to the full House. The result is that at periods when Scottish political feeling is most out of touch with that in England the delay on needed Scottish legislation is likely to be greatest.

In some of the legislative needs of the country, particularly where the need has been less serious in Scotland than in England, the delay has been indefinite. Scotland has not yet received the twentieth-century law revision comparable to the English work of the 1920s. There are by now features in Scottish civil law which fit badly into the social structure of the modern world. The social conservatism of the small legal caste in Scotland, and its concentration in a few cities and universities, prevents it generating much pressure for reform by itself. Yet a country needs a thorough legal reform every century or so. This is one of the ways in which the tightness of the parliamentary timetable is an argument, one of the strongest arguments, for some sort of devolution of legislative functions. That this argument is noticed most by people who, because of it, are considerably over-worked and anxious not to increase their overload, is perhaps the reason why it has not often figured in nationalist discussion.

The other weakness in Scottish government comes from the relationship of power within the Cabinet. The creation of new ministries for specific social or economic ends means that the concentration of an older group of functions under the Secretary of State for Scotland is anomalous. The increasing activity of the central government in these spheres, in response to increasing public pressure, makes the anomaly increasingly uncomfortable. There is always the risk that the divergence between the two areas of power will lead to conflict rather than co-operation. The enhanced power of the prime minister in the last thirty years also emphasizes the distinction between those political offices which are likely to be a step forward in a career aimed at the highest position, and those which are not. The Scottish office has not been conspicuous as an avenue of advancement. It is traditionally regarded as available only for a small section of members of Parliament, those who are Scots by upbringing and sentiment, and who also sit for Scottish seats. Only a few names can ever be considered for it. As a result, it is only under exceptional circumstances that it is held by someone capable and determined enough to use it well. The conspicuous example here was Tom Johnston in the Second World War. The wartime Cabinet was prepared to confer on the office exceptional powers, and Johnston, at the end of a political career, was a man prepared to confine his ambition to the few things that could be done in his period of office. The success of this period is to be measured not so much in specific enactments, such as the creation of the North of Scotland Hydro-Electric Board, but by the drive and penetration he gave to all aspects of the move for improved health and welfare. This has enabled Scotland to take full advantage of the opportunities for change created by the war.

In pushing the social needs of Scotland, Johnston could claim the existence of a real nationalist pressure. A core of nationalism had continued since the days of unrest on the Clyde in 1915. There were newspapers specifically tuned to it, and it had imparted a particular drive to the Independent Labour Party group in Parliament, of which

Johnston had been a member. The Scottish National Party, created in 1928, held only a part of this feeling, that of the more educated section, and like many movements with a well-educated membership and a basic appeal to generalized discontent, it suffered from schisms and disputes. The lack of a single dominant political party to stand for Scotland, as the Liberals had in the nineteenth century, meant that it was not easy for the Nationalists to form a positive and coherent programme beyond that of some sort of Home Rule. The result was that, whereas Scottish national feeling produced some interesting and vivid literature, particularly during the Second World War, and could rely on a wide, generalized support in the country, the actual party which professed its aims was regarded, both inside and outside Scotland, with a good deal of scorn. Many electors found that their genuine nationalist desires took second place to other political aims once they had heard a speech from a Nationalist candidate. At the end of the Second World War, Nationalism won a by-election at Motherwell, but lost the seat a few months later when the wartime party truce ended and real electoral issues were offered by the Labour and Conservative parties. This was symptomatic of the priorities in the public mind.

In the 1960s this changed. The membership of the S.N.P. went up into another order of magnitude. In 1967 the party gained a big vote in the Pollok by-election, and a few months later won the seat of Hamilton. This was an election into a Parliament which clearly had several more years of life, and brought an enormous infusion of new members to the party, resulting in a big swing in the local government elections in the spring of 1968. Much of this expansion was self-generating. Once the party had a prospect of immediate hope, it reduced its level of internal bickering, and became more attractive: new recruits reduced the proportional weight of the more extreme or sillier elements, and gave it a wider appeal. The special interest in the rapid expansion of the party rests on the fact that it is largely drawn from those who in the past have voted Labour. The swing to Labour that ousted the Conservative government in the 1964 election, and confirmed Labour power in that of 1966, was much more marked in Scotland than in England. Though shackled by an old-fashioned and incompetent party machinery in Scotland, it had looked as if, in the towns of the Lowlands, Labour might imitate the nineteenth-century dominance shown by the Liberal party, while the Highlands and the rural areas became the stronghold of a reviving Liberalism. Since then the drift from Labour has been striking, and much of it has gone to the Nationalists. The political map of Scotland is already completely different from that of the rest of the United Kingdom: it is likely to get more so. This difference must be accepted as indicating basic divergencies in political thought.

To some degree the changes in electoral history reflect negative rather than positive voting. The elections of 1964 and 1966, and the local elections of 1968, must be taken as votes against the existing framework and methods of government rather than as votes for any particular programme. This negativism has been produced by the feeling of pressure: the pressure of Britain's economic situation, which has kept the actual achievements and policies of both Conservative and Labour governments close together, and the pressures of the political world outside, which appear to give very little room for any line of action other than reluctant acquiescence. On the one hand any British government, faced with major political and economic problems, can only move within narrow limits. On the other hand, all post-war governments have interfered more and more with the conduct of industry, of agriculture, and of local affairs. Never has the central government appeared more pervasive and less effectual. Much of the sentiment behind national unrest in Scotland can be found, without any particular national element, in Manchester or Newcastle.

That a lot of nationalist feeling is negative in impulse can be seen from its lack of a simple and coherent programme. Instead, there is a collection of miscellaneous aims designed to attract particular elements. While this lack of clear lines of action makes the Nationalist party a valuable experimenter in local government, it may continue to keep down its support in national affairs. There is a great deal of confusion among those who are sympathetic to nationalism over the lengths to which they wish to go. As in past general elections, most people have found that they feel more clearly aligned with one or other general party than with the Nationalists, so today the number of people who put nationalist aims above all others is limited. Most people in Scotland would like to see less control of Scottish affairs exercised in London and more vigour in local life (there is no certainty that the former would lead to the latter). They would welcome a formal structure of government in which it was harder for English-men and foreigners to use the word 'England' as a synonym for Britain. They have a real wish for the recognition of the dignity of Scotland's nationhood. But for many this is the sum total of their nationalism, and they do not go on to a wish to separate from England in cultural, economic, or financial matters. When Irish nationalism developed in the nineteenth century it could point to real differences between Ireland and England in religion, in cultural and economic life, that made it natural for many Irishmen to see no advantage in a close connection between the two countries. This is not the case between Scotland and England, and most people recognize this fact.

Another element in national feeling is that in the twentieth century there are advantages for some elements of the community in a small national unit. With the developing authority of the United Nations, the independence of countries that do not possess the strength to defend themselves has become a practical proposition, unless they belong to the Warsaw Pact. There can be flexibility and experiment in a country of five million people in a way there cannot be with fifty million. But Scotland is unsuited to such a future because of the un-balanced industrial and geographical features of the country. Scotland's great conurbation on the Clyde is a far larger proportion of her population and wealth than any single urban aggregate, even London, in Britain as a whole. It contains 38 per cent of the popula-tion, and employs them in a one-sided industrial pattern. Though some of the new and necessary ideas of the nineteenth-century expansion of local government were developed in Clydeside, the social performance of the area in this century has been neither inspired nor inspiring. There is a further unbalance on the rural side. Scotland has vigorous and productive lowland farming, but she has also the scattered and unprogressive farm settlements of the High-lands, which present problems of remoteness and marginal viability to a degree not found elsewhere in Britain. The forms of economic regulation and social security worked out for an industrial society have not fitted well into the Highlands, yet there is no reason to think that most Scots would wish to see them drastically changed if the country was left to its own resources. Within either a still-unified Britain or an independent Scotland some step soon must be made to create a better balance between local and national needs, to devise methods of controlling the economy as a whole without accentuating the gulf between the prosperous and unprosperous sections. The successful mechanization of agriculture in the lowlands has also created problems. Population is leaking away from the farmlands as it has leaked away from the Highlands, and areas of successful farming may soon be approaching a position in which they are socially unviable.

The problem of the right encouragement and control of regional development is not peculiar to Scotland, but it reaches an acute form here. The two major problems of the country are the economic backwardness of the Highlands, and the tradition and material facts of overcrowding in housing which, though found all over Scotland, are most manifest in the dense settlement on Clydeside. For the former, a regional organization has in practice been frequently established: the Highland Development Board is the latest in a succession of special government agencies for this purpose. None of these has been armed with sufficient powers to do its job effectively, and none of them has yet found good methods of enlisting local support and effort in their work. For the latter problem a regional unit might provide new thinking, and might be big enough to recruit real talent, but here again the necessity is for local support. The tradition of Scottish house-building has had good as well as bad features. It has, for instance, been done with a high level of control of the quality of the structure. In some way this needs to be joined to a more imaginative grasp of the social and visual problems of planning, and a higher allowance of family space. It is possible that a separate Scottish legislature might find the initiative to tackle Scotland's special regional problems: it is also possible that it would not. The example of the semi-dependent legislature of Northern Ireland is not encouraging.

Another element in nationalist opinion is the belief that Scotland has been paying more in taxation to the central government than she has received in benefits. Figures with respectable arithmetic in support of this opinion have not yet been produced. Indeed it seemed likely, even before almost the whole of Scotland was named as a development area, that in the simple form of direct payments from the Exchequer, Scotland as an area with a higher birth rate, unemployment rate, and sickness rate than the average for Britain, was likely to be getting disproportionately high shares of social security benefits. The more difficult element to assess has been government-supported specialized establishments, from railway workshops to research laboratories, the government contribution to the arts, science, and defence. There are real difficulties in estimating anyway what the true shares of the different parts of Britain really are in taxation, since the money for taxes may be earned in a part of Britain where it is not in fact received. A government-sponsored investigation may well show that one or another part of the United Kingdom is doing more than its share in supporting the other parts, but it is difficult to see how such information can be added to the core of the nationalist case, which is a plea for a recognition of the dignity of Scottish national identity. At the same time, if Scotland were found to be a debtor and not a creditor in the general balance, this would not be an effective argument against some sort of legislative independence. A country may well choose to lower its level of income and social security for the sake of separate identity.

The real weakness of the nationalist argument is not, or should not be, a matter of pounds, shillings, and pence; but is the fact that the great bulk of nationalist discussion ignores the vast content of common British culture. Common economic development, the free movement of people, a great body of common social provision and law, a shared language and a large part of shared religious and historical experience, have tied the two countries together in a multitude of ways. The Scot who seeks work in England hardly regards this as going abroad, and the people among whom he settles do not treat him as a foreigner. In the less frequent event of an Englishman coming to Scotland, the situation is not quite the same. The English habit of regarding Scots as honorary Englishmen, which is not fully reciprocated, means that it is not the cultural but the physical climate that a visiting Englishman expects to find different. But since English penetration takes place into a smaller community, it is more often noticed, and sometimes resented.

There was an attempt to bring the established Churches of the two countries into communion, and perhaps ultimately union, in the 1950s. The initial difficulty here was the Anglican inability to recognize clerical orders other than those obtained through Episcopal means. This revealed the belief widely held in some Scottish presby-

teries and among some of the laity that there was something intrinsically sinister in the existence of bishops and hence of any association
with them. If the Anglican tenet of apostolically derived orders meant
that some sort of structure of an episcopal order had to be accepted
for union, this could in practice have been divorced from the principle
of episcopal control of the Church. But the outcry against bishops
showed that many people in Scotland were still fighting the issues of
the seventeenth century. In fact, the two Churches have grown very
similar in the last hundred years. The Church of England has
created a somewhat emasculated Church Assembly, and a large
clerical administrative body in the Kirk of Scotland has grown up in
spite of the Melvillian ideal of no clergy divorced from the specific
cure of souls. In worship too there are marked resemblances. The
Kirk has reduced the sermon's share of the service to fit in with a
society with other forms of amusement, and developed its own
liturgies in the 1860s and 1870s. Even the use of the organ, the 'kist of
whistles', has been accepted. Both Churches experienced intellectual
crises in the later nineteenth century, and have since abandoned the
crude fundamentalism of a hundred years ago. Both now cover a wide
spectrum of belief and practice.[1] There may still be a feeling reminiscent of 1638 at times in Scotland, but it has little intellectual justification, and is likely to succumb before the threat of modern atheism.

It is worth while considering which aspects of Scottish culture
appear to be viable on their own. Education, though it has been
separately organized in a system designed to keep out English
infiltration, has not had a particularly distinguished record this
century, except at the university level, where it has been open to
English influence. Though the formal doctrinal content of Calvinism
is little emphasized, or even understood, in Scottish schools today,
the derivative opinion that there is something intrinsically wrong
with activities such as learning when they can be pursued with
enjoyment has had a pernicious effect. In a period of changing need
the relatively rigid structure of teaching and curricula has been a
handicap unaccompanied by any apparent advantage. In literature
there is the community of the English-speaking world, in which
national differences are only minor distinctions, and though within

1. Even the veneration of saints has had a popular rebirth in the Kirk of today, as
can be seen on a visit to the Livingstone memorial at Blantyre.

this, some areas or nations make specific contributions it is not possible, at least today, to speak of a Scottish school of writing. At no period of history has there been a body of Scottish writers able to support themselves by their sales within Scotland. Though the visual arts have not for several centuries been an area in which the Celtic world has distinguished itself, lowland Scotland has developed a school of painters and a local market for their work in the last twenty years that many small nations might well envy. Scotland had achieved two portrait painters of distinction in the eighteenth century, Allan Ramsay and Raeburn. She had also a splendid tradition of architecture throughout the period known as Georgian, ending with the later suburbs of Edinburgh's new town. But after that, architecture and painting won little fame until this century. The recent development has been unexpected, and points a regional or even nationalist moral: that whereas literature needs a large scale on which to work, and seems to flourish best when national boundaries are breaking or overridden, the advantages of a local market in which painters can develop the taste of the public for their individual styles, can be very real.

Probably this assessment of national viability is the wrong approach. Increasingly, since the Second World War, it has been shown that there is a community of the western world and within that a community of Europe. It would be ambitious to expect Scotland to make the impact on the latter that she achieved in the later eighteenth century. The question that must interest us is whether the exchange of ideas and vision between one country and the rest of the community is likely to become more or less vital as the result of political change. There can be particular combinations of political and social forces that enable a people to contribute creatively to the rest of the world. The question of the 1960s is whether a degree of separation of Scottish government from that of England would enhance the prospect of this. There has been in the past no simple relationship between independence and creativity, or between the solution of problems of government and the fostering of new ideas. Two striking examples of these facts come from the period of the quarter century before the First World War, when the Austro-Hungarian Empire was perhaps the richest part of Europe in new ideas, and when much of the most impressive literature in the English language came from an

Ireland which had not attained independence. On the other hand, the aesthetic and social achievements of the Scandinavian countries in the last fifty years are witness to what small countries can do to show new methods to the world. There is reason to believe that some reconstruction of the relationship between the two main parts of the United Kingdom, if approached with honesty and humility (not virtues in which nationalist movements usually excel), might lead to something of value to the world at large.

Monarchs of Scotland
since the early eleventh century

Malcolm II	1005–34	James II	1437–60
Duncan I	1034–40	James III	1460–88
Macbeth	1040–57	James IV	1488–1513
Lulach	1057–8	James V	1513–42
Malcolm III 'Can-		Mary (I)	1542–67
more'	1058–93	James VI	1567–1625
Donald Ban	1093–4	Charles I	1625–49
	1094–7	Charles II	1649–85
Duncan II	1094	James VII (James	
Edgar	1097–1107	II of England)	1685–8
Alexander I	1107–24	William 'III' and	
David I	1124–53	Mary II	1689–94
Malcolm IV	1153–65	William 'III'	1694–1702
William I 'The		Anne	1702–14
Lion'	1165–1214	George I	1714–27
Alexander II	1214–49	George II	1727–60
Alexander III	1249–86	George III	1760–1820
John Balliol	1292–6	George IV	1820–9
Robert Bruce		William 'IV'	1829–37
(Robert I)	1306–29	Victoria	1837–1901
David II	1329–71	Edward 'VII'	1901–10
Robert II (the		George V	1910–36
Stewart)	1371–90	Edward 'VIII'	1936
Robert III	1390–1406	George VI	1936–52
James I	1406–37	Elizabeth 'II'	1952–

Dates of some of the principal battles and other events in Scottish History[1]

c. 563	Columba's arrival on Iona.
794	The start of Viking attacks on Scotland.
c. 843	Kenneth MacAlpin, King of both Scots and Picts.
c. 971	Edgar gives Lothian to Kenneth II.
1066	Norman conquest of England.
c. 1069	Marriage of Malcolm III to Margaret.
1073	Malcolm III becomes the man of William I.
1134	Annexation of Moray by the Crown.
1138	The Battle of the Standard.
1174	William the Lion defeated at Alnwick.
1189	The quitclaim of Canterbury.
1192	The Scottish church is made a special daughter of the Roman see.
1237	Treaty of York.
1263	Battle of Largs.
1266	Treaty of Perth.
1290	Treaty of Birgham. Death of the Maid of Norway.
1295	First Franco–Scottish alliance against England.
1297	Rising of William Wallace.
1305	Edward I's Ordinance for the government of Scotland. Execution of Wallace.
1306	Robert Bruce's murder of the Red Comyn and rebellion.
1314	Battle of Bannockburn.
1320	Declaration of Arbroath.
1328	Treaty of Northampton.
1332	Renewal of the War of Independence.

1. It is scarcely necessary to remind the serious student of history that most major historical developments cannot be included in this type of catalogue because they cannot be ascribed to specific dates, and that many events that took place outside Scotland have as great a bearing on Scottish history as those recorded here.

1346	Battle of Neville's Cross.
1349–50	The Black Death.
1412	Foundation of St Andrews University.
1424	Return of James I from captivity.
1455	Fall of the Black Douglases.
1468	Marriage of James III and Margaret of Denmark.
1468–9	Pledging of the Northern Isles.
1472	Erection of the see of St Andrews to archiepiscopal status.
1493	Forfeiture of the Lordship of the Isles.
1503	Marriage of James IV and Margaret Tudor.
1513	Battle of Flodden.
1517	Treaty of Rouen.
1528	Start of James V's personal reign.
1542	Battle of Solway Moss.
1546	Murder of Cardinal Beaton.
1547	Battle of Pinkie.
1558	Marriage of Mary and Francis II of France.
1560	Treaty of Edinburgh.
	The Reformation Parliament.
1561	The return of Mary.
1565	Marriage of Mary and Henry Darnley.
1567	Murder of Darnley.
	Abdication of Mary.
1568	Mary's flight to England.
1570	Murder of Regent Moray.
1573	Final defeat of the queen's party.
1581	Fall of Regent Morton.
1582	Ruthven raid.
1603	Union of the Crowns of England and Scotland.
1609	Statutes of Icolmkill.
1618	Five Articles of Perth.
1625	Charles I's Act of Revocation.
1637	The Scottish Prayer Book.
1638	The Covenant.
1639	First Bishops' War.
1640	Second Bishops' War.
1643	The Solemn League and Covenant.

1644	Scottish Invasion of England.
	Battle of Marston Moor.
1645	Battle of Philiphaugh.
1646	Surrender of Charles I.
1647	The Engagement.
1648	The Whiggamore Raid.
1649	Execution of Charles I.
1650	Battle of Dunbar.
1651	Battle of Worcester.
1651–8	The rule of Cromwell.
1660	The Restoration of the Monarchy.
1669 } 1672	Indulgences to Presbyterian ministers.
1679	Battle of Bothwell Brig.
1689	The Revolution.
	Battle of Killiecrankie.
1690	Establishment of Presbyterianism.
1696	Act for Settling Schools.
1698	Darien expedition.
1707	Act of Union.
1708	Abolition of the Scottish Privy Council.
1712	Restoration of patronage.
1715–16	Jacobite rebellion.
1719	Jacobite rebellion in Glenshiel.
1725	Shawfield riots.
1727	Founding of the Board of Trustees.
1739	Hume's *Treatise of Human Nature*.
1745–6	Jacobite rebellion.
1746	Battle of Culloden.
1814	Publication of the first Waverley novel.
1820	'Radical War.'
1832	First Reform Act.
1833	Burgh Reform Acts.
1843	The Disruption.
1845–6	Potato failure.
1885	Creation of the Scottish Secretaryship.
1886	Crofters' Holdings Act.
1929	Union of the Church of Scotland and the Free Church.

Materials for the study
of Scottish History

SOME OF THE MOST valuable materials available are not books but objects. The terrain and climate of Scotland, to those who know them well, are still today illustrations of forces that shaped her development. The names of Scottish hamlets and towns, the tracks upon the hills, the harbours and firths, the tide-races in the narrows off the north and west coasts, are all memorials of past events. Castles still stud the land; often in remarkably good preservation, for they were used later here than in more settled countries and by families who often could not afford to adapt them expensively to the taste of successive generations. Many of these have been studied, and their history and changing structure explained, particularly in the work of the late W. Douglas Simpson. In the older burghs of the country there are walls or houses of early date and distinctive style and, in the museums, household goods and weapons. Scottish silver in the Royal Scottish Museum in Edinburgh, or Scottish coins in the Ashmolean Museum in Oxford, provide artefacts that had a life of use as well as beauty. That the country benefited by ideas from elsewhere is borne out in the styles of her cathedral churches, the Dutch gables of houses in the eastern coastal towns, and the successful incorporation of the classicism of Diocletian's empire in the stately houses designed by Robert Adam. And to the student prepared to get information by ear, the unique richness and depth of two streams of folksong, Gaelic and Scottish, is an illustration of the feeling of the nation.

All the same, the historian must reckon to get his detailed history from the written word. Scottish literature has given us several imaginative re-creations of the country's past, among which Sir Walter Scott's *Old Mortality* and *The Heart of Midlothian* are pre-eminent. The historiography of Scotland, after a splendid start in the eighteenth century, lapsed severely, and in the nineteenth and early twentieth centuries has not, in general, been a suitable place for national pride. But there are elements in it which are creditable. The works mentioned here are those from which this outline has mainly been compiled, and are, in most cases, the obvious resorts for further work.

There is a large body of printed original material provided by the Maitland, Abbotsford, and Bannatyne Clubs of the last century, by the Scottish History Society, the Wodrow Society, the Scottish Text Society, and the Scottish Record Society, and the nucleus of state papers from the English and Scottish Record Offices. Major reference collections are available, such as the 8 volumes of the *Fasti Ecclesiae Scoticanae* (H. Scott, 1915–28, 1950) and the 9 volumes of *The Scottish Peerage* (J. E. Paul, 1909–14). The emphasis of these primary materials lies in the seventeenth century, which is particularly valuable since until very recently there was no major modern study of Scotland in that period. There has recently been a welcome increase in the quantity of serious and original work published, and some of it has even abandoned the singularly poor level of indexing acquiesced in by Scottish historians in the past. Articles on Scottish history in journals based on an English market, or in collections of general historical studies, and the existence outside Scotland of scholars contributing to Scottish history, indicate a recent maturity of historical perception both in Scotland and beyond. There has been, and is again, an important journal, the *Scottish Historical Review* (the *S.H.R.* in the rest of this chapter), and another for the history of Catholic Scotland, the *Innes Review*. *The Source Book of Scottish History* in three volumes (2nd edition, 1958–61) provides an indispensable text-book up till 1707, and Agnes Mure Mackenzie, *Scottish Pageant* (4 vol., 1946–50), is an anthology with a remarkably wide range and stimulating commentary. Of the projected four volumes of the new Edinburgh History of Scotland, two have become available while this book was in preparation, Gordon Donaldson, *Scotland, James V to James VII* (1965), and W. Ferguson, *Scotland, 1689 to the Present Day* (1968): both have full bibliographies and together they provide at last the ingredients for an understanding of modern Scotland in modern terms: they should be borne in mind in all the modern section of this chapter.

The history of early Scotland is relatively well supplied with books. Besides the indispensable two volumes of A. O. Anderson, *Early Sources of Scottish History* (1922), there is the symposium edited by F. T. Wainwright, *The Problem of the Picts* (1955), Isabel Henderson, *The Picts* (1967), and Nora Chadwick, *Celtic Britain* (1963). For Norse Scotland and its overseas connections Eric Linklater, *The Ultimate Viking* (1955), is an especially enjoyable introduction.

Relatively less is available for the **feudal** period. W. C. Dickinson, *Scotland from the Earliest Times to 1603* (2nd edition, 1965), has a limited historical vision but a real narrative sense, and G. W. S. Barrow, *Feudal Britain* (1956), enables the student to compare the institutions and development of Scotland with those of another feudal country. In his introduction to *The Acts of Malcolm IV* (1960) the latter author provides the best available examination of the working of the central government. R. L. G. Ritchie, *The Normans in Scotland* (1954), though miscellaneous in its approach, has value. Two important articles on Anglo-Scottish relations are A. O. Anderson, 'Anglo-Scottish Relations from Constantine to William', *S.H.R.*, vol. 42 (1963), and A. A. M. Duncan, 'The Earliest Scottish Charters', *S.H.R.*, vol. 37 (1958).

There is as yet no adequate book on the Scottish **medieval Church**. J. A. Duke, *The Columban Church* (1932), continues to be useful on the early period. Articles of importance are Dermot Fahy, 'The Historical Reality of St Ninia', *Innes Review*, vol. 15 (1964); G. W. S. Barrow, 'Scottish Rulers and the Religious Orders', *Transactions of the Royal Historical Society*, 5th series, vol. 3 (1953), and 'From Queen Margaret to David I, Benedictions and Tironians', *Innes Review*, vol. 11 (1960); and I. B. Cowan, 'The Development of the Parochial System in Mediaeval Scotland', *S.H.R.*, vol. 40 (1961).

For Scottish **economic history in the Middle Ages** Miss I. F. Grant, *Social and Economic Development of Scotland before 1603* (1930), was a pioneer study and remains unsuperseded. W. Mackay Mackenzie, *The Scottish Burghs* (1948), is a useful introduction to the organization of town life. Two distinguished specialized studies, I. H. Stewart, *The Scottish Coinage* (1955), and Stewart Cruden, *The Scottish Castle* (1960), have economic bearing. Unexpected aspects of the past can be found in L. A. Barbé, *Sidelights on the History, Industries and Social Life of Scotland* (1919).

The **War of Independence** has recently received serious attention by careful scholars and the result is a valuable group of works. For the origin and early stages there are G. W. S. Barrow, *Robert Bruce* (1965), E. L. G. Stones, *Anglo-Scottish Relations, 1174–1328* (1965), and A. A. M. Duncan, 'The community of the realm of Scotland and Robert Bruce', a review in *S.H.R.*, vol. 45 (1966). On the interconnected questions of the continuation of the war and the quality of David II as monarch there are the following recent articles: Bruce Webster, 'David II and the government of fourteenth-century Scotland', *Transactions of the Royal Historical Society*, 5th series, vol. 16 (1966); James Campbell, 'England, Scotland and the Hundred Years War in the fourteenth Century', in J. R. Hale, *Europe in the late Middle Ages* (1965); E. W. M. Balfour Melville, *Edward III and David II* (Historical Association Pamphlet, 1954); and Ranald Nicholson, 'David II, the Historians and the Chroniclers', *S.H.R.*, vol. 45 (1966). Miss May McKisack's volume in the Oxford History of England, *The Fourteenth Century* (1954), is also of use. Two other specialized studies on the structure of Scotland in the late Middle Ages are A. A. M. Duncan, 'The Early Parliaments of Scotland', *S.H.R.*, vol. 45 (1966), and Miss I. F. Grant, *The Lordship of the Isles* (1935).

Little modern work on **fifteenth-century Scotland** has yet reached publication, but there are two old-fashioned biographies, E. W. M. Balfour Melville, *James I King of Scots* (1936), and R. L. Mackie, *King James IV of Scotland* (1958). A suggestive and stimulating article is Monsignor David McRoberts, 'The Scottish Church and Nationalism in the Fifteenth Century', *Innes Review*, vol. 19 (1968). The correspondence of both James IV and James V are in print; the former edited by R. K. Hannay (1953) and the latter by the same author and Denys Hay (1954). The Scottish History Society has also published *The Scottish Correspondence of Mary of Lorraine*, edited by Annie L. Cameron (1927). J. D. Mackie, *A History of Scotland* (1964), can be used for the reign of James IV. W. H. Merriman, 'The Assured Scots: Scottish collaboration with England during the rough wooing', *S.H.R.*, vol. 47 (1968), is a detailed study of the relationship between power and loyalty. Though Scotland is poor in medieval historians, the Scottish Text Society's editions of John Barbour, *The Bruce*, 2 vol. (1904), and of Robert Lindesay of Pitscottie, *Historie and Chronicles of Scotland*, 3 vol. (1909–11), provide good reading.

The remarkable level of egregious error in Scottish ecclesiastical historians of the nineteenth and early twentieth centuries, whether dealing with their own or foreign religious movements, was, presumably, based on the conviction that those who hold divine truth can afford considerable latitude over its secular counterpart. Fortunately, things have improved in recent decades. J. H. S. Burleigh, *A Church History of Scotland* (1962), makes a real attempt at impartiality; G. D. Henderson, *Religious Life in Seventeenth Century Scotland* (1937), an important study, puts that period in a new perspective, and there are two specialized volumes on the Reformation, a collection of articles from the *Innes Review* republished as *Essays in the Scottish Reformation* (1962) edited by Monsignor David McRoberts, and Gordon Donaldson, *The Scottish Reformation* (1960). An interesting bibliographical supplement is Maurice Lee, 'The Scottish Reformation after 400 years', *S.H.R.*, vol. 44 (1965). W. C. Dickinson's edition of John Knox, *History of the Reformation in Scotland*, 2 vol. (1949), makes more available this vivid if one-sided account and also includes other contemporary documents: it should be read with Maurice Lee, 'John Knox and his History', *S.H.R.*, vol. 45 (1966). Hugh Trevor Roper, *George Buchanan and the Ancient Scottish Constitution* (Supplement to the *English Historical Review*, 1966), gives another aspect to the period.

The incidence of **sixteenth-century biography** is uneven. There is still none that can be recommended of Mary Queen of Scots, or of many of her courtiers, but Maurice Lee provides one for *James Stewart, Earl of Moray* (1953) and for *John Maitland of Thirlestane* (1959). There has recently appeared Jasper Ridley, *John Knox* (1968). Two lives of James VI supplement each other in opinion and emphasis; D. H. Willson, *King James VI and I* (1956), and Charles W. S. Williams, *James I* (reissued 1951).

Certain recent works on English history have a notable bearing on **Anglo-Scottish relations**: Conyers Read, *Mr Secretary Cecil and Queen Elizabeth* (1955) and *Lord Burghley and Queen Elizabeth* (1960). There is also A. L. Rowse, *The Expansion of Elizabethan England* (1955). All these are useful for the frontier question, which is considered in its Scottish aspect in T. I. Rae, *The Administration of the Scottish Frontier 1513–1603* (1966), and D. W. L. Tough, *The Last Years of a Frontier* (1928). For a later date, the frontier in general is discussed in Penry Williams, 'The Northern Border under the Early Stuarts', in *Historical Essays 1600–1750, presented to David Ogg*, ed. H. E. Bell and R. L. Ollard (1963).

Between the publication of W. L. Mathieson, *Politics and Religion in Scotland*, 2 vol. (1902), and Gordon Donaldson's Edinburgh History volume there was no serious and mature study of the **political history** of Scotland through the **seventeenth century**. Writers of English history, with the notable exception of Miss C. V. Wedgewood (e.g. *The King's War* (1958)) have also avoided any real consideration of the Scottish bearing of events. Because of this gap, any student of this vital period must spend time hewing out his material for himself from the primary materials in print. Fortunately these are many. Some part of them is published in J. G. Fyfe, *Scottish Diaries and Memoirs 1550–1843*, 2 vol. (1928 and 1942), but the main force and flavour of such works requires that they be read in full. Serious study of the period starts with the newsletters sent by Robert Baillie to his relative in the Netherlands, which show the gradual changes of opinion in Scotland, and are printed in his *Letters and Journals*, 3 vol. (1841–2), and with the opposition point of view expressed in John Spalding, *History of the Troubles*, 2 vol. (1828–9); a useful later source is John Nicoll, *Diary 1650–67* (1836); all these are Bannatyne Club publications. There are also Sir James Turner *Memoirs 1632–70* (1829), James Nimmo, *Narrative* (1889), and John Erskine of Carnock, *Journal* (1893); the last two produced by the Scottish History Society. This Society has given space in four volumes to Archibald Johnston of Wariston's *Diary*, published between 1896–1940, though a very small amount of this suffices for anyone who is not a psychiatrist. It has also made specialized collections in the period of the Great Rebellion: *Scotland and the Commonwealth* (1895) and *Scotland and the Protectorate* (1899), both edited by C. H. Firth; *The Army of the Covenant*, 2 vol. (1916–17), and *The Cromwellian Union* (1902), both edited by C. S. Terry; and three volumes of *General Assembly Commission Records 1646–52* (1892, 1896, and 1909). *Montereul Correspondence*, 2 vol. (1898–9), edited by J. G. Fotheringham, gives interesting documentation of the negotiations at the end of the first Civil War. Though Scotland lacks local historical societies of the strength of those in England the Spalding Society till recently appeared to be an exception to this generalization, and its *Presbytery Book of Strathbogie 1631–54* (1843) gives a picture of the local machinery of Church control. There are also Robert Law, *Memorials* (1818): the two Maitland Club volumes, *Memorials of Montrose* (1848 and 1850), and the Abbotsford Club's *Memoirs of Sir Ewen Cameron of Locheill* (1842).

There are fortunately also some useful studies in secondary sources. David Mathew, *Scotland under Charles I* (1955), is an interesting approach vitiated by too narrow a documentary base. John Buchan's life of *Montrose* (1928) is of a level far above most biographies set in the seventeenth century and has a particularly good assessment of the rival characters, Argyll and Montrose; the same author's *Oliver Cromwell* (1934) is well worth using too. A Cunningham, *The Loyal Clans* (1932), though long-winded and sometimes one-sided, shows understanding of the Highlands, and they are dealt with in briefer form by W. R. Kermack, *The Scottish Highlands* (1957). H. Trevor Roper in an article in *Religion, the Reformation and Social Change* (1967) considers **Cromwell's policy in Scotland**, and is to some degree rebutted by Paul J. Pinckney, 'The Scottish representation in the Cromwellian Parliament of 1656', *S.H.R.*, vol. 46 (1967). Three articles on the **Covenanters** give different aspects of their aims and beliefs, Miss C. V. Wedgewood, 'The Covenanters in the First Civil War', *S.H.R.*, vol. 39 (1960), I. B. Cowan, 'The Covenanters. A revision article', *S.H.R.*, vol. 46 (1967), and S. A. Burrell, 'The Apocalyptic Vision of the Early Covenanters', *S.H.R.*, vol. 43 (1964). Some of the articles in D. Shaw (ed.), *Reformation and Revolution, essays presented to the Very Rev. Hugh Watt* (1967), are of significance and W. R. Foster, *Bishop and Presbytery* (1958), is a sympathetic study of the Restoration Church. A. McKerral, *Kintyre in the Seventeenth Century* (1948), is of more than local interest.

The **politics of the Restoration period** are fully, if tendentiously, illustrated by contemporary narrative. As well as the Covenanting diaries already listed on their own or in Fyfe, there is the view of a supporter of government, Sir George Mackenzie (of Rosehaugh), *Memoirs of the Affairs of Scotland from the Restoration of King Charles II* (1821). Gilbert Burnet, *History of My Own Time*, 2 vol. (1724 and 1734), is thoroughly unreliable and most readable: it is best used in the eighteenth-century edition for then at least the reader has only the author's misrepresentations to allow for and not those of his nineteenth-century editor, O. Airy. Mr Airy's edition for the Camden Society of *The Lauderdale Papers*, 3 vol. (1884–5), reaches a low point in a period of poor historical standards, but the reader who is prepared to sort the letters into order of date, ignore the commentary, and correct the occasional obvious misreadings, can gain a lot from it. Sir John Lauder of Fountainhall, *Historical Observes* (1840) and *Historical Notices 1661–88*, 2 vol. (1848), both Bannatyne Club, contain a wealth of detail. The best delineation of the view of the Covenanting extremists is in *Naphtali* (1667) and *The Hind Let Loose* (1687), both anonymous. R. K. Chambers, *Domestic Annals of Scotland*, 3 vol. (1858 and 1861), is an enjoyable anthology, covering many aspects of life.

The economic development of the late sixteenth and the seventeenth century is well covered by S. G. E. Lythe, *The Economy of Scotland 1550–1625* (1960), and T. C. Smout, *Scottish Trade on the Eve of Union* (1963). There are numerous books on Scottish emigration in the seventeenth century but none that answer any of the major questions the historian of Scotland is likely to ask. T. Keith, *Commercial Relations of England and Scotland 1603–1707* (1910), has its uses and the same author (as T. Pagan) has also written a study of *The Convention of the Royal Burghs* (1926). W. R. Scott's comprehensive three volumes, *The Constitution and Finance of English, Scottish and Irish Joint-Stock Companies*, 3 vol. (1910–12), have information on seventeenth-century industries, and T. C. Smout and A. Fenton, 'Scottish Farming before the Improvers', *Agricultural History Review*, vol. XIII (1965), is a stimulating description of this aspect.

T. C. Smout's work on trade, already mentioned, has altered our understanding of the economic motives for Union. On the political side the major standard work is still James Mackinnon, *The Union of England and Scotland* (1896); the minor standard one is G. Pryde, *The Treaty of Union of Scotland and England 1707* (1950). Two recent articles offer reasons for a new view of events; W. Ferguson, 'The Making of the Treaty of Union of 1707', *S.H.R.*, vol. 43 (1964), and P. W. J. Riley, 'The Scottish Parliament of 1703', *S.H.R.*, vol. 47 (1968). The latter author's *The English Ministers and Scotland* (1964) and G. S. Holmes, 'The Hamilton Affair of 1711–12', *English Historical Review*, vol. 77 (1962), illustrate other aspects of the love–hate relationship of the two countries.

After 1714 there is a dearth of major **political studies**. Only two of the leading Scottish politicians of the eighteenth century have had adequate biographies, *Duncan Forbes of Culloden* by G. Menary (1936), and *Henry Dundas, 1st Viscount Melville* by H. Furber (1934). Scottish politics at Westminster have received no adequate study. The electoral scene is better covered, indeed covered well for the short period on which the History of Parliament Trust has published its results, *1754–83*, 3 volumes (1964). Besides this, there are a few articles of use: Sir James Fergusson, 'Making Interest in Scottish County Elections', *S.H.R.*, vol. 26 (1947), and W. Ferguson, 'Dingwall Burgh Politics and the Parliamentary Franchise in the Eighteenth Century', *S.H.R.*, vol. 38 (1959), as well as the detailed, anonymous analysis usually attributed to W. Adam, *The Political State of Scotland in 1788* (1887). **Jacobitism** is a subject which has attracted much poor historical writing: the most frequent weaknesses are an over-simplified romantic partisanship and the belief that a collection of facts can be left to stand for itself. Sir Charles Petrie, *The Jacobite Movement* (1959), and G. H. Jones, *The main stream of Jacobitism* (1954), are of a better calibre. On the **massacre of Glencoe** there is a valuable collection by the Maitland Club, *Papers Illustrative of the Political Condition of the Highlands of Scotland 1689–96* (1845). For modern accounts, there are Miss Cunningham's book, already mentioned, and D. J. Macdonald, *Slaughter under Trust* (1965). Two recent studies of special aspects of the 1745 rising deserve mention, Sir James Fergusson, *Argyll in the 'Forty-five* (1951), and John Gibson, *Ships of the '45* (1967). The first half of J. Prebble, *Culloden* (1961), is excellent historical journalism. As a postscript to Jacobitism and to the general problem of government in the Highlands there is the anonymous account, *The Highlands of Scotland in 1750*, edited by Andrew Lang (1898).

The sparseness revealed in the political historiography of **eighteenth-century** Scotland is not paralleled on the **economic** side. R. H. Campbell's *Scotland since 1707* (1965) is a useful outline, particularly perceptive for the eighteenth century, and there has recently appeared a valuable supplement to it, R. H. Campbell and J. B. A. Dow, *A Source Book of Scottish Economic and Social History* (1968). H. Hamilton, *An Economic History of Scotland in the Eighteenth Century* (1963), though very thorough, has not entirely supplanted his earlier pioneer study, *The Industrial Revolution in Scotland* (1932), particularly since this latter study carries well on into the nineteenth century. Specialized studies of value are R. H. Campbell, *Carron Company* (1961), and 'The Industrial Revolution: a revision article', *S.H.R.*, vol. 46 (1967); T. C. Smout, 'Lead-mining in Scotland, 1650–1850', in P. L. Payne, *Studies in Scottish Business History* (1967); and the stimulating chapter on Scottish banking in Rondo Cameron, *Banking in the Early Stages of Industrialization* (1967). For rural Scotland there is J. Handley, *Scottish Farming in the Eighteenth Century* (1953), and the enjoyable A. R. B. Haldane, *The Drove Roads of Scotland*. For detail on this aspect there is I. F. Grant, *Everyday Life on an Old Highland Farm* (1934). The economics of the Highland problem are set out rather gloomily in M. Gray, *The Highland Economy, 1750–1850* (1957), and in the first chapter of Philip Gaskell, *Morvern Transformed* (1968). All these secondary sources together enable a sound understanding of most of the main features of economic development to be held, though there are still some unexplained problems. What is specially valuable on this aspect is the amount of original material already in print or about to appear. The Scottish History Society has published several volumes of estate papers, of which two examples are E. Cregeen, *Argyll Estate Instructions* (1964), and H. Hamilton, *Monymusk Papers* (1945). D. Defoe's *Tour*, 4 vol. (1727), is only one of many contemporary comments on Scotland, and Samuel Johnson, *A Journey to the Western Islands of Scotland* (1775). reminds us that even if sociology was invented by the Scottish universities its practice was not confined to them even in the eighteenth century. *The Household Books of Lady Grizel Baillie*, Scottish History Society, ed. R. Scott Moncrieff (1911), are a fascinating picture of how a noble family lived; the papers of John Ramsay of Ochtertyre, edited by A. Allardyce (1888) in two volumes as *Scotland and Scotsmen in the Eighteenth Century*, give us the interests and activities of the gentry; and G. Robertson, *Rural Recollections* (1829), supplies the same information for the ordinary farmers.

Scottish intellectual life has several works available, but there is as yet no good study concentrating on the Scottish Enlightenment. D. B. Horn, *A Short History of Edinburgh University* (1967), is a helpful introduction to Scottish education. The best work on Scottish

P

schooling is Alexander Law, *Education in Edinburgh in the Eighteenth Century* (1965). David Craig, *Scottish Literature and the Scottish People* (1961), is a good place to study the background to literature, and G. Bryson, *Man and Society* (1945), is an introduction to the social studies of eighteenth-century Scotland. L. Schneider (ed.), *The Scottish Moralists* (1967), provides samples of the philosophy.

For the period of the **late eighteenth and early nineteenth centuries** there are several old works that still have bearing. H. W. Meikle, *Scotland and the French Revolution* (1812), and W. L. Mathieson, *Church and Reform in Scotland, 1797–1843* (1912), give insight into political history. There are many vivid first-hand accounts of life in this period among which the two most readable and memorable are Lord Cockburn's *Memorials* (1856) and Elizabeth Grant of Rothiemurchus, *Memoirs of a Highland Lady*, edited by Lady Strachey (reissued 1928). Of modern works, the outstanding one is L. J. Saunders, *Scottish Democracy 1815–1840* (1950), a pioneer study reconstructing the varying elements and pressures of society, for which there is no corresponding work for the later part of the nineteenth century. Two studies of social conditions are useful, T. Ferguson's two volumes, *The Dawn of Scottish Social Welfare* (1948) and *Scottish Social Welfare* (1958), and the short but more penetrating J. H. F. Brotherston, *Observations on the Early Public Health Movement in Scotland* (1952). A. R. B. Haldane, *New Ways through the Glen* (1962), tells the story of the building of the parliamentary roads and Caledonian canal in the early nineteenth century. The sense of sociology and history so strong in eighteenth-century Scotland culminated in *The Statistical Account of Scotland*, 21 vol. (1791–9); this example was followed by *The New Statistical Account*, 15 vol. (1845), and is being repeated now in *The Third Statistical Account* (1952–). These detailed local studies still provide a valuable quarry for the systematic inquirer, but all three Accounts are very uneven in their standards and basic concepts.

The main source of study of Scotland in the period **after 1830** must for a long time remain the great Royal Commissions and other Reports on various topics that took place. Here are listed those I have found particularly valuable, but there are others of perhaps equal importance. The two major studies of the Poor Law are the Report on *The Administration and Practical Operation of the Poor Laws in Scotland*,

P.P. 1844 XX, and the Report on *The Poor Law, Scotland*, P.P. 1909 XXXVIII. On similar topics are *The Report to the Board of Supervision* by Sir John McNeill on *The Western Highlands and Islands*, P.P. 1851 XXVI, and Edwin Chadwick's famous *Report on the Sanitary Condition of the Labouring Population of Scotland*, P.P. 1842 XXVIII. On education there are the *Report on the State of the Universities of Scotland*, P.P. 1831 XII, and *The Report on the Universities of Scotland*, P.P. 1878 XXXII. The actual Report of the Argyll Commission on Scottish Education is only one of the many volumes produced by this Royal Commission and is P.P. 1867 XXV. The famous Napier report on *The Conditions of the Crofters and Cotters in the Highlands and Islands*, P.P. 1884 XXXII, and *The Report on the State of Municipal Corporations in Scotland*, P.P. 1835 XXIX and 1836 XXIII, both need to be handled with detachment and care. There are two twentieth-century reports on housing; that on *The Housing of the Industrial Population of Scotland*, P.P. 1917–18 XIV, and the *Report of the Departmental Committee on Scottish Housing*, P.P. 1933–4 XII. Another important report which is not the product of a Royal Commission is the Toothill Report, *The Inquiry into the Scottish Economy*, for the Scottish Council (Development and Industry) (1962).

Against the weight of these materials there is not much serious historical study to set before the student, but in this period, in which Scottish history is closely integrated with English, most studies of individual politicians, events, or industries have a bearing on Scotland. J. G. Kellas, *Modern Scotland* (1968), is useful but lacks a deep historical perspective; H. J. Hanham, 'The Creation of the Scottish Office 1881–7', in *Juridical Review*, N.S. X (1965); and R. K. Middlemas, *The Clydesiders* (1965), are political studies of value. R. K. Webb, 'Literacy among the Working Classes in Nineteenth Century Scotland', *S.H.R.*, vol. 33 (1954), is a useful article, as is J. T. Ward, 'The Factory Reform Movement in Scotland', *S.H.R.*, vol. 41 (1962). There are many substantial biographies of Church figures of which the two with greatest historical significance are probably P. C. Simpson, *Life of Principal Rainy*, 2 vol. (1909), a study of Free Church politics in the nineteenth century, and C. A. Muir, *John White* (1958), a study of the twentieth-century reunion. Scotland's economic situation in the twentieth century is described in A.

Cairncross (ed.), *The Scottish Economy* (1954), to which G. McCrone, *Scotland's Economic Progress 1951–60* (1965), adds a slight postscript. W. R. Scott and J. Cunnison, *Industries of the Clyde Valley during the War* (1924), has political as well as economic interest. On the Highlands, J. P. Day, *Public Administration in the Highlands and Islands* (1918), has its uses, though it is not very readable: A. Collier, *The Crofting Problem* (1953), and F. Fraser Darling, *West Highland Survey* (1955), are more valuable because they cover both social and economic aspects. The standard works on Scottish government are D. Milne, *The Scottish Office and other Scottish Government Departments* (1958), and G. Pryde, *Central and Local Government in Scotland since 1707* (1960), but they should be supplemented by J. P. Mackintosh, *The Devolution of Power* (1968).

This account of reading matter cannot be regarded as comprehensive. Its purpose has been dual: on the one hand to give the authority behind the judgements and assertions of this book, and on the other it is, as is the book itself, introductory – it aims at showing the serious reader some of the varied stages that lie ahead. It has been difficult to know where to draw the line in this latter aim. Books which are so dull or so bad as to put people off the subject altogether have been left out, and I hope that readers will not allow themselves to be disconcerted by the apparent weight of some of the primary sources included. If any penetrate through to these, or find themselves looking at the 12 volumes of the *Acts of the Parliaments of Scotland* or consulting the serried ranks of the *Register of the Privy Council of Scotland*, they should realize that real history is just beginning for them and that behind the assertions of the historians lie, only partly exploited, the public records of Scotland and other manuscript collections. If one single reader is eventually drawn to enter the Manuscript Room of the National Library of Scotland, or the Historical Search Room of the Scottish Public Record Office, this book will have fulfilled its function. And that reader may be assured that in both these places he will be treated with a kindliness and courtesy which may not be above his deserts, but will surely be above his expectations.

Postscript

While this book was in the press other historical writings of importance have appeared. The *S.H.R.* of April 1969, vol. 48, is devoted to the norse element in Scotland and includes two articles on the acquisition of the northern isles, Barbara E. Crawford, 'The pawning of Orkney and Shetland: a reconsideration of the events of 1460–9', and Kai Hørby, 'Christian I and the pawning of Orkney: some reflections on Scandinavian foreign policy 1460–8'. Lady Antonia Fraser has produced a major biography of *Mary, Queen of Scots* (1969). H. J. Hanham has written a social and political study in *Scottish Nationalism* (1969), and a detailed study of the disturbances of the 1880s in 'The Problem of Highland Discontent 1880–1885', *Transactions of the Royal Historical Society*, 5th series, vol. 19, 1969. Dr T. C. Smout has advanced the whole concept of social history with his *History of the Scottish People, 1560–1830* (1969), and in 'The Road to Union' in *Britain after the Glorious Revolution*, ed. Geoffrey Holmes (1969), has opened new perspectives in the political history of the Revolution period.

MAPS

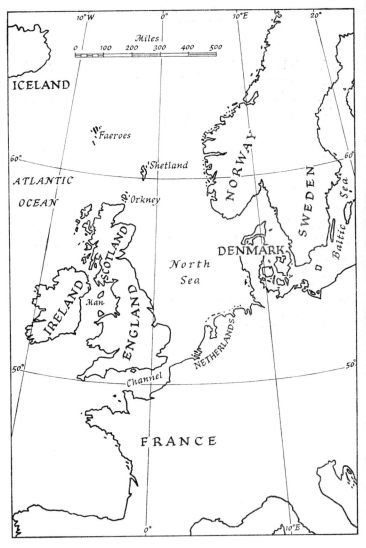

MAP I

Scotland and her neighbours

MAP 2

Map of some of the Scottish Regions

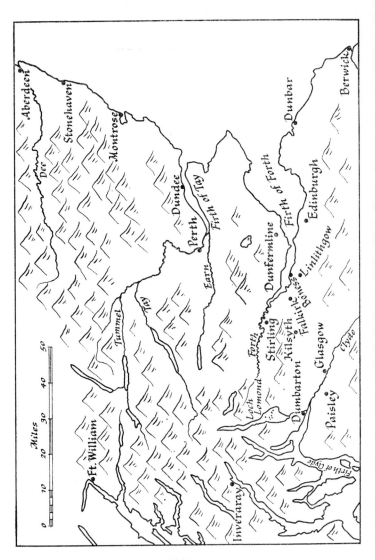

MAP 3
The Towns of Central Scotland

Index